The Poor Indians

EARLY AMERICAN STUDIES

Daniel K. Richter and Kathleen M. Brown, Series Editors

Exploring neglected aspects of our colonial, revolutionary, and early national history and culture, Early American Studies reinterprets familiar themes and events in fresh ways. Interdisciplinary in character, and with a special emphasis on the period from about 1600 to 1850, the series is published in partnership with the McNeil Center for Early American Studies.

A complete list of books in the series is available from the publisher.

The Poor Indians

British Missionaries, Native Americans, and Colonial Sensibility

Laura M. Stevens

PENN

University of Pennsylvania Press
Philadelphia

10   9   8   7   6   5   4   3   2   1

Published by
University of Pennsylvania Press
Philadelphia, Pennsylvania 19104-4011

Library of Congress Cataloging-in-Publication Data

Stevens, Laura M.
    The poor Indians : British missionaries, Native Americans, and colonial sensibility /
Laura M. Stevens.
        p. cm. — (Early American studies)
    Includes bibliographical references (p.   ) and index.
    ISBN 0-8122-3812-5 (cloth : alk. paper)
    1. Indians of North America—Missions.   2. Indians of North America—Public opinion.   3.
Indians of North America—History—Colonial period, ca. 1600–1775.   4. Missionaries—
Great Britain—Attitudes.   5. Anglicans—Missions—United States—History.   6. Protestants—
Missions—United States—History.   7. Public opinion—Great Britain.   8. Great Britain—
Colonies—America.   9. United States—History—Colonial period, ca. 1600–1775.   I. Title.
II. Series.
E98.M6S75 2004
266'.02341'008997—dc22   2004042027

For Tom

Contents

Introduction: "The Common Bowels of Pity to the Miserable"   1

1   Gold for Glass, Seeds to Fruit: Husbandry and Trade in Missionary Writings   34

2   "I Have Received Your Christian and Very Loving Letter": Epistolarity and Transatlantic Community   62

3   "The Reservoir of National Charity": The Role of the Missionary Society   84

4   Indians, Deists, and the Anglican Quest for Compassion: The Sermons of the Society for the Propagation of the Gospel in Foreign Parts   111

5   The Sacrifice of Self: Emotional Expenditure and Transatlantic Ties in Brainerd's and Sergeant's Biographies   138

6   "Like Snow Against the Sun": The Christian Origins of the Vanishing Indian   160

Conclusion   195

Notes   203

Index   249

Acknowledgments   261

Introduction
"The Common Bowels of Pity to the Miserable"

In Daniel Defoe's *Life and Strange and Surprizing Adventures of Robinson Crusoe*, Crusoe tells us that in his eighteenth year as a castaway he stumbled across the remnants of a cannibalistic feast. Repulsed by "this horrid Spectacle," he "gave God Thanks that had cast my first Lot in a Part of the World, where I was distinguish'd from such dreadful Creatures as these." He then spent several weeks plotting "how I might destroy some of these Monsters in their cruel bloody Entertainment." After a while, though, he gave up these fantasies, as he considered the injustice of "so outragious an Execution as the killing twenty or thirty naked Savages." Several factors prompted this change of heart. Crusoe admitted that the Caribes had not hurt him by slaughtering each other. He considered that any attack might result in his own death. He began to pity the Caribes, "who it seems had been suffer'd by Providence in his wise Disposition of the World, to have no other Guide than that of their own abominable and vitiated Passions." He wondered, how could God want him to kill Indians for their sinful acts when he had never told them those acts were sins?[1]

The real change, though, occurred when he realized that killing cannibals "would justify the Conduct of the Spaniards in all their Barbarities practis'd in America." After all, the Indians of Mexico "had several bloody and barbarous Rites in their Customs," but they were "yet, as to the Spaniards, very innocent People." To kill these Caribes would make Crusoe just like the Spanish, who, he categorically proclaimed, were "without Principles of Tenderness, or the common Bowels of Pity to the Miserable."[2] Crusoe gave up on murdering the Caribes because he pitied them, but more because he could not bear to think of himself as a man without pity. His response was ponderous and self-conscious, precisely because it emerged from his need to think of himself as one who, unlike the Spanish, spontaneously felt pity. A few years later he did find an opportunity to be both compassionate and violent. After dreaming of and planning for such an occasion, he killed two Caribes in order to rescue and enslave one of their captives, another Caribe he named Friday. Although Crusoe was pleased to hear reports from Friday of some white men nearby who had killed many people, "by all which I understood, he meant the *Spaniards*, whose Cruelties in *America* had been spread over the whole Countries," his hopes for rescue from the island did not distract from his need to understand himself as a more compassionate colonist.[3]

The primary expression of Crusoe's benevolence, the action that provided him with a sense of his difference from the Spanish, was his effort to convert Friday to Protestant Christianity. Crusoe assures his readers, "I was not wanting to lay a Foundation of Religious Knowledge in his Mind," and he relates some of their conversations about religion. Stymied by difficult questions from his student, he "seriously pray'd to God that he would enable me to instruct savingly this poor Savage, assisting by his Spirit the Heart of the poor ignorant Creature." Finally, after three years he concluded that "the Savage was now a good Christian, a much better than I." Friday's conversion solidified Crusoe's own reform, and it offered evidence to Crusoe of his own religious sensibility, so that "a secret Joy run through every Part of my Soul."[4]

The process by which Crusoe sublimated his hatred and his fear into heroic violence and evangelical fervor, while distinguishing himself from the cruel Spanish, has been a common one in the history of Britain's colonial encounters.[5] Assisted by Protestant propaganda, the horror the "civilized" person feels at the spectacle of "savagery" is overcome by a deeper need to establish difference between the people who feel compassion and those who can or will not. The ability to replace fear and disgust with pity, to transform the instinct to kill into the desire to convert, marks Crusoe, to himself, as civilized.

Joseph Conrad presented a reversal of this process, or a revelation of its underlying reality, almost two centuries later in *Heart of Darkness*. In this novel the ivory trader Kurtz, described to the narrator as "an emissary of pity" and a model of efficiency, cut off the platitudes in his report to the International Society for the Suppression of Savage Customs by scrawling, "Exterminate all the Brutes!" Imperialist pity, manifested in efforts to eradicate savagery and welcome new members into the circle of the civilized, is revealed to be a veil over exploitation and murderous desire, part of what inspires Kurtz's famous dying words, "The Horror! The Horror!"[6] His mission, supposedly a convergence of efficiency and compassion seen in his effort to transform the Congolese into organized exporters of ivory, has converted him into a man of unimaginable brutality. He has become as incapable of pity as the Spaniards to whom Crusoe could not bear to compare himself, and his transformation has exposed imperialists' pretensions to benevolence.

Examined together, these two stories trace an arc in British attitudes to colonization. They shift from horror at the savage other, to a pity that inspires efforts to convert the other into a version of the self, then finally to a horror that is as much of the self's own behavior as of the other's. In a way, they describe the rise and then the fall of an imperial rhetoric built on the claims of compassion. This book is a study of the pity that British people expressed for Indians in the years preceding the American Revolution. It focuses on the pity they expressed for Indians' souls, which prompted declarations of hopes to convert them to Protestant Christianity. It explores what this emotion, as articulated in missionary writings, tells us about seventeenth- and eighteenth-century British attitudes to Indians, to the British themselves, and to the ethical value of feeling.

"Pitty to Mens Soules": Protestant Structures of Feeling

The history of British mission in North America was one in which words outweighed deeds and textual production exceeded conversions. From the time they began to explore America, the British talked a great deal about their desire to convert the continent's indigenous peoples to Christianity. These intentions did translate into efforts, but they were few and feeble, especially in comparison with the work of the Spanish and the French. When missions did not fail through the resistance of Indians or the indifference of the British, war and disease rendered the work tragically redundant, destroying those native peoples who had accepted their invaders' religion.

This failure was an eloquent one, however. Although they did not create widespread conversions among Indians, the British people devoted much paper and ink to expressing their evangelical aspirations and seeking funds for missions. They produced many sermons, journals, letters, tracts, and even a few poems. Ironically, these writings are the primary accomplishment of British mission in the American colonies, as their influence often exceeded the effectiveness of the projects they were written to promote.

British missionary efforts among American Indians have received much attention from historians, but the documents produced in connection with these projects rarely have been examined as works of rhetorical complexity and depth.[7] In the past decade literary scholars such as Thomas Scanlan and Gordon Sayre have incorporated these texts into studies of colonial travel writings, ethnographies, and literature.[8] Others, such as Joshua Bellin, Sandra Gustafson, and Hilary Wyss, have examined some of them for evidence of the active but erased role Indians played in shaping colonial America or in maintaining their own culture in the face of conquest.[9] Together these projects show us much about the responses indigenous peoples had to the colonizing force of Christianity, as well as the ways in which the British portrayed Indians.

Rather than asking what missionary writings tell us about Indians and their responses to a colonial presence, this book asks how these texts encouraged their readers to think about their own emotional responses. I have taken this approach in an effort to untangle the knot of ambivalent benevolence that is at the center of many British and American attitudes to Indians and that still influences portrayals of Indians. In taking this approach I have been inspired by Toni Morrison's *Playing in the Dark.* Morrison describes her book as a study of "the impact of racism on those who perpetuate it," as part of an effort to break a "pattern of thinking about racialism in terms of its consequence on the victim—of always defining it asymmetrically from the perspective of its impact on the object of racist policy and attitudes."[10] While attending to the differences between race and religion as rationales for categorization, I have tried to translate Morrison's approach into the complex attitudes that produced and followed from missionary projects. I have considered the ways in which the tenor of Britain's imperialism developed through reference to Indians in the same way that Morrison suggests figures such as the American "frontier gentleman" were "backgrounded by slavery."[11]

Many missionary writings were basically advertisements for a charitable cause. As advertisements, they encouraged their readers to desire something they may not have known they wanted: the conversion of America's natives. Sometimes they persuaded their readers to support this work by stressing the practical benefits of Indian conversion, such as the promotion of trade. What they sold most often, though, was pity. While the British expressed pity for all non-Christians and non-Europeans, Indians offered a uniquely poignant object for the expression of this sentiment. Unknown to Europe until recent times, absent from and unaware of the Bible, impoverished in countless ways but rich with the potential to be remade in the image of their invaders, they promised the British all sorts of fulfillment as by-products of their effort to fill the Indians' need.

As soon as they encountered the native peoples of the New World, Europeans expressed their intentions to convert and "civilize" them. The propagation of the gospel was a traditional duty based on Jesus' command, "Go ye . . . and teach all nations."[12] Europe had an obligation to extend the benefits of Christianity to heathen lands, just as it had been Christianized centuries before. When he asked the Archbishop of York to oversee collections for a school for Indians at Jamestown's Henrico College in 1615, King James I did so by writing, "Wee doubt not but that yow, and all others, who wishe well to the increase of Christian Religion, wilbe willing to give all assistance and furtherance yow maie."[13] His logic was clear: to be Christian was to support the increase of Christianity. Millenarian beliefs that the conversion of heathens and Jews must precede the Final Judgment enhanced this obligation, as did many theories that Indians were descended from the lost tribes of Israel.[14]

While it drew upon traditional Christian duties, early modern missionary discourse acquired distinct characteristics from its development in the context of the Reformation and the rise of the nation-state. With the exception of the Jesuit Andrew White's attempts to convert Algonquians in Maryland in the 1630s and 1640s, British projects were emphatically Protestant.[15] Their characterization in fund-raising texts reflected the erratic and violent response of the British Isles to the Reformation in the Tudor years, as well as ongoing conflicts with Catholic powers. Defensive about the hundred-year head start Spain had acquired in the Americas, the English and Scots condemned Catholic missionary accomplishments as the result of tyranny. Claims about the deceptions of French Jesuits, who along with other missionary orders had made enviable progress among native groups in Canada, followed. As they contrasted the quantity of Catholic conversions with the quality of English and Scottish concern for Indian souls, they made benevolence central to an ideology of Englishness or Scottishness, and later of Britishness. The writings acknowledged a Christian mission to America as their duty, but they described it as a fervent desire generated from pity for a people who had never heard the gospel. This pity marked England, Scotland, and then Britain as the antidote to Catholic cruelty and proof that its people were the true people of God.[16]

In 1641 William Castell, a minister of Northamptonshire, published a petition to Parliament "for the Propagating of the Gospel in America."[17] In this petition, which was signed by more than seventy English and Scottish ministers, Castell asked Parliament to fund a settlement, just south of the Virginia colony, which would be focused on the conversion of Indians. He argued that England must compete with Spain, and he stressed the benefits of transplanting England's excess population abroad. At the core of his petition, though, was a basic complaint that the colonization of the Americas had "never beene generally undertaken in pitty to mens soules."[18]

To illustrate this absence of pity, Castell attacked Spanish "boasts" to have converted the natives of their colonies by describing the "monstrous cruelties" that the missionary Bartolomé de Las Casas had said his own countrymen committed in America: "[T]hey cut downe men as they did corne without any compassion. . . . They lodged them like bruite beasts under the planks of their ships, till their flesh rotted from their backs: And if any failed in the full performance of his daily taske, hee was sure to bee whipped till his body distilled with goar blood." Castell delivered this gruesome vignette not only to prove that the Spanish were "without any compassion," but also to provoke compensatory pity in his readers for Spain's victims. He defined a religious mandate as an emotional response, "compassion to mens soules."[19] This pamphlet precedes by at least twenty years an era often described as one of sensibility, in which philosophers argued that humans were inherently good because they felt sorrow at the sight of suffering.[20] His petition, one of the first attempts to muster English and Scottish support for the conversion of Indians through the printed word, suggests an earlier starting date for an era of preoccupation with benevolent feeling. It also shows how the tendency to mark compassion as a sign of goodness found expression through Europeans' efforts to understand their relation to the natives of foreign lands.

English missionary writings did not have the popularity of sentimental novels such as Richardson's *Pamela*, nor did they have the lasting intellectual influence of philosophical tracts such as Adam Smith's *Theory of Moral Sentiments*. But as they linked Britain's imperial self-image to the compassion its people felt for heathens and used that emotion to encourage donations, they anticipated many of the ideas and gestures that would constitute the culture of sensibility. Early missionary writings described the support of distant conversion efforts as an activity of national importance and a point of national pride. That is, they insisted that missions to Indians were crucial to securing English and then British interests abroad, while at the same time describing the concern that residents in Britain felt for Indians as a quality that demonstrated the country's moral superiority over powers such as France and Spain. While early missionary writings seem to have stressed their readers' pity in order to elicit financial support, the texts' discussions of shared feeling came to have an importance that overshadowed missionary work. They influenced debates about emotion, and they helped foster the idea—commonplace in the present day—that voluntary participation in a large-scale charitable enterprise is in and of itself a virtuous and pleasing thing, making oneself feel part of a collective endeavor while maximizing one's own potential to do good. Such notions had important implications for the development of British national feeling and for the culture of sensibility.

Perhaps the most significant contribution they made to this culture was to supply a mental framework for extending the emotional connections and obligations Britons felt they should feel. Asking why the British abolished the slave trade in the early nineteenth century, Thomas Haskell has argued that one cause of a widespread humanitarian sensibility was the rise of a capitalist market, which "inculcate[d] altered perceptions of causation in human affairs." The vast networks of investment and trade that the market made possible also propelled "an enhancement of causal perception," which "extend[ed] moral responsibility beyond its former limits."[21] This book suggests that if the market was the primary cause of this cognitive and ethical shift, the rhetoric of Protestant mission provided crucial preconditions for it.

Missionary writings often equated financial transactions with spiritual ones, and the spiritual links they envisioned among humans offered precursors to the webs of economic interdependence that would develop with colonial trade. Through the evangelical mandate of Christianity they linked pity metaphorically with profit, making possible stronger connections between economic and emotional discourse. By insisting on the effects that pity for Indians would have when translated into prayers and funds, they encouraged readers to understand emotion not just as something felt or expressed, but also as something that circulates, transacts, and connects. In this way missionary writings reinforced a transatlantic British consciousness, teaching their readers to imagine themselves connected to distant compatriots as they shared feeling for a pitied object. While they elevated the importance of emotion to ethics, these texts also called attention to the problems that an emotionally centered morality produced. In many ways, then, missionary writings can help us understand the complex status that emotion held in eighteenth-century Britain and its American colonies.

Between Christians: Pity, Sympathy, Proximity, and Distance

I tend to use the words *pity* and *compassion* in this book, rather than *empathy*, *sympathy*, *sensibility*, or *sentimentality*, to describe British attitudes toward unconverted Indians. All of these words connote an emotional response to scenes of suffering, but there are important differences among them. Missionary writings were more likely to ask for readers' pity than their sympathy for Indians, and for good reason. *Sympathy*—which comes from the Greek word *pathos*, meaning feeling or suffering, and a prefix meaning *like* or *the same*—has to do, of course, with an imagined or authentic experience of shared feeling. *Empathy*—which combines *pathos* with the Greek prefix *en* or *in*—also suggests intimacy between one who witnesses and one who feels an emotion.

Pity comes from the Latin word *pietas*, or *piety*, which in turn comes from the word *pius*, meaning duty. In its most literal form this word does not describe an emotion born of sameness, but rather the mercy born of religious devotion. The King James Bible, the translation that would have been familiar to most English readers after its publication in 1611, only uses the term *sympathy* a few times in the Epistles (Phil. 2:1; 1 Pet. 3:8), but it uses *pity* (or the lack of it) to describe how God treats sinners and Israel treats its enemies (Deut. 7:16, Hos. 1:6, 2:23). *Sympathy* has narrow use, applying only to relationships within the Christian community, while *pity* applies to a broad spectrum of relations among humans or between humans and God. *Pity* also tends to describe relationships marked by an imbalance of power between those feeling and those provoking this emotion, suggesting in particular the omnipotence of God. The Geneva Bible, first published in 1560 and in print until 1644, does not even use the word *sympathy* when the King James does, translating *pity* in Philippians and *compassion* in 1 Peter.[22] The terms the King James Bible uses most often to describe a reaction to the sight of suffering are *mercy*, derived from the Latin word for "reward," and *compassion*, meaning "to suffer with," a term that suggests imagined identification but not sameness.[23] The missionaries often referred to "compassion," and I sometimes use it interchangeably with "pity."

Milton also distinguished between sympathy and pity in *Paradise Lost* (1667). When the Son of God decides to clothe the fallen Adam and Eve, he does so because he is "pitying how they stood / Before him naked to the air."[24] At the same moment, Satan's monstrous daughter Sin is able to sense, from her place at the gates of Hell, that the Fall has occurred in Eden. She attributes this awareness to

. . . sympathy, or some connatural force
Powerful greatest distance to unite
With secret amity things of like kind
By secretest conveyance.[25]

"Sympathy," as Milton uses it here, is a morally neutral term that conveys an awareness of shared feeling. "Pity," on the other hand, suggests the benevolence bestowed by an all-powerful God.

In the seventeenth century pity usually was understood as an emotion that emerged from an acknowledgment of obligation, suggesting the goodness of the one who feels it. When expressed for one deprived of salvation, therefore, "pity" can suggest a gap of morality and entitlement between those feeling and those receiving it. An address by Cotton Mather to the Indians of New England configured "pity" in this way: "[I]t is God that has caused us to desire his glory in your salvation; and our hearts have bled with pity over you, when we have seen how horribly the devil *oppressed* you in this, and *destroyed* you in another world."[26] In this text the bleeding hearts of the English distinguish them from the Indians, evidencing their blessing as much as it suggests the Indians' damnation.

While earlier usage gave "pity" a connotation quite different from the similarity suggested by "sympathy," these terms began to overlap in the eighteenth century. Many writers and speakers in this era came to connect "sympathy" with sorrow for another creature's suffering by rooting that sorrow in the ability to imagine oneself in the situation of the sufferer. This connection, established by moral philosophers and popular novelists alike, fostered a popular culture of "sensibility," a term Janet Todd has defined as "the capacity for refined emotion and a quickness to display compassion for suffering."[27]

Missionary writings intersected pity with sympathy, although in a less direct manner. This intersection was the result of the writers' attempts to answer a difficult question: Why should British readers contribute to the assistance of a foreign people when there were dire needs at their own doors? However commendable and however useful for competition with France and Spain, missions in America were not obviously connected to most readers' immediate concerns. The proponents of mission had to develop ways of linking their readers conceptually to this distant work.

Some missionary texts simply relied on the boundless compassion of their audience. When he delivered the sermon of 1763 before the Society in Scotland for the Propagation of Christian Knowledge (SSPCK), Thomas Randall, a minister of Inchture, titled his text *Christian Benevolence.* Throughout this sermon, delivered just as "so many Indian tribes ha[d] fallen under the dominion of Great Britain" at the end of the Seven Years' War, Randall encouraged his listeners to support missions to Indians as an expression of their "desir[e for] the happiness of others."[28] He rehearsed pragmatic arguments for missionary projects, such as "the unceasing activity of the priests of Rome . . . to pervert more of these Heathen tribes," but his focus was on the pleasure his audience would feel at "a happy opportunity for exerting our Christian benevolence."²⁹ As a reward for their charity he offered only "an elevation in their minds" while they imagined the joy brought to converts, and an enhanced closeness with others: "[B]y . . . communication with the knowledge of others, their love, and their attainments, we enter into their joys, and make them all our own."³⁰ If they extended their sympathy throughout Britain's empire, donors in Scotland would enrich their own sense of self.

Randall's assumption of his audience's boundless compassion reflected a tradition of optimistic moral philosophy that extended from the Cambridge Platonists of the Restoration through early eighteenth-century deists to the moral philosophers of the Scottish Enlightenment. Reacting against cynical visions of an egoistic human nature developed by Thomas Hobbes and then by Bernard Mandeville, many British intellectuals had come to rely on emotion, particularly a tendency to feel sorrow at the sight of suffering, as proof of humans' natural selflessness.³¹ Early in the century the third Earl of Shaftesbury linked the moral sense to taste, suggesting that most humans would find what was good also to be pleasing. Francis Hutcheson extended this view by "reducing reason to an ancillary role in ethics," as Norman Fiering has noted, and by asserting the universal range of human compassion.³² Randall's sermon emerged from the efforts of orthodox Scottish Presbyterians to integrate secular enlightened principles with evangelical Calvinist ones after the transatlantic revivals of the mid-eighteenth century.³³

Writing at a moment of imperial optimism and in the midst of a culture steeped in ideals of benevolence, Randall alluded to his audience's limitless compassion as an obvious matter. Yet few authors of missionary tracts, especially earlier ones, so casually assumed that their readers would be able or willing to extend their compassion across an ocean to a foreign recipient.³⁴ While some philosophers argued for the limitless range of pity, others denied that humans could feel compassion across a distance. David Hume insisted in 1739 that "pity depends, in a great measure, on the contiguity, and even the sight of the object."³⁵ Although he granted pity a wider range, Adam Smith insisted that humans were not obliged to extend it into distant quarters. In his *Theory of Moral Sentiments* (1759), he berated "those whining and melancholy moralists" who suggest that no one should feel pleasure while a single person in the world suffers.³⁶ Rather than arguing that one might feel joy by expressing compassion, Smith described bound-less pity as an obstacle to pleasure. Even as he made intelligible the complex global systems that make distant suffering discernable, he denied the emo-tional tug of that suffering.[37]

Smith suggested that when compassion is stretched too far, it depletes the spectator without benefit to the sufferer. This distaste for the "artificial commiseration"[38] the sentimental spectator feels for distant sufferers be-came more pronounced as Smith revised this text. When he added a discus-sion of benevolence to the sixth edition in 1790, he juxtaposed the infinite scope of benevolent feeling with its limited effectiveness: "Though our ef-fectual good offices can very seldom be extended to any wider society than that of our own country; our good-will is circumscribed by no boundary, but may embrace the immensity of the universe."[39] While they feel sorrow at the most distant distress, humans should help those nearest themselves and leave the rest to God's care: "The care of the universal happiness of all rational and sensible beings, is the business of God and not of man. To man is allotted a much humbler department . . . the care of his own happiness, of that of his family, his friends, his country: that he is occupied in contem-plating the more sublime, can never be an excuse for his neglecting the more humble department" (VI.ii.3.6, p. 237). This commentary expanded on Smith's theory that sympathy, which he defined as a sense of shared feeling and situation, directs one's pity, which he defined as "fellow-feeling with the sorrow of others."[40] Benevolent feeling may be universal, but be-nevolent action should be local. Echoing classical definitions of pity, such as Aristotle's, but incorporating aspects of the egoistic philosophy for-warded by Mandeville, he argued that selfishness guides selflessness.[41]

When they asked readers in Britain to assist in alleviating the spiritual plight of Indians, missionaries would seem to have fit within Smith's cate-gory of "whining and melancholy moralists." If it were even possible for them to extend their readers' sympathetic capacity across a great distance and a vast cultural gap, their depictions of Indians threatened to ruin the happiness of British readers and distract them from more appropriate ob-jects of their care. But it is clear that whatever their motivations, many Britons expressed interest in the spiritual fate of Indians. If the most obvi-ous aspect of British missionary projects in America was their failure to convert many Indians, one of the most surprising was their success in rais-ing funds for those endeavors. The New England Company gathered £15,000 between 1649 and 1660, the Mohegan and Presbyterian minister Samson Occom raised more than £10,000 during his preaching tour of

Britain in 1766–68, and several times the Society for the Propagation of the Gospel in Foreign Parts (SPG) supplemented its annual subscriptions with lucrative nation wide parish collections.[42] Missionary charity dried up during Anglo-Indian wars, but it persistently returned, even amid domestic unrest. The New England Company's collection began weeks after the execution of Charles I, while Occom's tour occurred shortly after the Seven Years' War. The SPG and the SSPCK continued to collect funds in the wake of the South Sea Bubble, during riots and Jacobite invasions, and in spite of glaring local poverty.

We may well wonder how such projects could have made sense to those donors who had never left Britain. What could have made them care enough to contribute? It is one thing to assemble a discourse of imperial validation through claims to be saving heathen souls, but giving funds to carry out this claim is another matter. What gains did donors think they were getting for their generosity? Was it the case that, as Smith's work might suggest, they were "occupied in contemplating the more sublime" cases of need, while neglecting their own humble department? Should we attribute these donations to a basic sense of duty, to millenarian apprehension, to fear of Catholics, to self-promotional displays of generosity, to guilt?

I believe all these motivations applied, in varying degrees, to donors, but we still need to account for the complex discursive process by which the promoters of missions in America made readers in Britain care about distant projects and feel empowered to assist them. Ann Jessie Van Sant has described the widely held eighteenth-century view that "sympathetic feelings, which require vividness and proximity, arise through an act of the imagination largely dependent on sight."[43] This visually oriented understanding of pity underlay the fund-raising strategies that charities such as the Magdalen House for reformed prostitutes deployed, especially ceremonies that placed objects of charity before the gaze of their benefactors. She writes, "Contemplation of the fortunes of others, with the actual eye or the mind's eye, allows an imaginative exchange of place that 'makes real' and 'brings near' experience not one's own."[44] Compassion is enabled by a visual aid, especially when it is propelled by the evangelical fantasy of making the other spiritually similar.

The desire to make Indians visible did govern much of the discourse of mission. Promoters were well aware of the boosts their projects were likely to receive when they presented living Indians to a metropolitan audience. The widely celebrated visit to London in 1710 of "the four Indian kings," representatives of the Iroquois nations, inspired much British interest in missions, as did Occom's visit in 1766–68.[45] Because they rarely could present living Indian converts to benefactors in Britain, however, fund-raising tracts often fabricated such spectacles by presenting detailed portrayals of Indians complete with evocative descriptions of emotional turmoil.

But in spite of efforts to include affecting portraits of Indians, few missionary texts truly asked readers to feel sympathy for them. Even if the figure of the Indian had not had to compete in British minds with images of murderous savages from captivity narratives, the writers of these texts seem to have anticipated, and perhaps themselves felt, an inability to express sympathy for a people so distant—culturally or geographically—from themselves. British depictions of Indians often elicited less emotional connection than spectatorial objectification from their audience. This is always a hazard of such portrayals, but it was especially likely with Indians, whose depictions had been overdetermined by their displays as "New World artifacts and curiosities placed in 'Raree Shows' near Bible-thumping chapels," as Polly Stevens Fields has noted, as well as in travel writings.[46] Occom demonstrated his painful awareness of the function his visit to Britain had served when he reminded his teacher, Eleazar Wheelock, "[I]f you had not this Indian Buck you would not [have] Collected a quarter of the Money you did, one gentleman in Particular in England said to me, *if he hadn't Seen my face* he woudnt have given a tuppence but now I have 50 pounds freely."[47] Much of the money Occom raised seems to have emerged more from fascination at his racial difference than from a sense of shared situation.

Instead of eliciting sympathy, many missionary writings asked readers to feel pity for the Indians presented to them, but then encouraged readers to feel sympathy for other British people, and sometimes for non-British Protestants, who were trying to save the Indians. Through a variety of strategies that I will explore in this book, these writings operated within an understanding of "sympathy" that anticipated and transcended Smith's dichotomy between global and local. For although missionary texts beckoned their readers' compassionate gazes to faraway lands, they often marked that imagined connection as a self-referential one to other British people. The readers of these texts were encouraged to think of Christian mission as a duty placed within their inner circles of obligation. This duty emerged from self-interest, as it would help secure Britain's interests abroad, its safety at home, its moral purity, and—for some audiences—the second coming of Christ. To assist missionary projects was also, however, to help English or

Scottish people in the colonies, and to prove the compassion that all Britons felt for the spiritually needy. Even while stressing the Indians' foreignness, missionary writings thus presented Indians as the focal point for a triangulated expression of closeness between other English, Scots, or Europeans.

While eliciting pity, and while stressing the profits of promoting the gospel, the writers of these texts at once evoked and peddled a transatlantic sense of togetherness. That is, they insisted that everyone must help in this endeavor if it was to succeed, but they also suggested that one reward of such charity would be an enhanced collective identity. English people would feel themselves to be part of a great and divinely blessed endeavor if they all helped their compatriots in the colonies spread the gospel among America's Indians. In the preface to an account of Puritan New England missions, the Independent preacher Joseph Caryl proclaimed in 1655, "Beloved Brethren, Yee may now see and taste the fruit of those Prophecies, which ye have been helping to birth."[48] Suggesting the tangible rewards of mission through the medium of the text, Caryl also marked his readers as "Brethren" connected by their midwifery to a spiritual birth. As he sought funds in 1650 for the conversion of the Indians he thought were the lost tribes of Israel, Thomas Thorowgood insisted, "[S]urely the poore natives will not be a little encouraged to looke after the glorious Gospel of Christ, when they shall understand that not onely the English among them, but wee all here are daily sutors for them at the throne of grace."[49] Thorowgood described two triangles of affection: the first between the English, their counterparts in America, and the Indians, and the second between the English, the Indians, and God.

Collective acts of giving, Thorowgood suggested, are mutually enriching because they strengthen these triangulated relations. By pooling their resources for Indians, the English can connect with their brethren abroad: "And let these words be understood as awakenings to those of our nation there and our selves also that wee all labour mutually and from our hearts, to propagate the Gospell there because wee, who eate every man of his owne vine, and of his owne figtree and drinke every man water out of his owne cisterne (Esa 36.16) should witnesse our thankfulnesse unto God, for these favours, by sympathizing affections toward our brethren there, and the natives."[50] Sealing transatlantic ties, mission also promises reciprocal profit: "Honour will redound to this England, not onely from ours there, who professe truly, if they prosper, we shall be the more glorious, but the Natives enlightened by us will return hither the tribute of their abundant thankfulness."[51] The text argues that advocacy for Indians will enhance England's own case for salvation, just as underwriting mission will increase trade. Money becomes the medium of, and a metaphor for, mutual redemption. It provides the channel through which networks of sympathy are extended to include others by remaining focused on those closest to oneself. Collective missionary endeavor promotes profit, but collective identity also is the profit.

This economically articulated triangle of compassion between colonial missionaries, their metropolitan readers, and the Indians they were trying to save shares much with the erotic triangles studied by Eve Sedgwick and René Girard.[52] Just as men often are portrayed in literature as manifesting attraction to each other through romantic rivalry for a feminine object, the writers of missionary texts expressed affinity and sought mutual benefit through their pity for Indians. In terms of the rhetorical categories developed by Aristotle, missionary writings rooted their *pathos* in their *ethos*, and they defined *ethos* largely as a matter of shared *pathos*.[53] That is, these texts generated emotion (*pathos*) for their cause by establishing the character of the text's author (*ethos*), and they established the author's character by stressing his closeness—in situation, nationality, affect, and belief—to the audience. The pity for Indians that the audience was asked to feel was generated through affinity with the texts' authors. Shared pity for Indians, in turn, fostered ties between British people on both sides of the Atlantic, leading to affectionate correspondences between individuals, collaborations between groups, and suggestions that the effort to save Indians souls united all Britons, in Britain and America, in a shared endeavor. Several marginal groups also claimed that missionary projects generated from shared pity for Indians would contribute to national solidarity and strength in order to assert their affective membership in a developing national community that might otherwise have ignored them. Congregationalists, Anglicans, Presbyterians, and other denominations each described missions in ways that made their work seem central to Britain, even as they described the multidenominational and transatlantic unity that assisted and followed from such work.

It will not be lost on many readers that this description of collectivity draws on the work of Benedict Anderson and others on nationalism. Anderson has outlined the ways in which novels and newspapers reconfigured the cognitive boundaries of their readers, prompting them to understand themselves as engaged in shared acts of readership and connected with distant horizons of activity.[54] In the last decade much scholarship has charted a causal trajectory from discourse to discursive community, showing how the reading of new types of texts generated modern forms of social feeling. These sentiments crossed the gaps of geography and urban anonymity, affectively linking disparate people.[55]

Missionary writings served purposes similar to an effect often attributed to the newspaper, periodical, or novel: the enhancement of collective identities and norms of civility. Like newspapers (and, to some degree, novels), they conveyed a sense of things happening all over the world, at one time, which the reader could read about and imagine.[56] Like essay periodicals and sentimental novels they presented various affective responses as signs of internal inclinations and beliefs, modeling reactions that their readers could imitate if they wanted to feel included in communities of the civilized or genteel. The contribution that missionary texts made to this process, though, was more complicated than those made by secular genres. For they helped construct a modern vision of civil society, of a nation, and sometimes of a supra-national collective by alluding to what we might consider one of the earliest geographically dispersed and imagined communities, the early Christian Church.[57] As articulated in the New Testament, this community defined itself by a set of religious beliefs and in the enactment of a compassion most vividly expressed in efforts to expand the community's membership through the propagation of its creed. The great differences between the early Christian Church and modern nations do not eclipse the consistent phenomenon of a group in which people are made to feel membership through shared emotions and beliefs that find expression through circulating texts.

Whether such rhetoric actually helped to create a transatlantic nationalism felt throughout Britain and the colonies is hard to say, but it is clear that such claims were used to develop transoceanic networks among members of the same religious communities, such as seventeenth-century Puritans and eighteenth-century evangelicals. The notion of a nation characterized by benevolent feeling certainly became a component of the ideology of both Britain and the United States, and arguably is still an important aspect of both nations' self-images. Studying the ways in which these texts sought to expand their readers' capacity for sympathetic engagement and charity, by triangulating pity for Indians with empathy for the Indians' missionaries and British neighbors, helps us see how these texts provided a religious template for increasingly secular forms of collective sentiment. Linking group identity to emotion and emphasizing the ability of spectators to assist in distant work, these writings prompted their readers to see themselves not just as part of an imagined community but also as participants in a vicariously enacted one.[58]

"Poor Indians" and the Ethics of Emotion

As it influenced depictions of Indians, pity became a crucial component of the British people's developing sense of themselves as a people whose boundaries would extend as far as their ability to feel sorrow for suffering did. It presented a simple way to govern ethical obligations amid enlarged webs of human relations, especially those resulting from colonialism, slavery, and intercontinental trade. It proved to be a problematic basis for moral judgment, however, so that in the late eighteenth century the philosopher Immanuel Kant excluded emotions from the arena of morality.[59] While Indians offered useful occasions for the expression of pity, attempts to convert them compelled the British to contemplate the implications of equating pity with goodness. These writings thus provide a focal point for examining some of the questions and debates that developed around the use of emotion as a moral touchstone.

An immediate question was the trustworthiness of expressions of pity. One of the most obvious statements one can make about Europe's colonial projects is that they often caused great suffering in the name of alleviating suffering. It is tempting to interpret this paradox entirely as the result of dishonesty. Conrad seemed to reach this conclusion when he wrote about *Heart of Darkness,* "All the bitterness of those days . . . —all my indignation at masquerading philanthropy—have been with me again, while I wrote. . . . I have divested myself of everything but pity—and some scorn—while putting down the insignificant events that bring on the catastrophe."[60] Conrad suggested that as he stripped a veneer of benevolence from the reality of imperial exploitation, he was motivated by pity. True sorrow at the sight of suffering prompted him to attack an insincere pity that caused suffering.

It is important, however, to see that pity can be morally problematic even when authentically felt. The moral implications of pity become especially complex when it is expressed as a desire to save another's soul. As they elicited compassion arising less from sensory data than religious conviction, missionary writings encouraged readers to pity a people who did not necessarily feel that they were in pain. They prompted readers to feel compassion for another precisely because of his or her spiritual otherness. Yet they exhorted their readers to channel that emotion toward adopting that foreign other into their own religion. They enunciated the distance between self and other and then sought to bridge that distance through an intensive process of spiritual transformation and rigorous acculturation.

Because distance—both cultural and geographical—is such a prominent aspect of missionary writings, these texts provide a useful site for examining the ethical dilemmas that arose from the detachment inherent in texts evoking sympathy or pity. As Karen Halttunen has observed, "Although spectatorial sympathy claimed to demolish social distance, it actually rested on social distance—a distance reinforced, in sentimental art, by the interposition of written text, stage, or canvas between the virtuous spectator and the (imaginary) suffering victim."[61] This problem became prominent in the sentimental culture of the mid-eighteenth century. It was in this era that many literary texts were devoted to eliciting intense feeling for the sufferings of their main characters to convey moral lessons, but also to entertain. "The literary scenario of suffering, which made ethics a matter of viewing the pain of another, from the outset lent itself to an aggressive kind of voyeurism."[62] Pushed to its logical conclusion, this voyeurism led to the "pornography of pain" that Halttunen has analyzed in humanitarian, sensationalist, and erotic publications of the nineteenth century. Along with concerns about the inauthenticity of vicarious feeling, these worries about voyeurism also led to a pejorative connotation of "sentimentality" in the late eighteenth century.[63] Whether it excited its viewers or not, the spectacle of pain could end up inspiring more emotion than action.

The complex role that pity played in missionary writings is suggested by the shifting meaning of the adjective missionaries most often used to describe Indians: "the poor Indians," or sometimes "the poor heathens."[64] As Joseph Caryl wrote, "The poor, naked, ignorant *Indians*, who lately knew no civill Order, now beg to be brought into Church Order, to live under the Government, and enjoy the holy ordinances of our Lord Jesus Christ."[65] The word *poor* was used often in the seventeenth and eighteenth centuries to describe any figure worthy of pity. In Puritan context it also connoted a soul in need of salvation, but it appeared with unusual frequency in relation to Indians. In missionary writings the word *poor* conveys several meanings at once: it indicates material need, a lack of civilization, spiritual impoverishment, and brutal treatment by Catholic colonists. Central to missionary writings, the figure of the "poor Indian" also appeared in texts such as Pope's *Essay on Man*:

Lo! the poor Indian, whose untutor'd mind
Sees God in clouds, or hears him in the wind;
His soul proud Science never taught to stray
Far as the solar walk, or milky way;
Yet simple Nature to his hope has giv'n,
Behind the cloud-topt hill, an humbler heav'n;
Some safer world in depth of woods embrac'd,
Some happier island in the watry waste,
Where slaves once more their native lands behold,
No fiends torment, no Christians thirst for gold!
To Be, contents his natural desire,
He asks no Angel's wing, no Seraph's fire;
But thinks, admitted to that equal sky,
His faithful dog shall bear him company.[66]

In this passage Pope links the scientist's hubris with the Indian's naïveté, chiding both for reducing God's power to a finite scope. Better off than the scientist, the Indian still merits our pity and perhaps our amusement for his simplistic faith. Our pity takes many forms as several meanings of the word *poor* coincide. Deprived of civilization and abstract thought, the Indian also is oppressed by brutal colonists who pretend to embody the word *Christian*. Most of all, he is spiritually bereft. Replacing angels with dogs and heaven with happy hunting grounds, he misses out on the blessings of a rational yet revealed religion. Unlike in missionary writings, his poverty does not demand action from the reader. Rather, his marking as "poor" helps construct a consensus between Pope and his readers, unifying them through their reaction to the Indian as he illustrates what they should not believe. Between a missionary tract of 1655 and this poem of 1733–34, the "poor Indian" has changed from an image impelling charitable action to a vehicle of erudite discussion and moral education.

As Pope's reference to the tormenting "Christians" suggests, the figure of the poor Indian borrowed much from the noble savage, whose moral simplicity was used to set off Europeans' contrasting hypocrisy. Ultimately, though, these figures oppose each other. Poor Indians are defined through their need for the very things that noble savages do not need, Christianity and European civilization. This trope was not unique to English texts, as the French, the Spanish, and other colonizers also were inclined to describe Indians as pitiable. The English phrase, "the poor Indians," shares much with the Spanish word *miserable,* which was a legal term for Indians that at least theoretically granted them protections under Spanish rule.[67] This resemblance is ironic, because what often makes Indians "poor" in English writings is their mistreatment by the Spanish. It also is ironic because in English the term *poor* invoked no legal privileges, only emotion.

Along with moral philosophers, many authors of missionary writings were aware of the problems suggested by the reactions they sought from readers. Even as they generated an emotional response to raise funds and convert heathen souls, they worried that such emotion could be alienating and ineffectual. They debated whether pity involved identification with the sufferer and led to alleviating that suffering, or whether it simply became a source of pleasure at the cost of another's pain. These writings thus offer a case study for examining not only how the British generated connections with each other through their shared feeling for the victims of suffering, but also how and why they came to feel conflicted over such feeling.

The ways in which Indian converts interpreted this term also suggest the variable status of pity in a colonial framework. In *A further Accompt of the Progresse of the Gospel* (1659), the missionary John Eliot recorded the speeches of several "praying Indians" to display their preparedness for admission to full communion. One of these Indians, Piumbubbon, tailored the beatitude "Blessed are the poor in spirit, for they shall inherit the earth" (Matt. 5:1), to his Massachusett audience: "For poverty of spirit, we are the most poor, feeble, despicable people in the world, but let us look in what case our spirits be, for if our hearts be answerably poor, and low, as our outward condition is, then we are in the way to be made truly rich, for the Kingdome of heaven is promised to such as are poor in spirit."[68] To the degree that we can acknowledge these lines fully as Piumbubbon's, they reveal a Christian convert transforming the word *poor* from a signifier of humility and destitution to a path toward salvation. Piumbubbon essentially accepted a pejorative portrayal of Indians by English colonists, but he used the logic and the language of Christianity to eradicate the negative implications of that portrayal.

The faith that Piumbubbon expressed in the salvific and leveling connotations of "poor," an optimistic outlook that best fits the earlier stages of missionary work, was belied over a century later by Samson Occom's use of the same word at the end of his autobiography. After detailing the many ways in which the ministerial establishment of the colonies had insulted him, Occom compared his own status to that of a "Poor Indian Boy" who was beaten by the master to whom he was indentured. Noting that when asked why his master beat him so much, the boy replied, "'because I am an Indian,'" Occom applied this conclusion to his own situation: "So I am ready to Say, they have used me thus, because I Can't Instruct the Indians so well as other missionaries; but I can assure them I have endeavoured to teach them as well as I know how;—but I must Say, 'I believe it is because I am a poor Indian.' I Can't help that God has made me So; I did not make my self so."[69] Occom expressed his anger at the racial discrimination he suffered by resorting to an ironic use of the very term that helped inspire missionary projects. In so doing he detached this term from the compassion that originally produced it, revealing the abysmal treatment that such pity rationalized.

One of the greatest factors separating Piumbubbon's and Occom's uses of "poor" is the action that they saw connected to this word. Piumbubbon felt that Indians' poverty—which he marked as a depletion of material wealth and status—accelerated their admission to a Christian community within which they found salvation and spiritual wealth. He did not focus on the actions of the English people who pitied Indians; rather, he attended to the action of the Indians as they sought a Christian god. Poverty was for Piumbubbon a spiritual opportunity. While he shared Piumbubbon's faith in the salvation "poor" Indians could receive, Occom saw the insidious potential of this term as he described the discrimination it could obscure. He also played with the word's various meanings, shifting from a general connotation of piteousness to a focus on financial dearth. Occom was poor because he was paid less than white missionaries and received less respect. His poverty was the result of British behavior, not the motivating force behind it.

As he revised the trope of the "poor Indian" to expose the hypocrisy of his would-be benefactors, Occom revealed the processes by which pity, under the auspices of the word *poor*, can be linked to the very sorts of treatment that would seem to inspire it in the first place. While I argue that missionary writings often were more about their readers than their Indian subjects, the understandings of benevolence that they developed had an immense impact on the indigenous peoples of America. The U.S. policy of Indian removal could not have been established as easily as it was without the conflicted sentiment with which the British came to regard Indians. Although this sentiment eventually shed its religious origins, it could not have developed as quickly as it did outside of a missionary context, with its concern for the fate of heathen souls. When, in *The Farther Adventures of Robinson Crusoe*, Crusoe passively witnessed and then mourned the death of Friday, he was imitating the missionaries as much as he had done when he first converted his fantastically loyal servant.[70]

The final chapter of this book comments on the history of American Indians' erasure—in British minds if not in reality—through religious pity and ineffectual benevolence. One of my goals in writing this book has been to prevent the continued repetition of this sentimental erasure in our contemporary culture. I have worked from the conviction that we will never be able truly to hear Indians within texts authored by colonizers until we understand how it is that colonial discourse silenced them. Precisely because they often expressed sincere pity for Indians, and because they protested their own culture's treatment of Indians even as they gave their culture the rhetorical tools to support that treatment, missionary writings present an important area for analysis. My hope is that studies like this one will complement the work of other scholars to illuminate imperial history from the perspective of Indians and other conquered peoples. Only by understanding the mechanics by which benevolence can erase its object, especially in a sentimental and a colonial framework, can we then see those pitied objects more accurately as real people who actively sought to resist or mitigate the effects of colonization on their own cultures.

What Is a Missionary Writing?

Because I am more concerned with portrayals of mission than with the events of missionary work, I use the term *missionary writing* loosely. It denotes the journals, letters, and reports written by ministers trying to convert American Indians and other non-Christian peoples, but it also includes sermons, letters, and genres usually marked as literary, written by people raising money for, or merely thinking about, missionary work. My concerns with transatlantic reception and the culture of sensibility as well as my footing in literary study often steer me to focus on the latter group of texts. I make some references to the earliest Indian converts in English colonies and to the first organized English attempt to convert Indians, the establishment of Henrico College in Jamestown from 1620 until the Powhatan massacre of 1622. I also occasionally draw upon promotional writings of the Virginia Company.[71] For the most part, however, my study ranges from the beginning of the English Civil War in 1642 to the beginning of the American Revolution in 1776.

I chose these dates because they coincide roughly with the beginnings and ends of sustained, as opposed to extremely short-lived, missionary efforts in the parts of America that would become the United States. I also chose them because they bracket an era when missionaries would rely on the transatlantic circulation of print to generate an English and then British identity through shared feeling for America's Indians. The parish collection authorized by James I in 1616 would seem to provide the only English missionary writings that precede this era.[72] While the few letters printed for this project may have provided a model for later writings, they did not have to demand their audience's attention within the larger and less regulated print culture that developed during the English Civil War.[73] They also did not have to construct English cohesion against the background of domestic conflict, a factor that enhanced the unifying force of later missionary projects. While sharing much with their predecessors, English-language missionary writings produced after the American Revolution were markedly different in their imaginative range, their audience, and their tone. Emerging from evangelical movements and from the dynamic leadership of figures such as William Carey, late eighteenth- and nineteenth-century missionary writings reflected a new global consciousness, an altered sense of national and imperial identity, and an enlarged audience that openly included women.[74]

Although most of the texts I study were composed in English and for a transatlantic British audience, it is important also to understand their place within an international framework. Many writers of English missionary texts were aware of missions launched from other European countries. Sometimes these dealt with Protestant projects, such as August Hermann Francke's *Missionsnachrichten*, an account of Danish and German efforts in India and then in other lands that he began to publish serially in 1710.[75] More often British missionaries worked under the shadow of Roman Catholic missionary orders, especially the Jesuits, whose *Relations* had been distributed throughout Europe since the early seventeenth century. After his conversion to Roman Catholicism, John Dryden dedicated his translation of Dominick Bohours's *Life of St. Francis Xavier* to Queen Mary of Modena shortly after the birth of her son. This text constituted a celebration of a Catholic successor to the throne as well as an implicit critique of the Church of England's failure to show substantial concern for heathen souls.[76] English writings displayed defensiveness about Protestant projects, which revealed some acquaintance with Catholic successes. In their refutation of Catholic mission, these texts were central to the forging of a modern Protestant and British identity against the foil of Catholicism.

The missionary writings divide into five basic groups connected with the main denominations active in North America before the American Revolution.[77] The first group includes texts connected with The President and Society for the Propagation of the Gospel in New England. Established by the Long Parliament in 1649 and rechartered after the Restoration as the Company for the Propagation of the Gospel in New England and the parts adjacent in America, the New England Company (as it was commonly called and as I shall refer to it) was at first a corporation of sixteen persons, merchants and Independent or Presbyterian clergymen, who publicized the cause of converting Indians, collected funds in England, and sent money across the Atlantic to be distributed by the Commissioners of the United Colonies.[78] Robert Boyle, better known for his scientific work, became the company's president after the Restoration. From the Restoration until Boyle's death in 1691 the group's membership covered a moderately wide range of religious and class positions.[79] On the whole, however, the group retained a Dissenting majority. The missionaries it supported emphasized a Calvinist, mostly Congregational creed.

These missionaries included John Eliot, who established the praying Indian towns that housed more than one thousand Massachusett and Narragansett converts in New England, several generations of the Mayhew family (who converted the Wampanoags of Martha's Vineyard and Nantucket), and a handful of ministers scattered throughout the Plymouth and Massachusetts Bay colonies. In the eighteenth century this group helped fund Jonathan Sergeant's work with the Housatonic Indians of Stockbridge, the work of Gideon Hawley among the Mashpees of Cape Cod, and Joseph Fish's efforts among the Narragansetts of Rhode Island.[80] When the American Revolution began, the company abandoned its efforts in New England to focus on Canada. Although several figures were connected with both groups, the New England Company is different from the Society for Propagating Christian Knowledge among the Indians in North America, which was established by the Massachusetts General Assembly in 1762. This organization failed to obtain royal confirmation for its founding, but it was reestablished in 1787 as the Society for Propagating the Gospel among the Indians and others in North America.[81]

The New England Company printed some of the eleven "Indian tracts" during the seventeenth century, which contain reports from missionaries, testimonials from Indian converts, letters from supporters, and pleas for money, prayers, and supplies.[82] It also subsidized the publishing of Algonquian translations of the Bible, an Indian primer, and several religious tracts, which John Eliot completed with the help of Nesuton and James Printer, two native assistants.[83] Eliot published other texts relating to his work, such as the *Indian dialogues* (1671) and *The Dying Speeches of several Indians* (1685). Eighteenth-century publications connected with projects funded by the New England Company included Cotton Mather's *India Christiana* (1721), Experience Mayhew's *Indian converts* (1727), and Samuel Hopkins's *Historical Memoirs, Relating to the Housatunnuk Indians* (1753). Texts including Thomas Thorowgood's *Iewes in America, or, Probabilities That the Americans are of that Race* (1650) were not officially connected with the company but promoted its work. Although Roger Williams was exiled from the Massachusetts Bay Colony and resisted active missionary work on theological grounds, I also include some of his writings, especially his *Key into the Language of America* (1643), here.

The second collection includes the texts produced by the Church of England's Society for the Propagation of the Gospel in Foreign Parts (SPG), which was founded in 1701.[84] Made up mostly of high-ranking churchmen and affluent laymen interested in the establishment of Anglican churches in America, the SPG devoted much textual attention to the spiritual state of Indians. Of British missionary organizations, the SPG was the least involved in actual missionary operations, but it did have some success with the Mohawks. Individual SPG missionaries made occasional attempts to convert Indians, including John Wesley, who along with his brother Charles briefly collaborated with Moravians to convert a group of Yamacraw Indians in the Georgia colony.[85]

The central SPG publications were the anniversary sermons. Every February throughout the eighteenth century the society invited a bishop or dean to deliver a sermon at London's Mary-le-Bow parish church amid some fanfare, advertising in the London *Gazette* and inviting the city's leading citizens to attend. The society then distributed the sermon to its missionaries, members, and correspondents in Britain, Europe, and America. These usually were printed with "Abstracts," which included descriptions of the society's accomplishments, reports from ministers in the colonies, financial accounts, membership lists, and template forms for donations and bequests. From time to time it published broadsides, including requests for parish collections authorized by the monarch, requests for missionaries, and instructions to its ministers. As with the New England Company there are associated texts that promoted the SPG's work, such as *An Essay Towards an Instruction For the Indians* (1740), by Thomas Wilson, the Bishop of Sodor and Man, and *A Pindaric Poem on the Propagation of the Gospel in Foreign Parts* (1711) by Elkanah Settle, the laureate poet of the City of London.

The third group involves texts published in connection with the Presbyterian Society in Scotland for the Propagation of Christian Knowledge in the Highlands and Islands and the Foreign Parts of the World (SSPCK), which was chartered in 1709. The original mission of this group was to establish schools and distribute ministers throughout the Highlands and Islands of Scotland. In 1717, however, the Dissenting clergyman Daniel Williams left the SSPCK a generous bequest on the condition that it send at least three ministers to preach among non-Christian peoples of foreign lands.[86] After thirteen years the society began to dispatch missionaries to Indians in Connecticut and Long Island. Throughout the century it subsidized several projects through its colonial Boards of Correspondents. Among these were David Brainerd's mission to the Delawares (which was taken over by his brother John after his death) and Eleazar Wheelock's establishment of Moor's Indian Charity School and then of Dartmouth College.[87] The SSPCK also organized part of the visit to Britain in 1766–68 by Nathaniel Whitaker and Samson Occom.[88] Most of the ministers supported by the SSPCK adhered to a Presbyterian creed, and some of them supported the transatlantic revivals of the mid-eighteenth century.[89] The membership of its Boards of Commissioners in New York, Boston, and Connecticut overlapped with the membership of the New England Company's board, and missionaries employed by these groups sometimes worked together.[90]

Like the SPG, the SSPCK published anniversary sermons, accounts, and histories of its work. The missionaries employed by this society produced a variety of texts, such as David Brainerd's famous journal and the *Narrative[s] of the Indian Charity-School* (1766–75) published by Wheelock. Occom also wrote the first English publication to be authored by an American Indian, *A Sermon, Preached at the Execution of Moses Paul* (1772).

The fourth group is a small and diffuse collection of texts relating to the missionary efforts of the Quakers, or the Society of Friends. Although the Quakers developed close relations with many indigenous groups, and although some individual Friends preached to Indians, they did not undertake organized missions until 1794.[91] The Friends published few missionary writings during this era. I do, however, draw on George Fox's *Journal* along with a few texts suggesting Quaker efforts, such as John Cripps's *A True Account of the Dying Words of Ockanickon, an Indian King* (1682).

The fifth group includes texts relating to the work of the United Brethren, or Moravians. They were descended from Hussites, named after John Hus, a Roman Catholic priest of Prague who was burned at the stake in

1415 for preaching against church corruption. His followers built a reformist movement and in 1467 established their own ministry. Almost eradicated during the Counter-Reformation, the Moravians remained largely in hiding until 1722, when they migrated to Saxony and settled on the lands of Nicholas Ludwig Count von Zinzendorf, a Lutheran pietist who became their bishop. Evangelical concerns, especially a desire to convert Indians and African slaves, motivated Moravian emigration to the new colony of Georgia, via a small settlement in England, in 1735. Establishing Bethlehem, Pennsylvania, as their central settlement, they launched successful missions throughout the British colonies. Although they and their Indian converts suffered persecution from other colonists for their radical theology, Zinzendorf was able to establish some legitimacy for his church in England, so that in 1749 Parliament formally declared the United Brethren to be an ancient Episcopal Church.[92] The Church of England remained supportive of the Moravians throughout the eighteenth century, and in 1765 it hired the Moravian Christian Frederick Post, who had lived among the Mohegans for seventeen years, to preach to the Moskito Indians of present-day Honduras.[93]

In spite of their success in converting Indians, the Moravians occupy a minor position in my book because they produced few missionary writings for a British audience. Many Moravians did keep journals and write letters about their work, however. Most of these accounts were circulated within the Moravian community, and they may have encouraged contributions from Moravians in Europe. Except for the Society for the Furtherance of the Gospel, which existed from 1745 to 1764 and sought external support, the Moravians did not publicize their work with a British audience for quite a while.[94] John Heckewelder's journal was not published in English until 1820, and it was not until 1769 that a fund-raising tract for the Moravians' work, Heckewelder's *A Letter to a Friend*, appeared in London.[95]

Linguistic barriers and tensions with British colonists account partly for the dearth of published texts. Primarily, however, the Moravians neglected to publish many texts because their intense dedication and their communal ethos led them to fund their missions through a socialist economy supported by a variety of industries in Bethlehem. Moravians also were willing to live in poorer conditions than many British ministers were.[96] This group illustrates a central irony of my project: there often seems to have been an inversely proportional relation between the degree to which early modern Europeans talked about their desires to convert Indians and the degree to which they actually labored toward this end.

Alongside these publications I read documents written for private audiences. These texts include the correspondence of John Eliot and Richard Baxter, the minutes of the SPG's Standing Committee, the journals and letters of missionaries, and the Moravian papers. Besides providing additional information about the missionary work, these writings serve as a counterpoint to the published ones. They suggest how the carefully crafted portrayals of missionary projects related to the ways in which Indians, missionaries, and their supporters in Britain evaluated those efforts when they were removed from a public gaze.

These texts make up a vast and diverse corpus, especially because they include denominations that waged fierce disagreements with each other and underwent significant changes in the century and a half that this book covers. Any one of these collections would provide sufficient material for a book-length study of missionary discourse, as would any twenty or thirty years within the study. A book encompassing all of this data must overlook topics that would inform more specialized studies, such as the nuances of the Great Awakening or the finer points of debate between Calvinists and Arminians over salvation. From the earliest stages of this project I elected to examine the writings of all Protestant missions connected with Britain because I wanted to see the full range of representational strategies that developed through efforts to convert Indians. As I read more of these texts I became struck less with the range than with the rhetorical uniformity of these writings, which in spite of conflicting theological stances display a remarkably stable approach to the tasks of describing Indians and raising readers' interest in their conversion. My approach throughout most of this book thus has been to focus on the common discursive features of Protestant missionary writings, leaving doctrinal variety in the background except for those points where it produced significant rhetorical differences. The result, I hope, is a study that emphasizes similarity without ignoring important differences in various denominations' portrayals of Indians.

If I could have expanded my project without making it too cumbersome for a single book, I would have examined missionaries' depictions of both African slaves and Indians. Certainly any study would have to examine depictions of both groups if it were to provide a comprehensive account of the British encounter, both textual and actual, with "heathens" in America. Such a study also would reflect the parallel status Indians and Africans held in many missionary projects and texts. Groups such as the Moravians and the SPG simultaneously undertook missions to Indians and Africans, and discussions of both peoples often appeared alongside each other in fund-raising tracts. The enslavement of Indians as well as intermarriage between Indians and Africans also led to some blurring of categories in British or colonial writings, especially in an era before race was identified primarily through skin color.[97]

In spite of these overlaps, British missionaries tended to treat Africans and Indians as separate groups whose conversion required different strategies and whose existence, as "heathen" or Christian, provoked distinct emotions and debates. As Chapter 4 will show, the complete isolation of Indians from the Christian world until the fifteenth century produced a theological quandary that Africans, who at least theoretically had had access to the gospel, did not. The noble savage produced forms of pathos related to but still distinct from the emotions that met images of African slaves, and slaveholders' concerns about the legality of owning Christians created particular obstacles for missionaries that were different from the difficulties they encountered preaching to Indians. The complex differences between these two missionary efforts, as well as the sheer quantity of material produced in connection with them, proved too vast for this study. A comparative examination of British missionaries' depictions of Africans and Indians, especially a close analysis of the subtle affective differences between them, surely would yield important information, and it would be a worthwhile topic for future work.

How Widely Read Were Missionary Writings?

As with any question about early modern reader reception, there is no easy answer. Data on the distribution of the published writings are limited, but in general it seems that while few people read many missionary writings, many people were aware of a few of them. The three main organizations printed most of their texts with an eye toward distributing them to members and to associates who might contribute to their cause.[98] The Journal of the SPG's Standing Committee reveals that the society published its sermons in numbers ranging from 500 to more than 3,000, basing their decision sometimes on the reputation of the preacher.[99] William Kellaway has noted that the New England Company's members had trouble distributing more than 1,500 copies of their tracts.[100] With the exception of blockbusters such as Jonathan Edward's *Account of the Life of the Late Reverend Mr. David Brainerd,* the readership of these texts seems to have ranged into, but not past, the low thousands.[101] Many of these texts were distributed in the

American colonies and Europe as well as Britain, but the anticipated audience usually was a British metropolitan one. Having encountered copies of SPG sermons in rare-book rooms with the pages still uncut, I also suspect that some texts were received but not read. Certainly this reaction would fit with the response many of us today have to fund-raising texts.

When estimating the impact of these texts on British culture, though, it is important that we consider the multiple paths by which readers and listeners would have become aware of them. Although most of these texts had a select audience, fragments of them reached much of England, Wales, and Scotland in written or spoken form. Announcements of collections were often read aloud during church services, and newspapers occasionally published letters from missionaries or extracts from fund-raising sermons.[102] Events such as the "four Indian kings'" visit and Occom's tour heightened the public's awareness of missionary projects, as did calls for nationwide or citywide collections by the monarch. These events were publicized through broadsides and pamphlets. We should also consider the symbolic importance attached to missionary images, such as charters, seals, and portraits of the "four Indian kings," and we might consider texts presented for their iconic rather than textual value. After all, much was made of the presentation of Eliot's "Indian Bible" to King Charles II, the Lord Chancellor, and other public officials in 1664, although none of these recipients could read the Massachusett translation.[103] Such icons symbolized the ongoing salvation of foreigners through the rendering of well-known texts into dramatically illegible signs. If the vision of collective evangelical endeavor usually assumed a select core of gentlemen with financial means and feelings for "heathen" peoples, the references to national endeavor and the varying patterns of text distribution imply a series of concentric circles of emotionally invested citizens surrounding the missionary groups.

Chapter Outline

Missionary writings were only one subset of the many texts that early modern Europeans wrote about the Americas. Chapter 1 describes missionary tracts in relation to this broader context by surveying two prominent tropes of colonial endeavor. These are the images of husbandry—meaning the tending of the domestic sphere through farming, accounting, or housekeeping—and trade. They provided a religious validation for the plantation-style colonialism propagated by the British, and they enhanced anti-Spanish and anti-Catholic rhetoric. As they persuaded readers through these images to save Indians, the missionary writings depicted British pity as an exportable commodity and an instrument of husbandry, the spiritual profits of which benefited Indians more than colonialism impoverished them. Ironically, these writings helped transform a symbol of exploitation, the exchange of American gold for European trinkets or glass, into an image of the priceless spiritual "gold" with which the British purchased America's wealth.

Chapter 2 examines the importance of epistolarity to seventeenth-century English missionary writings. It shows how the letters that missionaries and their supporters wrote to each other, and often published for the consumption of a wider audience, constructed a transatlantic community through a shared desire to save America's Indians. The boundaries and tenor of these communities shifted with the concerns of different writers and times. The New England Company's publications, for example, stressed the importance of England's links with Puritan colonists in New England, while Henry Jessey, a London Baptist, used accounts of missions in Taiwan and New England to strengthen Anglo-Dutch ties. Late seventeenth-century writings stressed interdenominational cooperation in a way that mid-century writings did not, reflecting the political changes England underwent in this era. If the qualities of the community described in these texts altered, the basic idea of a transatlantic connection did not.

Chapter 3 continues to examine the sympathetic network described in Chapter 2 by showing how the publications of two missionary societies founded in the early eighteenth century presented a voluntary society as the unifying center and active agent of Britain's compassion. The Anglican SPG and the Presbyterian SSPCK drew on earlier models of cooperative endeavor for a worthy cause, but they refined those models to stress the utility of a central organization that maximized widespread benevolence. The publications set these groups apart from the public while making their operations trustworthy and admirable. They also configured prayer and financial donations as forms of active but displaced involvement that made readers feel included in the groups' endeavors. Through their emphasis on collective pity for heathen souls they provided a religious template for what would become a secular model of imperial sentiment constructed as emotional involvement.

The missionaries' emphasis on shared emotion enhanced Britain's benevolent self-image, but it also introduced concerns about the moral status of pity. Chapter 4 shows how the anniversary sermons of the SPG grappled with the ethics of pity while debating the necessity of Indian conversion. As they encouraged contributions to support Anglican ministers in America, the authors of these sermons used descriptions of Indians to defend Christianity from challenges posed by heterodox thinkers, especially the idea that God had been cruel in denying Indians earlier access to the gospel. By arguing that the savage behavior of Indians proved the necessity of Christian conversion for salvation, and asserting that God had delayed revealing himself to heathens so that Christians would save them, most of the sermons' authors sought to recuperate the compassionate character of God as they insisted on the necessity of their faith. These texts illustrate some of the ways in which the idea of Indians provoked debates about the capacity and moral consequences of pity.

Producing concerns about the ethics of compassion, Indians also propelled developments in the portrayal of emotion. Chapter 5 shows how mid-eighteenth-century missionary writings intersected with a broader culture increasingly interested in the depiction of feeling. I contrast the framing of emotion and human relations in two edited memoirs: Jonathan Edwards's *Life of David Brainerd,* which describes how Brainerd evangelized several groups of Indians over a four-year period until his death in 1747, and Samuel Hopkins's *Historical Memoirs, Relating to the Housatunnuck Indians,* which describes the work of John Sergeant at the Stockbridge mission of western Massachusetts from 1734 until his death in 1749. Unlike earlier tracts, these memoirs present a missionary not only as an extension of collective feeling but also as an object of emulation. While Edwards's text focuses on the solipsistic emotions of an isolated missionary and inscribes a transatlantic community through collective spectatorship of Brainerd's spiritual experience, Hopkins's account positions Sergeant within a network of transatlantic feeling. Together these texts suggest the effects that the culture of sensibility and the Great Awakening had on the representation of Christian mission, even as they imply the importance of Indians to eighteenth-century accounts of emotion. They also show how missionaries began to supersede Indians as the central figures of promotional writings, paralleling a developing British fascination with vanishing Indians.

Chapter 6 illustrates some of the ethical problems that emerged from depictions of Indians in missionary writings, as it argues that missionaries unwittingly helped create the dying Indians that were so useful to Romantic literature and the claims of manifest destiny. It shows that while they evoked pity for the wasteful deaths of unconverted Indians, especially through violence, missionaries also surrounded the exemplary deaths of

Indian converts with abundant detail and emotional response. The texts thus encouraged their readers to mourn the deaths of Christian Indians but also to feel pleasure at the recuperation of lost souls, which they saw as the outcome of British benevolence. Missionary writings prepared their readers to expect the disappearance of the Indians from America, associating the death of their bodies with the cultivation of their souls.

British missionary writings had a limited influence on seventeenth- and eighteenth-century readers. Their impact did not equal that of genres such as captivity narratives or travel writings, and the piteous figures presented in these texts received less attention than the noble savages and incorrigibly cruel brutes that filled more popular publications. Nonetheless, they exerted a subtle influence on Euro-American culture. They helped shape attitudes to Indians throughout the nineteenth and twentieth centuries, contributing in particular to notions that Indians should be pitied, saved, and mourned, sometimes all at once. They played a major role in the development of a benevolent imperialist rhetoric, the impact of which is still felt in the United States and Britain, indeed throughout the world. Finally, as they assisted in the construction of an optimistic moral philosophy intertwined with a culture of sensibility, they presented especially vivid examples of the dramatic transformations that emotion could provoke. What exactly those changes were, and whether they occurred for the better, were questions with answers that did not always match the expectations of the texts' authors and audience. This book explores some of those answers, and their implications, for the twenty-first century as well as for the era of Britain's colonization of America.

Chapter 1
Gold for Glass, Seeds to Fruit: Husbandry and Trade in Missionary Writings

"Your Spiritual Factory in New England"

In July 1649, a few months after the execution of King Charles I, Parliament established the Society for the Propagation of the Gospel in New England to subsidize the efforts of John Eliot, Thomas Mayhew, and other Puritan ministers to convert the Algonquian-speaking Indians of Massachusetts and Martha's Vineyard.[1] By 1655, the society had received several thousand pounds from a nationwide parish collection commanded by Parliament.[2] It used those funds to purchase land throughout England, some of which had just been confiscated by Parliament from loyalists to the king.[3] Besides subsidizing a few missionaries and sending supplies abroad, the rents from these lands funded the printing of several tracts, among them *A Late and Further Manifestation of the Progress of the Gospel*. Joseph Caryl, an Independent preacher of London, introduced this tract with a letter endorsing the organization's work:

Read this short discourse, and it will tell you that the Lord hath blesed the labours of the Messengers of *Sion* in *New-England*, with the Conversion of some (I may say, of a considerable number) of the *Indians*, to be a kind of first fruits of his (new) Creatures there. O let old England rejoyce in this, that our brethren who with extream difficulties and expences have Planted themselves in the Indian Wildernesses, have also laboured night and day with prayers and teares and Exhortations to Plant the Indians as a spirituall Garden, into which Christ might come and eat his pleasant fruits. Let the gaining of any of their souls to Christ . . . be more pretious in our eyes then the greatest gaine or return of Gold and Silver. This gaine of soules is a Merchandize worth the glorying in upon all the Exchanges, or rather in all the Churches throughout the world. This Merchandize is Holinesse to the Lord: And of this the ensuing Discourse presents you with a Bill of many particulars, from your spiritual Factory in New England.[4]

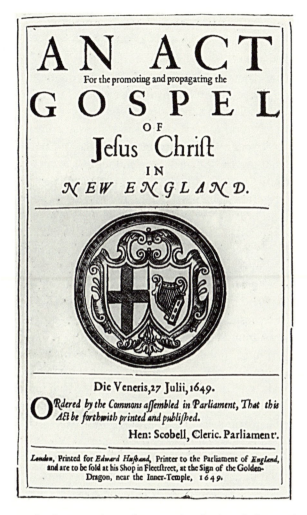

Figure 1. *An Act for the Promoting and Propagating the Gospel of Jesus Christ in New England* established the first voluntary missionary organization in England. It founded a corporation of sixteen men in England for the collection of donations, named the Commissioners of the United Colonies as agent for the disbursement of funds, ordered that the act be read in every parish of England and Wales, asked that ministers "exhort the people to a chearful and liberal contribution," and commanded parish officials to undertake a door-to-door collection. The act linked England's piety and charity to emotion both felt and observed, as it "rejoyce[d]" that "the heathen Natives" of New England "give great testimony of the power of God drawing them from death and darkness ... which appeareth by their diligent attending on the Word so preached unto them, with tears lamenting their mis-spent lives." (The John Carter Brown Library at Brown University)

As the exuberant tone and elaborate conceits of this passage suggest, English missionary projects sometimes enjoyed a richer existence in print than in reality. For many people in England, texts such as Caryl's may have been the only outcome they would witness of their contributions to missionary work. As they offered a visible return on generosity and then sought more funds, descriptions like his superseded the activities of mission, and in this excess of representation re-created the worlds they described. Caryl himself never went to America, never encountered its natives, never experienced the difficulties of persuading them to abandon their own customs for alien beliefs. Unlike the writers of countless travel narratives, who claimed the authority of experience, he invented a land and its people from what he read, heard, and believed. While he presented a textually fabricated world to his readers, he compelled them to will a dramatic transformation of it.

These lines replicated England's early colonial aspirations in miniature, linking the pursuit of material prosperity to spiritual growth and presenting Indian converts as the symbolic profits of both endeavors. Thomas Scanlon has noted, "In his characterization of the missionary enterprise as a mercantile adventure, Caryl accentuates the fact that the Indian discourse functioned as a commodity for England."[5] I would add that this depiction is positioned within a frame of agriculture and manufacture. Mission takes place first through metaphors of plantation, so that America is transformed into an orchard. Wild inhabitants of an uncultivated land, Indians become a "spirituall Garden," the fruits of cultivation. The text then replaces gardens with gold, placing plantation within commerce. As Christ eats the garden's "pleasant fruits," images of these spiritual products are returned across the Atlantic, circulated among readers, and accepted as imported goods. The tone of the last sentence resembles a report to stockholders, promising a "Bill of many particulars," as if it were a list of assets and expenses. Mission in America is made to suggest the accrual of English wealth.

Churches become orchards and factories, while mission becomes inseparable from commerce. The figure of the heathen, then Christian, Indian—cultivated, transported, and consumed—stands for the settlement and trade already undertaken by England. By focusing on the Indian, Caryl's readers could visualize colonial settlement, follow paths of trade, and feel themselves to be benefactors and beneficiaries in this enterprise. The idea of the converted Indian made colonialism imaginatively possible. With a coyness worthy of modern advertising strategies, Caryl allured readers with a secular object that he then proclaimed they really did not want. He also offered them a spiritual object that he assumed their virtue must make them desire. This apparent disowning of greed merely brackets the real object he was selling: a sense of belonging, through shared desire and emotional response, to a transatlantic community.

Caryl was able to accomplish this rhetorical feat because of the way in which he drew on two of the tropes, or figures of speech, used most frequently in English missionary writings. These were the metaphors of husbandry—which described agriculture, thrift, and the careful management of the household—and trade. Both images have ample scriptural precursors, especially gospel parables about the talents, the sower, the vineyard, and the mustard seed. The combination of these images stressed the profitability of promoting Christian mission, even as it insisted that the English really cared about Indian souls. The vision of budding Indian converts in the newly cultivated wilderness must have been an appealing one to an audience that was emerging from a civil war and that had recently witnessed the execution of their king.

It also offered an important counter to the bloody images of Spanish conquest in America, with which anti-Spanish propaganda had made the English familiar.[6] When he wrote, "Let the gaining of any of their souls to Christ . . . be more pretious in our eyes then the greatest gaine or return of Gold and Silver," Caryl did not just contrast two objects of desire. He also alluded to the violence that made possible the wealth of the Spanish Empire. Gold leaves a trail of blood, he suggested, that orchard groves do not. If they valued Indian souls over gold, the English would prove their superiority to the Spanish. His comment was a moral caution against greed, but it was more emphatically a boast about English virtue.

One of the ironies of missionary writings, however, is that by adopting scriptural images to the scene of colonial encounter, these texts altered the point of those images, validating the same acquisitiveness they seemed to shun. This tension emerges in Caryl's letter as he sells the idea of saving Indian souls through images of agricultural abundance and intercontinental trade. In particular, many missionary texts played a pivotal role in the development of a British imperial rhetoric by borrowing, and then rereading through the lens of scripture, a prominent scene of early modern travel writings. This scene was that of American gold traded for the glass and other trinkets offered to Indians by European travelers. First symbolizing the exploitation of colonized peoples, and then more generally the bilking of the powerless, this image came to signify the opposite of its original connotation. This change took place as the trope was combined with images of husbandry and applied to Christian conversion. It was this rhetorical shift that made possible the catastrophe wryly summarized by Vine Deloria: "It has been said of missionaries that when they arrived they had only the Book and we had the land; now we have the Book and they have the land."[7]

Several scholars have commented on the tendency of British missionaries to characterize their project as a mutually beneficial trade.[8] This chapter charts a rhetorical history of this tendency, placing the missionaries' descriptions in a broader discourse that begins with the Bible. Through their biblical allusions missionary writings transformed the trope of gold exchanged for glass into a sign, first, of Britain's obligations to its colonies and, then, of the intangible but eternal rewards that conquest would bring to the conquered. Focusing on Paul's comment in Romans 15:27 that "if the Gentiles have been made partakers of [the Jews'] spiritual things, their duty is also to minister unto them in carnal things," along with his rhetorical question in 1 Corinthians 9:11, "If we have sown unto you spiritual things, is it a great thing if we shall reap your carnal things?" these texts presented colonialism as a reciprocal circum-Atlantic exchange involving an endlessly replenished and exportable commodity: the prayers and pity of the British people. The piteous spectacle of Indians being cheated by Europeans, refracted through Paul's description of a charitable collection and framed by images of husbandry, reconfigured the idea of intercontinental commerce. Seeking to convert the "poor Indians" of America, these texts inverted an image that had been used to condemn the exploitation of those Indians. On a rhetorical level, then, selling the idea of saving souls helped make possible the idea of selling Europe's glass for America's gold.

"They Bartered Like Idiots": Early Modern Images of Indian Trade

It is well known that the missionary and imperial aspirations of early modern Europe were intertwined. Whether European desires to save the souls of America's indigenous peoples were sincere or not, the public expression of those desires rationalized efforts to conquer those peoples and own the resources of their land. Columbus's first descriptions of the islands upon which he had stumbled made this point clear. Emphasizing that the Taino Indians there "do not carry arms and do not know of them," he suggested simultaneously that they would be easy to conquer and convert. "They ought to make good slaves," he wrote, "for they are of quick intelligence since I notice that they are quick to repeat what is said to them, and I believe that they could very easily become Christians, for it seemed to me that they had no religion of their own."⁹ Besides their mimicry, paltry weaponry, and apparent lack of religion, one of the strongest signs of their pliability was their inability to negotiate a profitable trade. As Columbus noted in the same letter, the poignancy of the Indians' overly generous bartering proved the ease with which Europe could rob or redeem these people: "They . . . give objects of great value for trifles, and content themselves with very little or nothing in return. . . . It even happened that a sailor received for a leather strap as much gold as was worth three golden nobles, and for things of more trifling value offered by our men, . . . the Indians would give whatever the seller required. . . . Thus they bartered, like idiots, cotton and gold for fragments of bows, glasses, bottles, and jars."¹⁰ In describing this exchange Columbus failed to recognize the expectations of reciprocity and the nuances of status-determination that surrounded indigenous American systems of gift giving.¹¹ He also neglected the possibility that the Taino found gold to be as inconsequential as the sailors considered their own "trifles," or that they attached a metaphorical and ceremonial importance to the glass.¹² With stunning confidence in his interpretive ability, he was quick to see this exchange as evidence of economic innocence. Showing that "Columbus reads the Indian system of valuation (whatever it was) as an empty prefiguration of his own," Joshua Bellin has observed, "a glass bead is worthless and a pearl precious only in systems of exchange value."¹³ Echoing Stephen Greenblatt's comment that this letter epitomizes the European fantasy of "the grossly unequal gift exchange: I give you a glass bead and you give me a pearl worth half your tribe," Bellin has pointed out that Columbus describes the Indians as "naive consumers beyond Europe's wildest dreams."¹⁴ The profits of a few sailors suggest the effortless gain of future treasures.

Moral self-congratulation accompanied the coy assessment of potential wealth in this letter. Columbus juxtaposed his sailors' eagerness to exploit the Indians with his own insistence that they be treated favorably: "I forbad [these trades] as being unjust, and myself gave them many beautiful and acceptable articles which I had brought with me, taking nothing from them in return; I did this in order that I might more easily conciliate them, that they might be led to become Christians, and be inclined to entertain a regard for the King and Queen, our Princes and all Spaniards, and that I might induce them to take an interest in seeking out, and collecting, and delivering to us such things as they possessed in abundance, but which we greatly needed."[15] With this narrative Columbus set in place a vision of intercontinental contact that would unite diverse expressions of European desire.[16] Wonder at the Indians' financial naïveté, concern to save them from injustice and divine wrath, fervent hopes to win their "regard" and hence receive their wealth—all these reactions became central to the discourse of colonialism. Underlining the contrast between unjust sailors and the just admiral who commands them is a distinction between shortsightedness and foresight that is more intellectual than moral. Columbus's initial insistence on fair trade will, he hopes, encourage the Indians' excessive reciprocity. It is an investment, promising a payoff in gold and labor. Christian conversion plays a dual role in a vision of reciprocal exchange: fair trade by Columbus will help lead the Indians to Christianity, and Christianity will keep the trade fair. For what except the gospel can match the wealth that the Indians "abundantly possess" but Spain "greatly need[s]"? Christianity is the only commodity that can balance the intercontinental books for Columbus, offering compensation for conquest.

At the core of Columbus's formulation is this vision of "gold for glasse," of true wealth bartered for its shiny imitation. This trope of trade became central to descriptions of global exploration. It also acquired a broad metaphorical register in the early modern period, suggesting many forms of poor judgment. After killing his wife Desdemona out of ill-founded suspicions of infidelity, for example, Shakespeare's Othello referred to himself as

> [O]ne whose hand,
> Like the base Indian, threw a pearl away
> Richer than all his tribe. (5.2.344–46)

Shakespeare's choice of metaphor, if he did refer to an American Indian here, emphasizes Othello's gullibility in the face of Iago's manipulation.[17] Stressing his tendency to trust appearance over deeper truth, these lines also link prodigality to naïveté. Othello does not really trade; rather, he throws his treasure away. Instead of focusing on a desire for what glitters, this reference emphasizes a prerequisite eagerness to discard what is more valuable than it seems. Indians toss away pearls because they do not understand their value. Othello, likewise, has tossed away the love of his wife because he was made to distrust its authenticity. The absence of any trade, even for glass, heightens his suicidal sense of loss.

More than a century later Eliza Haywood echoed Shakespeare's romantic inflection of this trope in *The City Jilt* (1726), a narrative of love betrayed by greed. Near the end of this story the callous Melladore, who had seduced and then abandoned the heroine Glicera so that he could marry a wealthier woman, finds that Glicera has obtained ownership of the deed to his now bankrupt estate. Throwing himself on her mercy, Melladore writes, "Like the foolish *Indians*, I have barter'd *Gold* for *Glass*, exchang'd the *best* for one of the *vilest* that ever disgraced the name of Woman."[18] Although Melladore describes himself as bartering rather than discarding a treasure, the emphasis on poor discernment echoes Othello's use of this trope. Like Othello, he has judged badly in matters of love, failing to see the value of true gold.

Besides asserting the cost of ignorance, the trope of trade also could suggest the exploitation of innocence. This meaning applied especially when intangible resources were balanced against material ones. John Milton used this image at the beginning of the Civil War in *The Reason of Church Government Urg'd against Prelaty* (1642). In an autobiographical interlude he pondered the moral burdens that accompany the acquisition of spiritual knowledge, justifying his criticism of England's bishops as a duty placed on him by the privilege of his education. Those who have received gifts of knowledge should share them, he argued, not hoard them while they sell false treasures at a high price. This autobiographical defense enhanced his attack on the Church of England, because he then contrasted his own generosity with episcopal greed. England's church hierarchy had failed to meet its duty to the intellectually impoverished, exploiting the common people just as merchants cheat "poor Indians" with cheap trinkets. Expanding on the "burden" of the educated, Milton wrote:

And that which aggravates the burden more is that (having received amongst his allotted parcels certain precious truths of such an orient lustre as no diamond can equal, which nevertheless he has in charge to put off at any cheap rate, yea for nothing to them that will) the great merchants of this world, fearing that this course would soon discover and disgrace the false glitter of their deceitful wares wherewith they abuse the people, *like poor Indians with beads and glasses,* practise by all means how they may suppress the venting of such rarities, and such a cheapness as would undo them, and turn their trash upon their hands. Therefore by gratifying the corrupt desires of men in fleshly doctrines, they stir them up to persecute with hatred and contempt all those that seek to bear themselves uprightly in this their spiritual factory.[19]

Overlapping images of global commerce become a vehicle of Puritan attack in Milton's text. While cheating "poor Indians" by selling them glittering

trash, England's bishops have hoarded the treasures entrusted to them by
God, those truths of "orient lustre" that they were supposed to give away.
Europe's exploitation of other lands becomes a symbol of England's exploi-
tation by its church.

As he applied this trope to the domestic realm, Milton added a spiritual dimension. The suggestion of simony, the selling of religious benefits
for material gain, created an intersection between axes of spiritual and material worth. Through this accusation Milton made explicit Columbus's implied vision of an intercontinental reciprocity involving a payment of
Christianity for gold, compensating for the false currency of glass. The
"spiritual factory," the same term Joseph Caryl used thirteen years later
to advertise America as the place where the English convert Indians, here
condemned England's ecclesiastical corruption through analogy with the
cheating of Indians.[20]

Other seventeenth-century writers used the trope in similar ways.
Robert Boyle, best known for his scientific work, invoked this image in his
moral writings. "The Aretology" (1645) one of his (until recently) unpublished essays, notes that "Vertu by an aduantagious Exchange for vs, serves
her followers as the [silly] Indians do our Mariners, giuing them for Beads
and Whistles and Gugaws, precious wares and substantiall meat."[21] Rather
than taking the perspective of the cheated Indians, Boyle focused on the
"aduantagious Exchange" that the virtuous enjoy for their avoidance of
vice, just as European sailors gain from trades with Indians. The essay "Of
Felicity" (1646), by the Interregnum writer John Hall, also used the trope
of gold for glass to mourn the abandonment of spiritual happiness for
material gain: "We have [felicity] brought home to our own doores; . . .
[T]hose happy soules that *claspe* hold of it. . . . They can set a true *estimation* of those *sublunarie* things, that others are contented so to overbuy,
more Sottish then the Barbarous *Indians* to exchange *Gold* for *Glasse*."[22] As
with *Othello* and *The City Jilt,* Hall's reference to Indians signifies a poor
bargain prompted by the duplicity of appearance. Like Boyle and Milton,
he harnessed a moral prescription to the image of the duped Indian, warning his readers not to make an equally poor bargain.

Clearly a variety of seventeenth-century writings replicated Columbus's depiction of naive Indians exchanging their treasures for the trash of
those who would become their conquerors. In their appropriation of this
trope they took for granted the distinction between real and apparent worth
suggested by exchange. That is, the allusion to Indians and trade conveyed
the supremacy not only of reality over appearance, but also of the intangi-

ble—whether romantic or moral—over the quantifiable. These texts also took for granted the idea that exchange was to the detriment of Indians.

Ironically, this interpretation did not apply to the texts that claimed to be most interested in the welfare of Indians: missionary writings. While they also adopted the trope of gold for glass, they realigned the meanings Columbus had assigned to it by diminishing the real worth of gold in the face of spiritual goods. This change makes sense when we consider the delicate task these writers faced: raising funds to convert Indians by soliciting many of the very people gaining wealth from the exploitation of Indians. This adjustment made it possible to invoke a sense of moral obligation while presenting a model of fair exchange that would not alienate an English or British audience. Understandable though their motives were, the writers of these texts played an important role in developing a rhetorical justification for colonialism. What Columbus took as an example of exploitation that he had rectified to make possible the Indians' acceptance of Christianity, British missionaries later presented as an emblem of salvation.

"First Fruits": The Husbandry of Souls

Because it conveyed that the British were giving something valuable to America, the trope of husbandry was crucial to interpretation of gold traded for glass in missionary writings. Husbandry already was a central Christian metaphor, and it became especially prominent in the seventeenth century. Besides suggesting the spread of the gospel, it conveyed the ordering and tending of the self. Both ideas were attractive ones in Protestant thought, with its emphasis on individual faith and moral accountability unmediated by priests. The pragmatic connotations of this trope also fit into the increasingly secular and financially saturated perspective of early modern Europe. As Richard Allestree noted in *The Whole Duty of Man*, a popular book of Anglican practical piety, "There is a husbandry of the soul, as well as of the estate."[23] Teaching its practitioners to tend the estate along with the soul, the notion of husbandry helped individuals operate virtuously within the world rather than separate from it.

This trope occupied a prominent position in the rhetoric of colonization because it validated the plantation model that English and Scottish settlers practiced. As Samuel Sewall wrote in the history of Puritan missionary work that prefaced his *Phaenomena quaedam Apocalyptica* (1697), "They who remove from one Land to another, there to dwell; that settlement of theirs is call'd a Plantation. Especially, when a Land, before rude and unfurnish'd, is by the New-comers replenished with usefull Arts, Vegetables, Animals."[24] The British applied this trope with ease to the topic of Indian conversion. Except for a tendency to depict the spread of the gospel through a contrast between pagan darkness and Christian light, the missionary texts seem most often to describe the conversion of Indians through images of trade or cultivation. Metaphors of husbandry were most prominent in Puritan writings, even in titles such as *New Englands First Fruits* (1643). In *The Glorious progress of the Gospel amongst the Indians in New England* (1649), the writer J. D., or John Dury, prayed "that those sometimes poor, now precious Indians . . . may be as the first fruits of the glorious harvest."[25] In *The Light Appearing More and More Towards the Perfect Day,* (1651), Thomas Mayhew, Jr., asked his readers to pray "that the Indians in this small begining [*sic*], being Gods husbandry, and Gods building, may be a fruitful glorious spreading Vine, and building together for an habitation of God through the Spirit."[26] Urging for more missionary efforts several decades later, Cotton Mather warned his readers, "Verily, our GOD will not look on us as a *Thankful People,* if we are not also a *Fruitful People.*"[27]

Although used most vividly in Puritan writings, the rhetoric of husbandry pervaded missionary texts of all denominations. John Wynne, Bishop of Asaph, concluded his sermon of 1725 before the SPG by saying, "Let us then beseech Him, who alone, whatever pains we may take in planting and watering the Gospel, is able to give the Increase."[28] In his *History of the Propagation of Christianity,* Robert Millar, an affiliate of the Society in Scotland for the Promotion of Christian Knowledge (SSPCK), said of America, "The blessing of God, and the pouring out of his spirit from on high, are necessary to turn this wilderness into a fruitful field."[29] In a sermon of 1766 before the SSPCK, George Muir described Indians as "Ignorant of God,—unacquainted with themselves,—their reason, like their fields, quite uncultivated."[30] Whether the earth in which the gospel is seeded or the harvest of that earth, Indians appear in these texts as the objects of cultivation.

The real husbandry that missionaries taught underscored this rhetoric. Most promoters of mission assumed that "culture" or "civilization" – by which they usually meant the acquisition of British clothing and behavior – must accompany conversion.[31] The practice of husbandry was crucial to both goals. As Claire Jowitt has explained, "From the end of the sixteenth century until the nineteenth century the main sense of 'culture' was to mean 'human development', especially in relation to an earlier connotation of husbandry."[32] The New England minister Solomon Stoddard saw conversion occurring along with training in husbandry and trade: "Many Nations, when they were in their Heathenism, lived miserably as to this World. . . . But since their imbracing the Gospel, they are got into a flourishing condition. God leads them in ways of wisdom, to follow *Husbandry, Trades* and *Merchandize,* and to live honourably and plentifully."[33]

Of course the Indians of the eastern seaboard did farm and in fact had taught the English to cultivate indigenous crops. This escaped the notice of most proponents of mission, however. Cotton Mather took the Indians' initial resistance to adopting English husbandry as the greatest sign of their depravity. Describing the first interactions between New England's colonists and natives, he wrote, "Tho' [they]. . . . saw this People Replenishing their *Fields*, with *Trees* and with *Grains*, and useful *Animals*, which until now they had been wholly Strangers to; yet they did not seem touch'd in the least, with any *Ambition* to come at such Desireable Circumstances, or with any *Curiosity* to enquire after the *Religion* that was attended with them."[34] Although there were ample reasons why the Indians did not accept English-style agriculture, their refusal only enhanced their "barbarous" qualities in his eyes.[35] A group of Boston ministers signing a preface to Experience Mayhew's *Indian Converts* (1727) acknowledged one of their greatest failures to be that *"We cannot get the* Indians *to improve so far in* English *Ingenuity, and Industry, and Husbandry, as we would wish for.*"[36] More optimistically, John Sergeant reported in 1736 that the Stockbridge Indians "'gave very much into *Husbandry, . . .* planted more this Year than ever they did before.'"[37] The degree to which Indians settled into houses and plantations thus often directed how successful the British felt their missions were.

This rhetoric, along with the economy that supported it, was so pervasive that it shaped how Christian Indians talked about themselves. In *Indian Converts* Experience Mayhew quotes one Mary Coshomon, who "declared, that she look'd on the Officers of the Church of Christ, as Dressers of the Trees planted in God's Vineyard; and that she greatly needed to be under such Cultivations, . . . as Members of Churches might expect to enjoy."[38] Clearly the trope of husbandry served multiple purposes for the missionaries. First, it was useful for fund-raising. As authoritative and accessible as the parables they imitate, these images were appealing to their audience, suggesting a link between initial contributions and long-term results. As the last example indicates, this rhetoric also seems to have offered at least some Indians a way of reconciling themselves to the rigors of conversion. More broadly, it presented Indians as unrealized organic potential. They are described as waiting for the British to save them, not only from the pains of hell but also from a limbo of sterility and waste.

This understanding of the Indians as a people who did not cultivate their land's resources and did not allow themselves to be "cultivated" was central to the justifications the British developed for their usurpation of American territory. John Locke's famous comment on America summarizes this perspective: "[I]t is labour indeed that puts the difference of value on everything. . . . There cannot be a clearer demonstration of anything than several nations of the Americas are of this, who are rich in land and poor in all the comforts of life. . . . [L]and that is left wholly to nature, that hath no improvement of pasturage, tillage, or planting, is called, as indeed it is, waste."[39] Because they derived rightful ownership from the maximal "improvement" of available resources and acknowledged only narrow definitions of improvement, such formulations allowed the British to define themselves as the caretakers of the American continent. Missionaries added to this understanding even as their projects benefited from it.

This claim becomes especially potent if we consider "husbandry" to connote not just farming but also frugality and the management of a household. As the prefatory letter to *The Clear Sun-shine of the Gospel* (1648) proclaims, "An account is here given to thee, of the conquest of the Lord Jesus upon these poor out-casts, who have thus long been estranged from him, spilt like water upon the ground and none to gather them."[40] The image of spilt water transforms colonial conquest into miraculous recovery. That they conceived of their work in these terms may help explain why many found it so easy to believe that Indians were the lost tribes of Israel. Gathering and cultivating scattered souls, missionaries saw themselves engaged in spiritual husbandry.

Images of husbandry also suggest a Protestant distaste for what were perceived to be the baroque excesses of all things Catholic. The Black Legend, the collection of stories that marked Spain as the center of Catholic tyranny and cruelty, assisted in the propagation of this assertion.[41] Early modern anti-Spanish propaganda, especially translations of Bartolomé de Las Casas's *Brief Relation of the Destruction of the Indies*, linked the cruelty of the conquistadores in America to their prodigality and greed.[42] In these translations, references to English harvests sometimes were contrasted with images of Mexico's blood-soaked land. As *The Tears of the Indians*, a translation of Las Casas's *Brevissima relacion*, said of the conquest of Jamaica,

"So lavish were the swords of the bloud of these poor souls, scarce two hundred more remaining; the rest perished without the least knowledge of God."[43] The text juxtaposed the abundance of America's population and agricultural production before the conquest with the destruction perpetrated by the Spanish. Mexico had been "a pleasant Country, now swarming with multitudes of People, but immediately all depopulated, and drown'd in a Deluge of Bloud." The translator's preface quoted from scripture to emphasize the countless souls who could have been saved from hell:

Never had we so just cause to exclaim in the words of the Prophet *Jeremiah; O that our heads were waters, and our eyes fountains of tears, that we might weep* for the Effusion of so much Innocent Blood which provok'd these sad Relations of devout CASAUS, by reason of the cruel Slaughters and Butcheries of the Jesuitical Spaniards, perpetrated upon so many Millions of poor innocent Heathens, who having onely the light of Nature, not knowing their Saviour Jesus Christ, were sacrificed to the Politick Interest and Avarice of the wicked Spaniards.[44]

The Spanish are cruel, and they are poor managers of wealth. Greedy for gold, they have destroyed a fortune in agricultural revenues and a rich harvest in souls. The only product of their venture has been an "Effusion of . . . Innocent Blood." As they weep the English offer a compensatory outpouring of emotion to the sight of extravagant slaughter. They juxtapose Protestant pity with Catholic coldness, matching both affects to the contrasted tropes of conservation and waste.

David Humphries, the secretary of the SPG, summarized this anti-Catholic perspective in his history of the society (1730). Distinguishing between Spanish and English colonies, he wrote, "All the Riches drawn from these Lands now by the English, is owing chiefly to their own honest Labour, scarce any Thing to that of the Natives; whereas the Wealth of the Spaniards, is to this Day dug out of the Mines, at the Expense and Sweat and Blood of the miserable Natives and Negroes."[45] Humphries set English settlement apart from Indian indolence and Spanish violence, both of which waste land. The English deserve America, he suggested, because they are good caretakers, matching agricultural toil with spiritual labor.

Allusions to husbandry or trade often accompanied literary appropriations of the Black Legend such as John Dryden's *The Indian Emperour* (1667), a heroic tragedy based on the conquest of Mexico. In the final act of this play a priest and several Spanish soldiers torture Montezuma, who heroically refuses to abandon his gods or his gold. Frustrated by Montezuma's resistance, the priest says:

Mark how this impious Heathen justifies
His own false gods, and our true God denies;
How wickedly he has refus'd his wealth,
And hid his Gold, from Christian hands, by stealth:
Down with him, Kill him, merit heaven thereby.[46]

In a gruesome parody of the trope of gold for glass, the priest attempts at once to force Christianity upon, and extort gold from, Montezuma. The promise to the soldiers that they should "merit" heaven by killing Montezuma marks the priest's economic paradigm of redemption as perverse. The Aztec king's ensuing death becomes the only reward for their violent exertion, suggesting the inefficiency as well as the cruelty of the Spanish.

In contrast, British missionaries stressed their role as caretakers. In *The Day-Breaking, if not the Sun-Rising of the Gospell* (1647), John Eliot's colleague Thomas Shepard juxtaposed English and Spanish missions in exactly this way. Defending the Massachusetts Bay colonists against accusations that they had not converted enough Indians, he stressed "the vast distance of Natives from common civility" and contrasted the quantity of false Catholic converts with the quality of Puritan ones: "[W]ee have not learnt as yet that art of coyning Christians, or putting Christs name and Image upon copper mettle."[47] The description of "coyn[ed]" Christians suggests spiritual counterfeit, and it alludes to the mines that were known to have helped the Spanish build their empire with the blood of indigenous Americans. In contrast, Shepard described New England's missionary project through analogy to its agricultural one:

[M]e thinks now that it is with the Indians as it was with our New-English ground when we first came over, there was scarce any man that could beleeve that English graine would grow, or that the Plow could doe any good in this woody and rocky soile. And thus they continued in this supine unbeliefe for some yeares, till experience taught them otherwise, and now all see it to bee scarce inferior to Old English tillage, but beares very good burdens; for wee have thought of our Indian people, and therefore have beene discouraged to put plow to such dry and rocky ground, but God having begun thus with some few it may bee they are better soile for the Gospel than wee can thinke.[48]

This comparison helped Shepard stress the difficulty of civilizing Indians, even as it contrasted a true return with the false profits created by Catholic counterfeiting.

Shepard presented other images of husbandry and organic growth that proved central to the developing discourse of Protestant mission. His insistence that "it must certainly be a spirit of life from God . . . which must put flesh and sinewes unto these dry bones" implied a promise fulfilled in later New England Company tracts.⁴⁹ Listing the questions Indians asked missionaries four years later, John Eliot told his readers, "You might perceive how these dry bones begin to gather flesh and sinnews."⁵⁰ As he implied the presence of a divine spirit at work, Eliot sounded like an anxious parent fretting over a sickly child. He emphasized this parent-child relationship in letters to Robert Boyle, president of the New England Company from 1662 until his death in 1691. Eliot began a letter of 1684 by addressing Boyle as "Right honorable nursing Father" and then wrote, "Your hungry Indians doe still cry unto your honor for the milk of the word in the whole book of God, & for the bread of life."⁵¹ The description of Boyle as a "nursing Father," a term traditionally applied to monarchs in allusion to Isaiah's prophecy, "Thou . . . shalt suck the breast of kings" (60:16), also echoes references to nursing from the biblical epistles. These references stress spiritual immaturity, as when the epistle to the Hebrews notes, "[E]very one who useth milk is unskilled in the word of righteousness" (Heb. 5:12), even as they assert a desire for spiritual nurturance in response to 1 Peter's advice, "As newborn babes, desire the sincere milk of the word" (2:2). In both private correspondence and published fund-raising texts, the heathen soul was described as an emaciated or infantile body nurtured by the English.

As poet laureate for the City of London, Elkanah Settle also discriminated between a nurturing British mission and the cruel incursions of Catholics. In the preface to his *Pindaric Poem on the Propagation of the Gospel in Foreign Parts* (1711), he praised Queen Anne for supporting the SPG's plans to establish a mission among the Mohawks by distinguishing her "bloodless Crosade" from medieval crusades and Catholic missions: "Yes, Royal Christian Heroine, You send Your Deputed Champions over to those pitied Infidels, on a more sacred Expedition; whilst by thus truly performing the Vicegerency [*sic*] of God in so shining and so merciful a Charity to so many Thousand wandring Souls, You set up the Standart of Your own British Cross amongst them, not like the Romish nor Spanish Cruelty, for the sacrificing of so many innocent Lives; but laying them the Foundation of your own Eternal One."⁵² British mission is described here as a curative endeavor. While the Spanish sacrifice America's innocents, the British minister to them. Under the guidance of their benevolent queen they express their pity through charity, alleviating the effects of Spain's empire.

Settle relied on Anne's gender as well as her domestic initiatives to create an image of British benevolence. Howard Weinbrot has shown that in their efforts to imitate but morally supersede classical poetic models, many eighteenth-century odes supplanted the glory of Rome's military empire with a British empire of peaceful commerce. "Many [odes] celebrate not Marlborough's victory at, say, Ramillies or Blenheim, but Queen Anne's arms as extended by Marlborough on behalf of the nation."[53] Settle exemplified this effort as he praised Anne for building new churches throughout London and supporting the SPG, describing her as a nursing mother to British and foreign Christians: "What a Glorious Aera of Christianity shall this Age commence . . . when turning our Eyes into our Holy Temples, we find not only so many Trebble Voices added to the Hallelujah Song, in the Religious Infant Nurseries now spread around the Kingdom: But not content with bounding so tender a Compassion to her own Native Sphere alone, we see the Royal Piety laying those yet greater Plans of Glory, resolv'd to make her Britannia, with such expanded Arms and flowing Breasts, a more Universal Nursing Mother in so extensive a Filial Adoption."[54] The references to motherhood, painfully ironic when considered alongside Anne's ill-fated attempts to bear children, translate physical into spiritual fertility and personal into national maternity. They echo Isaiah's vision of Jerusalem as a mother suckling her children (Isa. 66:10–11). Britain becomes a boundless, compassionate body engaged in the nurturing of foreign souls, all of whom will rejoice with the new Jerusalem.

All these images valorize British mission by linking it to the tending of the domestic sphere. This spacial association echoes an ancient Greek distinction between the *oikos*, the private household space of agriculture and economics, and the *polis*, the arena of war and public affairs. The rhetoric of husbandry, when understood in its broadest sense, thus insists on the domestic and peaceful character of British mission. It let the British think of themselves as giving more to the Indians than they took from them.

"To Barter Gold for Brass, and Pearl for Trifles": Missionaries and the Trope of Trade

When British missionaries and their supporters raised funds to convert Indians, they often did so by invoking their readers' sense of Christian duty even as they evoked their acquisitive desire. Sometimes they attempted this twofold task directly, arguing that contributions to missions would enhance Britain's colonial wealth. Martin Benson, Bishop of Gloucester, insisted in his SPG sermon, "For were we but wise enough to consider only the Advantage of our Trade in *America* . . . we should take care to propagate the Christian Revelation which . . . enjoins all those Virtues that make Commerce gainful, and prohibits all those Vices that bring Poverty in their Rear."[55] Nathaniel Eells, a minister involved with Wheelock's Indian school, paired a commercial mission with a Christian one: "[T]he vast Consumption of british Manufactures among ym," he claimed, "would teach the Nation how to make a *Gain* by promoting *Godliness*."[56] Although they would lose short-term profits through their charity, contributors to mission would enhance colonial wealth in the long run, turning savages into consumers as well as Christians.

Most missionary texts did not make so direct a link between charity and trade. Rather, they spoke through a metaphorical language that imitated the Gospels' treatment of riches. In the gospel of Matthew, Jesus emphasizes the importance of giving up wealth, because " 'It is easier for a camel to go through the eye of a needle than for a rich man to enter into the kingdom of God' " (19:24). But he also relied on the language of wealth to emphasize the value of this kingdom: "[T]he kingdom of heaven is like unto a merchant man, seeking goodly pearls: Who, when he had found one pearl of great price, went and sold all that he had, and bought it' "(13: 44–46). Such images allowed Jesus to use material acquisition as a metaphor for spiritual gain, even as he demeaned riches in the face of spiritual reward. These images also can be seen to equate material with spiritual value. The Kingdom of God may be greater than all one's wealth, but there is a suggestion of equivalence in the parables, brought about by references to purchase. The Kingdom of God is costly and more valuable than all earthly treasure. Although it is priceless, it is like something that can be bought. Whether it is meant by its writers to do so, the Gospels' adoption of a metaphorical economy can lend itself to an economic vision of religion.

In his epistle to the Romans, Paul also juxtaposes material with spiritual wealth. At the end of his letter to the church in Rome, he wrote, "But now I go unto Jerusalem to minister unto the saints. For it hath pleased them of Macedonia and Achaia to make a certain contribution for the poor saints which are at Jerusalem. It hath pleased them verily; and their debtors they are. For if the Gentiles have been made partakers of their spiritual things, their duty is also to minister unto them in carnal things" (15.25–27). Paul's formulation suggests not just the virtue of charity but also the imperative of spiritual and material exchange. Unlike the gospel parables, Paul asks his readers to take literally the exchangeability of money with spiritual wealth. Describing the gentiles' charity as a debt for the Jewish church's

communication of the good news has the effect of placing a fulcrum between the balanced values of material and spiritual wealth. Generosity is
there, but it is prompted by obligation. As Paul would have it, the conversion of the gentiles has merited material compensation to the Christian
Jews.

Drawing on these references, many writers of missionary texts evoked
images of wealth to make two claims. First, they communicated that the
conversion of heathens was as valuable as it was costly, meriting donations
and superseding in importance any wealth the British would gain from
colonial trade. Second, they suggested that Christianity was a compensation
Indians deserved for the wealth they had lost. Taken together, and read
through Paul's formulation, these claims could be (and eventually were)
made to suggest a fair payment of Christian conversion for colonial wealth.
A survey of the missionaries' references to exchange suggests a gradual shift
from stressing the debt owed to America's natives for their loss of material
gold to emphasizing the spiritual gold that England or Britain brought to
America.[57]

John Dury stressed the expense and importance of conversion in one
of the earliest missionary texts, *The Glorious Progress of the Gospel, amongst
the Indians in New England.* He exhorted his readers, "*Come forth ye Mas-
ters of money,* part with your Gold to promote the Gospel; let the gift of
God in temporal things make way, for the Indian receipt of spirituals."[58]
Rather than suggesting a transatlantic reciprocity, he pinned his appeal on
Christian obligation: "If you give any thing yearly," he concluded, "Remember Christ will be your Pensioner." The main compensation suggested
for these contributions was spiritual. For parting with their gold the English
would underwrite the Indians' reception of spiritual wealth and receive the
blessing of God.

Dury's preface was written in the early, optimistic stages of Christian
missions in America. By the end of the seventeenth century, especially after
King Philip's War had destroyed most of New England's praying Indians,
missionaries began to acquire a tone of pessimism and urgency.[59] While
they adapted images of exchange to their projects, they did so less to emphasize the value of Indian conversion than to stress the debt England owed
America's natives for what they had suffered. This shift may have reflected
a growing familiarity with the language of debt, especially after the founding of the Bank of England in 1690.[60] It also, however, was a response to
glaring evidence of colonial exploitation, Indian demise, and evangelical
failure.

In 1693 Patrick Gordon, a Scottish Episcopalian minister, appended a proposal for spreading the gospel in pagan countries to his *Geography Anatomized,* a cultural survey of the globe.[61] Of North America Gordon wrote of the great embarrassment to England, "That those very *Indians* who inhabit near on the English Pale . . . should still continue in most wretched ignorance. . . . O Christians. Shall we covet and thirst after their *Talents* of Gold? and yet keep hid in a Napkin that *Talent* entrusted to us. Shall we greedily bereave them of their *Precious Pearls?* And not declare unto them the knowledge of the Pearl of Price. No! No! Let us not act as others have done in making *Gold* our *God,* and *Gain* the sole design of our Trading."[62] Focused on what he saw as the theft of America by the English, Gordon did not even mention trade. Citing parables about the Kingdom of God, he stressed the kingdom's value and reminded his readers of their duty not to hoard its blessings. He sharpened this reminder by pairing the allusion to the spiritual gold of God's kingdom with a reference to the Indians' material gold. Rather than selling the idea of supporting missions by alluding to the riches of America, he suggested that those who have acquired wealth from the Americas owe some return.

Gordon drafted part of this proposal in a letter to the SPG, and it was transcribed into the society's journal in 1701.[63] The next year the SPG sent Gordon to Jamaica, Long Island, as one of its first missionaries.[64] Although Gordon's death shortly after his arrival prevented any sustained contribution to the SPG's efforts, his publication may have influenced the society's preachers. In 1704 Gilbert Burnet, the well-known Latitudinarian and chronicler of the Civil War, appealed to merchants, noting, "You great Dealers in Trade, who have had so plentiful a Harvest in Temporal things, from the Productions of those Countries, and from the Industry of our Colonies settled among them, are, in a more especial manner, bound to minister to them in Spiritual things."[65] As he alluded to Paul's formulation Burnet told his audience they owed America a spiritual debt that could be repaid through the contribution of funds. He thus suggested that financing missionary work translated into a spiritual expiation for material gain.

Other SPG preachers, like George Stanhope, the Dean of Canterbury, emphasized the idea of spiritual debt by comparing merchants to sailors acquiring Indian gold with European glass. Presenting this image with reference to Paul's vision of spiritual-material exchange in 1714, however, he reversed the usual description of transatlantic trade. Emphasizing the "obligation" of all Christians to spread the word of God, he wrote:

But this Obligation seems to be drawn yet closer, upon All, whose Fortunes are owing to any Commerce with those Ignorants and Unbelievers. For, may I not be allowed to turn to *St. Paul's* Argument, and affirm upon this Occasion, that to Them, whose Strength and Toil is consumed in the Service of your Carnal Things, Some Debt is contracted, Some Title thereby convey'd, to the Spiritual Advantages, they might receive from you? This were to act like generous Traders indeed; To barter Gold for Brass, and Pearl for Trifles; in returning the noblest and most useful Treasure, for Riches, which they knew not either the Use, or the Value of.[66]

While gentile Christians of the early church offered material help to Jewish ones in return for sharing the spiritual wealth of Christ, Stanhope suggested that the British owed a spiritual debt to those who had given them material wealth. The change was subtle but significant. Material acquisition preceded spiritual generosity. The order and the origin of exchange were overturned. This reversal allowed Stanhope to validate the very trade that the image of gold for glass condemned. The Indians gave away gold because they did not understand the use of it. By taking their gold and repaying them with spiritual wealth, the British were donating spiritual pearls for material trinkets.

Rather than badgering his audience into charity, Stanhope tried to prompt their generosity by offering a pleasing image of mutually profitable trade. A few years later Edward Chandler, Bishop of Coventry and Litchfield, expanded on Stanhope's strategy by presenting a moral vision based on reciprocity: "Natural Justice guides Men to be kind to that People, and Benefactors to those Places, by whom, and where they live, thrive, and prosper. . . . The moral sense whereof is this, that we return good, wherever we receive good: Return it not in Beads and Baubles, but in a Species, which may indeed cost us little, but to them, that are without Christ, and without God in the World, is of inestimable Value."[67] Although he cited "natural Justice," Chandler echoed Paul's description of exchange when he stressed the importance of repaying goodness. His goal may have been the gathering of money for mission, but he approached it by describing colonialism as an exchange of gifts rather than exploitation. Describing America as England's "benefactor," Chandler called his audience to express thanks by offering America a gift of "inestimable value," the knowledge of Christ.

The idea of mission allowed Chandler to reverse the usual vision of gold traded for glass. Britain would give true gold instead of the "beads and baubles" other colonists offered for the wealth of America. At first cheated of their treasure, the Indians would now receive something more lasting and useful. Their gain did not required Britain's loss but in fact enabled its continued enrichment.

"We are more poor, they more rich by this"

The idea of spiritual wealth flowing to America in exchange for temporal riches became a cliché in missionary writings, especially Anglican ones, through the mid-eighteenth century. In 1709 William Dawes, Bishop of Chester, said in a sermon before the SPG, "[W]e cannot make them a more rich amends, for all these Advantages, for all these their *carnal Things,* than by letting them *reap our spiritual ones.*"[68] Several decades later Martin Benson, Bishop of Gloucester, proclaimed, "We *abundantly reap temporal things* thence, and it is just therefore that we should *sow spiritual things* there."[69] Reminding his readers of their Christian duty as he alluded to their profits, Benson drew simultaneously on images of husbandry and trade, combining the Gospels' evocations of God's vineyard with Paul's juxtaposition of spiritual and material wealth. Perhaps John Waugh, the Dean of Gloucester, made the point most persuasively in 1722 when he wrote,

Nor can we otherwise do Justice, or express our Gratitude to those poor Infidels, from whose Countries we have drawn such immense Wealth . . . than by repaying them *spiritual* for *temporal* Riches. This, as it is an easie Expence to the Contributors, for so great Gains, so will it be a Means of procuring to those that receive the Advantage of it, a Treasure of inestimable Value, *The Knowledge of the only true God, and Jesus Christ whom he hath sent.* A Treasure, which St. Paul set so great a Value upon, that he looked upon the most pretious things as nothing worth, as *Dung* and *Dross.*[70]

By referring to Paul's epistle, Waugh was able to suggest the worthlessness of worldly goods even as he stressed the bargain that his readers would enjoy by funding missions. The British suffer only an "easie Expence," in exchange for which they receive both material wealth and the awareness of Indian conversion. The "Infidels" of foreign lands lose wealth they hardly knew existed, and in return they receive the invaluable word of God. Everyone gains and nobody loses in this vision of intercontinental exchange.

The trope of trade allowed the British in their most optimistic moments to imagine an inexhaustible circulation of wealth around the Atlantic basin, enriching every participant and saving every soul. As Philip Bisse, the Bishop of Hereford, said, "All Zeal naturally spreadeth, without spending its Force; and rather increaseth its Fervour, the farther it goes."[71] Long before Adam Smith wrote the *Wealth of Nations,* missionary texts taught their readers to transcend the zero-sum game of a mercantilist vision, seeing piles of wealth made endlessly expandable through global circulation. While raising money for the salvation of the Indians, they transformed a symbol of the Indians' exploitation into one of their spiritual compensation.

Later missionaries were focused far less on tropes of exchange. In his fund-raising narratives of the Indian Charity School, written in the 1760s and 1770s, Eleazar Wheelock rarely described his work as part of a trade with or a debt owed to Indians. When he discussed his school in financial terms he was more likely to stress the comparative bargain Indian conversion presented in comparison with the price of waging war. Near the conclusion of the Seven Years' War he speculated, "[I]f one half which has been, for so many Years past expended in building Forts . . . had been prudently laid out in supporting faithful Missionaries . . . the instructed and civilized Party would have been a fair better Defence than all our expensive Fortresses, and prevented the laying waste so many Towns and Villages."[72] After he announced his intention to focus on the education of Anglo-American missionaries rather than Indians, his focus shifted altogether.[73]

Factors including the Seven Years' War, a growing sense of British entitlement, and a weakening of transatlantic ties between Britain and the colonies probably influenced this rhetorical shift in missionary writings.[74] Another important factor no doubt was the growing poverty of those Indians who remained in areas now filled with European colonists. In his SPG sermon of 1766 William Warburton, Bishop of Gloucester, juxtaposed spiritual with material wealth, but with an important change. He wrote, "[T]he Aborigines of the Country, Savages without Law or Religion, are the principal Objects of our Charity. Their *temporal,* as well as *spiritual,* condition calls loudly for our assistance."[75] Unlike his predecessors, Warburton did not refer to an exchange, reciprocal or not, but rather stressed the Indians' temporal *and* spiritual needs. A sense of specific obligation disappeared under the general rubric of charity.

In 1633, George Herbert's "Church Militant," the penultimate poem of his collection *The Temple,* included a prophecy of true religion moving westward from its seat in England to a new home in America. Prompting this transfer was an eastward flow of wealth from America to Europe, which it was corrupting. Of America Herbert wrote,

My God, thou dost prepare for them a way,
By carrying first their gold from them away,
For gold and grace did never yet agree;
Religion always sides with poverty.

We think we rob them, but we think amiss:
We are more poor—they are more rich by this.[76]

Celebrating the arrival of Protestants in the New World, Herbert portrayed the church on the brink of transition, about to abandon a corrupt Europe for an innocent America from which the Spanish already had taken much wealth.[77] He transformed the impoverishment of America into enrichment, toying with the term as he linked colonialism to divine will. By having the Spanish take their gold, God prepares Indians for Christianity. The English also help the natives by making them financially poor, while transforming that poverty into spiritual wealth.

Writing when the only English attempt to convert America's indigenous peoples had been the abortive establishment of Henrico College near Jamestown, Herbert reversed Paul's description of financial generosity repaying spiritual, by seeing spiritual conversion as a compensation for theft. That his vision influenced at least some missionaries is suggested by the fact that these lines appeared forty years later in Daniel Gookin's *Historical Collections of the Indians in New England*. Gookin, who was the superintendent of Indian affairs in Massachusetts during King Philip's War and a supporter of Eliot, quoted this poem as he described the piety of the praying Indians, mourned their treatment during the war, and called for more missionary efforts.[78] Two of Herbert's lines also appeared in Thomas Randall's SSPCK sermon of 1763. Randall suggested that his audience could prevent the flight of religion from Britain by returning some of their wealth to the society's mission in America.[79]

Many poems of the Restoration and the eighteenth century expanded on this vision of riches flowing eastward from America in exchange for intangible forms of wealth. Herbert's poem also influenced British understandings of empire, although the alterations made to his vision of exchange are as telling as its appropriations. After Herbert, English and then British visions of empire rarely saw gold and grace flowing in opposite directions. Rather, they imagined an organic expansion of grace both prompted and proved by the wealth that the world brought to Europe. In *Annus Mirabilis* (1667), John Dryden adapted Isaiah's prophecy of gentiles worshipping Yahweh (Isa. 60) to a future in which merchants flock toward a glorious, gold-paved London like "suppliants" before a beautiful woman.[80] Christopher Smart's "On the Goodness of the Supreme Being" (1756) envisions a scene of worldwide thanksgiving, in which peoples across the globe converge to offer their wealth to God and a well-armed "Europa" guards the loot. After describing caravans of elephants bearing "frankincense and myrh" from Araby and trains of camels bearing gold ingots from Africa, Smart addresses an American Indian maiden:

And thou, fair Indian, whose immense domain
To counterpoise the Hemisphere extends,
Haste from the West, and with thy fruits and flow'rs,
Thy mines and med'cines, wealthy maid, attend.
More than the plenteousness so fam'd to flow
By fabling bards from Amalthea's horn
Is thine; thine therefore be a portion due
Of thanks and praise: come with thy brilliant crown
And vest of furr; and from thy fragrant lap
Pomegranates and the rich ananas pour.[81]

Identified with organic abundance rather than the luxury of the east, the "fair Indian" also mirrors and belies the bodies of upper-class British women who displayed the wealth of colonial commerce.[82] Described as Amalthea, who nourished the infant Jupiter with goat's milk, she is termed "wealthy" because of the "fruits and flow'rs . . . mines and med'cines" with which she can enrich others. Identified with the products of a fertile and generous land, she becomes inseparable from them.

Although both America and Europe are female, Smart deploys their gender in different ways, illustrating the power dynamics between the continents. America is a nurturing Amalthea, but "Europa" is a fierce Athena, "Clad in the armour of the living God," whom the poet beckons:

Approach, unsheath the spirit's flaming sword;
Faith's shield, Salvation's glory,—compass'd helm
With fortitude assume, and o'er your heart
Fair trust's invulnerable breast-plate spread. (ll. 119–23)

Smart describes Europe in terms of her military might but the other continents in terms of their available products. The peoples of America, Africa, and Asia offer the riches of their lands for the glorification of an altar guarded by Europa. In exchange for this generosity, America receives only "a portion . . . of thanks and praise." Charitable as her intentions may be, Europa wages a crusade of conquest and becomes the caretaker of God's wealth.

Such expectations of gifts from America also directed the ways in which real Indians were treated and discussed. After the "four Indian kings" of the Iroquois Nations visited London in 1710, for example, an apocryphal story circulated that they had offered some of their land to the "Poor Palatines," German religious refugees camped out on the hills of Blackheath.[83] That this legend circulated at all is significant, especially in light of the attention the visitors' request to the queen and the Church of England for a mission received.[84] This story was not the only episode that connected the visitors with pity and generosity. While touring London, the kings were reported to have given alms to a poor woman in a scene that affected the crowds watching them.[85] I suspect that the vision of Indian Kings remedying the material poverty of pitied Europeans suffering from Catholic persecution was viewed as the complement to their highly publicized desire for Protestant missionaries, reinforcing the model of spiritual-material exchange.

But the more vividly English poets identified Indians with luxury, the more impoverished real Indians, especially those on the eastern seaboard, became. A letter from the missionary Gideon Hawley to the Massachusetts Historical Society, describing his almost forty years of work with the Mashpee Indians on Cape Cod, presents us with a wry fulfillment of Herbert's prophecy. Writing in 1794, Hawley described his first meeting with the Mashpees in the late 1750s: "The natives here appeared in a very abject state. . . . They were dressed in English mode; but in old tattered garments and appeared below a half naked Indian in possession of his Liberty. . . . Their children were sold or bound as security for the payment of their fathers' debts. . . . These Indians and their children were transferred from one to another master like slaves. Nevertheless to console them they had the Christian religion."[86] Like Herbert, Hawley paired material poverty with spiritual wealth. He described the latter as compensation for the former, "consoling" the Mashpees for the loss of their wealth and freedom. Although Hawley did depict himself as trying to ameliorate the Mashpee's material conditions, his description of their status presents an uncanny repetition of Herbert's vision.

The metaphors of husbandry and trade were pervasive enough that they shaped the articulation of the early Indian policy of the United States. In an address to Congress in 1803, President Thomas Jefferson noted, "The Indian tribes residing within the limits of the United States have for a considerable time been growing more and more uneasy at the constant diminution of the territory they occupy, although effected by their voluntary sales." Because some tribes had begun to protect their land by refusing to sell it, he argued that the government should convert the Indians entirely to a sedentary, agriculturally based economy supported by federally subsidized trading posts. Because farming required less land than hunting, "the extensive forests necessary in the hunting life will then become useless" to them. This project, combined with efforts to "multiply trading houses among them, and place within their reach those things which will contribute more to their domestic comfort than the possession of extensive but uncultivated wilds," would make the Indians more willing to sell their lands. After all, he predicted, "Experience and reflection will develop to them the wisdom of exchanging what they can spare and we want for what we can spare and they want."[87] Like many a missionary, Jefferson sought to reduce the Indians to a civility marked by land enclosure, and he sold this scheme as a mutually profitable exchange.

In this public address Jefferson insisted, "I trust and believe we are acting for [the Indians'] greatest good." In a private letter, though, he described a less benevolent plan: "To promote this disposition to exchange lands, which they have to spare and we want, for necessaries, which we have to spare and they want, we shall push our trading houses, and be glad to see the good and influential individuals among them run in debt, because we observe that when these debts get beyond what the individuals can pay, they become willing to lop them off by a cession of lands."[88] Jefferson described a transaction that, while more complex, amounted to the same trade Columbus's soldiers had made of their glass for the Indians' gold. In exchange for the lasting wealth of land, he offered only the fleeting "comfort" of manufactured goods, the alleviation of a debt in which the government had entrapped them, and the skills to farm their diminished land. He was able to describe his plan in the way he did because the discourse of mission had transformed this symbol of unfair exchange into an expression of benevolence.

Stephen Greenblatt has observed that "the whole achievement of the discourse of Christian imperialism is to represent desires as convertible and in a constant process of exchange. . . . The rhetorical task of Christian imperialism then is to bring together commodity conversion and spiritual conversion."[89] This chapter has explored one such aspect of this intersection. From the time of Columbus's first encounter with the natives of what would be called America, one of the most important images of that encounter became the trade of gold for glass. It is one of the cruel ironies of imperial history that even as they condemned the exploitation of America and sought to save the souls of its indigenous residents, British missionaries set in place a rhetoric that bridged the benevolent and acquisitive desires of

Europe in relation to America. Describing colonial commerce through biblical references to charity and the Kingdom of God, they made it possible to see Christian conversion as fair compensation for the vast sufferings of America's natives.

Ironically, the proponents of mission used the tropes of husbandry and trade to align their work with the domestic sphere, even as they helped define the burgeoning public sphere. They sought nationwide charitable collections, established some of Britain's earliest philanthropic organizations, and reified the idea of voluntary collective endeavor. With Indian visitors such as the Iroquois in 1710 and Samson Occom in 1766–68 they gave Britain some of its most memorable public spectacles. As they presented the pitiable state of Indians to their readers, the texts of British mission developed new ways of expressing shared and public sentiment. Yet they did all this while separating British mission rhetorically from the world of politics and violence. How missionary letters and sermons contributed to the development of collective identity and shared sentiment is the topic of the next two chapters.

Chapter 2

"I Have Received Your Christian and Very Loving Letter": Epistolarity and Transatlantic Community

Early British missionary writings encompass an eclectic corpus of narratives, dictionaries, biographies, and journals, but one of the most prominent genres is the letter. The British hardly set precedent here, as the vast collection of letters making up *The Jesuit Relations* testifies. The earliest English effort at fund-raising for a mission in America was organized through letters from James I to the archbishops, and then from the archbishops to their church wardens, who raised money at the parish level.[1] Most of the "Indian Tracts" describing work in New England are made up of letters between ministers on either side of the Atlantic, along with epistles to the reader, Parliament, and Cromwell. The SPG's annual reports include abstracts of letters from missionaries, and from 1708 to 1718 this group also published a series of letters from one of its members to a friend in London.[2] The SSPCK published some of its texts, such as *A Genuine Letter from Mr. John Brainard* [sic] (1752), in epistolary form. The Moravians' first fund-raising publications, such as Latrobe's *Succinct View of the Missions Established Among the Heathen by the Church of the Brethren, or Unitas Fratrum* (1771), were written, as the text's subtitle notes, "In a Letter to a Friend."

Letters, of course, were central to missionary operations, as the vast correspondence that fills the archives of both Catholic and Protestant missionary groups suggests. From requesting funds to reporting conversions, these documents provided channels for information exchange between organizations, their supporters, and their employees. But however unremarkable as choices for the discussion of missions, they also were uniquely suited to their fund-raising task because of their formal properties. The letter form also helped construct the community of feeling evoked by missionary writings.

Letters define and describe ties between individuals or groups. The formal elements that mark a letter—a salutation, second-person address, or a signature—are also what define it as the conduit of human connection. If, as James Watson has observed, "letters of love and friendship declare their intimacy in the circumstances of their writing as they describe them,"[3] letters mediating less familiar relations fill corresponding functions, articulating the social ties from which they emerge. Julia Stern's description of novelistic epistolary as "a formal category that bridges the apparent divide" between "the poetics and the politics of fictive form" is applicable here. Studying the role of letters in the formation of the early republic and its literature, Stern has noted that although epistolarity "functions as a narrative mode that is both outwardly directed and disembodied," it also "provid[es] a vital bridge between a developing public sphere and an emerging private realm" through its capacity to suggest a writer's voice and body: "[T]hrough a unique form of theatricality, both self and other are forged in an act of imaginative projection and inscription. Conveying the vicissitudes of solitary individuals, epistolarity puts a premium on the affective component of such exchange; in that regard, it becomes a dedicated channel for the reflection of fellow feeling, an appropriate forum for the sort of sympathy Adam Smith describes in his *Theory of Moral Sentiments*."[4] Elizabeth Heckendorn Cook has developed a similar explanation of eighteenth-century epistolarity, arguing, "The epistolary genre was central to the construction and definition of public and private that we have inherited from Enlightenment social and political traditions."[5] Rather than establishing an absolute divide between these arenas, a letter could combine the form of the private with the substance of the public, evoking intimacy and "the somatic terrain of the emotions," while "keeping its actual function as an agent of the public exchange of knowledge."[6] In this way letters complicated the division between public and private that historians and political theories have rooted in the eighteenth century, making possible a great deal of crossover and rhetorical masquerade. The earliest missionary letters preceded this era by several decades, but they share—perhaps anticipate—this tendency to shape relationships by articulating them through reference to both public and private realms. They were adept at bridging physical or social distance by describing relationships in spiritually intimate terms, relying on the affective ties developed from a shared concern for Indian souls.

Apprehending the rhetorical purposes of missionary letters is easier if we understand them as acting in counterpoint to narratives that contained or were contained within them. The narratives take the form of journals, biographies of converts, institutional histories, and mission histories. While they present their accounts of missionary work to passive readers, letters reach out to those readers, asking them to become active contributors to the work. The narratives often refer to biblical prophecies and histories, while letters extend this connection by alluding to the scriptural epistles. As the narratives describe the spread of Christianity, the epistles enact that expansion by addressing members of the church. Sometimes they refer to Paul's epistle to the Romans, which asks of the gentiles, "[H]ow are they to believe in one of whom they have never heard? And how are they to hear without someone to proclaim him?" (10:14–15). Such comments, as incorporated into missionary texts, link the spiritual fate of Christians with that of distant heathens. They also replicate the vision of a dispersed but spiritually united community forwarded in the New Testament. The urge toward vicarious involvement, as expressed for example in this command from the epistle to the Hebrews, "Remember those who are in prison, as though you were in prison with them; those who are being tortured, as though you yourselves were being tortured" (13:3), informs many missionary letters.

Most of the letters John Eliot wrote to supporters served a similar purpose. In July 1652 Eliot wrote to Jonathan Hanmer, a minister of Barnstable who had organized the exportation of some linen for Indian converts, "I have received your letters . . . wherin the Lord hath made you an unexpected instrument, and messenger of incouragment, and supply unto this work of the Lord among these poore Indians."[7] He linked Hanmer to the Indians in a triangulated structure, defining him as an agent of God. Later letters, such as one written on October 7, enhanced their relationship, noting, "I received letters from you full of love, both in acknowledgment and incouragement in this work of the Lord among the Indians."[8] Such comments defined Hanmer increasingly as an intimate friend, just as Hanmer himself—from Eliot's description of his letters—seems to have done. Letters to other supporters, such as one written the very next day to the New England Company, described their contributions in similar terms. Eliot wrote, "Worshipfull and much respected Gentlemen, You are called unto a service of Christ, w[hich] by his blessing upon it, may greatly further the advancement of his kingdome."[9] Like the first letter to Hanmer, this one strengthened a financial relationship by defining it via God.

Missionaries' letters also shaped closer relationships, such as the friendship that developed between the Nonconformist theologian Richard Baxter and John Eliot. Baxter had quietly assisted with the reorganization of the New England Company after the Restoration, and Eliot began a personal transatlantic correspondence with him in 1665.[10] He did so by emphasizing their spiritual connections: "Though I am a stranger to you by face, yet in neere bonds by faith, and we dayly meet at the throne of grace."[11] Their letters are filled with spirited theological debate, but often they focused on Eliot's mission. Indians provided a point of common concern that balanced disagreements, and it was in their communications about the mission that the men used some of their most affectionate language. In his first letter, Baxter expressed concern for Eliot's health, but in connection with the mission: "I know no worke in all ye world yt I think more highly and honorably of yn yors; and consequently no p'son whom I more honor for his works sake; and therefore none whose loss or disablement would be more grievous to me."[12] The work with Indians provided the grounds for Baxter to express how much Eliot's pain vicariously affected him. In response Eliot wrote, "I have received your Christian and very loving letter wherein your deepe sense of my infirmity and eminent acceptance of my poore labours among the Indians, doth minister to my spirit."[13] In a later letter he described difficulties his congregations had encountered, and concluded, "We greatly need your prayers and doe crave ym."[14] Discussions that focused on the Indians allowed them to express their esteem for each other and describe an awareness of their friendship. Although the two men never met, and although Baxter was uninvolved in actual missionary labor, Eliot raised his participation to the level of a partnership in his letters. Baxter became a minister to the missionary. Whether out of sincerity or politeness, Eliot described his role as a vital one.

"Let Your Hands Reach Them Now for Good": Sympathy and Simultaneity in the New England Company's Epistles

The impact of these ostensibly private letters between missionaries and supporters expanded as some were published in the "Indian Tracts" connected with the New England Company. The goal of raising funds for the cash-poor Massachusetts Bay colony and its missions, foremost in the minds of the tracts' authors and editors, determined much of their style and structure.[15] Most obviously, the tracts consistently stressed the trustworthiness of the agents who would collect and disburse charitable contributions. Such emphasis was understandable, given the accusations of mismanagement and theft that had broken out over an earlier project to ship English orphans to the colony.[16] This focus on reliability often led the texts' editors to depict an unbroken chain of personal yet verifiable connections between

England and its colony, which relayed the concerns and good wishes of the English people along with their generous funds. This approach met political goals along with financial ones, giving Puritan New England, as Kristina Bross and William Kellaway have both argued, a renewed sense of mission after the Civil War threatened the colonies with irrelevance.[17] Thomas Scanlan also has noted that these tracts portrayed Indian conversion as a unifying cause that would offer England spiritual renewal.[18]

The epistolary form of most of these tracts was important to their political and promotional ends. It also assisted in the rhetorical convergence of these goals, describing financial and political relationships through allusion to closer personal ties. While unpublished letters gathered support by articulating the relations informing that correspondence, published letters invited readers to feel included in a transatlantic community defined by a shared concern for America's natives. Letters were useful for both projects, because no other genre is able to replicate a sense of intimacy for an expanding audience in quite the way that a letter is. No other kind of text simultaneously unfolds from and crafts interpersonal links as letters do. Although essays, plays, and novels often gesture toward an intimacy between writer and reader, or between performer and audience, they do so with an anonymity that letters do not—or pretend to not—allow. Letters usually name and claim to know their audience. While the audience of a letter can expand, it is difficult for new readers to ignore the original one. To be a secondary reader of these texts is to read over the shoulder of the first reader(s), but to read such texts is also to be drawn into the relationships described by them. This dynamic applies especially to letters with an audience that is ostensibly personal but actually public. Placing epistolarity in a performative context, such letters deploy a form of "overheard" direct address. That is, they seem to communicate privately, but they place their message before a public audience. Gesturing toward intimacy and promising authenticity even as they welcome an expanding readership, satisfying both curiosity and a desire to be included in an inner sphere, published letters can be useful vehicles for gathering interest, emotion, and funds.

In the "Indian Tracts" written by Eliot and others, letters served several related purposes. First, they offered readers a sense of transatlantic simultaneity, of events happening throughout America and England to assist the Indians' conversion. Second, the multiplication of letters and testimonials emphasized the expanding consensus surrounding the projects. And third, the implied reciprocity of the epistolary format suggested a collective endeavor that the reader could passively watch or actively assist. The texts made room for the readers' involvement occasionally by addressing them directly but most often by using overheard direct address.

In Thomas Shepard's *The Day-Breaking, if not the Sun-Rising of the Gospell* (1647), the earliest New England tract devoted to missionary work, a single, anonymous letter serves all these ends.[19] Describing a series of meetings between Eliot, Shepard, two other ministers, and a group of Indians who formed one of the praying Indian towns of New England, *The Day-Breaking* presents portraits of spiritually needy Indians within a letter from one minister to another. The intimacy and detail of the narrative within the letter, which never directly addresses the readers, enhances the document's claims to reliability, as does an opening endorsement by Nathaniel Ward, a minister recently returned from Massachusetts. More important, the epistolary form allows Shepard to shift quickly from modes of pathetic display to petition, allowing readers to overhear and be drawn into his requests for help.

The text's epistolarity is understated, appearing through lapses into second-person address rather than through an opening salutation. It begins in a first-person narrative mode, describing the first meeting between the Indians of Nonantum and the Puritan ministers. Throughout the text Indians are at the center of Shepard's gaze, and he presents vivid descriptions of their attentiveness to the gospel. Of their first session of prayer, he writes, "It was a glorious affecting spectacle to see a company of perishing, forlorne outcasts, diligently attending to the blessed word of salvation."[20] Indians are made visible to readers in sentences such as this one, but an emotionally persuasive mode of representation supersedes a mimetic one. That is, Shepard tells how what he saw "affect[ed]" him, before actually telling what he saw. The text's indirect trajectory of address helps him prompt readers to imitate his own reactions to the Indians.

Emotion plays a central role in the tract. The Indians spend most of their time weeping in response to the word of God, and Shepard spends most of his time rejoicing over their tears. The Indian who would not cry out under torture but who would weep at the word of God was a favorite trope of missionaries, because this figure suggested the benevolent power of Christianity. Tears also constituted proof of the Indians' initial repentance while making their spiritual suffering visible.[21] Shepard's descriptions of his own emotions suggest how the audience should respond, through identification with him, to the Indians. He comments at one point, "[I]t might not be amisse to take notice of the mighty power of the word which visibly appeared especially in one of them, who in hearing of these things about sinne and hell, and Jesus Christ, powred out many teares and shewed much affliction without affectation of being seene, desiring rather to conceale his griefe which (as was gathered from his carriage) the Lord forced from him."[22] Several portraits of weeping Indians follow. With each portrait Shepard assesses the authenticity of these reluctant tears and explains their significance, while sharing his own reaction. In one description we follow him through stages of observation, analysis, and then response: "[O]ne of them I cast my eye upon, was hanging downe his head with his rag before his eyes weeping; at first I feared it was some sorenesse of his eyes, but lifting up his head againe, having wiped his eyes (as not desirous to be seene) I easily perceived his eyes were not sore, yet somewhat red with crying; and so held up his head for a while, yet such was the presence and mighty power of the Lord Jesus on his heart that hee hung downe his head againe, and covered his eyes againe and so fell wiping and wiping of them weeping abundantly."[23] As he presents the reader with a pathetic picture of distress and an exemplary emblem of spiritual self-hatred, Shepard shows how he came to understand and respond to this scene.[24] At first he "fear[s]" that the Indian's red eyes are merely a symptom of soreness, before realizing that these eyes are exhibiting "the presence and mighty power of the Lord." Lest there be any doubt about the significance of these tears, Shepard reiterates their meaning several times.[25]

Halfway through the tract he shifts from a mode of display to one of overheard direct address. This shift allows him, after having sought emotions from his readers that imitate his own, to seek a more active response. He writes, "Thus I have as faithfully as I could remember given you a true account of our beginnings with the Indians within our owne bounds; which cannot but bee matter of more serious thoughts what farther to doe with these poore Natives the dregs of mankinde."[26] First showing readers how they should feel, he then asks his correspondent—and, by implication, his larger audience—to consider what they can do for the Indians.

Having made room for an active response, Shepard finally asks for prayers: "[T]here is the greater hope of great heart-breakings . . . if ever God brings them effectually home, for which we should affectionately pray."[27] The implied agreement between Shepard and his addressee forms a consensus that readers are invited to join. A flattering description of those who would contribute to the mission enhances this invitation, as Shepard meekly asks his correspondent to gather funds: "I did think never to have opened my mouth to any, to desire those in England to further any good worke here, but now I see so many things inviting to speak in this businesse, that it were well if you did lay before those that are prudent and able these considerations."[28] This sentence constructs a collective of "those in England" who are united by their ability, prudence, and concern for the Indians. Epistemological reliability combines with an imitative affective response, as readers are invited to join a privileged community through their contributions.

The Clear Sun-shine of the Gospel Breaking Forth upon the Indians in New-England (1648), published by the Massachusetts Bay Company's agent Henry Whitfield, extends the strategies of Shepard's text with a compilation of epistles that construct a transatlantic community. The text opens by announcing, to Parliament, its task as the bridging of distance with spiritual exertion and emotion: "These few sheets present unto your view a short but welcome discourse of the visitations of the *most High* upon the *saddest* spectacles of *degeneracy* upon earth, the *poore Indian People:* the *distance* of place (or our *spirits* be right) will be no *lessening* of mercy, nor of our *thankfulnesse* . . . that the *Gospel* doth any where find *footing*." As in the biblical epistles, the imagination of suffering bridges distance. Pity for Indians does not lead to a connection with them, however. Rather, the text encourages its readers to feel links with other English people through their shared concern for these "spectacles of degeneracy." It seeks this sympathetic response through an epistolary structure that suggests widening consensus even as it depicts a community bound by feeling and faith.

The Clear Sun-shine contains five letters: the first from twelve well-known English clergymen to Parliament; the second from the same group to the reader; the third from Thomas Flint and Simon Willard, a fur merchant who introduced John Eliot to indigenous tribes along the Merrimac River; the fourth from Thomas Shepard; and the fifth from Eliot to Shepard. Beginning in the halls of Westminster and ending in the missions of Massachusetts, moving from English ministers to colonial lay witnesses and then to the missionaries themselves, the letters pull readers' gazes across the Atlantic until they are made the implied recipients of Shepard's and Eliot's accounts. While readers are escorted across the Atlantic they are drawn rhetorically inward, as the letters progress from the formality of the opening epistle to the intimacy of the missionaries' correspondence. Shepard, for example, explains his minimal account by noting, "[Y]ou know the neare relation between me and the fire side usually all winter time," evoking the closeness of a friendly chat.[29]

Addressed as "[T]he Godly and well affected of this Kingdome of England, who pray for, and rejoyce in, the thrivings of the Gospel of our Lord

Jesus," readers are defined as a people united by their desire. The tract urges readers to action by illustrating responses to missionaries' requests. This strategy is deployed across letters with the implied rhythm of a correspondence, suggesting a collaborative effort. The opening letter to the reader asks for clothes for the Indians, noting, "they want . . . cast-garments to throw upon those bodies, that their loins may blesse you, whose souls Christ hath cloathed." Shepard later describes the effects of past generosity: "I marvailed to see so many Indian men, women, and children in English apparell . . . which they have got, partly by gift from the English, and partly by their own labours . . . and you would scarce know them from English." These two letters encapsulate a cycle of transatlantic charity, providing a return to readers, in the form of the text, for their anticipated gifts. Shepard marvels, "To think that a poor blind Indian that scarce ever heard of God before, That he should see not only God in his cloths but mercy also in a promise of a cast off worne sute of cloths, which were given him." He presents a clothed and converted Indian, in imitation of the English, as a virtual payment for charity. He also suggests an expansion of an English religious community through the incorporation of the converted other. The conclusion emphasizes the transactional equivalence established between letter and donated cloth: "Thus you have a true, but somewhat rent and ragged relation of these things; it may be sutable to the story of rent and ragged men." Readers see philanthropy unfolding before their eyes and can envision themselves assisting it.[30]

Throughout the tract promises of payback for charity are indirectly conveyed. All the letters allude to profit, and they enact forms of exchange. Even as he offers affecting portrayals of his Indian converts, noting that "one especially did weep very much," Eliot stresses the Indians' burgeoning productivity, evidenced in their transformation from a hunting to a farming economy and in the brooms and baskets they produce for sale. Thomas Flint and Simon Willard describe "that mean esteem many of [the Indian converts] have of themselves, and therefore will call themselves poor Creatures, when they see and heare of their great distance from others of the English." Such depictions hold up an Indian mirror to the evangelical desire anticipated in the reader. This gesture suggests the same kind of reciprocity and mutual profit promised by the trope of trade outlined in Chapter 1.[31]

The letters urge a vicarious mode of engagement inspired by the scriptural epistles. For their contributions readers are promised a sense of connection with the missionaries in spite of the ocean that divides them. The opening letter rhetorically asks, "In *order* to this what doth God *require* of us, but that we should *strengthen* the hands, *incourage* the hearts of those who are at *work* for him?" The missionaries "desire to have *dependnce* [*sic*] on you they . . . desire the countenance and incouragement of their friends." To support the missionaries, the text implies, is to be understood as their friends. "Let your hands reach them now for good," the letter urges, and in a sense it promises what it requests. It suggests that readers in England can reach out and feel linked to their counterparts in America, while together they pity Indians.

The *Glorious Progress of the Gospel amongst the Indians in New England*, published in 1649 by another agent of the Massachusetts Bay Company, Edward Winslow, expanded on these rhetorical strategies as the mission's supporters lobbied Parliament to establish the New England Company. Like the earlier tracts, this one stresses the active role people in England can play in the conversion of Indians through the mechanism of overheard petitions and thanks, and it displays the results of prior charity through descriptions of the Indians' improved spiritual and material lives. As in *Tears of Repentance*, Eliot's tract of 1653, vivid portrayals of the Indians, including quotations of their speeches and questions, enhance the readers' awareness of the need for and results of their charity. Eliot would carry this approach further in his last publications, such as *A Briefe Narrative of the Progress of the Gospel* (1671) and *The Dying Speeches of Several Indians* (1685), both of which featured the translated speeches—public confessions on the one hand, and deathbed speeches on the other—of Massachusett converts. An assumption of readers' familiarity with the idea of Indian converts might have prompted this shift, as well as a need to present the evidence of on-going missionary projects after the immense destruction resulting from King Philip's War in 1675–77.

The missionaries still mediate connections between Indians and readers in these texts, however, suggesting how readers might react to these portrayals. After listing the questions that Indians have asked in *The Glorious Progress*, such as "Shall we see God in Heaven?" and "What is Salvation?" Eliot offers an interpretation: "By these questions you may see they somewhat savour the things of God and Christ, and that their soules be in a searching condition." In the conclusion to his letter he reinserts himself into the transatlantic link he has established, asking readers to pray for the Indians and himself: "I doubt not but they will be acceptable tidings to your heart, and will be an occasion of quickning your prayers for them,

and for me also, that utterance may be given mee."³² The link between
readers and Indians remains a mediated one.

This emphasis on the Indians' promising reactions to the gospel en-
ables Winslow to present an especially poignant plea to Parliament, imagining a direct petition from the Indians. Noting that he is "daily and earnestly
called upon to publish [the missionaries' letters], that the whole Nation
may be acquainted therewith," he stresses Parliament's responsibility to
help the Indians: "I took it to be my duty to present it in the first place to
this honourable House, and the Councel of State; that your HONOURS
might perceive how these poor Creatures cry out for help; Oh come unto
us, teach us the knowledge of God, tarry longer with us, come and dwell
amongst us, at least depart not so soon from us."³³ Winslow stresses the
transatlantic unity of the English by imagining them all hearing the Indians'
pleas. The compassion of what he assumes to be all English people becomes
articulated in the Indians' ventriloquized desire for closeness to their colonizers. Their desire to be saved mirrors the English people's desire to save
them, and only Parliament, he suggests, can fulfill both needs. What the
title page to this tract calls "the hungring desires of many people" for the
gospel becomes the focal point for the articulation of a unanimous goal,
the salvation of New England's Indians.

In *Strength out of Weakness*, published a few years after the founding
of the New England Company, missionaries evoke a transatlantic community by praising their "Brethren" in England. In a letter to Henry Whitfield,
a minister of Winchester, Thomas Mayhew writes, "Sir, assure your selfe,
and let all our beloved Friends know, that what is done by you together in
this behalf, doth not only strengthen my hands, and give me advantage to
be more helpful to the Indians, but also is a further encouragement unto
my heart from the Lord." As in Eliot's letters to Baxter, the missionaries
elevate the importance of good wishes from readers, granting them a crucial
role in their labor. Eliot describes an exchange of feeling through Christ's
mediation: "Worshipfull and much Honoured in the Lord: It is through
the grace of Christ who hath called you into the fellowship of his Kingdome, that you are willing to take such care and paines for the advancement
. . . of his Kingdome, and the Lord fill your hearts with the Consolations of
his holy Spirit."³⁴ Blessings move from the English to Eliot and back in
a triangulated flow that propels the exportation of funds. A transatlantic
circulation of feeling frames the mission. The English are described as
drawing together while they envelop the Indians within their world.

Although in some senses an obvious choice for a transatlantic report or request, the epistolary format did more than communicate information. In the "Indian Tracts" letters enhanced the sympathetic ties between England's residents and colonists by encouraging readers to imagine themselves linked with other English people through the collective act of contemplating unconverted Indians. Pity for the souls of America's natives provided an affective occasion for the assumption of common desires and concerns, as the tracts' letters assured their readers that they were included among the writers' brethren.

Our Dutch Brethren: Henry Jessey's Supra-National Collectivity

While the collective identity generated by English missionary writings in the seventeenth century usually was described as national, it was not entirely so. There were occasional gestures toward an international or supra-national[35] Protestant consciousness, such as the appearance in 1650 of a pamphlet titled *Of the Conversion of Five Thousand and Nine Hundred East-Indians, in the Isle of Formosa, neere China, to the Profession of the True God, in Jesus Christ.*[36] Published by Henry Jessey, a Baptist minister of London, this text presents a translated account of a Dutch minister's successes in Taiwan alongside extracts from three of the "Indian Tracts," *The Day-Breaking, The Clear Sun-shine,* and *The Glorious Progress of the Gospel,* and a new letter from Eliot. The pamphlet extols Protestant efforts to convert the heathen peoples of America and Asia and then exhorts its readers to support the New England mission.[37]

Understanding Jessey's position within Interregnum religious networks and beliefs is helpful to interpreting this text.[38] At first a Separatist Puritan who had considered immigrating to New England in 1637, Jessey became a Particular Baptist who retained a Calvinist understanding of "particular" salvation but insisted on believers' baptism. Although he had close ties to the Puritan communities of both England and New England, he was an early proponent of religious toleration among Protestants.[39] He also was immersed in the millenarian consciousness that was so prevalent among Separatists in the mid-seventeenth century and that propelled desire for the conversion of heathens among Eliot and many others.[40] His preface to Mary Cary's *The Little Horns Doome and Downfall* (1651) did not share her confidence in predicting 1656 for the Second Coming, but it shared her hopes.[41] The possibility that the world's end was imminent made it imperative that the conversion of Jews and gentiles occur.

These connections and beliefs led Jessey to stress collaborative missionary efforts that superseded national or denominational boundaries. Through the vision of a heathen world turned Christian, he communicated his dream of a fractious world made communal and thus prepared for the end of time. The title page of *Of the Conversion of Five Thousand* suggests a worldwide spiritual unification through allusion to Isaiah 49:12: "*Behold, these shall come from farre; and loe, these from the* NORTH, *and these from the* WEST, *and these from the land of* SINIM." It then cites Ptolomy to explain that "CHINA *is called* SINARUM Regio," implying that such unity will come from Christian missions to Asia. The section on New England also begins by quoting Isaiah 59:19: "*From the WEST they shall feare the name of JEHOVAH, and from the Rising of the Sun his Glory,*" establishing a parallel for the title page's claim. In a prefatory address "To his Christian Friends, in ENGLAND, NEW ENGLAND, or elsewhere, that pray for *the Comming in of the fullnesse of the* Gentiles," Jessey explicitly links Isaiah's prophecies to his present-day hopes. Addressing the readers as "*Dearely beloved,*" he proclaims that the "*things* that (with many of you) I have greatly *longed* for, soon will be fulfilled."[42] From beginning to end the text reinforces these hopes by presenting geographically polarized vignettes of heathen conversion within a millenarian framework.

Like the "Indian Tracts" connected with the New England Company, Jessey's document uses letters to verify his claims about distant events but also to instill an expanding consensus around an endeavor in which readers can participate. Through a translated Latin letter by one Caspar Sibellius, Jessey tells of a Dutch minister named Robert Junius who converted thousands of people in Formosa (modern-day Taiwan) to Christianity. Over twelve years he baptized almost 6,000 natives, taught 600 to read and write, established churches in more than 23 towns, and translated parts of the Bible into the native Formosan language. Echoing the emphases of the New England writings, Sibellius notes that many of the Taiwanese pray "with such comelinesse and fitnesse of speech . . . that may provoke teares to such as heare and behold them." Junius concluded his mission in 1641, after his wife died and he became ill. Before he departed for Holland the native Taiwanese "*shewed great affection to him, . . . desired him to promise, either that he himselfe would returne to them, or else what* [sic] *he would instruct one in their Language, and send him over to them.*" Jessey concludes this section by assuring us that as of December 25, 1649, the missionary work has continued, with the Dutch East India Company supporting four ministers in Taiwan and planning to send three more.[43]

In spite of its hagiographic tenor, this account accurately reflects much of the history of Dutch mission in Taiwan. Until its capture in 1662 by Coxinga, who led a group of loyalist Ming refugees from the Manchu invasion of China, Taiwan was one of the few places where approximately 1,000 missionaries dispatched to Asia by the Dutch East India Company enjoyed some success. The 32 ministers who worked in Taiwan between 1627 and 1662 were able to indoctrinate large numbers of the natives in the principles and practices of the Calvinist Dutch Reformed Church.[44]

Robert Junius, who arrived at the village of Sakam to assist the company's first minister in Taiwan, George Candidius, was an especially successful missionary. The colonial government's efforts to require children's school attendance and prohibit indigenous religious practices assisted the missionary endeavors, as did the government's willingness to manipulate rivalries between neighboring villages. In 1631 Formosa's governor Hans Putmans reported, "We have just had an expedition against Mattau, a place that has always been at enmity with Sinkan; and which expedition, according to Candidius and Junius, was our most efficient means for extending the Christian religion."[45] The quantity and the quality of reported conversions no doubt were inflated; Gustav Warneck has noted that the practice of *disciplegeld*, or fees based on the number of baptisms performed, prompted the Dutch East India Company's missionaries to encourage superficial conversions and mass baptisms.[46] Exaggerations notwithstanding, the success of Junius and other Dutch Reformed ministers was great enough to raise the hopes of Protestants both in and outside of the Netherlands that they could compete with Catholic missionaries on a global scale.

The story of the Dutch mission is simple, but the layers of epistle and authentication surrounding it are more complicated than the document's length (thirty-six pages) would seem to accommodate. Rather than just telling us about the mission, Jessey tells us the good news as he has heard and verified it. He notes that he heard the news from a friend of Edward Cresset, raced to Chelsea to hear the report, talked to Cresset's wife, received a letter from Cresset's wife, received a letter from Cresset, and finally received letters from Junius and Sibellius. With every epistolary layer are character references from friends of Jessey or from prominent figures, such as members of Parliament, aristocrats, and ministers from the Westminster Assembly. Cresset himself offers to corroborate his story with that of "*M. Halhead,* who . . . lived neere two yeares in my house at *Delft,* and being a Scholar, had convers'd with M. *Junius.*" These references become increasingly trivial, as Jessey tells us that Cresset left his book from Junius with

"Lady Mayerne, wife to Sir Theodore Mayerne, Baron of Albone," for him to pick up.[47] Almost no one appears in the text without connections drawn from him or her to Jessey and to other well-known people.

The attention Jessey devotes to the means by which he acquired his knowledge of the missions verifies his story, but it also highlights the breadth of the missionary networks. He positions paired images of indigenous American and Taiwanese converts in a tightly knit network of correspondence, involving several layers of multilingual communication among the Netherlands, England, America, and Taiwan. In so doing he reifies a Protestant Christianity unrestricted by boundaries and undivided by sect. Dutch and English missions emerge as parallel projects, moving in opposite directions around the earth to fulfill a shared goal. We leave the text not only with the awareness that ministers are hard at work at every edge of the earth, but also with the sense that Christians are joined across countries and continents by their prayers for that work.

The articulation of this vision makes sense historically, considering its publication shortly after the execution of Charles I. It also makes sense if we consider its appearance two years after the United Provinces of the Netherlands had won its war for independence from Spain, but just as William II of Orange, Stadholder of the Dutch Republic, was plotting a coup on July 30, 1650, to install himself as absolute monarch. Only William's death from smallpox in November 1650 prevented the completion of this coup, which may well have resulted in military support for an invasion of England by William's brother-in-law, Charles II.[48] Jessey compiled this text during a period of increased public awareness of missions and of heightened republican anxiety. To many of his Puritan readers, few endeavors could have served to stress the legitimacy of their precariously maintained political entity as well as a Christian mission did.

Of the Conversion of Five Thousand shows us how at least one mid-seventeenth-century Protestant interpreted the idea of converting foreign peoples through his expectation that the end of the world was at hand. It also suggests a short-lived era of hope about alliances between the republics of England and the Netherlands, a hope that collapsed with the outbreak of the first Anglo-Dutch war in 1652. Finally, this text reveals that the conversion of heathens could be presented to enhance a sense of unity not only among English readers but more broadly among Christians of different countries and creeds.

Although Jessey's millenarian framework resonated with other Separatist writings from his time, including the New England Indian tracts, his vision was less typical of English writings during the Interregnum. Thomas Thorowgood's *Jewes in America,* for example, which also appeared in 1650 and also supported New England's missions because of millenarian expectations, promoted an explicitly English mission to Christianize the indigenous Americans that Thorowgood, like many of his contemporaries, suspected were the lost tribes of Israel. As Claire Jowitt has shown, Thorowgood described Indians in ways that justified and demanded English expansion into North America.[49] Unlike Jessey, who stressed a supra-national community, Thorowgood urged his readers to support American missions so *"that thy affections may bee warmed towards thy Countreymen, and they receive encouragement in the planting of themselves, and the Gospel among the Natives."*[50] In spite of their shared topics, concerns, and times, Thorowgood's and Jessey's texts differ markedly in the geopolitical framework they use.

Jessey began his opening letter by expressing his hopes "that all [God's] people may be one visibly, and serve Jehovah with one shoulder; and all differences and envies amongst them may be removed farre away." That five years before he published this text Jessey also had written to acquaintances in New England gently protesting their persecution of Baptists hints at the larger message he wished to send through his celebration of a multidenominational Protestant mission.[51] His inclusion of a letter from John Eliot to Hugh Peter, the former agent of the Massachusetts Bay Colony, also suggests that his vision may have clashed with the agenda of those who wished to tie Indian conversion exclusively to the promotion of New England. While he focused on forwarding his millenarian hopes Jessey seems to have been ignorant of or indifferent to the accusations of mismanagement and embezzlement that had been hurled at Peter years before, as well as the hatred he had inspired among moderates for his approval of the king's execution.[52] An emblem of intercultural convergence, the heathen convert stood for all Jessey wished for from a Christian world that was not torn apart by persecution, national competition, and civil war.

"As Well in *Head* as *Heart*": New England's Ecumenical Turn

In spite of Jessey's call for closer Anglo-Dutch and interdenominational collaboration, the New England Company's publications continued to focus on generating explicitly English transatlantic ties. These emotional ties had a material basis, as Eliot suggested in *A Late and Further Manifesta-*

tion of the Gospel (1655) when he attributed difficulties in his work to ship-ping delays. Hoping to use the transcribed confessions of several Indians to prove their readiness for church membership, he related, "I having sent their Confessions to be published in *England*, I did much desire to hear what acceptance the Lord gave unto them, in the hearts of the people there. . . . As also my desire was, that by such Books as might be sent hither, the knowledge of their Confessions might be spread here."[53] Relying on the English not only to approve his work but also to publicize it in his own colony, Eliot asserted the interdependence of English and New English Christians in the conversion of America's Indians.

Throughout the seventeenth century, missionary writings consistently sought to generate metropolitan interest and generate transatlantic ties through epistolary appeals, but the nature of these emotional links altered with political circumstances. During the Interregnum these texts responded to the tensions of the Civil War by connecting antiroyalist sentiment with missionary work. In *The Glorious Progress of the Gospel* Edward Winslow explained that several letters sent from New England in 1648 had "miscar-ried . . . in that the Ship that brought them was taken by the Prince of Wales," thereby marking the royalist cause as an obstacle to missionary efforts.[54] Subtle comments like this, along with direct addresses to Parlia-ment, constructed a community of saints and revolutionaries who proved their worth by saving Indian souls.

The restoration of Charles II to the throne altered missionaries' de-scriptions of their work in subtle but significant ways. As in earlier tracts they sought to validate the Massachusetts Bay Colony through their mis-sions to Indians, but for a different audience. In *A Further Accompt of the Progress of the Gospel,* published in 1659, the year of uncertainty between the death of Cromwell and the Restoration of the monarchy, Edward Reynolds emphasized the moral good that had resulted from the Puritan migration. He declared that the tract, a compilation of confessions by Massachusett Indians, demonstrated "*How much those winds and shakings which carried many good men of* Old *into* New England *have made way to the publishing of the name of Christ in those barbarous places.*" Such claims implied a greater good resulting from persecution and revolution, whatever each reader's opinions of those political events was. Like earlier tracts connected with the New England mission, this text envisioned a transatlantic partner-ship through the tropes of husbandry and trade. Through a remarkable assortment of metaphors Edwards proclaimed: "*[T]ruly it cannot but be matter . . . of great comfort and encouragement unto all those whose hearts the Lord has stirred up, either here in a way of liberall contribution, to honour* *him with their substance, and to bring Silver and Gold unto the name of the* *Lord, that their merchandize may be* Holinesse unto him: *or there, in a way* *of labour and service, setting their heart and hand to snatch poor souls as* *brands out of the fire, to see . . . such seeds of the* Everlasting Gospel *come up* *in so barren and desolate a soile.*[55] The transformation of silver and gold into seeds planted in Indian souls not only refutes the greed of Catholic colonists, it also valorizes England's efforts to assist a worthy cause. Contributions from England are matched by the labor of New England, proving the moral legitimacy of a country defined by its people's desire to spread the gospel. Such evocations of collectivity put the best face on a country's violent history, asserting the distant goodness that emerged from domestic conflict.

As late seventeenth-century politics led New England missionaries to stress the appeal of their work to Dissenters and Anglicans alike, it also prompted some of them to reach beyond national boundaries in the way that Jessey had so much earlier.[56] This shift became most apparent in 1695, when Matthew Mayhew concluded *The Conquests and Triumphs of Grace:* *Being a Brief Narrative of the Success which the Gospel hath had among the* *Indians of Martha's Vineyard* with an English translation of a Latin letter written in 1687 from Increase Mather to John Leufden, "a Hebrew Professor in the University of Utrecht." This was a response to Leufden's request for information about the praying Indians of New England. Preceding Mather's transatlantic missive are several letters from ministers describing ongoing missionary efforts throughout New England. The penultimate letter is from a Dutch minister named Dellius, who preached to Mohawks near Albany.[57]

While attending only to American missions, *The Conquests and Triumphs of Grace* shows its English audience, through the inclusion of Dellius's and Mather's letters, that the Dutch are included in a Protestant network of the evangelically inclined. Letters from America, along with endorsements from Dissenting ministers of London such as Increase Mather's brother Nathaniel, verify reports and enlarge readers' awareness of collective endeavor.[58] Dedications to the governor, lieutenant governor, and major general of Massachusetts, to Increase Mather as president of Harvard, and to Charles Morton, the pastor of Charlestown, expand this consensus by linking the mission to governmental, religious, and educational institutions. The text replicates the strategies of earlier tracts, displaying Indians to readers and asking for donations through overheard direct address. It also builds on earlier texts by presenting a history of transatlantic philanthropy that readers are asked to continue.

It should not be surprising that New England missionaries and their supporters stressed their connections to the Dutch in the years following the Glorious Revolution. With William III of the Netherlands' House of Orange on the English throne, and with a new era of Anglo-Dutch peace, Dutch and English proponents of mission understandably would have sought to communicate with each other. It also is not surprising that the Congregationalists writing this text emphasized their ties to other Protestant groups after the passage of the Toleration Act in 1689. The Revocation of the Edict of Nantes in 1685, which had granted some protections to Huguenots in France, may also have prompted a desire to overlook lesser differences among Protestants. At the same time, a growing Anglican opposition to Calvinist theology—a trend John Spurr has used to contextualize the term "Latitudinarianism" in the seventeenth century—may have encouraged New England Puritans to emphasize their devotion to saving heathen souls.[59] Perhaps most important, the renegotiation of a charter for the Massachusetts Bay Colony in 1691, after its revocation in 1684 and after its release from the governance of Edmund Andros, prompted efforts among New England's clergy to stress the colony's moderate religious stance and its ties to other Protestant groups.[60] That Andros "had chided New Englanders for their abominable treatment both of Indians and of Englishmen who dissented from their particular religious way" in 1684, as Louise Breen has noted, only could have enhanced their emphasis on Christian mission.[61]

Breen also has shown that Cotton Mather undertook a similar project in his *Magnalia Christi Americana,* a history of the New England colony written throughout the 1690s. Coming of age in the uncertain era of King Philip's War and the Andros governance, Mather devoted much of his writing to the task of rendering New England acceptable to an audience in England. The topic of Indian conversion was central to this project: "To have a good reputation as integrators of native peoples into the imperial web was useful not only in establishing ties with fellow dissenters in London who contributed to the New England Company, and who had helped Increase Mather to negotiate a new charter in 1691, but also for proving to metropolitan authorities that Massachusetts was a responsible member of the imperial community."[62] Throughout the *Magnalia* Mather contrasted the missionary efforts of New England's ministers with the deceptive strategies of Catholics and wrote a lengthy biography of Eliot. He described these projects in moderate terms, stressing the uncontroversial nature of New England's mission.

Matthew Mayhew undertook a similar approach in his depiction of the Mayhew family's mission. Relating the beginnings of his family's work on Martha's Vineyard, he notes that the major obstacle to Indians' conversions was the jealousy of princes who feared they would lose power by converting. Thomas Mayhew, he says, responded to this fear by assuring the Indians that "*Religion* and *Government* were distinct things."[63] While earlier Puritan publications such as Eliot's *Indian Dialogues* also had described the reluctance of Indian leaders to convert, they did not suggest that missionaries assuaged Indians' fears by promising a separation of church and state. Indeed, it is hard to imagine Puritans of an earlier era conceiving of such a separation. The common cause of saving heathens provided a vehicle for the further validation of English and New English Dissenters, as Nathaniel Mather suggested in his introduction to the text. After contrasting the purity of Protestant mission with the corruptive influence of Jesuits, and after expressing his hopes that other English colonies would convert Indians, he writes, "Never let it be said, nor let there be occasion given for it to be thought, that the *English* Prelacy, Liturgy, and Ceremonies, will not admit of the Gospel's being Preached to blind perishing Heathens, that they might be saved."[64] Even as he challenges Anglicans to launch their own missions, he argues that competing with Catholics and saving Indian souls is a goal shared by all Protestants, regardless of their proclivity for "prelacy."

Mayhew's text reflected new concerns about the rights of Dissenters in the developing British empire, as well as what Bruce Tucker has called a "reinvention of New England" after the Massachusetts charter of 1691 eradicated an established Puritan government.[65] Building on Tucker's observation, Ned Landsman has noted that "with their coreligionists in England joining with other Reformed denominations under the banner of Protestant unity, New Englanders proclaimed that religious liberty rather than ecclesiastical purity had been the founders' motive" in the late seventeenth century. This was part of a broader process by which the residents of the British colonies came to see themselves less as members of separate colonies than as provincial Britons, holding distinct outlooks yet linked to London and other provincial areas such as Scotland through correspondence, trade, and the protections of British law.[66]

The Conquests and Triumphs of Grace shows how New England Congregationalists sought to fit themselves within the religious map of England after the Glorious Revolution by stressing their efforts to save Indian souls. Pairing Matthew Mayhew's text with Jessey's *Of the Conversion of Five Thousand* as well as with earlier New England writings helps us distinguish between the consistent and variable features of the collective identities generated through missionary tracts. In all of these texts readers' pity for unconverted Indians was sought in tandem with fellow-feeling for distant Christians. Protestant missionary fund-raising both required and promised a sense of individual participation in collective endeavor. While the nature and boundary of that Christian collective varied greatly, what remained consistent was the placement of an unconverted Indian at the center of a compassionate gaze.

*   *   *

An appropriate, even obvious vehicle for the exchange of information, letters also offered a discursive mode through which colonial missionaries and their metropolitan supporters could develop a transatlantic network of people connected by their desire to save American Indian souls. A fluid alternation between modes of narration and direct address allowed these texts to present vignettes of spiritual suffering to readers, displaying Indians as missionaries claimed to see them, but then reaching out to those readers, calling them to modes of active involvement in missionary work. This rhetorical strategy, one reliant on the conventions of epistolarity and generated from the assumption that compassion was likely to prompt a desire to alleviate suffering, became a basic feature of most missionary tracts and indeed of much philanthropic rhetoric.

While the religious mandate and the millenarian hopes underlying most seventeenth-century tracts could have prompted their authors to stress the limitless extent of Christian feeling, few of them asked their readers simply to feel benevolence toward Indians. Rather, they asked readers to share the perspective of other Christians trying to convert Indians by looking over the shoulders of missionaries and hearing their requests for help. The epistolary forms used by these writings also proved crucial to this approach, for they displayed the many links in the chain of correspondence binding this network together, they invited readers to join this group through overheard direct address, and through the back-and-forth of correspondence they displayed the conversions and emotional connections that would result from charity. The size and boundaries of the community constructed through these writings varied a great deal with the goals of each tract's authors and with the shifting politics of seventeenth-century England. What remained consistent was the assertion of a community—national or supra-national, Puritan or multidenominational—built through shared feeling for Indians.

Accompanying the beliefs that pity would produce action and that shared feeling sustained a transatlantic community was an assertion, discussed more tacitly than directly, that individual actions could produce significant results when organized by a reliable group. The next chapter will examine the origins and implications of that assertion. It will show how a discourse of "associated" philanthropy, developed initially by missionary groups, taught readers to imagine a wide circle of spectators supporting the charitable endeavors of a select few. Responding to pragmatic needs for smaller organizations that could concentrate widespread philanthropy, this discourse distinguished between different forms of sympathetic response to the sight of suffering. It accommodated the horizontal model of a community delineated by shared feeling to a hierarchical structure, it presented a new, positive model of masculine sensibility, and it forwarded an ideal of nondenominational philanthropy that could assist the pursuit of sectarian and partisan goals. As with the vision of a transatlantic community developed by the seventeenth-century missionary tracts, this model placed at its center a figure for whom all true Britons and all true Christians should feel pity—the poor Indian.

Chapter 3
"The Reservoir of National Charity": The Role of the Missionary Society

"Unio Fidelium"

While the Anglo-Dutch collaboration envisioned by Jessey's *Of the Conversion of Five Thousand* was unusual when it was published in 1650, the inclusion of a Dutch readership in *The Conquests and Triumphs of Grace* marked a nascent internationalism of the late seventeenth century expressed through references to evangelical endeavor. Over the next three decades Increase and then Cotton Mather published letters to and from Dutch, Danish, and Prussian ministers. Anglican proponents of mission also developed correspondences throughout the continent and attempted international collaborations. A handful of well-positioned individuals—Anthony Boehm, the chaplain-in-ordinary to Queen Anne's consort Prince George of Denmark, August Hermann Franke, a professor of divinity in the city of Halle, Westphalia, and Daniel Ernest Jablonsky, senior bishop of the Church of the United Brethren and court-chaplain to the king of Prussia—engineered many of these communications.[1]

Rivalry sometimes undercut collaboration, as when the United Ministers of Boston who signed a preface to Experience Mayhew's *Indian Converts* claimed that the Dutch mission in the East Indies was not as pious as their own "more vital" work.[2] Competition was especially present between Anglican and Dissenting groups, except for rare moments when they united through their opposition to Catholicism. Even when there was intense rivalry between missionaries of different denominations, however, their members tended publicly to espouse the ideal of "Unio Fidelium," or "the Union of the Faithful," as Cotton Mather titled a description of German and Danish work in Malabar.[3]

While reflecting political changes such as the succession of the elector of Hanover to Britain's throne, and some early eighteenth-century attempts to create an international union of Protestants, this shift also was propelled by the establishment throughout northern Europe of voluntary societies devoted to the promotion of philanthropic goals.[4] Cotton Mather heralded this development by proclaiming, "May sufficient numbers of great, wise, rich, learned, and godly men in the three kingdoms, procure well-composed *societies*, by whose united counsels, the noble design of evangelizing the world may be more effectually carried on."[5] This was an era of what David Owen terms "associated philanthropy," in which "groups of Englishmen arranged to pool their efforts in voluntary societies dedicated to . . . accomplishing special charitable aims."[6] F.W.B. Bullock has traced the emergence of these groups to the rise of pietism and to Reformation theories of "ecclesiolae ecclesia," or little churches within a church.[7] The moralistic inclinations of William III and Mary's reign led to the growth in England of religious societies, which offered support for individual spiritual development, and Societies for the Reformation of Manners, which sought to eradicate immoral offenses through public pressure and legal prosecutions.[8] Although part of a broader emergence of clubs and secret societies, these religious groups dissociated themselves from secular ones, especially those reputed to be environments for the voicing of radical beliefs.[9] Related to what Margaret Jacob has described as the emergence of "a new private society with which mercantile and literate elites could identify," such groups flourished in a public sphere characterized by civil discourse and developing religious toleration even as they reacted against heterodox views that developed in that sphere.[10]

This chapter explores the ways in which eighteenth-century British missionary organizations, especially the Church of England's Society for the Propagation of the Gospel in Foreign Parts and the Presbyterian Society in Scotland for the Propagation of Christian Knowledge, crafted a discourse of associated philanthropy. While distinct because of their ties to the established churches of England and Scotland, as well as their male-only membership, these organizations described themselves in ways that would become central to later philanthropic and missionary societies.[11] American Indians were helpful to this discourse, for although their conversion was not the only goal of either group, the figure of the pitied heathen shaped the texts' claims of affective ties between their members and their readers.

Both the SPG and the SSPCK presented themselves as groups whose dedication to the eradication of heathenism, immorality, and atheism both asked for and instilled cooperation. This focus on unity in the name of a philanthropic goal helped validate the Church of England and the Church of Scotland as they confronted political and doctrinal problems around the turn of the eighteenth century. Defining their male, educated, and moneyed membership through shared compassion and morality, these societies contributed to the development of an eighteenth-century ideal of gentlemanly masculinity marked through civility and Christian faith. These basic similarities in the rhetoric of both societies were present in spite of significant differences in their theology, structure, projects, and relations with colonial Americans.

This assertion of collective endeavor was not without complication. While these groups claimed to be leading a unified effort to save souls, they did so by setting the philanthropic societies apart from and above the very public whose compassion they were supposed to render useful. Through annual reports, self-aggrandizing histories, subscription lists, rules for admission to membership, and an ongoing litany of praise for their work, they forwarded an exclusive vision of a club at odds with the inclusive vision of a broad community also evoked in their fund-raising texts. That is, the very rhetoric that asserted the societies' reliability and made membership in their groups seem worthwhile also distinguished them from an audience of potential contributors.

As the societies' fund-raising texts sought to bridge this gap, they helped articulate the relations of modern private societies and the public. They depicted a voluntary society that was separate from, but transparent to, a public audience whose religious desires the society claimed to represent. They did so partly by describing an economy of prayer that was focused on Indians and channeled through the society. Through requests for prayers, that is, these writings encouraged their readers to engage vicariously with distant events through the mediation of a smaller organization. They constructed that engagement as a contribution that consoled other British people even more than it helped Indians, the objects ostensibly at the center of their work.

"This Laudable Society": The Rhetoric of Association

In 1701 Thomas Bray, the Church of England's commissary to Maryland, founded the Society for the Propagation of the Gospel in Foreign Parts, three years after establishing the Society for the Promotion of Christian Knowledge (SPCK).[12] Sharing many members, these organizations pursued global and domestic aspects of the same mission. They sought to enhance the nation's moral fabric, as they combatted the spread of atheism, immorality, and Catholicism. The SPCK originated in efforts to support the moral education of the English populace by building charity schools and distributing books, some of which they sent abroad, while the SPG was founded to subsidize the establishment of Anglican clergy throughout most of the colonies.[13] Generally, the SPG claimed a three-part mission: to improve the moral and religious climate of the colonies by establishing more ministers, churches, and libraries there; to convert African slaves; and to bring the gospel to American Indians.[14] More quietly and controversially, some SPG ministers also sought to convert Dissenters to the Anglican creed.[15]

These organizations emerged as the Church of England was suffering several crises in the wake of the Glorious Revolution. The refusal of one-tenth of its clergy to take oaths of loyalty to the new monarchs, the legalization of Dissenting churches under the Toleration Act, and the failure of efforts to include moderate Dissenters within the established church all threatened the church's viability.[16] These various issues contributed to internal tensions between Latitudinarians and High Churchmen, who differed most of all on the degree of toleration they felt should be extended to Dissenters, High Churchmen preferring to outlaw the occasional conformity that gave some Dissenters access to government and university positions. Such tensions erupted into heated disputes surrounding the trial in 1710 of Henry Sacheverell, whose virulently High Church and anti-Dissenting sermons provoked riots throughout London, and the disbanding of Convocation, a representative body of the clergy, in 1717. The Anglican orthodoxy also faced theological challenges from Deists and other heterodox thinkers whose texts were reaching a large audience with the lapse of the Licensing Act in 1695. The founding of these two voluntary societies was partly an effort to help the church regain its legitimacy and overcome internal conflict with a renewed pastoral focus.[17]

The SPG publicized its activities by printing a wide range of texts. Foremost among these were the anniversary sermons, which were delivered every February by a prominent divine and published along with accounts, lists of members, forms for subscriptions or bequests, and abstracts of the society's charter. Together these texts claimed that a voluntary society of reputable gentlemen authorized by the monarch and headed by the Archbishop of Canterbury was the most effective agent for accomplishing that goal.

By the time of the SPG's founding, England's clergy had a century-old tradition of generating domestic interest in the colonization of North America. The Virginia Company had paid many ministers to deliver promotional sermons, and clergy such as William Crashaw and Samuel Purchas had established the basic tropes of England's colonial rhetoric.[18] They had linked England's interest to colonial settlement and Christian mission, while the joint-stock model developed by the Virginia Company, the Merchant Adventurers, and other groups probably influenced later visions of collective philanthropy.[19]

Another possible influence on this discourse of associated philanthropy was the ideal of apolitical intellectual collaboration developed by the Royal Society. As Thomas Sprat narrated of the society's members in his *History of the Royal Society,* "Their purpose was no more, than onely the satisfaction of breathing a freer air, and of conversing in quiet one with another, without being ingag'd in the passions, and madness of that dismal Age."[20] In the uneasy stability of the Restoration, the Royal Society encouraged civil discussion without political conflict. Emphasis on the collective witnessing of experiments added to the society's collegial nature.[21] Links between scientific and missionary societies were not as improbable as might seem in the twenty-first century, as Robert Boyle's central position in both the New England Company and the Royal Society suggests. In 1700 the Berlin Academy of Sciences was founded with a mission to convert heathens while promoting investigations of the natural world. The philosopher and mathematician Gottfried Wilhelm von Leibnitz seems to have come up with this idea, although in 1712 the king of Prussia's chaplain told the SPG that their founding had inspired the king to give the academy a missionary mandate.[22]

The New England Company also may have played a role. Although it was founded in the regicidal environment of the Rump Parliament, this group remade itself after the Restoration, relying on the unifying force of pity for Indians. Richard Baxter oversaw this transformation by persuading its more radical members to step down and asking the widely respected Boyle to become the group's president.[23] The corporation was granted a charter by Charles II in 1662 as "The Company for the Propagation of the Gospel in New England and the parts adjacent in America," and it was allowed to retain ownership of lands that had been confiscated from Royalists during the Civil War. It featured a new, diverse membership, including George Monck, the general who had escorted Charles II back to England, and the Lord Chancellor Edward Hyde, Earl of Clarendon.[24]

Were there not records that the SPG discovered the New England

Company in 1705 and fretted about how to treat this organization, we might conclude that the SPG was modeled on it.[25] The connection between these groups was less direct, however. Thomas Bray seems to have developed his vision of the SPG while helping to determine the best use of a bequest by the New England Company's president Robert Boyle. He and others founded the Christian Faith Society in 1691 from this bequest, which sent most of its funds to William and Mary University until 1794, after which point it supported the conversion of West Indian slaves. In a "Memorial Prepar'd for the Clergy of Maryland," which dealt with Boyle's gift and with another legacy, he stressed the importance of having a small, reputable group to organize the proceeds of a nation's benevolence.[26]

The Presbyterian Society in Scotland for the Propagation of Christian Knowledge was founded in 1709, two years after the Act of Union between England and Scotland.[27] Cofounded by a Scottish Presbyterian aristocrat, Sir Francis Grant, Lord Cullen, and an Episcopal priest from Edinburgh, James Kirkwood, the SSPCK was partly a response to one of the more awkward aspects of the union, the coexistence of different established churches in England and Scotland. In its inception it seems to have embodied a desire for collaboration among Anglicans, Scottish Episcopalians, and Scottish Presbyterians in the name of an ostensibly nonsectarian cause, the establishment of charity schools and the distribution of religious texts throughout Scotland. That these schools promoted British acculturation and English proficiency as much as they spread Christian values no doubt enhanced English support for them. The SSPCK based much of its organization on a copy it had been given of the SPCK's standing orders, and it set up a London Board of Correspondents, which coordinated domestic programs with the SPCK. The crown also supported this group, for in 1725 George I started a tradition of granting the Church of Scotland £1000 a year to fund the SSPCK's programs.[28]

The ecumenical sentiments that seem to have inspired the SSPCK's founding became more selective over time, drifting away from links to Episcopalians while building connections with Dissenting ministers in England, Presbyterians and Congregationalists in North America, and continental European Protestants. Robert Kent Donovan has observed that most SSPCK members aligned themselves with the Church of Scotland's Popular party, also called High or Evangelical, rather than with the Moderate Party. Many members of the Popular party, who differed from the Moderate through a stricter adherence to Calvinist theology, "a fervent experiential spirituality," and a desire to promote more lay participation in parish decisions, welcomed the evangelical revivals of the mid-eighteenth century. Their support for revivals inspired more interest in the conversion of Indians while strengthening the connections ministers had formed with clergy in America over many years.[29] The evangelical network that was nurtured by the SSPCK overlapped very little with that of the SPG. Nonetheless, the SSPCK, like the SPG, tended to articulate an ecumenical ideal in its publications, stressing the desirability of Protestant unity.

While the Society in Scotland was at first domestically focused like the SPCK, it undertook missions to Indians in order to meet the conditions of a bequest by the Dissenting English clergyman Daniel Williams.[30] In 1729 it appointed a Board of Correspondents in New England, which then sent three missionaries to separate forts on the frontier, from which they were to minister to neighboring Indian groups. These initial attempts failed, but the society later saw some success with the work of David Brainerd, John Brainerd, Eleazar Wheelock, Samson Occom, and others.[31] It promoted projects in Scotland and America through the publication of texts modeled on those distributed by the SPG and SPCK, especially anniversary sermons, lists of members, templates for donations, and regular accounts.

Regardless of specific links between these groups, both the SPG and the SSPCK drew on an extant, if diffuse, discourse of associated philanthropy. Unlike the New England Company's seventeenth-century texts, which generated direct lines of identification between readers and missionaries as they shared pity for Indians, the SPG's and Scottish society's texts spent more time establishing the organizations' intermediary role between readers and the objects of their pity. These newer publications praised the society's members, developed institutional histories, and established concentric circles that delineated levels of involvement.

The SPG's concern with developing an appropriate institutional image becomes clear from a survey of its earliest documents. During its first meetings, the society's Standing Committee spent most of its time creating a seal and motto, designing organizational procedures, drumming up contributions, and deciding how to present itself to the world.[32] The seal, which showed a clergyman standing at the prow of a ship, holding out a Bible toward a group of figures running toward the shore, downplayed domestic conflicts by drawing the reader's eye toward the overriding difference between Christian and heathen (see figure 2). While the seal replicates the standard iconography of Euro-American contact, its accompanying motto, "transiens adjuva nos" ("Coming over to help us"), written over the ship and under a benevolently shining sun, quotes from the dream that St. Paul

Figure 2. Seal, Society for the Propagation of the Gospel in Foreign Parts. The seal imitated the iconography of early modern contact narratives, displaying a clergyman holding out a Bible from a ship's prow to a group of unclothed figures running toward shore. The seal and the motto, "Coming over to help us," which alluded to the dream St. Paul interpreted as God's command to bring the gospel to gentiles (Acts 16:9–10), implicitly placed a stronger emphasis on a mission to indigenous Americans than the SPG's own charter did. While the seal attempted to evoke a nonsectarian mission that would inspire Christian unity, colonial Congregationalists and Presbyterians later accused the SPG of fraud for its failure to live up to this image, converting white Dissenters to the established church while neglecting Indians and African slaves. (Courtesy of the United Society for the Propagation of the Gospel and The John Carter Brown Library at Brown University)

interpreted as a divine mandate to convert the gentiles (Acts 16:9–10). This quotation, which also had appeared coming from the mouth of an Indian in the seal of the Massachusetts Bay Colony, suggests a convergence of English hopes for America.

A year after the society's founding the Standing Committee decided to publish the group's charter and first sermon, so that "such of the Members as intend to speak to the Lord Mayor and Aldermen and other Eminent Citizens of London about the Designs of the society [could] present them with copies." At the same meeting "A Motion was made to Consider of some Methods to be taken in order to make the Designs of the Society more known and Publick."[33] None of the many texts printed by the SPG in its first decade appeared without extensive review by the Standing Committee, and this focus on public relations resulted in a polished image.

The unwavering structure and style of the SPG's publications played almost as important a role as the content of individual texts did in developing this institutional image. The seriality of the anniversary sermon publications in particular evoked a sense of timeless ritual, which connected the present with the distant past of salvation history and enveloped independent activity within the smooth operations of a group. Although individually authored and slightly varied in topic, the sermons convey little change in tone. They appeared with almost the same title (*A Sermon Preached before the Incorporated Society. . . .*), delivered in the same church every February to the same audience for the same end. The supplementary documents published with the sermons absorbed individual voices into a collective one, especially by including abstracts of letters from missionaries rather than reprinting the actual letters.

The SPG's descriptions of itself featured a fine balance between invocations of a widespread collective endeavor for a cause that superseded many differences, and suggestions of virtuous, elite male clubbishness. While ostensibly diverse in membership, the society marked itself as careful in the selection of its members. It published its criteria for membership and its many rules for missionaries,[34] but it also insisted that everyone could and should support the group's labor. In the society's first sermon Richard Willis, the Dean of Lincoln, proclaimed, "His *Majesty* has been pleased to erect a *Society* or *Corporation* consisting of many of the greatest Persons both in *Church* and *State*, and of a considerable number of others of almost all Ranks and Professions among us. These are enabled by His Majesty's *Charter* to contribute *themselves*, and to *receive* the Contributions of *others*, and to *dispose* of both in such Methods as shall appear most likely to promote this great Work."[35] With this description Willis established the basic elements of the image the society would consistently present: unwavering support from the monarch, a mixture of members from secular and clerical spheres, and a nonpartisan focus on pooling efforts to achieve a laudable Christian goal. Succeeding sermons emphasized the honesty and reliability of the society's members, as when John Moore, the Bishop of Ely, said, "As for you, the worthy Members of this Society, none can suspect that Covetousness was at the Root of your good Undertaking; for, on the contrary, with a large and constant Expence, . . . you have advanced your Work to so high a Pitch, and spread it far and near."[36] Such comments removed the society from arenas of self-interest and partisanship while conveying that funds donated to this group would be channeled to their appropriate and charitable ends.

Other texts added to this praise by commemorating the early history of the society, as Matthew Mayhew had done for the New England Company. Gilbert Burnet began this process in 1704, recollecting that "This *Corporation* was no sooner formed than a great many more came in and concurred in it: some in the Church and others of the Laity, noble by their Blood, but much nobler by their Faith and Charity, joined to set the Work a going."[37] Early *Accounts* of the society continued this strategy, as they narrated the group's efforts to recruit members and publicize their mission.[38] An *Account* of 1705 began by citing "the chief Care of Apostolical Men in all Ages downwards, to execute that *Commission* for the Good of Souls, and the Honour of their Blessed Redeemer," and then relating the SPG's efforts. Noting that "Twas during the Reign of King *William* III. that this glorious Design for advancing the Kingdom of the *Blessed Jesus* was first effectually set on foot," the *Account* explained how the society survived William's death by receiving the patronage of Queen Anne.[39] Later publications, such as a history of the SPG written by the society's secretary David Humphreys in 1730, praised the early organizers for their exemplary generosity: "[T]he Society were diligent to consider of farther and more effectual Ways and Means, to obtain Subscriptions and Contributions, sufficient to enable them to bear the Expence of sending many Missionaries abroad. They immediately agreed that the best Argument to Mankind was Example, and the most effectual means to engage others to contribute, was to lead the Way themselves, by subscribing towards the Support of the Work."[40] Assuring readers of the group's reliability, such commemorations also heightened the status attached to membership in an organization with a revered tradition. At the same time these descriptions of the society's founding marked the group as transparent, distinguishing itself from clubs or secret societies that were reputed by High Church Anglicans to be hotbeds of atheist or revolutionary thought.[41]

The SSPCK adopted many of the rhetorical strategies of the SPG, but it did so while adopting a provincial outlook more focused on Scotland and America than England. Its publications stressed the Scottish society's role in strengthening the British union, especially through its efforts to protect Britain from Jacobite invasions by eradicating what the society's *Account* of 1714 called the "Ignorance, Atheism, Popery, and Impiety, that did so much abound in the Highlands and Isles of Scotland."[42] This idea of defending the nation through the conversion of Highlanders could be translated easily to focus on Indians who were being wooed to French alliances by Jesuits, so the society's rhetoric did not change very much when it first attempted an Indian mission. Sometimes the society attempted to combine these efforts, as when it described plans in 1741 to send a missionary to a colony of "Argyle-shire Highlanders" in North Carolina, who also would minister to local Indians.[43]

An Abridgment of the Statutes and Rules of the Society in Scotland for Propagating Christian Knowledge (1732), which was printed partly to reflect the society's new focus on Indians, began by presenting an institutional history stretching back to the first royal letters patent issued by Queen Anne.[44] It related the early history of the group, attending to the care its members took to develop the group's image and seek contributions. It described how the society's members chose their seal, "*A Hand holding out an open Bible,* with these Words written out upon it, THE HOLY BIBLE, and this Inscription above it, POST TENEBRAS LUX."[45] Having forwarded a mission and an image of which few Protestants could disapprove, the text then stressed the unimpeachable character of the society's members by reciting the standing order, "That none shall be admitted Members of this Society, but such as are of the true reformed Protestant Religion, of a sober and religious Conversation, and of an humble and charitable Disposition, and who are Subscribers or Contributors to the Society's Fund."[46] The text avoided the finer distinctions of doctrine as it stressed its members' solid Protestant credentials, morality, and ability to contribute to the group's work.

Both groups devoted much of their own publicity to making membership in these societies admirable. Although the SPG and the SSPCK included more clergymen than merchants, their patterns of establishing prestige through collective charity shared much with those outlined by

Linda Colley in relation to Thomas Coram's mid-century philanthropic organizations.[47] Emphasizing the Christian merit of the groups' work, the social and moral quality of their members, and the governmental validation of their projects, these texts presented voluntary societies as the worthy agents of Britain's compassion and charity.

"Like the Rays of the Sun": The Missionary Society as the Agent of National Sentiment

As they forwarded the idea of a voluntary missionary society, the SPG and the SSPCK presented new ways of thinking about masculinity within this model. While the groups defined their membership entirely as male, they acknowledged donations from individual women, who often asked to remain incognito.[48] In 1759 the SPG began to include a brief list of women subscribers, and the SSPCK soon followed suit.[49] Through such gestures the societies expressed gentlemanly deference to female modesty while maintaining a gendered distinction between private and public space. The pious concern the groups' members displayed for non-Christians thus accompanied the broader efforts of the SPCK and other reformists to encourage gentle manners among men.[50]

The texts of both groups described their members as national heroes even as they redefined traditional understandings of heroism. When he wrote his *Pindaric Poem on the Propagation of the Gospel* in 1711, Elkanah Settle described the SPG's missionaries as the greatest in a series of British champions going back to medieval crusaders. Addressing Queen Anne in the poem's preface, he wrote, "Our Albion Chronicles, Most Excellent Princess, have justly resounded the Glories of those Crown'd Heads, Your Royal Predecessors, the British Heroes of Old, so zealously active for the Reduction of the Holy Land, an Undertaking, how praise worthy soever, yet far far short of the Glory of this Nobler Christian Atchievement."[51] The description of Christian mission as a bloodless crusade not only helped Settle distinguish between British benevolence and Spanish violence, as we saw in Chapter 1, but also to describe missionaries through traditional terms of male bravado. The poem describes missionaries rushing to the aid of distant heathens who repeat the call of the Macedonian in St. Paul's dream:

Help Us (by Heav'nly Instinct) sayes the Wild,
In Ignorance, not Innocence, a Child,

Begging with earnest Voice, & eager Eyes,
While thro' the Indian Foam the British Vessel flyes.
'Tis done: From England see the Star appears,
It dawns, and starts from the Britannic Spheres. (ll. 57–62)

In these lines Settle showed a missionary harnessing Britain's naval might in the service of religious need, describing the labor of religious conversion through images of chivalric rescue. In so doing he marked religious benevolence as a heroic response to poignant suffering.

While lionizing the Church of England's missionaries, Settle also praised those SPG members who helped to administer and fund distant missions. He thus extended his revision of British heroism to include less energetic and dramatic activities. The creation of the SPG's charter, for example, becomes a sign of national stability and moral strength, and Queen Anne's willingness to support a project begun by William III suggests continuity across different reigns:

A Charter from a British King,
        Which did from prompting Virtue spring,
        Supported by a Queen like Ours,
        Two Pious, Two Britannic Pow'rs,
    Must needs be Solid, Lasting, and Secure,
        And Ages, worthy such a Rise, endure. (ll. 409–14)

The domestic solidarity emblematized by the SPG's charter buttresses the activity of the missionaries, who are exhorted to "Go, Plant your Saviour, where you plant your Queen" (l. 324). Internal unity allows for spiritual exertion abroad, strengthening the spiritual sway of Britain in foreign lands.

Settle made a particular effort to mark philanthropy as heroic. After depicting the epic spread of Christian light over a dark pagan earth, and after relating the dramatic conversion of an Indian by an SPG missionary, he turned to the society's members, saying,

And now, Ye Patrons of this Great Croisade
In which so much of Heav'nly Zeal's display'd,
urge on the Glorious Task, as You've begun,
Nor leave till You the Mighty Web have spun,
And, the yet distant Palm of Conquest, won. (ll. 585–89)

Foreign souls become the objects of spiritual conquest, while the benefactors and fundraisers of the society, hardly involved in the actual labor of conversion, appear as the domestic agents of this bloodless crusade. Through decidedly unmartial activity, the society's members are heroic because of their efforts to weave the web of a spiritual empire, one that "transport[s], to the remotest Sky, / Not Coin, nor Traffic, but Christianity" (ll. 594–95).

After urging the SPG's members to a religious conquest of the earth, Settle described them withdrawing from the public gaze to stand anonymously behind the figure of "Charity." This figure, who also alludes to Queen Anne, becomes a figurehead for the society's collective generosity:

See how Majestic Charity appears
    With pon'drous Gold, and weighty Sums!
She's veild, when she the Contribution bears,
While You admire from whom the Bounty comes.
    As the Sum was of Quality,
So also was her Bright Humility
. . . .
We see, and own the Benefits reveal'd,
And yet the Benefactors are concel'd. (ll. 596–601, 604–5)

A reversal of traditional gender roles takes place as self-effacing men stand behind a woman. Traditional feminine modesty becomes a sign of male generosity. Even as she obscures the men, the figure of Charity fixes their masculinity in a homosocial context. Like the "Lady Credit" of Addison and Steele's *Spectator* and Defoe's *Review*, Lady Charity channels and stabilizes economic and emotional circulation through the conventions of masculine heterosexual desire.[52] That is, the poem valorizes the cooperative endeavors of men united by their desire to save heathens and by the collective channeling of their beneficence through a virtuous female icon. It also presents a gentlemanly heroism in keeping with new norms of sentimental and pious masculinity.

Settle's masculine ideal becomes especially striking when contrasted with another reaction a group of men were reported to have had to the visit of the "four Indian kings": the founding of a street gang named the Mohawks. As Richard Steele reported in *The Spectator,* through a letter from one "Philanthropos," the "Mohocks" named themselves after "a Sort of *Cannibals* in *India*" and distinguished themselves through "the various Kinds of Barbarities which they execute upon their Prisoners," such as gouging out eyes and sexually assaulting women while standing them on their heads.[53] Competing images of Indians thus provoked a contest between two British models of masculinity.

Sometimes the preachers of the anniversary sermons made explicit their desire to present what G. J. Barker-Benfield has termed "a style of manhood" that would counter a libertine tendency to define masculinity through an extravagant and violent search for pleasure.[54] In 1750 Richard Trevor, the Bishop of St. Davids, digressed from his description of the global expanse of heathenism to comment on a growing immorality he described as rash of effeminacy: "[I]nstead of that serious and manly Temper which Religion, when rightly understood, does so naturally inspire, a general Dissoluteness and Effeminacy of Mind and Manners have prevailed in every Rank and Order of Men among us." In response to this threat Trevor exhorted his audience to exhibit Christian courage, steeling them for conflict as though they were soldiers holding a battle line: "In such Circumstances, no small Degree of Courage and Constancy is required in every good Man to stem the Torrent, and to assert the Cause of Christianity."[55] Like Settle, Trevor described the propagation of the gospel as a feat that only real men could accomplish. He made Christianity the hallmark of a modern masculinity.

Through these and other descriptions the SPG portrayed itself as an agent of national sentiment, concentrating widespread feeling and magnifying its effect. As John Ewer, the Bishop of Llandaff, said in the SPG's sermon of 1768, "This Corporation is . . . the reservoir of national charity in this kind, wherein the bounty of each individual, which singly had been fruitless, being collected together, and directed one and the same way, like the rays of the sun concentrated on the same point, hath wrought much greater effects, than otherwise could have been produced."[56] Drawing on traditional descriptions of mission as the husbandry of souls, Ewer described British light pouring into fertile American soil. The society focuses the beneficence that Britain radiates, translating intention into result. Through the labor of an elite organization the British people could see their charity made fertile in foreign worlds.

References to harmonious relations among the group's members allowed the SPG to connect its particular agenda with a broader vision of national concord. "We are all Soldiers under one Banner," wrote Richard Willis in the society's sermon of 1702, as he linked foreign mission to domestic unity and universal salvation. It is crucial, he stressed, "that we stand fast in one Spirit, with one Mind; that we don't break into Factions and Parties, but with united Hearts and Strength promote the Common Cause of the Gospel of Christ."[57] An emphasis on the unifying force of a missionary society became especially important amid the intense partisanship of

Queen Anne's reign, which began in 1702 just after the SPG's founding. It is striking that during its first decade the society's sermons were preached by divines whose positions ran the gamut from High to Low Church, although the organization's emphasis on widespread moral education, voluntary association, and active participation by the laity marked it to some degree as a Low Church enterprise.[58] The Bishop of Chester William Dawes, who delivered the sermon of 1708, was a supporter of Sacheverell and had voted in the House of Lords to acquit him.[59] The Bishop of Norwich Charles Trimnel, who delivered the sermon the following year, voted for Sacheverell's guilt, as did William Fleetwood, the staunchly Whig Bishop of St. Asaph, who preached the SPG sermon of 1711 a few months after publishing an aggressive attack on Sacheverell.[60] That bishops of such divergent views could unite for the SPG's work demonstrated the unifying effect of the missionary cause.

Many SPG sermons implied that the society's goals motivated its members to rise above petty disputes. John Hough, Bishop of Litchfield and Coventry, noted in the sermon of 1705, "Private Persons have partial Affections, and sometimes unreasonable Disgusts, so that they neither know how to give or with-hold in the right place: But Societies are commonly more free from these Impressions."[61] Trimnel, preaching during the Sacheverell controversy, said with some urgency, "I hope, that all Persons concerned in this Trust, will so entirely divest themselves of particular Views . . . as to be sollicitous only for the sending of . . . Labourers into the Vineyard."[62] An emphasis on cooperative endeavor stressed the society's nonpartisan nature, as well as its trustworthiness. In his sermon of 1718 Philip Bisse, Bishop of Hereford, contrasted the clean flow of funds from societies with the potential corruption of private patrons: "It is by the good Providence of GOD, that, in this degenerate Age, many Charities . . . have been cast into these Channels, wherein they run clear and free of all such Defilements, as might corrupt the most flowing Liberalities of private Men."[63]

Such gestures toward the common good did, in fact, make possible an unprecedented degree of international collaboration even as the society itself stressed its national importance. These cooperative endeavors took place against the background of some early eighteenth-century efforts to forge a formal union of Protestants, especially between the Church of England and German Protestants, but they outlasted most of those attempts to negotiate a shared liturgy and common articles of faith.[64] The SPG routinely sent French translations of its publications to corresponding members on the continent and featured these correspondents in its domestic publications. As George Stanhope, the Dean of Canterbury, noted in his sermon of 1714, "The Fruits of [the SPG's] Charity are already so visible, as to draw other Countries to an Imitation of it; And Persons, of eminent Figure abroad, have already deemed it an Honour, to become Members of this Body."[65] The SPG helped the king of Prussia's chaplain establish a similar society, it supported Denmark's missionary work in Tranquebar along with the SPCK, and in other ways positioned itself publicly within an international Protestant network.[66] It acknowledged the assistance of the Church of Ireland, which organized collections for the SPG after its first decade. These acknowledgments stressed the paired missions of the Church of Ireland and the SPG, as it "promot[ed] within herself a Design similar, or subordinate, by instilling Christian Knowledge into the Hearts, and introducing true Devotion into Practice with her ignorant, or bigotted *Natives*."[67]

The Society in Scotland also stressed the unifying force of Christian mission, especially in connection with loyalty to the Hanoverian monarchs. In his sermon of 1735 John Gowdie, a professor of divinity at the University of Edinburgh, bemoaned the fact that "Christians have been, and are as much at variance, as ever Pagans were."[68] Asserting that "Charity is the bond of peace, and links men together in the closest and truest friendship," he urged the SSPCK's members to eradicate such disunity by continuing their work in Scotland and North America.[69] Documents such as the Scottish society's *Account* of 1720 noted that its members "are zealous for the Protestant Religion, and loyal to His Majesty King GEORGE, and are for the Protestant Succession in his Royal Family, without regard to other smaller Differences."[70] As late as 1795 Henry Hunter described the SSPCK's mission to the Highlands as the fruit of the Act of Union: "No sooner had England and Scotland embraced as friends, than they turned their eyes together to the bleak regions of the North, with the olive branch extended."[71]

Such nationalist sentiments emerged from England as well as Scotland and America. When he dedicated an abridgement of David Brainerd's *Journal* to the Scottish society in 1748, Phillip Doddridge, one of the society's London correspondents, hoped that Brainerd's journal, as well as the grief that so many felt for the death of this young missionary, would inspire more support for missions in both Scotland and America: "Nor can I forbear expressing my Desire and my Hope, that the important Facts mentioned in this Abstract . . . may be a Means of exciting many to join your useful Society. . . . While I offer my best Wishes for its Success abroad, I cannot but express them likewise for the Prosperity of your Missionaries to the Highlands of Scotland, that the rude and untaught Inhabitants of that Part of our Country, may be subdued to the Discipline of true Religion, and by a natural and happy Consequence to a due Sense of their Happiness under the present Government." Doddridge emphasized the ecumenical sympathies of the Scottish society, "which," he noted, "receives Protestants of all Denominations, in Prosecution of a Design in which all are equally concerned." This was an important point to make just a few years after the Jacobite rebellion of 1745, which had drawn much of its strength from Catholics in the Highlands of Scotland. His focus on the society's ecumenical and transatlantic range allowed him to reiterate its importance in rectifying "[t]he Calamities lately produced by the Want of" Protestantism in the Highlands. He concluded by offering his hopes that the society would be so successful in civilizing northern Scotland that it then could focus entirely on America's Indians.[72]

Whether gesturing towards national or international endeavors, whether focusing on Scottish or English activity, the publications of both the SPG and SSPCK argued that a voluntary society, especially a well organized society populated with respectable members and receiving the support of eminent peoples, was indispensable to the accomplishment of ambitious charitable projects. As Thomas Newton, the Bishop of Bristol, said in the SPG's sermon of 1769, "[N]othing considerable can be done, no great information be gained, no great influence be preserved but under the direction and conduct of a regular society."[73] Such an organization was especially important to transatlantic projects, as Thomas Randall indicated in his SSPCK sermon of 1763, emphasizing the stability of a "formed and legal society" with a parallel "board of correspondents in New England," who could appropriately "caus[e] our benignity [to] flow" from Scotland to America.[74] Such organizations could facilitate complex transatlantic transactions, while the well-known reliability of their members combined with the self-scrutiny of an organization could assure donors that contributions would find their way across the ocean to assist in the conversion of Indians.

While promising the honest and useful dispensation of charity abroad through the intermediary of a voluntary society, the SPG and SSPCK argued that through their eminent presence societies would encourage many individuals to emulate their generosity. Philip Bisse outlined the exemplary role that voluntary "corporations" such as the SPG performed: "Corporations erected for Charitable Uses, are, in their Nature, made to be seen of Men. They are as that City set on an Hill, which cannot be hid. The greater Applause they obtain in the World, the more zealous will others be induced to assist in the Work: And that Pomp and Appearance, almost of Ostentation, wherein they are sometimes shewn to the Eyes of the Multitude, hath its Use; and infuseth, as it were, a Spirit of Charity into the Mass of Mankind."[75] Although Bisse's quoting of Paul's "City on a Hill" to describe ecclesiastical pageantry may have infuriated John Winthrop, who famously used this phrase to describe the Massachusetts Bay Colony, both preachers cited this phrase to express a goal of inspiring moral imitation through self-conscious display. While seeking contributions to their work, the SPG's members set themselves above these wider networks of support, marking their mission as particular and urgent. Thus while advancing the Anglican Church in foreign lands, the SPG created a discourse of institutional philanthropy, describing a collaboration of elites in the name of a pitied object.

It is important to stress that in spite of the parallel discourses developed in the writings of the SPG and the SSPCK, these groups did not always meet their own rhetoric with actions, especially in relation to each other. However much their words were alike, in reality these groups established separate networks that developed different characteristics and competing projects. The SPG in particular was only intermittently successful at presenting itself as the focus of ecumenical endeavor. In the years preceding the American Revolution it became a lightning rod for transatlantic tensions, as colonists criticized the society's feeble missionary attempts with Africans and Indians and condemned the Church of England's efforts to establish a bishop in America.[76] Collaboration proved more successful between the SSPCK and the New England Company than between these two groups and the SPG, mostly because the SPG's conflicts with Dissenters in America became too severe.[77] The SPG also developed a vision of transatlantic Protestant cooperation that was oriented toward London and Canterbury, while the SSPCK developed a broader, less hierarchical network articulating the perspectives of provincial centers in Scotland and North America.[78] In spite of this failure to cooperate, and in spite of the many differences between these groups, they both insisted that the conversion of Indians was a goal for which all Protestants should strive.

They also developed new ways of thinking about collective identity and the imaginative construction of empire. Most of all, they presented a model of a voluntary association that was linked to church and state, revising perceptions, especially among High Church Anglicans, of societies or clubs as secular, secretive, and revolutionary. By praising a missionary group, and by requesting support for the group's work, these texts tried to inculcate in readers an imitative volunteerism that would extend to a global arena.

"Many Can Do Nothing but Pray": Christian Fellowship and the Economy of Prayer

As they applauded their organization's members, the SPG and the SSPCK defined a role for general readers that made them feel affiliated with an elite organization rather than left out of it. The abstracts and reports of both groups took care to praise the smallest donations, as when the SPG's abstract of 1712 reported, "[A]t this last Anniversary Meeting, a *poor Body* laid at the Vestry Door, a small Parcel of the Church Catechisms, with a Note, desiring they might be accepted, and sent to the Plantations."[79] Such poignant donations were not always available, however, so they accomplished this task mostly by elaborating on the active role that prayers played in their work.

Requests for prayers had been crucial to the promotion of mission throughout the colonial period because they assisted in the construction of active reader response. Missionaries frequently sought prayers from their readers, and they did so with an urgency that marked these requests as more than empty platitudes or euphemisms for financial petitions. "Sir," wrote Eliot in a published letter, "I doe earnestly beg your prayers,"[80] while John Brainerd wrote a century later, "I would . . . desire a Remembrance in your Address to the Throne of Grace."[81] Such texts marked prayer as crucial contributions, at least as important as financial ones.

Often prayer and money appear in these texts within parallel systems of desire and exchange. But while they paired requests for money and for prayers, missionaries were careful to describe prayer in ways that separated it from a financial context. Reactions against Catholic configurations of prayer no doubt informed this approach, as Protestant writers shied away from the idea that one could buy or earn the salvation of a soul.[82] Rather, they described prayer as a mode of active involvement. As something that could be promised, exerted, and performed, but not transported or consumed, prayer stood at a point of liminality, negotiating between the spiritual arena of religious conversion and the material arena of objects supporting that conversion. A mode of urgent desire, prayer also constituted a form of labor that connected distant spectators with participants, making them feel invested in missionary work. Samson Occom described prayer in just this way when he began a sermon in England by acknowledging, "Without Doubt many of you have been praying for the poor *American* Heathens, that the Lord would turn their Hearts; and I am firmly persuaded, that the Lord has now begun his Work amongst them, and many cry out after the Gospel."[83] By assuming their prayers Occom tried to draw his listeners within the circle of those concerned for Indians' souls. John Dury did the same when, in the conclusion to *The Glorious Progress of the Gospel* (1649), he described prayer as an act of emotional exertion that linked readers with distant missions. "Pray that an effectual door may be openned there. Remember Mr. Eliot. Forget not Mr. Mayhew, and all that labour in their hands. Pray for them that Christs [*sic*] work may prosper in their hands. Christ calls upon you by these letters."[84] By alternating petitions for prayer and for remembrance, Dury enlarged the significance of his readers' exertions.

Sometimes portrayals of prayer as labor extended to descriptions of vicarious suffering. The narrator of *The Day-Breaking, if not the Sun-Rising, of the Gospell* (1647) wrote, "[S]urely [God] heares the prayers of the destitute and that have long lien downe in the dust before God for these poore prisoners of the pit."[85] The text suggests that as they pray for Indians the English humble themselves. Through prayer they replicate the system of vicarious salvation set in place by Jesus' death. Prayer is not a gesture to persuade the Indians but a performance to win Christ's mercy for them.[86]

In most missionary writings, prayer provided an arena of imaginative participation that connected a select group with a larger audience. In many publications of the SPG and the SSPCK, these requests also achieved a more specific goal, presenting the missionary society as a conduit for contributions and a focal point for emotional outreach. In the SPG sermon of 1707 William Beveridge, the Bishop of St. Asaph, preached on St. Paul's compliment to the Corinthian church for their charity, "your Zeal hath provoked very many" (2 Cor. 9:2). He praised the SPG for its tendency to "provoke" charity from a wider group of Christians who imitate the generosity of the society's members. He called his audience to support the spread of the gospel in America, not only because Britain's accrual of wealth from American lands made it morally imperative, but also because the establishment of the SPG made such work feasible. "[T]he Care and Management of this great Affair is committed by a Royal Charter," even as "God hath opened the Hearts of so many good Christians, to pity the sad Estate of the Heathen, and hath inclined others to go and help them." His comments urged tighter links between the actions of a small society and the feelings of all British Christians. All should assist the SPG, he concluded, at least with their prayers if not with their own funds: "All that have any true Love for God, for Christ, for themselves, or for the Souls of other Men, must now shew it. They must all contribute, every one as God hath prospered him, to the Maintenance and Support of those who go into Foreign Parts to promote and propagate the Gospel of our ever Blessed Redeemer. And they who can do no more, must at least assist them with their daily Prayers."[87] Prayer provides a way of making all British Christians, no matter how poor, participate in the SPG's work. The request for prayers stresses the breadth and unity of Beveridge's audience, translating feelings into actions and funds.

In the SPG sermon of 1709 William Dawes went so far as to present a hierarchy of contributions British people should make to the society according to their rank. Beginning the list with the bishops and ministers who spread the gospel, then turning to "all Persons of Quality, Wealth and Character" who could fund the work and merchants who could transport ministers to America, Dawes finally addressed "all other Christians, whose particular Stations and Circumstances of Life, do not give them any special Opportunities of doing service to this great Work."[88] Even if they could not provide moral examples to the Indians, as colonists could, Dawes stressed that in their actions and thoughts everyone could assist this work. Lastly, he sought "Alms and Prayers," which were "in the Power of every Christian upon the Face of the Earth." To encourage such contributions he concluded by suggesting a prayer: "*Have Mercy upon all Jews, Turks, Infidels, and Hereticks, and take them from all Ignorance, Hardness of Heart, and Contempt of they word, and so fetch them Home, Blessed Lord, to thy Flock.*"[89] Dawes thus gave his readers a script they might follow to enhance their own participation in a distant mission.

In 1715 George Ash, Bishop of Clogher, Ireland, followed Dawes's example by suggesting different modes of support for different classes of people. Prayer provided the most common sort of participation, as it was what everyone should do even when they could do nothing else: "Doubtless Obligations are, in some Measure, laid upon every Order and Degree of Men among us, to contribute to so Christian a Design; we all pray daily, that God's *Kingdom* should *come*. . . . and ought not then every one to put his Hand some Way to this good Work? The Clergy, by Preaching, Writing, and personal Labours; and the Laity, by Advice, Encouragement, and liberal

Subscriptions; the Rich, by maintaining Missionaries, supporting Schools and Catechists; and the Poor, by most earnest Prayers to Almighty God."[90] Here Ash set in place a hierarchy of participation in missionary work, assigning various tasks to the different segments of the British people. He based his assignments not only on the resources of various classes, but also on the degree to which individuals profited from colonialism. Owners of American plantations and merchants engaged in transatlantic commerce thus bore an extra duty to return some of their wealth in the form of charitable contributions for missionary projects, echoing the trope of spiritual-material exchange explored in chapter 1. The implied function of the SPG in this passage is to collect these various contributions, channeling them into missions in America. Prayer not only provides a fallback form of participation for those unable to contribute in other ways, it also connects the British people spiritually and emotionally with the endeavors of the SPG. Prayer helps to delineate an imagined British nation, unifying it spiritually across the divisions of geography, class, wealth, and profession he demarcates by focusing everyone's energies on the SPG's efforts to spread the gospel in foreign lands.

In other sermons the coding of prayer as labor linked general British exertion with the propagation of the gospel abroad. In his sermon of 1727 before the SPG, John Leng, the Bishop of Norwich, argued that every Christian could contribute to the salvation of heathens through their daily lives: "[E]very Christian may at Home, in his own Native Country, contribute something towards the Advancing of Christ's Kingdom abroad in the World, if he will but live so in all holy Conversation and Godliness as to bring Credit and Reputation upon his Profession. If Christians in general would all live according to the Rules of the Gospel, their Light would by degrees communicate it self even to the most Remote Regions. This would be a Means of making all our Prayers for the Conversion of Heathen Nations, and all the Labours of our Missionaries effectual."[91] Like a mother scolding her children for not finishing their food when there are starving people in the world, Leng extrapolated great power from individual acts. Described almost as an expression of prayer, good conduct provided the missing link between a Christian's desire for the conversion of "Heathen Nations" and the fulfillment of that desire. Leng suggested an apotheosis of collectivity, catalyzed by individual prayer and professional, Christian conduct, and evidenced through the propagation of the gospel.

While elaborating on the pleasure of alleviating sorrow, these requests defined the outreach to Indians as an expression of shared feeling. They tacitly conveyed that to assist in the conversion of Indians was to enlarge the boundaries of the arena in which one could feel sympathy, because one saw one's own feelings reflected back by people culturally, and often nationally, linked to oneself. Petitions for and promises of prayer, that is, became the textual strands through which the readers and writers of these texts wove a web of affect that did not connect with the Indian objects of their feeling so much as it surrounded them.

The SSPCK, along with its correspondents in England and America, promoted a transatlantic network separate from that evoked in the SPG writings. Less hierarchical, more wide-ranging, and increasingly evangelical, especially after the revivalism of the mid-eighteenth century, it nonetheless shared basic characteristics with the community of prayer described in the Anglican writings. Like the Anglican writings, the Presbyterian writings sought to position Indians in the center of a transatlantic web of affect and prayer that would translate into missionary action. The main difference in the content of their texts was a greater tendency to pair references to the objects of missionary endeavor in both America and Britain. Benjamin Colman and Joseph Sewall, Presbyterian ministers of New England, envisioned such a scenario in their epistolary preface to Sewall's sermon at the ordination of three missionaries for the SSPCK. In their address to the members of the Society in Scotland, Colman and Sewall both offered and sought prayers for missions on both sides of the Atlantic. They asked "that the Knowledge of this Beginning of your *Mission* will excite *Prayers* for the Progress of it under the Smiles of His Providence and Grace," noting that they knew they would not need to ask for prayers from abroad. In return they promised "to pray for the *Honourable Society,* that the special Direction of GOD may ever attend their Counsels."[92] The request for prayers was accompanied by a petition for funds, but as it was reiterated throughout the text it also delineated the society's ties with its missionaries, correspondents, and readers.

In the ordination sermon Sewall said of "the Children of Men in Darkness,—*How deplorable is their Condition! How doth it Command our Pity and Prayers!*" He asked his audience to look to the society as a model, proclaiming that the "generous Compassion express'd towards this poor People by the *Honourable* SOCIETIES in *South* and *North Britain,* should provoke us to an holy Emulation." In conclusion he exhorted, "Let us Pray that the *Honourable* SOCIETY and their *Commissioners* may at all times enjoy the Direction and Assistance of GOD." Prayers for and from the society were then incorporated into the ordination ceremony: "The special

Blessings of Providence were ask'd on the *Honourable Society* in *Scotland*, and on the like in *England* and other Places, for propagating Christian Knowledge, 'That Grace, Mercy and Peace may be multiplied to them! and they that sow and those that reap may rejoyce together.'"[93] By relating the prayers of the ceremonies' participants, the text gestured to the transatlantic community supporting the Indian mission.

The references to prayer in a series of genres—a letter, a sermon, and a description of a ceremony—helped bridge the separation between a missionary society and its general supporters because they provided a way in which readers could transform from spectators to participants. Readers overhear the ministers asking for and promising prayers, then are asked to pray, and are invited to witness communal prayer. The ordaining minister's final prayer for the missionaries, that God will "Touch You with the most tender and condescending Pity for those wretched *Natives*," becomes a prayer that the readers also might feel directed to them.[94] That the missionaries will be able to channel this pity into more direct forms of action than can distant readers does not really matter, at least for the readers' own sense of involvement in this project, because the text has asserted, from beginning to end, the unifying force of prayer.

The vision these texts present of a global community created by prayer for and through an organization was realized more fully during the evangelical revivals of the mid-eighteenth century. It reached full expression through the Concert for United Extraordinary Prayer organized by ministers in both Scotland and America in 1747, "in which evangelical parishioners on both sides of the Atlantic for the revival of religion."[95] It also found expression through George Whitefield's English 'Letter Meetings,' where Whitefield's followers gathered to hear accounts of revivals from all over the world.[96] Timothy D. Hall has noted that these activities provided Christians with ways of imaginatively spanning the world "by self-consciously exploiting a potential to unite across vast distances in simultaneous activity." Revivalist publications thus fostered a "sense of participation in a movement of empirewide scope."[97] Ned Landsman also has observed that the concerts of prayer, along with the transatlantic correspondences fostered by revivals, contributed to Presbyterian-driven movements for Protestant union, assisting in the development of a transatlantic British identity that accommodated provincial perspectives. Although Indians were not at the center of these evangelical events, they did play an important role in the development of these networks, offering an uncontroversial cause for the generating of unified Christian sentiment and prayer.[98]

Near the end of the eighteenth century William Carey expanded on the networks of Christian fellowship established by the earlier groups. Carey, who sparked much of the evangelical fervor associated with the London Missionary Society, the Baptist Missionary Society, and other groups founded near the turn of the nineteenth century, expounded on the contributions that prayer alone could make to the conversion of heathens and the improvement of Christian nations: "Many can do nothing but pray, and prayer is perhaps the only thing in which Christians of all denominations can cordially, and unreservedly unite; but in this we may all be one, and in this the strictest unanimity ought to prevail. Were the whole body thus animated by one soul, with what pleasure would Christians attend on all the duties of religion, and with what delight would their ministers attend on all the business of their calling."[99] The heathen object seems to drop out of Carey's vision, as he becomes caught up in visualizing a Christian nation unified in its shared spiritual exertion. Prayer propels heathen conversion by mustering collective support for a distant project. It also provides an activity in which every Christian can participate, regardless of location or financial means, and therefore feel a personal investment.

*   *   *

Prayer provided the fabric of the transatlantic web from which missionary projects derived their support. Missionary writings argued that efforts to convert Indians, sustained by an economy of prayer, embodied the desire of many Christians. They also suggested that a disparate group of people, far away from and largely unacquainted with each other, could cement their ties by expressing their desires and hopes simultaneously to God. Although the particular vision of transatlantic British closeness articulated by some of these texts was shattered by the American Revolution, evocations of emotionally connected rather than geographically bounded communities would continue to propel missionary movements long after that event. They also would inform distinctively modern constructions of collective identity.

While these fund-raising texts demonstrate the intense feeling that could be aroused among British readers for the spiritual sufferings of Indians, they also display a tendency to overlook the Indians at the center of that sentiment. It is an odd but important characteristic of British missionary writings that they depicted the colonial venture as a fierce but unrequited aspiration to save the Indians, coupled with the abundantly requited desire of Britons—and sometimes European Christians— for closeness with each other. The fact that so many projects failed and that these failures were intertwined with the Indians' widespread deaths catalyzed the inherent affective tendencies of this discourse. For the inclinations of these texts are to move the by-products of the endeavors to centerstage, allowing the primary object of desire to disappear within a circle of shared emotion. Like the female object whose death, according to Eve Sedgwick, promotes the homosocial bonding of men, the Indians promote, through their sentimentalized and sanctified disappearance, emotional connections among those European Christians who pity them.

We are all familiar with the Romantic trope of the vanishing Indian but less so with its religious roots. As I will show later, the teleological preoccupations and triangular emotional trajectories of missionary writings prepared the British to expect the disappearance of the Indians from America, associating the deaths of their bodies with the cultivation of their souls. Missionary desire exceeded and inevitably failed to be fulfilled by its elusive object, the heathen convert. Precisely because it was unfulfilled, however, this desire allowed the British to envision plantation, settlement, and trade unfolding benevolently across the canvas of the Indians' souls, until they could look through this increasingly translucent image to each other.

Chapter 4

Indians, Deists, and the Anglican Quest for Compassion: The Sermons of the Society for the Propagation of the Gospel in Foreign Parts

The Problems of Pathetic Representations

Among British groups who attempted to convert Indians during the colonial period, the Church of England's Society for the Propagation of the Gospel was the least successful. A few Anglican ministers had preached to Indians since Alexander Whitaker's and George Thorpe's efforts in Jamestown before the massacre of 1622, and Morgan Godwyn, a minister of Barbados and Virginia, had published texts stressing the church's duty to convert Indians and African slaves, but the church otherwise had paid little attention to Indians in the seventeenth century.[1] After its founding in 1702 the society undertook a mission to the Mohawks (which received much attention after the visit of the "four Indian kings" to London in 1710) (see figure 3), it attempted to convert the Yamasee of South Carolina before the Yamasee war of 1713, and it hired the Moravian Christian Frederick Post to minister to the Miskito Indians of present-day Honduras.[2] Through Gideon Johnston, commissary to South Carolina, it brought "Prince George," the son of a Yamasee chief, to London to be educated (see figure 4), and throughout the century it encouraged its ministers in colonial parishes to preach to Indians as opportunity allowed.[3] With the exception of the Mohawks these efforts came to naught, and by the American Revolution the SPG was able to claim few heathen converts who were not the slaves of colonists.[4]

The failure of the SPG to convert many Indians is best explained as the result of the group's inability to provide sufficient resources for the religious needs of the colonies. Unlike the New England Company and the Scottish society, which had more narrowly defined goals, the SPG was de-

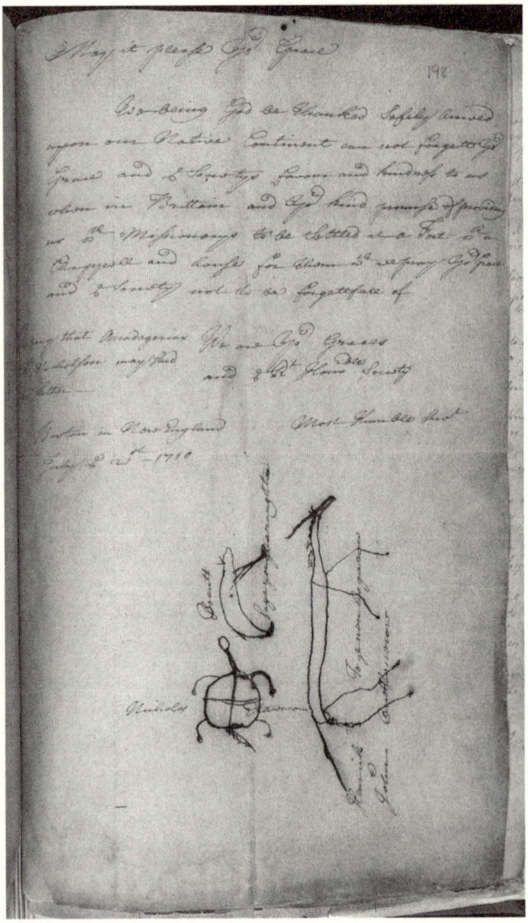

Figure 3. Letter from three "Indian Kings" to Archbishop of Canterbury, July 21, 1710. In 1710 Peter Schuyler brought "the four Indian kings," actually three Mohawks and one Mahican, to London to seek military assistance in campaigns against the French and their native allies and to petition for the construction of a fort and mission near Albany. In July 1710, after their return to America, three of the envoys signed this letter to the Archbishop of Canterbury with the totems of their clans. The letter, which Col. Francis Nicholson delivered to the Archbishop of Canterbury, thanked the archbishop for his hospitality and reminded him of his promise to assist with the construction of a chapel and fort. The SPG's Standing Committee discussed this letter on January 5, 1710/11, with Nicholson in attendance, and expedited their plans to dispatch a missionary and undertake work on a chapel. In the meantime the military expedition that had inspired the transatlantic visit had failed, largely through insufficient support from the British. (Courtesy of the United Society for the Propagation of the Gospel and Lambeth Palace Library, MS 711, folio 98)

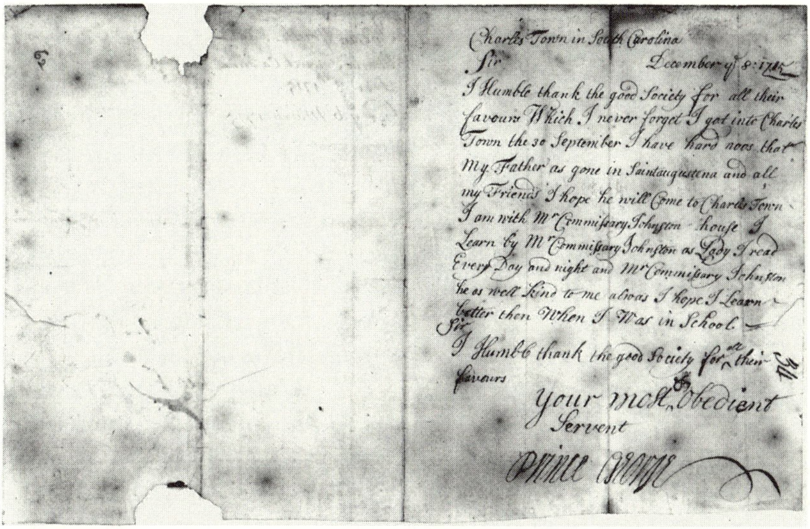
Charles Town in South Carolina
Sir December ye 8: 1715
I Humble thank the good Society for all their
favours Which I never forget I got into Charles
Town the 30 September I have hard noes that
My Father as gone in Saintaugustina and all
my Friends I hope he will Come to Charles Town
I am with Mr Commissary Johnston house I
Learn by Mr Commissary Johnston as Lady I read
Every Day and night and Mr Commissary Johnston
he as well kind to me always I hope I Learn
better then When I Was in School
Sir
I Humble thank the good Society for all their
favours
your most Obedient
Servent
Prince George

Figure 4. Letter from "Prince George" to SPG, December 8, 1715. In June 1713 Gideon Johnston, commissary of South Carolina, brought the son of a Yamasee chief to London to be educated at the cost of the SPG. This youth, who is named only as "Prince George" in the SPG's records, appeared before the SPG's Standing Committee, which also received regular updates from tutors about his progress. Prince George wrote this letter to the society after his return to South Carolina in 1715. The letter demonstrated his literacy and gratitude even as it conveyed concern about George's father's disappearance during the Yamasee war. The father later was discovered to have been enslaved, and after Johnston's death in 1716 the society received no more information about or from Prince George. (Courtesy of the United Society for the Propagation of the Gospel and the Bodleian Library of Commonwealth and African Studies at Rhodes House)

voted to supplying ministers, churches, and schoolmasters to colonists, their slaves,[5] and neighboring Indians in all colonies except for Virginia, Maryland, and the West Indies.[6] The society's inheritance in 1710 of Christopher Codrington's Barbados plantation, along with a mandate to maintain three hundred slaves there, made the conversion of slaves a more pressing priority than its members had anticipated.[7] As colonial populations became more ethnically diverse the society also ministered to French and German Protestants, persuading some to conform to Anglicanism.[8] When it was founded in 1717, the Associates of Dr. Bray assisted with the education of slaves, but the SPG still could not meet all its objectives. Even retaining competent missionaries in urban postings proved difficult, as ministers sometimes left their positions for more appealing ones, engaged in disreputable conduct, or died.[9] Finding men who would face the rigors of life among Indians and learn their language was all but impossible when such men could more easily minister to colonists.[10] The cause of converting Indians tended to be overshadowed by the society's efforts to provide ministers for colonial parishes, pay their salaries, and manage them from three thousand miles away.

Throughout the colonial era, however, the SPG expressed interest in its publications, especially the anniversary sermons, in converting Indians. The absence of Indians from the society's charter was quickly rectified when Richard Willis explained, in the society's first sermon, that "[t]he design is in the first place to settle the State of Religion as well as may be among our *own People* there, . . . and then to proceed in the best Methods they can toward the *Conversion* of the *Natives*."[11] Succeeding sermons referred to Indians with some frequency, as they compared them with ancient heathens, deplored their treatment by Catholics, expressed horror at their barbarities, and stressed the importance of converting them.

The SPG's attempts to convert Indians received frequent mention in the society's publications, and over the years a few clergy tried to launch new conversion projects through the printed word. In 1723 George Berkeley, Dean of Derry, Ireland, published a proposal to found a missionary college for Indians in Bermuda.[12] Berkeley's proposal angered members of the SPG because he had ignored the group's efforts with Indians, but he delivered the society's sermon of 1732 after spending several years in Rhode Island trying to establish his college.[13] In 1727 Thomas Bray, the SPG's founder, published *Missionalia*, a collection of texts regarding the conversion of Indians and Africans.[14] In 1740 Thomas Wilson, the Bishop of Sodor and Man, wrote *An Essay Towards an Instruction For the Indians,* a primer inspired by the renewed hopes for Indian conversion that accompanied the founding of the Georgia colony.[15]

This gap between abundant textual attention to Indians and meager attempts to convert them is at first puzzling, and in the eighteenth century it gave cause for suspicion among American Dissenters. The SPG had inspired ill will since its founding because it seemed to ignore other Protestant efforts to convert Indians.[16] Dissenters also resented the SPG because it had sent far more ministers to colonists than to Indians or slaves. Such actions suggested an effort to establish the Church of England as the official state church, a religious hegemony that many colonists and many Presbyterian Scots associated with political tyranny.[17] Criticisms of the SPG became especially strong in the second half of the century, when the Great Awakening exacerbated tensions between revivalists and nonrevivalists and the Church of England increased efforts to establish a bishop in America. John Brainerd, who took over his brother David's mission in New Jersey after his death, concluded a fund-raising letter in 1752 by noting that the SPG poured large sums of money into metropolitan New England churches "while our poor Heathen Neighbours lie almost utterly neglected."[18] The next year the Congregationalist Samuel Hopkins devoted several pages of his *Historical Memoirs, Relating to the Housatunnuk Indians* to chastise the SPG for granting half-hearted support to its own missionary to the Mohawks, Henry Barclay, while building churches in New England's cities.[19] Over the next two decades Congregationalist and Presbyterian ministers continued to depict the SPG as a group that neglected Indians in order to dominate the colonial religious establishment.

Peter M. Doll has corrected a tendency among historians to see the effort to establish an American bishop mainly as part of tensions leading up to the Revolution by showing that this effort also was a response to Catholic dominance in Canada, concerns over church administration, and debates about the function of a state church.[20] From its first years, however, the SPG did little to assuage worries that its hopes for Indian conversion provided a smokescreen for efforts to establish Anglican dominance in America. Just after its founding the society took four years to launch a mission to the Mohawks, largely at the prodding of the Lords Commissioners of Trade and Plantations, who worried that Jesuits were exerting too much influence on the Iroquois.[21] Well before this, however, it dispatched George Keith, a converted Quaker who had received Anglican ordination, to proselytize Quakers in the colonies.[22] The anniversary sermon of 1741 by Thomas Secker, then Bishop of Oxford and later Archbishop of Canterbury, also fueled these tensions by downplaying the group's mission to Indians and arguing that part of the society's task was to encourage conformity to the Church of England.[23]

The SPG came under its most severe attack in 1763, when Jonathan Mayhew, the pastor of Boston's West Church and son of the missionary Experience Mayhew, published *Observations of the Charter and Conduct of the Society for the Propagation of the Gospel in Foreign Parts.*[24] Mayhew published this text shortly after the Massachusetts General Assembly incorporated a "Society for Propagating Christian Knowledge among the Indians in North America" and while the SPG was lobbying to prevent royal and

parliamentary approval of this new organization.[25] Mayhew attacked the
SPG's sermons for dishonestly "induc[ing] good people of all denominations" to support the society, "chiefly for the sake of the poor heathen
slaves and savages in, or bordering on the English plantations." This fund-
raising, which "had doubtless drawn some thousands of pounds from Protestant dissenters in England,"[26] had occurred when the society had no intention of "propagating the gospel among the poor *Negroes* and *Indians*"
but instead sought "to support and increase the episcopal party."[27] The
society thus had exploited the powerful effects of "pathetic" depictions of
heathens at the cost of the residents—Indian, African, and European—of
Britain and America.

Mayhew's attack was based on a misreading of the SPG's publications,
which consistently stressed a mission to provide ministers for colonists as
well as slaves and neighboring Indians. His accusations did, however, accurately represent the tendency of these texts to discuss Indians in emotional
and intellectual terms more than pragmatic ones. Certainly George Stanhope, the Dean of Canterbury, had noted in the SPG's sermon of 1714, "To
propagate Christianity among the uncivilized Indians, hath been generally
thought a good Work, rather fit to be commended and well wished to, than
likely to be accomplished."[28] A few of the sermons' authors questioned the
feasibility of Indian conversion,[29] and many described missionary work, as
William Fleetwood had in 1711, as "a Work of such unspeakable Compassion" without dwelling on the details of that work.[30]

This inclination to abstraction rather than action does not necessarily
show that Mayhew was correct in his assessment of the SPG, for it is important to consider that these sermons were attempting to do more than raise
funds. Like all sermons, they clarified doctrine, prescribed moral conduct,
and interpreted scripture. They enhanced a sense of Christian community,
and they engaged in theological debate. Besides the usual work of their
genre and their obvious task of raising funds, these sermons provided a
public platform for the strengthening of Anglican identity through a missionary vision. The discussion of Indian conversion was to some degree
politically expedient, as Mayhew alleged, but it also was doctrinally crucial.
Ultimately the discussions of Indians in these texts had more to do with
theological controversy in Britain than with sectarian conflict in America.
They also had a great deal to do with moral philosophy and the culture of
sensibility, as they speculated on the emotional capacity and proclivities of
Indians, Christians, and God.

In addition to attempting, however feebly, to convert Indians, and trying, however assiduously, to establish Anglican churches throughout the colonies, the authors of the SPG's sermons used the idea of Indians to confront an ethical dilemma oddly connected to the one in which Mayhew implicated the society. Both Mayhew and the authors of the sermons articulated a concern with the ethics of eliciting feelings for the sufferings of others. The authors of the sermons addressed, even as they were accused of exploiting, the uncertain moral value of pity.

If we read the SPG's anniversary sermons against the backdrop of contemporaneous philosophy, we can see that many of these sermons used portrayals of Indians to buttress Anglicanism against one of the most significant challenges of its time: Deism, which denied the existence of a God who revealed himself to humans through anything but nature. This function was especially important in the sermons published during the first forty years of the eighteenth century, which coincided with the peak of the Deist controversy in England. As Frank Klingberg points out, "The Society . . . waged the ideological battles of the age, particularly those of deism."[31] The sermons' authors strove to establish the spiritual necessity of converting Indians. This assertion was a key response to longstanding but suddenly crucial questions about how God would judge the souls of humans who have never heard the gospel.[32] Through their ignorance of the Bible Indians introduced the possibility that God was unfair or that Christian doctrine was extraneous to a moral life. Thinking about Indian conversion thus proved crucial to the Church of England's confrontation with heterodoxy.[33]

This confrontation was one of doctrine, but it hinged on emotion: the concern that God might be so callous as to condemn a people ignorant of his command. Deists suggested that orthodox Christians who believed in such a God must themselves be callous. The arguments based on cool-headed reason favored by late seventeenth-century Latitudinarian divines, as outlined by Gerard Reedy, would not suffice to combat this particular attack.[34] Such strategies only would show apologists displaying the callousness that Deists refused to attribute to God. Anglican apologists not only had to explain why the case of the ignorant heathen did not undermine their vision of Christian salvation; they also had to show that they cared about those heathens.

As they sought replies to this challenge, the sermon authors enhanced their counterarguments through displays of sensitivity toward America's natives. Some of the sermons, especially earlier ones, insisted that God was too kind to condemn the uninformed, but most asserted that the Indians' cruelty proved the necessity of Christianity for salvation. The SPG's failure to support its talk about Indian conversion primarily shows that it saw the talk as important in its own right because it served an apologist purpose.

Framing their arguments with the tacit logic of sensibility, especially the idea that a capacity for feeling marked the difference between Christian and non-Christian, the preachers straddled otherwise insuperable inconsistencies in their position. They also contrasted their active concern for Indians with the Deists' passive sentiment. In so doing they formulated a concern about the ethics of witnessing suffering, especially what James H. Averill has called "the peculiar moral status of sentimental pleasure," which became central to the developing culture of sensibility.[35] Brooding on the plight of uninformed heathens thus constituted an effort by Anglican preachers to gain the upper hand in the intellectual *and* emotional components of theological debate. These strategies later would play an important role in the Church of England's response to the evangelical revivals of the mid-eighteenth century. Viewing the SPG's approach to Indian conversion as a response to Deism allows us to see this issue as one superseding proto-revolutionary sectarian conflict and detached from, although informed by, missions. It compels us to consider the importance of Christian mission to moral philosophy and the complex role of theological debate in the unfolding of eighteenth-century sensibility.

"To Indian Souls, and Worlds Discovered New": Deism and the Question of God's Compassion

The goal of raising funds determined much of the content of the SPG's sermons, which almost always stressed the pleasure and duty of charity and the worthiness of the society's work. Rather than dealing with the details of ongoing projects, a task left to the *Abstracts of Proceedings* that were published with the sermons from 1711 onward, most of the sermons concentrated on articulating the theology supporting charity and Christian mission. The sermons typically elaborated on the doctrine connected with a scriptural verse, applied that doctrine to the society's work, and then asked for money. Sometimes these verses dealt with charity, but more often they focused on the position heathens occupied in salvation history. This approach led most of the sermons to portray Christian mission with bold strokes, describing a grand vision of the gospel's progress across the earth and through time. As they emphasized the continuity of the society's mission with that of the early church, they asserted that Christianity required and assisted the spread of civilization, to which they juxtaposed both heathenism and Catholicism.

Unlike earlier English missionary writings, the sermons rarely presented vignettes of Indians or Africans that stressed their humanity and their desire for Christianity. Instead, the sermons positioned them within a scriptural frame as modern gentiles or heathens. This inclination was especially true for Indians, who, because they had been excluded entirely from knowledge of the Bible (or the Bible's knowledge of them) until Columbus's voyage, required more explanation. John Waugh, the Dean of Gloucester, noted in 1722, "The Natives . . . which we are to bring in, are as great Objects of our Compassion, and stand in as much need of our Help, as the Gentiles then did; they live in as thick Darkness, and in as gross Idolatry, are as vicious and neglectful of God's Worship, as those were."[36] In 1729 Henry Egerton, the Bishop of Hereford, concurred, as he stressed the "the special Instance of Christian Charity, now before us, that of converting Infidels. . . . Who are emphatically styl'd by St. Paul, Gal. ii. 15. Sinners of the Gentiles."[37] The sermons tended to describe Indians as literally outside biblical history but allegorically within it, as analogues of ancient gentiles.

This strategy shared much with the tendency to cast Indians as Canaanites to the Puritans' Israelites, but it softened this inimical vision with a looser allegorical frame and a stronger hope for conversion. As gentiles, the Indians appeared in the sermons as sinners who, without the redemption offered by Christianity, would be condemned to hell. Many of the sermons argued this point assertively, and they suggested that people who believed otherwise would undermine the social stability that Christianity also propagated.

This treatment of Indians in the sermons is easier to understand when we recall that the origins of the SPG, as with the SPCK and the various religious societies founded in the late seventeenth century, lay in concerns over internal as well as external threats to Britain's religious establishment.[38] One of the greatest threats to the Church of England was Deism.[39] Less a school of thought than a collection of heterodox critiques, Deism was an effort to pare organized religions down to their indisputable basics.[40] Emerging from early modern epistemological developments, Deism also was a skeptical response to the violence and confusion resulting from the Reformation and increased intercultural contact. As they searched for a verifiable core of what they praised as "Natural Religion," Deists attempted to strip belief of what they saw as ornate accoutrements, such as miracles, and corrupt elements, such as the dominance of priests. As the Deist Matthew Tindal wrote, "God's will is so clearly and fully manifested in the book of nature that he who runs may read it."[41] Tindal's implication that the least educated human can obtain access to divine truth also illustrates the Deist tendency to see civilization as corrupt.

Defining Deism is difficult because it was used as a general term of denunciation but also because in the wake of the Scientific Revolution, the English Civil War, and efforts to historicize the Bible, the distinction between eighteenth-century Christian orthodoxy and heterodoxy was not always clear.[42] Many thinkers who considered themselves orthodox Anglicans valued the idea of natural religion, especially as they sought to stress the rational aspects of their faith and separate their religion from the superstitions of Catholicism and the "enthusiasm" they associated with many Dissenters. S. Charles Bolton has pointed out that some of the SPG's missionaries to South Carolina "were interested in Indian customs in part because they hoped that primitive religious practices would prove that Christianity was a natural faith as well as a revealed religion."[43] Deists were controversial not because they stressed the natural basis of religion but rather because they insisted that religion was evident only through nature and reason, not through supernatural revelations. Most Deists also believed in a God who was not providentially involved in the universe he created, although they differed in the exact amount of involvement they attributed to God.[44]

Deist thought in England dates back at least to Lord Herbert of Cherbury, whose *De Veritate* (1624) forwarded what he called "five common notions concerning religion." As Leslie Stephen summarizes, "[T]hese affirm the existence of God, the duty of worshipping him, the importance of piety and virtue as the chief parts of this duty, the propriety of repentance, and the existence of a future state of rewards and punishments."[45] Deism became more prominent in England after the lapse of the Licensing Act in 1695, when John Toland's *Christianity Not Mysterious* (1696) appeared and when Charles Blount's *Works* (1695) expressed doubts about scriptural miracles and satirized the story of the Fall.[46] In *Characteristics of Men, Manners, Opinions and Times* (1711), Anthony Ashley Cooper, the Third Earl of Shaftesbury, grounded Deist ideas in sentimental moral philosophy.[47] The height of the controversy spanned the 1720s and 1730s, when Anthony Collins undermined biblical prophecy in his *Discourse on the Grounds and Reasons of the Christian Religion* (1724) by noting that scriptural prophecies were indistinguishable from those of other religions. Thomas Woolston was imprisoned for blasphemy after trying to disprove the Resurrection in six *Discourses on the Miracles of our Saviour* (1727–29), and Matthew Tindal wrote *Christianity as Old as the Creation* (1730), a text sometimes termed "The Deist Bible." Throughout the century Deism exerted a hold in France and North America, influencing figures such as Benjamin Franklin and Jean Jacques Rousseau.[48] In Britain, orthodox apologies combined with blasphemy prosecutions to create a general impression of its defeat by the 1740s.[49]

Several of the sermons' authors published tracts against Deists, the sermons themselves routinely invoked the threat of "free-thinkers," and a few, such as Thomas Sherlock's of 1716, focused on this topic.[50] This response was understandable, for the Church of England's rationalist inclinations in the early eighteenth century made it vulnerable to attacks on efforts to "prove" religious belief.[51] Deists also were a concern for the SPG because they used American Indians for their critiques of Christianity.[52] By emphasizing the Indians' idealized simplicity, they suggested an innate human ability to intuit moral tenets.[53] As John Toland said in his "Account of the Indians at Carolina," "We know our Saviour's precepts without observing them, and they observe them without knowing him."[54] In his entry titled "The Philosophy of the Canadians" in Diderot's *Encyclopédie*, Abbé Pestré transformed the Hurons into Deists, noting their belief that "[t]he Great Spirit has endowed men with reason to enable them to distinguish good from evil and follow the rules of justice and wisdom."[55] Benjamin Franklin later used images of Indians in similar ways.[56]

Indians also offered a more profound avenue of attack on organized religion. Because countless generations had never heard the gospel, they never had had the chance to choose Christianity. Through their mere existence they brought to crisis an old Christian quandary: How does God judge those people who never have heard of Christ? As Gerald McDermott has explained, this dilemma, which he terms "the scandal of particularity," is "the notion, galling to many, that God revealed himself to particular peoples at particular times rather than to all human beings from the very beginning."[57] Certainly this notion occurred to at least some of the Indians missionaries encountered. In *The Day-Breaking, if not the Sun-Rising of the Gospell* (1647), one of the earliest tracts publicizing Puritan missions, the Congregationalist Thomas Shepard recorded a question posed by a Massachusett Indian: "How the English come to know God so much and they so little?"[58] Two years later *The Glorious Progress of the Gospel* included a letter from John Eliot, who recollected another Indian's remark, "If it be thus as you teach, then all the world of Indians are gone to hell to be tormented for ever, until now a few may goe to Heaven and be saved."⁵⁹ These were serious questions, because to say that all heathens would go to hell undercut the idea that Christ died for everybody's sins; to say that they would be saved questioned the importance of faith. The problem was, as Phillip Harth has noted, "as old as Christianity itself,"⁶⁰ going back to Paul's discussion in the epistle to the Romans of gentiles who instinctively follow the law of God: "For not the hearers of the law are just before God, but the doers of the law shall be judged by the law; (For when the Gentiles, which have not the law, do by nature the things contained in the law, these, having not the law, are a law unto themselves: Which shew the work of the law written in their hearts, their conscience also bearing witness, and their thoughts the mean while accusing or else excusing one another;) In the day when God shall judge the secrets of men by Jesus Christ according to the gospel" (Rom. 2:13–16). Aligning Christian law with the heart, Paul expressed hope for the uninformed gentile. This hope set a high threshold, however, suggesting that heathens could—and thus should—find their way unaided to God. "[T]hat which may be known of God is manifest in them; for God hath shewed it unto them." (Rom. 1:19). If they ignored the knowledge of God available in nature and their hearts, they were "inexcusable" for lapsing into idolatry (Rom. 2:1). Paul's answer made room for the exceptional gentile. It did not, however, erase the impression that God held unfair standards for the ignorant.⁶¹

This question was one of recurring though minor concern through the Middle Ages. Dante placed such virtuous pagans as Homer and Socrates in "Limbo," the first circle of hell, where there is "sadness, without torments." As Virgil explained of the souls there, "[T]hey did not sin; but if they have merit, that does not suffice, for they did not have baptism, which is the portal of the faith you hold."⁶² Dante thus suggested that good works could ameliorate eternal punishment, but they could not earn a heathen entrance to heaven.

Such resolutions became less convincing to early modern Protestants, however. European contact with the Americas renewed the question of ancient pagans, while Reformation debates over redemption intensified dispute over the fate of heathens.⁶³ On the one hand, Congregationalist missionaries working in the seventeenth century had little trouble acknowledging a God who had denied knowledge of the gospel to Indians. This line of thought was based on a Calvinist belief in predestination but also on an assumption that Indians, perhaps descended from the lost tribes of Israel, had denied God long ago. While stressing the compassion that he and other ministers felt for "a company of perishing, forlorne outcasts" in 1647, Thomas Shepard conveyed no hesitation in their insistence that the "Indians['] forefathers were a stubborne and rebellious children, and would not heare the word."[64] Even at the end of the century Cotton Mather suggested that the devil had led Indians to America in order to remove them from the gospel.[65]

A belief that Indians had, through their own fault, lost God's favor held some sway throughout the eighteenth century, but developments in moral philosophy, especially theories of compassion and universal benevolence, created a climate of intellectuals eager to fret about God's fairness.[66] The idea that one might suffer in hell for one's ignorance (or that one might suffer in hell at all) began to strike many people as unthinkable, because it would evidence a God lacking in compassion.[67] Judith Shklar has rooted many of the intellectual changes brought about during the Enlightenment in a tendency to consider cruelty, as opposed to the seven deadly sins, as the greatest evil.[68] Ava Chamberlain has applied this argument to the gradual softening of Calvinist theology in eighteenth-century New England.[69] Growing concerns about cruelty contributed to the rise of Arminianism, named after the seventeenth-century Dutch theologian Jacobus Arminius, who argued against John Calvin and his followers that humans are not simply predestined for heaven or hell but can earn salvation through their conduct and faith.[70] While this theology seemed, to many Protestants, to deny the supremacy of God's will and resemble Roman Catholic notions of salvation, it also struck many as fairer than a Calvinist outlook, fitting a God who was not cruel.

Such changes pertained to at least some Calvinists in Britain, as the sermons of the Presbyterian SSPCK indicate. As early as 1730 John Matthisen preached on the question, "Why the Gospel is named *an hidden Mystery*," revealed to different peoples at different times. Noting that Deists had used such questions to provoke skepticism, he reminded his audience of the importance of maintaining faith even when one could not fathom God's reasons.[71] While many preachers of the Scottish society's sermons continued to blame the dearth of Christian awareness in the world on "the depravity of human nature," as David Plenderleath, author of the SSPCK sermon of 1754, did,[72] they showed growing concern with all forms of cruelty, including the apparent unfairness of salvation history. In 1746 Robert Wallace, a minister of Edinburgh, confronted the recent Jacobite rebellion through Psalm 74:20, "Have respect unto the covenant, for the dark places of the earth are full of the habitations of cruelty." He then itemized the injustices and cruelties perpetrated by Catholics and heathens that Protestant Christianity, through its compassion, could eradicate.[73] One of the first SSPCK sermons to defend God's apparent unfairness was that of 1755 by William Robertson, who was a leader of the Church of Scotland's Moderate Party, Principal of the University of Edinburgh, and a central figure of the Scottish Enlightenment. Robertson argued that revelation took place when and where humans were prepared to receive it, "not poured in upon mankind all at once, and with its full splendour."[74] The sermons of the Presbyterian SSPCK suggest a preoccupation with the implications of a Calvinist outlook and an effort to reconcile this theology with a growing abhorrence of cruelty.

Such concerns seem to have occurred earlier to those who did not hold strictly Calvinist views of salvation. As early as 1649 Thomas Fuller, a preacher known for his anti-Puritan but moderate stance during the Civil War, included the question of the Indians' damnation in a list of "Five things . . . in the primitive parts of Gods justice, which are very hard for men to conceive."[75] While he offered no explanation for the condemnation of "Americans" and did not suggest that God would offer them any mercy, the fact that he grouped this issue with inexplicable and painful events such as the deaths of children suggests the emotional heaviness with which he considered it. The existence of Indians was distressing enough to lead some divines, such as Richard Reynolds, Bishop of Lincoln, to theorize in the SPG sermon of 1728 that the Apostles actually had visited America.[76] No doubt this quandary also played a role in the many theories that America's natives were descended from the lost tribes of Israel. A bane to the orthodox, Indians were a boon to more radical groups. Thomas Hahn has noted that Quakers used Indians to "affirm one of [their] fundamental tenets, the universality of God's inspiration through the Inward Light."[77] While he was visiting the governor of North Carolina in 1671, George Fox used the example of an Indian's natural moral sense to defend his religious views from a "doctor's" disbelief in the inner "light and the spirit" of all human beings.[78] A century later Anthony Benezet, a Quaker of Philadelphia, prefaced his translation of *A Plain Path to Christian Perfection*, a fifteenth-century German tract, with an account of a neighboring Indian group that had initiated its own religious reformation. One Indian had led this movement because "strong desires were begot in his heart for a further knowledge of his Creator."[79] On their own this group detected most of the basic truths of Christian morality and faith, proving the simplicity and truth of Christianity.[80]

Helpful to Quakers, the figure of the virtuous but uninformed Indian was most useful to Deists arguing that traditional Christian theories of revelation could not be valid. As Charles Blount wrote: "That Rule which is necessary to our future Happiness, ought to be generally made known to all men. Therefore no Revealed Religion is necessary to future Happiness. . . . [W]itness the large Continent of *America*, not discover'd to all the World; where if there were any Reveal'd Religion, at least it was not the *Christian*."[81] Matthew Tindal reiterated Blount's point: "If *God's Ways are equal,* . . . how can we suppose he left all Mankind, for so many ages, & the greatest part, even at present, in a most miserable state of doubt . . . about the possibility of Man's being sav'd?"[82]

These arguments were neither sophisticated nor new, but they posed a basic challenge to Christian thought. When they argued that Christianity's God was unjust to Indians, Deists suggested that the person who believed in such a God must be callous to suffering. This strategy gave the Deist position rhetorical strength, allowing Tindal, for example, an indignant dismissal of Christian faith: "[N]othing, sure, can be more shocking, than to suppose the unchangeable God, *whose nature, and property is ever to forgive,* was not, at all times, equally willing to pardon repenting Sinners; and equally willing they shou'd have the satisfaction of knowing it."[83] Tindal used the language of masculine etiquette to insist that God must be more compassionate than Christian doctrine suggested. Like any gentleman, God would not refuse humans the "satisfaction" of knowing that he would forgive sins. This point was made just as British culture was reaching a consensus that "those who were coldly indifferent to suffering were, by definition, something less than human."[84] Deism was ostensibly rational, but the thrust of its argument here was emotional: by insisting on a God who would not unfairly condemn Indians, Deists challenged Christians to show their *caritas* and prove they were humane.

The strength of this challenge lay partly in the fact that by drawing on the trope of the noble savage while stressing the cruelty of Christianity, Deists attacked English Christians for their Englishness (and later for their Britishness) as much as for their Christianity. By 1700 England had spent more than fifty years developing a national image that relied on evoking horror at the cruelties propagated by the Spanish in America, and many SPG sermons contributed to this project. In his sermon of 1704, Gilbert Burnet described "the poor ignorant Natives" of America and disparaged "the unexampled Cruelties and Barbarities that almost exceed belief with which they were treated, as [the Spanish] destroyed the greatest part of them."[85] Both the Black Legend and the Deist challenge relied to some degree on an image of Indians as damaged innocents. Arguing against the Deists' attack almost inevitably involved undermining the very stereotype of Indians that had come to validate England's presence in America and define the English people's understanding of themselves in opposition to Catholics. The Deist challenge made it imperative that Anglican divines find some way to assert their capacity to feel for the sufferings of heathens. In this way compassion became a crucial possession of the Anglican Church, and indeed of England.

Responding to the question of heathen salvation was difficult, and apologists attempted several strategies. Before his Catholic conversion John Dryden defended Anglican theology in *Religio Laici* (1682) by addressing the question of Indian salvation. Quoting "the Deist," he wrote,

'Tis said the sound of a Messiah's birth
Is gone through all the habitable earth;
But still that text must be confined alone
To what was then inhabited, and known:
and what provision could from thence accrue
To Indian souls, and worlds discovered new?[86]

This argument was a serious one, he acknowledged, but not insuperable, "stagger[ing]" only "frail belief."[87] Its weakness was its reductive understanding of redemption, which Dryden rooted in Athanasius's ancient battles with the heterodox theologian Arius. He responded by refusing to accept the Deist premise that heathens would not be saved. Citing Romans 2:14–15, he insisted that a merciful God had provided the "bewildered souls" of heathens with a path to heaven.[88]

In the long run, however, Dryden's reply was insufficient. The reliance on God's kindness was a double-edged sword, as it was hard to stress that God was both charitable and consistent. To believe that heathens could be saved implied that they were better off than Christians. Missionaries might do more harm than good, because the knowledge they conveyed would make their hearers eligible for hell. Defoe summarized this problem in *The Serious Reflections of Robinson Crusoe*: "[I]f they are received to mercy in a future state . . . then their ignorance and pagan darkness is not a curse, but a felicity;. . . . [I]t may in a negative manner be true that the Christian religion is an efficient in the condemnation of sinners, and loses more than it saves."[89] The Puritans in *The Day-Breaking* seemed to agree about the damning effect of gospel knowledge, although they were less troubled by the implications of this idea. Shepard noted that he and three other ministers warned the Indians of Nonantum, near Boston, after having preached to them several times, "[I]f now they did repent it was not too late . . . , but if they did not come when they were thus called, God would be greatly angry with them, especially considering that now they must sinne against knowledge, whereas before we came to them they knew not anything of God at all."[90]

While it did not seem to bother seventeenth-century Puritans, this question created problems for Anglicans of the early eighteenth century, especially those who leaned toward Arminian views of universal salvation. Their moderate path was vulnerable to the questions Deists provoked them to ask about redemption. The fate of heathens sharpened the Anglican struggle to assert divine omnipotence and compassion, to make room at once for faith, charity, and rational thought.

As they quarreled with Deists about the question of heathen salvation, Anglicans were engaged in a contest for the turf of sociability and sentiment. Many Deists were thought by their opponents to be fracturing the culture of bourgeois civility, gentlemanly discourse, and moral reform that was developing in the wake of the Glorious Revolution.[91] Sympathy, as a basis for social cohesion, was central to this culture. That Deists such as Shaftesbury were central to the establishment of that same culture only emphasizes the uncertain alignment of orthodox religion with gentlemanly rhetoric in the early Enlightenment.[92] Maintaining a Christian perimeter around the *sensus communis,* Anglicans were engaged in a struggle to own new forms of cultural praxis. They were trying to mark as Christian a modern ideal of masculine conduct: the ideal of gentlemanly behavior based on gentle but manly feeling.[93] Deists challenged the Church of England to assert its social legitimacy through its pity for heathen souls.

"All the Strictest Bonds of Love": Cruelty and Compassion in the SPG Sermons

They rarely have been acknowledged as such, but the SPG's sermons provided a main site for the Church of England's response to the Deist controversy.[94] Most of the sermon authors saw the spread of Christianity abroad as intertwined with the defense of it at home, and they confronted Deists through their depictions of Indians. This unity of strategy is noteworthy given the range of views that Anglican divines held in this era. John Moore,

Bishop of Ely, who delivered the sermon of 1713, was a patron of William Whiston, whose theological writings were attacked as heterodox by many members of the Anglican establishment such as Richard Smallbroke, Bishop of Litchfield and Coventry, who authored the sermon of 1733.[95] Edward Waddington, author of the sermon of 1721, publicly supported the imprisonment of Thomas Woolston for blasphemy, while Francis Hare, author of the sermon of 1734, had published a tract in 1714 that was condemned by the Lower House of Convocation, the Church's governing body, for its skeptical treatment of Christian tradition.[96] While these divines fell on opposite sides of some lines of orthodox thought, and while these lines shifted during the century, they presented an almost unified response to claims that the question of heathen salvation proved a God who was not compassionate or did not require Christian belief.

Displays of compassion played a central role in the controversy. Deists and orthodox Christians accused each other of indifference as both sides tried to anchor their agendas with sympathy. In his sermon John Moore wrote, "[T]he Persons who entitle themselves *Free-Thinkers* . . . insinuate that the *Ministers* of our Lord Jesus Christ, and the *stupid Idolaters* of *Siam,* are upon the same Level. . . . Let these Persons . . . consider, that by this prophane Mockery . . . they crucify themselves the Son of God afresh."[97] Moore recast spiritual relativism as cruelty to Christ. This point surely was an effective one for his clerical audience, but he was preaching to the choir, begging questions Deists asked about religious intolerance. Hurling accusations of cruelty back at Deists could not be a useful tactic in the long run.

Rebutting the charge that Christianity was unfair, the preachers of these sermons had to chart a universal emotional economy that admitted the particular logic of Christianity. God's apparent indifference to heathens had to be made to signify Christian care. The SPG preachers responded to this challenge in two basic ways, sometimes in the same sermon. The first approach was to suggest that God was too kind to condemn the uninformed, and the second was to assert that the Indians' cruelty proved the necessity of Christianity for salvation. They either tried to match the Deists' displays of sensitivity, or they exposed this pity as ineffectual and morally bereft.

Those using the first approach conveyed that God would not be so callous as to condemn all heathens. Asserting that "no body can be said to assent to, or reject a Proposition of which he never heard," John Hough, Bishop of Litchfield and Coventry, speculated in 1705 that virtuous heathens would receive a minimum of both punishment and reward.[98] William Stanley, the Dean of St. Asaph, insisted in 1708 that Indians could not be worse off than insincere Christians: "The Ignorance of the *Indians and others*, we may justly think, will find more excuses than our Uncharitableness."[99] In the same sermon of 1713 that called Deists the new crucifiers of Christ, Moore pronounced of heathens: "[W]e safely leave them to the uncovenanted Mercies, and to the immense Goodness of God."[100] Nicholas Clagget, Bishop of St. Davids, summarized this approach in 1737 when he proclaimed of heathens, "*Ignoti nulla cupido.* As they have not heard the Joys of heaven, so it is not to be suppos'd, that want of knowing the Gospel can cause them uneasiness."[101] Many preachers thus stressed Paul's words on the law of the heart rather than his condemnation of the gentiles. Doing so, they foregrounded their feeling and competed with the Deists' compassion.

This argument was useful, but it left Christianity in the lurch of inconsistency. Taken to their logical extent, these arguments would invalidate the idea of formal creeds. When the sermons took a softer stance on salvation they also displayed a more passive form of pity. Because they relied on God to show mercy for heathens, the pressure on Christians to convert others was not as strong. This stance suggested, as Adam Smith later would, that humans could trust God to take care of distant cases of need.[102]

In 1706 John Williams, Bishop of Chichester, conveyed his concerns about an emphasis on God's mercy for heathens. Based on Acts 16:9, Paul's vision of the man in Macedonia who said, "come over and help us," this sermon was the first to emphasize a mission to Indians. Deism framed Williams's concern with Indian conversion in an encounter he imagined between an indigenous American and a missionary:

> Suppose now that a Missionary should address himself to a Native of these Countries, and labour to perswade him to . . . become a Christian. And he should reply. . . . [P]ray satisfie me in my Doubt . . . whether a Heathen continuing so to be, may not be saved, if he take Nature and Reason to be his Guide, and live soberly and virtuously?
> Now if the Answer of the Missionary be, that I dare not be positive in it. . . . [T]he Labour of the Missionary will be at an end. . . . For what is left is not Christianity, but Deism.[103]

Williams's point is not that Deism threatens missionary work. It is rather that Deism undermines Christianity by saying that missions are unnecessary.[104] Whether Williams really cared about converting Indians is not certain, but this topic served his apologist task. He responded to the Deists'

challenge with emotion, commenting, "[H]ow cold must all [the missionaries'] Arguments be, if they fall short of this; if a bare stock of Nature were
sufficient, and Morality might be our Salvation."[105] This assertion balanced
the hard stance he took on heathens' spiritual fate. Following Romans 1, he
argued that the Indians' "grossest Corruptions of Idolatry and Immorality"
showed that they had discarded their natural ability to lead a virtuous life.[106]
They were thus "without excuse" and "without hope."[107]

This sermon delivered a remarkably transparent assessment of a Christian mission's apologist function. Many sermon authors also took a hard
stance on the question of heathens, stressing the omnipotence and mystery
of God while refusing to grant heathens a loophole in the scheme of salvation. In 1730 Zachary Pearce, Vicar of St. Martins-in-the-Fields, argued that
"*Remission of Sins* . . . is what every Nation . . . stands in need of." The
Indians' ignorance of the gospel did not dissuade him from maintaining
this point. "[W]e know . . . how many Nations of that spacious Continent
have never yet had CHRIST preached unto them," he conceded, but "the
Divine Goodness [cannot] be called in Question upon this account." After
all, the point of salvation was that it involved no human entitlement.
"[T]he Scriptures always speak of the Gospel as the *Free-Gift* of God; and
what Nation . . . can justly complain, unless debar'd of some Right?"[108] For
Pearce, the Deist demand for universal redemption denied the importance
of God's mercy. Expressing compassion for heathens was less important
than defending God from charges of callousness.

John Denne, the Archdeacon of Rochester who had gained some reputation as an apologist by delivering the Boyle lectures from 1725 to 1728,
followed in Pearce's tracks the next year. Titling his sermon *Want of Universality no Just Objection to the Truth of the Christian Religion,* he presented
one of the society's most direct confrontations with this topic. He assured
his audience that God already had done enough for humans in giving them
reason and free will: "[W]e ought in Reason to expect no more of [God],
than that he do make Use of the most natural, and reasonable Means to
any End; and if those Means become insufficient for that End . . . thro' the
Fault of free and moral Agents, the Blame must rest on *them*, and not on
him."[109] He asserted that all humans had the power to choose God, even if
they did not know the name of Christ.

Many preachers insisted that heathens had perverted their innate sense
of God's word and thus brought damnation on themselves. When Martin
Benson, the Bishop of Gloucester, argued in 1740 that Deists were wrong
about natural religion, he did so by attacking the belief that Indians were

noble savages. Of the Deists he wrote, "They observe indeed that the *Indians* are free from several Vices, practised in civiliz'd Nations." This claim was unfounded, he asserted, because it confused true virtue with a lack of opportunity to practice vice: "They are innocent in these Respects, for the same Reason that Brutes are. . . . They have great need therefore of being instructed, in order to their being reformed."[110] This stance was hardly unique to Anglicans. In *The Doctrine of Original Sin Defended* (1758), Jonathan Edwards also had cited the savage practices of Indians as evidence that humans were not naturally able to follow God's will.[111] Rather than undercutting organized religion, Indians proved, in the Thomistic tradition of natural theology, that humans rarely could find virtue on their own.[112]

Many SPG sermons deployed a twofold strategy of excluding the Indians from salvation but then displaying concern for this exclusion by calling for increased missionary efforts. An emphasis on the Indians' cruelty helped accomplish this task, for the strongest evidence that they had perverted their innate awareness of God was their barbaric behavior. Indians were, as Thomas Secker said in his sermon of 1741, "engaged in almost perpetual Wars against each other, which they prosecute with Barbarities unheard of amongst the rest of Mankind . . . inhumanely negligent of Persons in Years; and . . . not scrupling to kill and eat their nearest Relations."[113] Isaac Maddox, the Dean of Wells, presented a similar viewpoint in 1734: "[G]reat Immoralities, *Rapin* and *horrid Cruelties,* are universally committed by them."[114] Such catalogs of malevolence showed that left to their own devices, humans were inclined to be inhumane.

The link between Christian faith and compassion was a central assertion of most SPG texts. No matter how civilized even ancient heathens might have been, they did not have the essential quality of kindness. They did not understand the idea of a caring God, for in ancient pagan writings "not much notice is taken of [God's] Love, his Affection, and his tender Care over all his Creatures."[115] In contrast, Christianity "instructs Men to act with Justice and Candour towards each other; to consider the whole Race of Man, as the Offspring of one Heavenly Father, entitled to the same Measure of Favour and Compassion."[116] The preachers asserted this idea and then performed it through their own reactions to heathen atrocities. As Isaac Maddox wrote, "[T]here are dark Corners of the Earth, now the Habitations of Cruelty. The Condition of whole Nations of bordering Indians, loudly calls for Pity and Assistance."[117] Because they dwelt in heathenish darkness, Indians lacked compassion, and their callousness acted as a foil to highlight his Christian sensibility.

Although it initially seemed to support Deist attacks by exhibiting callousness, insisting that heathens would go to hell, this tougher approach provided a stronger defense. Those who asserted that heathens were to blame for their damnation could express more urgent concern for them and defend Christianity's universality. They also delivered a more compelling critique of Deist sentiment. John Denne argued that the Deists' insistence on God's fairness could be taken to a ludicrous extreme. He asked, "Why do *Deists* make a violent Outcry against *partial* Revelations, as if *God* was on this Account *unmerciful* and *cruel*, whilst they are silent about a no less *partial* Distribution of *natural* Powers and *providential* Blessing?"[118] That some humans received more revelation than others was no less a sign of God's injustice than the fact that some humans were smarter or stronger than others. To question the distribution of blessings was not only blasphemous; it was childish.

In 1738 Thomas Herring, Bishop of Bangor, argued that such questions were ineffectual: "Whatever Nations are at present without the Gospel. . . . this we are very sure of, That we have it; and are we fretful and uneasy, that God has favoured us with so distinguishing a Privilege? There is no End of satisfying this captious and discontented Humour."[119] Herring dismissed Deism as mere petulance. His references to humors pathologized the tendency to "fret" about fairness, linking worries about privilege and passivity to melancholic excess. These worries, he insisted, distracted from the basic point of Christian obligation. They prevented humans who had Christian knowledge from converting those who did not.

While replying to Deists, these sermons formulated an ethical problem that would plague theorists of sensibility: the difference between passively witnessing suffering and actively alleviating it. This was a worry that, ironically, had been voiced early in the century by the Deist Shaftesbury, when he noted that "excessive pity renders us incapable of giving succor."[120] Later in the century such concerns about the incapacitating effects of excessive sensibility would become more fully articulated in satirical depictions of over-sensitive men, such as in Mackenzie's *Man of Feeling*. As Fiering has noted, "[O]ne of the things that happened to the man of feeling in the romantic period is that the enjoyment of the emotion of pity, the sympathetic identification with the sufferer, became an end in itself and the compulsion to relieve the suffering proportionately less urgent."[121] Stephen Cox has pointed out the problematic status of "sensibility as argument," which he defines as "persuasive discourse that tends to equate intellectual authority with the power to display or elicit emotional susceptibility" because it introduces the possibility of feeling standing in for beneficent action.[122] Paralleling worries that excessive feeling prevented action were concerns, voiced by thinkers such as Bernard Mandeville, about the inherently self-serving nature of pity.

In "An Essay on Charity and Charity-Schools," Mandeville argued for a distinction between charity and pity. "Charity," he wrote, "is that Virtue by which part of that sincere Love we have for our selves is transferr'd pure and unmix'd to others, not tyed to us by the Bonds of Friendship or Consanguinity."[123] In opposition to this response to another's need, he presented pity: "This Virtue [charity] is often counterfeited by a Passion of ours call'd Pity or Compassion, which consists in a Fellow-feeling and Condolance [*sic*] for the Misfortunes and Calamities of others. . . . It is raised in us, when the Sufferings and Misery of other Creatures make so forcible an Impression upon us, as to make us uneasy."[124] The problem with pity is that it emerges from a desire to relieve one's own discomfort rather than to help another. Hardly one to declaim self-interest, Mandeville condemned pity because it led people to act against their interest even as it failed to provide relief to those in need of help.

The preachers of the SPG sermons opposed Mandeville's egoistic philosophy, but in their approach to heathens they displayed a surprising overlap with his description of pity. The agreement lay in their suspicion of pity that was merely expressed, without being followed by the action of true charity. Feeling pity for the unfairness heathens seemed to suffer, they pointed out, was different from doing something about that pity. Real pity, the preachers claimed, would generate a desire to convert Indians. Shifting the burden of the heathens' fate from God to Christians, they asserted that heathens' ignorance made Christians responsible for their conversion. William Fleetwood warned, "[N]o Man living can assign a better and more justifiable Cause, for God's withholding Mercy from a *Christian*, than that *Christian's* with-holding the Mercy of *Christianity* from an *Unbeliever*."[125] Such comments suggested that sentiment was authentic only when it was Christian, because only Christian sentiment was active. "We cannot think, that God has brought us to our new Settlements in the neighbourhood of the Indians, barely to make us spectators of their deplorable condition," said Clagget.[126] The existence of a people ignorant of the gospel did not disprove Christianity. Rather, God showed Christians the Indians' depravity in order to prompt an evangelical response.

In this way the core of the Deist critique was appropriated to enhance a Christian emphasis on love. Heathens existed to make Christians be more

Christian. As Joseph Butler, Bishop of Bristol, noted in 1739, "God . . . could indeed miraculously have revealed every religious Truth . . . to every individual Man. . . . Yet he has not done this: but has appointed, that Men should be instructed by the Assistance of their Fellow-creatures, in both."[127] Butler, who is better known for his critique of egoistic moral philosophies in *The Analogy of Religion*,[128] argued that God's apparent neglect of Indians was part of his plan to enhance the human bonds of compassion. God had distributed revelation unevenly because he wanted to link humans more closely together, not because he did not care about Indians.

Francis Hare, Bishop of Chichester, declared in 1735 that a person with any "Love of his own species. . . . can't behold infinite Numbers of his Fellow-Creatures dead as it were while alive, and buried in Ignorance and gross Darkness, and not be sensibly touch'd at their great Unhappiness."[129] He suggested that for all their cries that Christianity was unfair, Deists really were the ones who did not care about the Indians. Rather than admitting the Indians' spiritual plight and trying to rectify it, they undercut the one religion that could save them from eternal misery. The fact that in the same sermon Hare stressed that the conversion of "wild Indians" would not occur without miracles akin to those described in the Acts of the Apostles did not diminish his emphasis on missionary aspirations.[130] What was important was that the society's members really cared for the Indians and at least imagined that they could be God's instrument for rescuing them from damnation. The British owed it to their sense of themselves as Christians to attempt to save heathens. Thomas Secker was grim about the prospects of missionary work among Indians, but he felt that the success of these projects was beside the point. "The natural Dictate of Piety and Virtue is, to try," he said. "By endeavouring to our Power that these things be done. . . . we shall give a Proof to our own Hearts, that we are indeed [Christ's] Disciples; and convince the World, that Zeal for Religion is not yet extinguished."[131] It was important to Secker and the SPG's members that they feel they were feeling for the Indians and doing something about their pity.

Of course, for all their efforts to distinguish their authentic pity from the Deists' false sentiments, most of the sermon authors were not concerned with actual missions. Rather, they were concerned that the society be concerned with this issue. Certain that the society should not devote itself to converting heathens, Charles Trimnel, Bishop of Norwich, still insisted that the society's members always should be prepared to do so. His understanding of preparedness was not organizational or financial, but spiritual and emotional: "We ought no doubt to take care to keep such a

Sense of the Christian Religion continually alive in our Hearts, as may dispose us upon all Opportunities to do every Thing for its Advancement."[132] Trimnel pinned his hopes for heathen conversion on the spiritual content of British hearts. He recast missionary endeavor as emotional exertion. This gesture suggests one of the most important purposes that Indians served in the sermons. They prompted an exploration of the British subjective interior.

*   *   *

The SPG sermons demonstrate that the Church of England was profoundly affected by the idea of the American Indian as heathen other. They also suggest that the gap between the SPG's discussions about Indians and its failure to convert them involved a complex intellectual dimension that rarely has been acknowledged. Real encounters between the SPG's preachers and Indians were minimal, but their encounter with the *concept* of indigenous Americans was an intense and troubled one. The idea of a continent of people who until recently had never heard the Bible crystallized problems with which Christian theologians already were grappling. These problems ranged from debates over Arminianism to concerns about the logical coherence of Christian faith. These doctrinal quandaries touched on questions of broader ethical concern, such as the limits of human benevolence, the value of pity, and the responsibility of humans to alleviate each other's suffering. The sermons of the Society for the Propagation of the Gospel in Foreign Parts offered a forum for sorting out these issues.

Many more issues were involved in the sermons' treatment of Indians than Jonathan Mayhew acknowledged. At a certain level, though, he was correct that the SPG had fabricated their concerns for Indians in order to strengthen the Church of England. That the "enemies" against which the preachers exaggerated their concerns for heathen souls were more often Deists than Dissenting colonists only renders more complex the concern they expressed with the authenticity of pity.

Roger L. Emerson has cited the interest Anglican divines expressed in the SPG's missionary work as evidence that Latitudinarians held a position quite distinct from that of Deists: "Had Christianity been merely the religion of nature in fancy dress there would have been less interest among the latitudinarians in missionary activities."[133] The society's first forty sermons demonstrate that the converse of his point also is true: emphasizing that heathens must be converted if they were to be saved provided Anglicanism with a rebuttal to Deists. The fact that it was not until 1742 that an SPG preacher, the Chancellor of Sarum Henry Stebbing, explicitly denied the society's dedication to an Indian mission, corroborates this point. That no preacher would deny the importance of Indian conversion until the Deist threat largely had abated in Britain suggests the importance of emphasizing feeling for Indians while the Church of England seemed to be under Deist attack.[134]

Anglicans needed to display their interest in converting Indians so that they could reply to a particularly challenging aspect of Deist thought. They had to undercut the idea of the noble savage as promoted by the Deists, and they had to explain why the exclusion of Indians from awareness of the gospel did not show that Christianity was cruel. While some hoped that God would not condemn heathens, others argued that Indians had perverted their God-given inner light of reason and thus needed Christians' help. Nothing proved this perversion more than the cruelties Indians exhibited. The crux of the Anglican response, then, was that God only *seemed* to be unfair. Most of the preachers insisted that feeling for the Indians required acknowledging their likely damnation. Accused of insensitivity, the authors of the SPG's sermons set out to reclaim compassion for their own side in this doctrinal dispute. They argued that it was the Deists who really were indifferent to the sufferings of others. Through this reply the SPG preachers distinguished between true and false sentiment, claiming the former as an exclusively Christian mode of expression.

Ironically, in presenting this reply to Deists, the Anglican preachers were developing a line of argument that intersected in surprising ways with the thought of skeptical moral philosophers such as Mandeville. What they shared was a growing worry that pity might not prompt ethically appropriate action. These concerns would find more specific articulations later in the century. While evangelical revivals would provoke debates about the reliability of intense spiritual experience, the sentimental novel and other popular productions of a culture steeped in sensibility would call attention to the curiosity and pleasure that accompanied the spectacle of suffering.[135]

Before the height of a popularized culture of sensibility, however, these issues received a great deal of attention in the theological discussions surrounding missionary projects. The past seventy years have seen some debate over the question of whether the culture of sensibility emerged from secular skepticism or Latitudinarian Christian theology.[136] This study of the SPG's early sermons would seem to suggest that whether they were more influenced by seventeenth-century Latitudinarians or skeptics, many early eighteenth-century Anglican divines made substantial contributions to the intellectual underpinnings of this culture. Understanding the SPG's approach to Indian conversion as a response to Deism compels us to consider the importance of Christian mission to moral philosophy and the role of theological debate in eighteenth-century Enlightenment philosophy. Most of all, in their grappling with the question of heathen salvation these sermons pushed forward interrogations of the ethical value of feeling, even if they failed to provide definitive answers to their questions. In these texts, emotional expression came to constitute action. The sermons show that Indians were, to paraphrase Clifford Geertz, useful to feel with.

Chapter 5
The Sacrifice of Self: Emotional Expenditure and Transatlantic Ties in Brainerd's and Sergeant's Biographies

One of the ironies of early British missionary writings is that the priority of eliciting readers' pity for Indians and closeness with distant missionaries resulted in some erasure of the missionaries. This erasure is distinct from that of the Indians, who are vividly portrayed within the texts but who often are more present as stereotypes than as real people. Missionaries, on the other hand, are not portrayed or depicted for readers. Rather, they are presented as extensions of their readers' perception. Readers rarely look at missionaries; they look through their eyes and are asked to feel what the missionaries feel. More lenses than objects of a gaze, missionaries often remained unknown within their own writings, while they and their readers observe Indians.

Most of the New England Company's publications tended to elide individuality as they focused on a collaborative endeavor brought to fruition by a generic "I" or "we." This was true even of John Eliot, the celebrated "apostle to the Indians," who described his perceptions and efforts far more than he portrayed himself in his published writings. This inclination was most evident in Eliot's *Indian Dialogues,* which erased the English entirely from missionary labor while featuring imagined conversations between Christianized Massachusett Indians and unconverted ones. Texts referring to missionaries often did so in ways that absorbed them into a collective voice. The *Accounts* of the SPG and SSPCK tended to include summaries of individual letters, pasting them into broader narratives and integrating them into a corporate identity. In a sense this flattening of individuality is not surprising, for these organizations were concerned with publicizing their work, not with presenting character studies of their employees. Nonetheless, it is of interest that such texts rarely sought to develop readers' sense of connection to missions by presenting missionaries as sympathetic or engaging figures. The lack of attention paid to missionaries' characters, let alone their internal complexity, reminds us that many of these writings preceded the fascination eighteenth-century British readers came to have with the exploration of individual consciousness, a phenomenon most often associated with autobiographies and novels.[1]

Perhaps the only texts that asked readers to look at, rather than through the eyes of, missionaries were their biographies. Often connected with funeral sermons, they imitated the tone of martyrologies or lives of saints. One of the earliest examples of this genre to appear in English was a Catholic text, John Dryden's translation of Dominick Bohours's *Life of St. Francis Xavier,* published in 1688.[2] Cotton Mather's biography of Eliot, which was featured in his *Magnalia Christi Americana,* may have constituted a Protestant reply to Dryden's text even as it brought an appealing image of Puritan New England to the notice of a broader readership.[3]

Protestant accounts of missionaries' lives were rarer than Catholic ones because Protestant missionaries themselves were rarer and their culture was less steeped in the traditions of hagiography.[4] This gap narrowed in 1749, however, when Jonathan Edwards published his *Life of David Brainerd.* This biography, largely drawn from Brainerd's diary, featured his reflections during four years of labor among native groups in western Massachusetts, Long Island, Pennsylvania, and New Jersey under the employment of the SSPCK. It narrated his initiation of a revival among a group of Delawares, providing an introspective complement to Brainerd's published account of the revival, and then described his early death in 1747 from tuberculosis.[5]

The most popular of Edwards's writings, the *Life of David Brainerd* was published in countless editions throughout the eighteenth and nineteenth centuries, translated into several languages, and presented as an inspiration for evangelical Christians.[6] As Joseph Conforti has noted, the text "served as the archetype for an important sub-genre of religious biography in America—the missionary memoir."[7] It was followed in 1753 by Samuel Hopkins's portrayal of John Sergeant, a missionary of western Massachusetts who had died in 1749, in *Historical Memoirs, Relating to the Housatunnuk Indians.*[8] Hired by the Boston Commissioners of the New England Company in 1734, Sergeant spent fourteen years ministering to a settlement of Mahican Indians who called themselves the "Muhhakaneok" or River Indians, also called the Housatonic after the river along which they lived.[9] Although Hopkins's *Historical Memoirs* did not have nearly the impact that the *Life of David Brainerd* did, there was sufficient demand for it that in 1757 Hopkins published a follow-up work, *An Abridgment*.[10]

This chapter will study these two narratives alongside each other, showing how they marked an expansion of missionary discourse that reflected a broader cultural interest in the exploration of individual subjectivity through genres such as memoirs. J. Paul Hunter has noted that as it "started from the self but then tried to encompass the world" and exhibited a previously private self to a curious audience, the memoir "represent[ed] . . . growing uncertainties about formal boundaries" between self and other.[11] Missionary memoirs served this function in ways matching their religious orientation. While negotiating one form of alterity, that between Christian and heathen, they sought to bridge another, that created by distance, through the collective experience of witnessing a man's devotion to the salvation of others. These narratives suggest how the figure of the missionary enriched the affective vocabulary of the eighteenth century even as he complicated the emotional networks that had developed from desire to convert Indians. Opposed to one culture and isolated from his own, this liminal figure provided readers with new ways of considering the boundaries between intra- and intersubjective feeling.

These two narratives, their authors, and their subjects were closely connected within the world of the New England clergy. Brainerd was an apprentice to Sergeant in western Massachusetts, where he ministered to a settlement of Iroquois a few miles from Stockbridge. Hopkins, a minister of West Springfield, was a brother-in-law and colleague of Edwards.[12] His nephew, a well-known abolitionist and theologian also named Samuel Hopkins, was a classmate of Brainerd's at Yale and later a student and friend of Edwards. After he became a minister in western Massachusetts, the younger Hopkins turned down an offer by the Boston Commissioners of the New England Company to replace Sergeant at the Stockbridge mission. He persuaded the commissioners to offer the post to Edwards, who had alienated his Northampton congregation through his desire to return to a stricter standard for admission to communion.[13] Seven years after Edwards's death in 1758 the younger Samuel Hopkins wrote a biography of him.[14]

Edwards's and Hopkins's texts have a great deal in common. Both tell stories of young men who ventured out from their community into the wilderness to save heathen souls. Both men overcame their initial repulsion to Indian culture not through acceptance but through a desire to alleviate the suffering they thought accompanied a life of heathen savagery. Both sought to remake a pagan Indian community in the image of a British Christian one, and both enjoyed successes that they and others publicized as signs of God's favor.[15] Both men died at a young age, in the midst of their labor, having ignored secular ambitions and expended their lives for the salvation of others.

Two factors had particular influence on the ways in which Edwards and Hopkins depicted their subjects. The first was a growing belief that efforts to convert Indians should take place in isolation from colonial settlements. Reflecting an emerging consensus that secular European culture corrupted Indians, this approach suggested that if Indians could not be isolated within colonial settlements through Eliot's model of the "praying Indian town," a missionary should leave his community to live near Indians.[16] To some degree this shift in method also reflected a departure from the prevailing opinion that Indians should be civilized before they were converted, although debates on this topic would continue.[17] The second was the series of religious revivals that swept through areas of Protestant Europe and the British colonies in the 1730s, which in America came to be termed the Great Awakening.[18] These revivals increased missionary efforts, prompted greater interest in Christianity among Indians, and affected the ways in which missions were publicized.[19] They also expanded participants' visions of their communities even as they moved the individual's interior religious experience to the center of theological thought.

As the new imperative that missionaries venture into the wilderness isolated them from their communities, the Great Awakening directed attention to the ways in which people experienced their own feelings of sinfulness and salvation. When a missionary left home to preach the word of God among native groups, his experiences became more arduous while they became interesting to a broader evangelical audience. The missionary's physical isolation also spoke to the new, more dynamic ways in which revivalists had come to configure community. For as revivalists encouraged the fear and trembling of the solitary sinner to spread through the large crowds to whom they preached, they built expansive epistolary networks and appropriated a developing consumer culture to disseminate their message.[20] As Timothy Hall has written, "Through sermons and in print [itinerant preachers] called on followers to envision the inhabitants of the Atlantic world as one vast company of lost people who needed desperately to hear the message of the New Birth and who could now be reached by new market-generated methods and media."[21] Besides providing a template for the development of sympathetic ties across a distance, the missionary offered a model, in his increased physical isolation, for an emotionally generated understanding of community.

The missionary's work in the wilderness thus presented a situation that intersected with interests fostered by revivalism. The influence of these concerns is clear in the structure of Edwards's and Hopkins's texts. Both feature subjects whose most distinguishing features are their efforts to exhaust themselves to the point of death for the glorification of God. In this way they adhered to a Christian ideal of *kenosis*, or emptying of self, exemplified in Paul's words to the Corinthian church, "I will very gladly spend and be spent for you, though the more abundantly I love you, the less I bee loved" (2 Cor. 12:15).[22] They also upheld a porous model of individuality, suggesting that the exemplary self is one who seeks not to be a self but rather a vessel of God's benevolence.

Both biographies also sketch a textually delineated religious network through the solitary missionary. This network contrasts with the missionary's exile from his own culture, mirroring his physical departure with a textual return. The letters, sermons, and tracts distributed along the network sometimes offer consolation to the missionaries, and they always welcome them, before and after their deaths, into the embrace of a spiritually bounded community. While the missionary expends his energy for the salvation of Indians, readers consume the narrative of his expenditure, incorporating it into their moral development as an example for emulation.

Indians were important to these formulations of individual and collective identity. Situated in the wilderness and initially resistant to the gospel, they presented an eminently suitable stage for the unfolding of a basic Christian drama, the soul's struggle to overcome selfishness and expend itself for God. They allowed Brainerd and Sergeant to approach the human limits of benevolence, exhausting themselves and transforming from individuals into examples of a Christian ideal. Treated as pitied object and as metonym for hardship, they offered a bridge between the missionary's immediate experience and the reader's vicarious one. They presented an explanatory framework for the missionary's physical exile from his community and a proving ground for his benevolence, inspiring readers' sympathy for the Indians' benefactor rather than for the Indians themselves.

The two accounts do differ in significant ways. Edwards subordinated the task of promoting missions to the exploration of Brainerd's exemplary life, while Hopkins did the opposite. Imitating but revising Edwards, Hopkins featured an element that remained in the background of Edwards's text: the network of supporters who offered letters and prayers to compensate for the missionary's isolation. In so doing he accommodated the penetrating gaze and the hagiographic tone of a missionary memoir to the promotional rhetoric of a fund-raising tract. He sought to shift readers from a passive position of spectation to an active one of charitable response. This combination of perspective, made possible through an interlacing of epistolary dialogue, diary, and description, helped make the sympathetic scrutiny of a missionary's character central to the invocation of a transatlantic community focused on the salvation of heathen souls. Whether focused more on the missionary's spiritual struggle or on the network surrounding that figure, these memoirs share a tendency to upstage the spiritual needs and conversions of Indians with the struggles of the people trying to save them. The emphasis on British interiority ultimately implied by the SPG's early eighteenth-century sermons becomes more explicit in these mid-century evangelical writings. Looked at in sequence, then, these writings suggest a trajectory that transcends denominational distinctions, shifting over the course of a century from a focus on saving distant heathens to a preoccupation with the heroic expenditure of British Christians—from other to self.

"God Gave me to Wrestle Earnestly for Others": The Spectacle of David Brainerd's Solitude

One of the observations most often made about Edwards's *Life of David Brainerd* is that the text pays less attention to the Indians Brainerd was trying to convert than it does to Brainerd's spiritual struggles. As Paul Harris has observed, the text is "first and foremost, a tale of a melancholy spiritual pilgrimage through the American wilderness" rather than a narrative of efforts to Christianize Indians.[23] Throughout the diary Indians briefly appear and then recede into the background of what Sandra Gustafson has termed Brainerd's "nearly incapacitating performance anxiety" as well as uncertainty about the fate of his soul.[24] Brainerd was correct as well as modest when he lamented to Eleazar Wheelock, "When I consider the doings of the Lord among these Indians, and then take a view of my journal, I must say 'tis a faint representation I have given of them."[25] Although his public journal attended more closely to the Indians' conversion than his private diary did, this comment is suggestively representative of his attitude toward Indians.

References to Indians throughout the diary indicate that they shaped

Brainerd's spiritual development to a degree neither he nor his biographer acknowledged. Gustafson has pointed out that "native Americans function primarily as externalized images of Brainerd's own 'brutish' self, a self threatening in its resistance to conversion and assimilation to the divine image."[26] As a revival spread through the Delaware community of Cross-weeksung, New Jersey—partly through Brainerd's appropriation of native performance strategies as well as the assistance of his interpreter Moses Tatamy—Brainerd's resistance to his own spiritual assimilation dissipated, leaving him feeling connected to God as he approached death.[27] Richard Pointer also has shown that Brainerd's "relationships with Indians increasingly shaped everything from his evangelistic method to his psychological health."[28] The diary reveals this influence in spite of itself, however. Brainerd could be quite direct about his inclination to focus on himself, as when he wrote, "I felt peace in my own soul; and was satisfied that if not one of the Indians should be profited by my preaching, but should all be damned, yet I should be accepted and rewarded as faithful."[29] Such comments reinforce observations made by both Pointer and Conforti that Brainerd replaced an external goal of converting Indians with an internal goal of exerting himself in an effort to convert them.[30]

Edwards enhanced this inclination in the presentation of his subject, using Indians to certify the difficulty of Brainerd's labor. He praised Brainerd as "one who himself was the instrument of a most remarkable awakening, and an exceeding wonderful . . . transformation of such subjects as do peculiarly render the change rare and astonishing." That Brainerd could initiate a revival among Indians, that is, firmly qualified him as an object of admiration. Edwards also built on Brainerd's tendency to displace external goals with internal ones by structuring the biography through an alternation between external action and internal emotion. He highlighted this contrast as a basis for the text's appeal, claiming that "the reader will have the opportunity to see, not only what were the external circumstances and remarkable incidents of the life of this person, . . . but also what passed in his own heart."[31] This juxtaposition suggested a corroborated account that supported several aspects of Edwards's theology.

Because Brainerd's diary revealed anxiety about his soul and a constant desire to spend his life in the service of God, it offered Edwards "an example of the good rather than the excessive 'effects' of experimental religion."[32] It thus refuted Arminian assertions that humans can choose salvation and Antinomian beliefs in a redemption that has no relation to Christian behavior.[33] Brainerd also provided him with a model for his concept of "disinterested" or "universal" benevolence, which emerged from a Christian disregard of self rather than particular sympathy.[34] It is perhaps surprising that this concept, which would motivate reformist movements as it was refined by the younger Samuel Hopkins,[35] would be exemplified in a person whose benevolence often collapsed into distaste for its recipients. Brainerd confessed little affection for Indians, writing of a Delaware community in Pennsylvania, "Their monstrous actions tended to excite ideas of horror." What fondness he did express was for Indians on the path to conversion, and it was intertwined with regard for his own labor. From Edwards's perspective, though, the unease Brainerd felt around Indians demonstrated his disinterested benevolence. That he "long[ed] for more compassion towards"[36] Indians rather than feeling it automatically, and that he devoted his life to converting a people he did not like, proved a true compassion that transcended sympathy or self-interest.

Edwards could make these points through Brainerd because the diary, which he aggressively edited, relates the missionary's "thoughts, affections and secret exercises."[37] The biography thus suggests an almost unprecedented level of intimacy through the medium of the written word, letting readers look at Brainerd even as they see the world through his eyes. For this reason the text offers its readers secular pleasures along with its religious message, offering a tantalizing glimpse into a person's private feelings and thoughts. What this multifaceted study—rich with the promise of intersubjective exploration and voyeuristic experience—ends up revealing is a person who both longed for and fled from contact with others. If the biography suggests unprecedented access to another person, it also presents a person who exhibited conflicted attitudes to interpersonal ties.

While Brainerd's comments on Indians have excited much scholarly interest, he himself seems to have expended more words on his relations with other British people. He often commented on the pleasures of visiting friends. "Rode to New Haven," he wrote while working on Long Island in 1742, "Saw some Christian friends there; had comfort in joining in prayer with them." Friends provided him with moments of consolation, and prayer with them granted him a closeness to God that he rarely felt otherwise. In February 1743 he wrote, "[S]pent some time with a dear Christian friend; felt sweetly serious, as on the brink of eternity; my soul enjoyed sweetness in lively apprehensions of standing before the glorious God."[38] Easing the alienation that otherwise defined his outlook, friends seemed to come from and provide access to God.

That Brainerd craved such companionship made isolation one of the greatest hardships of his mission, and the *Life* is in many ways a meditation on loneliness. While in Kaunaumeek he complained, "I live in the most lonesome wilderness. . . . I have no fellow Christian to whom I might unbosom myself and lay open my spiritual sorrows." He felt this isolation had been so damaging that in 1745 he set out on a trip to raise funds "to support a colleague with me in the wilderness (I having now spent two years in a very solitary manner) that we might be together; as Christ sent out his disciples, two and two." The proximity of Indians did not remove this loneliness, nor did the company of just any whites. Brainerd found more pain in the presence of non-Christians than he did in solitude. Over-hearing fellow guests at an inn speaking about secular matters, he exclaimed, "Oh, I thought what a hell it would be to live with such men to eternity!" Although his developing relations with Indians affected him in ways he did not often acknowledge, he revealed a constant awareness that he flourished in the company of the "few with whom [he could] talk religion itself."[39]

This desire was conflicted, however. As the biography grants its readers access to the missionary's psyche, it displays a man who sought to cure himself of loneliness less by fostering bonds with others than by weaning himself from closeness with them. Brainerd lamented, "My circumstances are such that I have no comfort of any kind but what I have in God," but this complaint was also a goal. He often expressed a desire for the same solitude that he dreaded. Recollecting the time of his spiritual awakening, he wrote, "My soul often mourned for want of more time and opportunity to be alone with God." He sometimes wished to escape his beloved friends, confiding to his diary, "had some refreshment and comfort in religious exercises with Christian friends; but longed for more retirement. Oh, the closest walk with God is the sweetest heaven that can be enjoyed on earth!"[40] The pleasure of friends was also a problem, for companions buffered the soul from trials and infringed upon the time he should be spending with God.

While unusually fervent, this desire reflected a traditional Christian emphasis on detachment from finite things to reach oneness with God. Brainerd's attitude to friendship resembles Augustine's conclusion, in the *Confessions*, that his attachment to a deceased friend had obstructed his relationship to God. "Our hearts find no peace until they rest in you," Augustine had written to God, and much of Brainerd's diary evidences a similar belief.[41] Even when writing to his brother Brainerd was "grieved that time slid away while I did so little for God." This desire for solitude became more pronounced near the end of his life, perhaps because his newly converted congregation offered him a stronger sense of community and placed more demands on him. In March 1745 he wrote, "I got alone and poured out my soul to God. . . . This was the dearest hour I have enjoyed for many days, if not weeks."[42] Such confessions seemed to prove his benevolence as much as his earlier longings for companionship had, for both desires highlighted the dedication of a man who found little pleasure through his ministry except for an awareness of serving God.

Ironically, it was in solitude that Brainerd really could reach out to and for others through prayer. "My soul was drawn out very much for the world," he wrote in April 1742. "I grasped for multitudes of souls." Sometimes he "enjoyed great sweetness in praying for absent friends," but often his prayers were for heathens or for all of humanity. After arriving at Crossweeksung he seems to have responded to his increased alienation among a new community by seeking physical solitude and then projecting himself imaginatively into a global space. He wrote, "In prayer my soul was enlarged. . . . I was much assisted in prayer for dear Christian friends and for others that I apprehended to be Christless; but was more especially concerned for the poor heathen and those of my own charge."[43] As he avoided direct contact with others, he sought a virtual closeness with them that was mediated by God. Seeking solitude, he found in prayer an expansion of his sense of self.

When read in light of Brainerd's preoccupations with interpersonal relations, *The Life of David Brainerd* is more than a missionary memoir or a study of spiritual experience. It features a juxtaposition between physical isolation and virtual intimacy made possible through prayer and the published word. Celebrating a man's willingness to suffer isolation for the salvation of Indians, the biography places him at the center of a wide circle of readership. It invokes a community through a collective act of voyeurism, encouraging readers to witness the workings of his mind and heart. That Brainerd thought he was called to exhaust himself for the salvation of others only enhanced the dynamic the biography established between reader and text. As they mourn him, admire him, and vicariously experience his arduous life, readers offer a posthumous compensation for Brainerd's exile. They mirror his attempts to reach into the world through prayer, penetrating to his interior through the written record of his subjective experience.

Indians were important to the forging of this link between the *Life* and its readers. Because their alterity highlighted the comparative similarity of Brainerd's and his readers' perspective, they ensured some shared experience between missionary and reader. Moments when readers looked at Indians along with Brainerd countered the biography's tendency to display the missionary to readers, and the narrative of Indian conversion supplied an external counterpoint to the story of Brainerd's painful progression toward assurance of his salvation.

Brainerd's work with Indians also gave his anomie an external framework for readers' understanding, rooting his solitude in dedication to God. Edwards stressed this theme in the summaries that are interspersed with the diary entries, linking Brainerd's solitude to his spiritual dedication. Of his willingness to transfer from Kaunaumeek to Crossweeksung he writes, "[H]aving spent about a twelve month in a lonely desert among these savages, where he had . . . been the subject of a train of outward and inward sorrows. . . . he chose still to go on with this business."[44] Minimizing the fact that Brainerd accepted his mission after being expelled from Yale, Edwards quoted him as one who "found myself willing (if God should so order it) to suffer banishment from my native land, among the heathen, that I might do something for their soul's salvation." Isolation among Indians became proof of a spiritual dedication that elicited the compensatory embrace of readers' admiration. As Brainerd wrote of his escape from a bout of despair, "God gave me to wrestle earnestly for others, for the kingdom of Christ in the world, and for dear Christian friends. I felt weaned from the world and from my own reputation amongst men, willing to be despised, and to be a gazing stock for the world to behold." Describing himself in Pauline terms as one willing to humiliate himself for God's glory, Brainerd transformed his isolation into apostolic emulation. He thus wrote himself into a spiritual community through his physical exile "in the wilderness, where I have none to converse with but the poor rude ignorant Indians."[45]

"The Ardent Desire of Being an Instrument": John Sergeant's Eager Isolation

In many ways Samuel Hopkins's *Historical Memoirs, Relating to the Housatunnuk Indians* complements Edwards's biography of Brainerd. Hopkins seems to have shared Edwards's desire to rebut the enthusiasm and Antinomianism that flourished after the Great Awakening, as he made clear that Sergeant "prefer'd the Satisfaction which proceeds from the calm, rational Exercise of practical Piety and Devotion, to those Emotions of the Mind."

His project was less to present evidence supporting his theology, however, than to inspire support for the Stockbridge mission. Throughout the narrative he mentions his aim of inspiring readers' support, explaining, for example, that he had included a description of an Indian ceremony not "so much for its being curious, as to excite Compassion towards such ignorant Creatures, and the charitable Endeavours of generous Minds." He projected this goal onto Sergeant's texts, introducing one of his sermons by writing, "[T]o move our Pity to the poor *Heathen* who are brought up in Ignorance, he proceeds thus."[46] His references to readers' compassion call attention to the spectators at the edge of the text, prodding them to a charitable response. These intentions also direct the narration of Sergeant's ministry, establishing a metonymic link between the life of a missionary and the salvation of heathens.

This goal matched Hopkins's subject, who was less melancholy than Brainerd and who left documents more focused on his missionary activities than his spiritual struggles.[47] It corresponded with the circumstances of Sergeant's work, which took place amid more companionship with other whites than Brainerd's did. While Brainerd almost always worked alone, Sergeant was assisted by Timothy Woodbridge, the schoolmaster to the Stockbridge Indians.[48] As part of an experiment to promote British acculturation while preserving separation from larger colonial settlements, four British families also took up residence next to the Stockbridge mission. This strategy proved damaging to the mission, as the white population grew to outnumber the native one and led most of the Muhhakaneok to join Samson Occom's Brothertown migration after the American Revolution.[49] The white settlement did provide Sergeant with some modicum of British community however and, after he married his neighbor Abigail Williams, a family.[50]

While exile in the wilderness is one of the text's central themes, Hopkins's narrative also stresses the social context of Sergeant's life. His biography unfolds within the story of the Stockbridge mission, the Indians who resided there, and the network that supported it. Although it shares with Brainerd's *Life* a tendency, as Hilary Wyss has shown, to overlook much of the Indians' perspective on the mission's history, the Muhhakaneok act as more than the landscape they provide to Brainerd's subjective interior.[51] Hopkins presents detailed descriptions of several of the mission's residents, he relates conversations with them, and he quotes messages the Muhhakaneok sent to nearby native groups and British benefactors. The *Historical Memoirs* begins by describing the Muhhakaneok, their history, and their settlement along the Housatonic River of western Massachusetts. An account of the people who founded the mission precedes any description of Sergeant, and a call for more support for the mission ends the text.[52]

Wyss has argued that Sergeant's "writings rhetorically structure his tenure there as a captivity." Stories of Indian captivity, which pervaded colonial culture, provided him with a paradigm to interpret his isolation from British culture and his "embattled" status in Stockbridge. "Both the missionary and the captive struggle in isolation to maintain their moral and spiritual superiority over the strangely seductive Natives who surround them, and both sacrifice bodily comfort for a greater spiritual good."[53] Wyss has also shown how Sergeant's work took place in counterpoint to the well-known captivity of Eunice Williams, whose brother Ephraim—and eventually Sergeant's father-in-law—lived next to the Stockbridge mission. Ephraim had been ransomed from the Iroquois after the Deerfield massacre of 1704, but Eunice had integrated fully into the community of her captors. She converted to Catholicism, married a Mohawk, and refused to return to her English family.[54] While this reading of Sergeant's writings, many of which are not included in Hopkins's *Historical Memoirs,* is convincing, it is important also to note that Hopkins's framing of Sergeant's life differs from Sergeant's own writings on exactly this issue. Hopkins describes Sergeant in ways that deliberately oppose his experience to that of a captive, stressing that Sergeant chose his residence among the Indians. This voluntary isolation becomes the organizing feature of his biography.

The biblical context through which Hopkins relates Sergeant's story distinguishes his experience from that of a captive. Many captivity narratives unfold through analogies to the Hebrew Bible, especially stories of the Israelites' captivity and Job's sufferings. In so doing they depict suffering as a purifying test by God. Within Hopkins's text the most important scriptural precursors for Sergeant's work are the New Testament stories of the Apostles. The epigraph on the title page is Peter's declaration, "I perceive that God is no respecter of persons: But in every nation, he that feareth him, and worketh righteousness, is accepted with him" (Acts 10.34–35). This quote marks Stockbridge as the continuation of the Apostles' efforts to bring the gospel to Jews and gentiles alike. The apostolic model shapes the depiction of Sergeant more than a captivity narrative does. Like Brainerd, Sergeant is described as having lived in imitation of the Apostles, who were called to go out and spread the good news. Like the Apostles he sacrifices much to respond to this call, and like most of the Apostles he dies in the midst of his work.

When Sergeant first appears in Hopkins's narrative the reader learns that while working as a tutor at Yale he had expressed a desire to evangelize heathens. The text then quotes Sergeant's journal account of the response he gave when asked to work in Stockbridge: "'I told the Gentlemen, that I was so far from being unwilling to devote myself to the Service of God in so good a Cause, that I was rather desirous, if none better qualify'd could be found, to improve what Abilities I had in such an Undertaking; tho' I was sensible, I must not only lose a great many agreable Amusements of Life, . . . but also expose myself to many Fatigues and Hardships, and I know not to what Dangers, among a barbarous People.'" This journal entry stresses not only Sergeant's sacrifice but also his awareness of what that sacrifice will entail. The references to what he will miss at Yale and what he will face at Stockbridge assure readers that he entered his mission with no expectation of pleasure except what would follow from an awareness of having done God's will. An additional comment that "'I should be asham'd to own myself a *Christian*, or even a *Man*'" without performing this work aligns his isolation with the valor of combat, displaying a masculine and active form of surrender.[55]

Hopkins quoted from Sergeant's letters to similar effect, stressing the heroic willingness with which he undertook his work. A letter from Sergeant to Adam Winthrop, Secretary to the Boston Commissioners of the New England Company, notes of his first months in Stockbridge, "'I have had the Approbation of my Conscience in the Business I have undertaken, nor have I been at all discontented.'" The sterile self-satisfaction of this comment conveys Sergeant's focus on pleasing his conscience to the exclusion of other desires. A letter he wrote from Yale to Stockbridge when he briefly returned to finish his education depicts his unfailing dedication to the Indians. It opens, "'My good Friends and Brethren, You are always in my Heart, and I cease not every Day to pray to God for you.'" A second letter sends an equally affectionate message, and a note to Benjamin Colman, minister of the Brattle Street Church of Boston, conveys his desire for a permanent position at Stockbridge: "'I am very willing (if the Gentlemen *Commissioners* please) to devote my Life to the Service of their Souls. And if God shall give Success in it, it will be the greatest Satisfaction to me.'"[56] The missionary's focus on pleasing God by converting others, even at immense cost to himself, becomes the primary message of this narrative.

Sergeant's descriptions of the Indians in the *Historical Memoirs* always emphasize the difficulty of converting them, as when he writes, "It is not easy for those, who are not acquainted with barbarous Nations to conceive, into what a Degree of Barbarity they are sunk; nor how difficult it is to recover them." Hopkins's concluding description of Sergeant also stresses the arduousness of his labor: "His Ministerial Labours were extreamly hard, more than double to those of other Ministers." These comments contribute to Hopkins's assessment of Sergeant: "He was indeed a rare instance of Diligence, Industry, and Painfulness, in his Work; and the Pains he took for the Good of the poor *Natives* are not to be express'd."[57] The gesture toward descriptive fatigue is doubly appropriate, for as Hopkins conveys his inability to represent Sergeant's benevolence he also suggests a man who based his identity on the spiritual welfare of others with a corresponding neglect of himself. He is at a loss to describe a man engaged in a pious erasure of himself.

Indeed, Hopkins presents a model of Christian self-denial in Sergeant, stressing that the missionary based his identity on dedication to the Indians. He claims this process began in Sergeant's youth: "[B]efore there was any Prospect of his being imploy'd among the Natives, his tender Mind was so affected with the Tho'ts of their perishing State, that it had been his Practice, for a long Time, to make it Daily an Article in his secret Addresses to God, that he would send him to the *Heathen*, and make him an Instrument in *turning them from Darkness to Light*." Hopkins conveys the fierceness of this desire to be God's "instrument" by describing the other desires with which it competed. He notes that just before leaving Yale, Sergeant contemplated several career opportunities, "yet he prefer'd a *Mission* to the *Heathen*: not from any Views he could have of Worldly Advantage from thence, but from a pious, generous and ardent Desire of being an Instrument in the Hand of God." That he gave up so much to be a missionary should only heighten the reader's estimation of his sacrifice. Lest the reader miss this point, Hopkins drives it home by connecting Sergeant's labor with his sensitive character: "Every one must be sensible, that, to one of so delicate a Make, it must be difficult and self-denying, to leave the College, that Seat of Learning, and other Delights, to dwell in a Wilderness: to change the polite society he had been us'd to, for the Conversation of a Number of Savages."[58] Juxtaposing the fragility of Sergeant's body and the refinement of his mind with his fierce determination suggests a man rendered heroic through compassion and spiritual courage rather than physical prowess.

Hopkins notes that Sergeant added to the inherent difficulty of his work an intense attachment to his labor, as when he quotes the missionary's reflection, "'I am sure nothing affects me with more Grief than to observe the little Fruit of my Labours.'" He later paraphrases this line when describing the exertions to which the Indians' sinfulness provoked Sergeant, observing, "His Concern on that Account is not to be expressed: many Days he spent in Fasting and Prayer, and *Sleep departed from his Eyes,* his tender Heart was almost broken, and he *forgot to eat his Bread;* and his Eyes *poured out Tears unto God.*"[59] The biographer's claim to verbal exhaustion once again mirrors Sergeant's expenditure of self.

Sergeant's internalization of ministerial failure shares much with Brainerd's, although it is a less garrulous version of his tendency to generate identity through attempts to save others. Unlike Brainerd, Sergeant seems not to have dwelt on his diminished sense of self. He left behind no details of the "*saving Change*" he experienced while at Yale, noting only that "'a great many Particulars are now escaped from my Memory.'" Hopkins attributes this oversight to modesty and fills the ensuing verbal gap. In place of a first-person account of Sergeant's conversion he supplies reports that he "was very constant and frequent in the Devotions of the Closet, pouring out his Soul to God in fervent Address of Prayer," and that "There were Instances of his Voice failing," as he was overwhelmed by "the glorious Perfections & incomprehensible Excellencies of the divine Being." The overall description of Sergeant is formulaic, noting only that he was even-tempered and likeable. The missionary is most memorable as an individual for his tendency to give himself up for others, to be "compassionate and tender-hearted to the Afflicted; . . . liberal and bountiful to the Poor."[60]

Hopkins's emphasis on third-person description, an emphasis made necessary through the minimal journals Sergeant left behind, results in a portrait of self-expenditure paradoxically stronger than that conveyed by Brainerd. While Brainerd minutely describes his self-hatred, Sergeant seems to have forgotten about himself. He writes letters to raise support for the mission instead of a journal that explores the flaws of his soul. Brainerd details his devotion to God and his lack of regard for self, but Hopkins depicts Sergeant performing this spiritual drama, simultaneously disappearing as a person and appearing as a vessel "of great Generosity and true Compassion to the Souls and Bodies of Men."[61] He seems to disappear before the readers' eyes as Hopkins relates the story of his life, transforming an individual into a metonym for Christian mission.

"'Let your Heart, *Dear Sir,* be Encourag'd'": The Communal Embrace of Sergeant's Exile

Sergeant is at the center of Hopkins's narrative, but he is hardly its only character. As he grants his readers a multifaceted awareness of Sergeant's identity, Hopkins surrounds him with correspondents who offer emotional and financial support. The depiction of this epistolary network serves a function very much like that performed by early missionary tracts, in which readers are encouraged to imitate the support that correspondents show missionaries. As readers watch other people venerating Sergeant for his pious expenditure of self, they see an epistolary community taking the place of a physically demarcated one. They also see an exhaustion of self compensated for by the emotional replenishments offered by distant correspondents.

When Sergeant briefly returned to Yale after his first six months in Stockbridge, his letters to the Muhhakaneok sought to bridge physical distance with affection. "'My Heart is with you,'" he wrote, "'tho' I am so far distant from you.'" Once he returned to Stockbridge he became the object rather than the source of such sentiments. Hopkins shows how correspondents connected with Sergeant in his exile, noting that "Mr. Sergeant's self-denying, generous, and pious Behaviour, discover'd in devoting himself to the Service of the Souls of the poor *Heathen*, as above, rais'd him very high in the Esteem of many." These "many" included influential figures in Britain and the colonies, such as the psalmist Isaac Watts, the philanthropist Thomas Coram, Governor Belcher of Massachusetts, and members of the New England Company and the Society in Scotland for the Propagation of Christian Knowledge. Hopkins includes letters from and to these people, noting, "[A]s many rejoic'd to see Mr. SERGEANT chearfully devote himself to the Service of *Christ*, in this self-denying Work, and to hear of the glorious Success he was favour'd with in it; so they said many kind and endearing Things to him by their Letters."[62] Devotion to the service of Christ produces epistolary affection, so that inter-personal connection fills the vacuum created by an expenditure of self.

Benjamin Colman wrote to Sergeant just after he had accepted a permanent post in Stockbridge, "'Our Esteem of Mr. SERGEANT is not to be express'd, who can chearfully deny himself for the Service of *Christ*, and the Souls that may look mean among Men, but are precious in the Sight of *God*.'" After Sergeant's ordination Colman wrote, "'May the Consolations of God refresh and enlarge your Soul from Time to Time, in all your Self-denials for the Sake of his Name, and of the dear Souls, for whom you are labouring.'" Secondhand communications accompanied these letters, as when Colman told Sergeant that Isaac Watts had written, "'*May Jesus . . . the Head of the Church and of Nations, attend your young Missionary with extraordinary Assistance, and Success. Methinks . . . I love him upon your*

Report, for his Courage, and Zeal.'" Colman also reported a pledge "'the honourable Samuel Holden of London'" had made to the mission, but he devoted more attention to the messages he and others had sent: "'Let your Heart, *dear Sir,* be encourag'd, and your Hands strengthen'd by the Love and Prayers of Men of God at such a Distance from you. They hear of you, and rejoyce and bless you, of whom you neither hear nor think.'"[63] The effect of these many communications is to present a group of people extending their words where they themselves cannot reach Sergeant.

While offering compliments and comfort these letters also presented advice on managing the hardships Sergeant faced. Governor Belcher suggested, "'Set before you the Example of the great Apostle of the Gentiles, for your Imitation, that you may approve yourself *a chosen Vessel* unto Christ.'" Nathaniel Appleton, pastor of Cambridge, Massachusetts, noted, "'[I]t was with great Pleasure, that I saw you so freely surrender up yourself to the Service of *Jesus Christ,* and of the Souls of the poor *Indians,*'" before he set about fortifying Sergeant's commitment. He advised: "'This is one of the best Tokens you can have, *that God is with you of a Truth:* For what can be a surer Mark of the promised *Presence* of *Christ,* than his spiriting you to preach, and opening their Hearts to receive? Therefore you must not complain of Solitude, when you hear *Christ* saying so plainly to you, *Lo I am with you.*'"[64] As with so many of Sergeant's correspondents, Appleton defines Sergeant through his willingness to "surrender up [him]self" for the Indians' conversion. Sergeant's sacrifice gives Appleton the motivation and the means to offer support. His advice that Sergeant hear Jesus' final words to his disciples echoes Belcher's suggestion that he emulate the Apostles, and together these comments bolster Hopkins's portrayal of the missionary.

The communications do not just move in one direction, and Hopkins quotes eloquent replies from Sergeant alongside the affectionate letters he received. These letters resemble but elaborate on the comments made by earlier missionaries such as Eliot. Sergeant wrote to Colman, for example, "'Next to the Blessing of God on my Endeavours, the Prayers and good Wishes of Men of God, yield to me the greatest Satisfaction. In their Favour I seem to enjoy the Pleasure of Society, in the deepest Solitude.'"[65] Belying his claims elsewhere to require nothing but the satisfaction of his conscience, Sergeant here confesses a need to feel connected with other "men of God." These letters filled a void of loneliness and made him feel part of a community from which he was physically separated. By quoting Sergeant's replies Hopkins emphasizes the emotional replenishment Sergeant's labors made necessary. He also makes room for readers' participation, encouraging them to anticipate the thanks with which their support would be received.

This reciprocity extends beyond Sergeant to the Indians. Hopkins relates, "Of these noble, and generous Instances of Liberality, Mr. SERGEANT inform'd the *Indians*, who were much affected with them, and very thankful to their pious Benefactors." He then quotes the translation of a letter that eleven Muhhakaneok wrote to the New England Company. This letter replicates the inclinations of British correspondents to overcome physical distance with spiritual closeness. The Muhhakaneok wrote, "'We are at a great Distance from you, and shall never see your Faces in this World, but hope it will be our Happiness . . . to rejoice with you in Heaven, our Father's House.'" Thanking God "that he has pitied us, and put it into your Hearts to use your Endeavours to communicate to us that Knowledge of divine Things," they hoped that through their prayers God would "repay our Benefactors a Thousand Fold into their Bosoms, for the Kindness they have shewn us."[66] That the Muhhakaneok imitated the rhetoric of the English letters so effectively suggests the thoroughness of their conversion.

This letter also demonstrates the absorption of Indians into the missionary network, a sure sign to Hopkins's readers of the project's success. While their letter to the New England Company holds up a mirror to missionary discourse, a belt of wampum to the "Showanoos" or Schaghticokes of New York, whom Sergeant visited, expands it. Like the English texts, the wampum circulates around and through Sergeant while drawing others into a Christian community. One belt of wampum reads, "'*Brother, this is our Teacher; we have brought him with us, thinking perhaps he may open your Eyes a little, that you may see the Way to eternal Life. We wish you would hear him.*'"[67] By including translations of the wampum Hopkins enlarges the network around Sergeant, and he emphasizes the multidirectional movement of sentiment that holds it together.

Besides showing readers how fondly Sergeant and the Indians replied to the letters they received, Hopkins forwards models of active, even exhausting, reader response. Sergeant is not the only figure who expends himself for the mission, and Hopkins memorializes other people who wore themselves out for the cause of converting Indians. Benjamin Colman, one of Sergeant's correspondents, provides the most significant model of this displaced expenditure of self. Hopkins quotes many letters from him, demonstrating how he became a conduit of transatlantic support to the mission by corresponding with benefactors in Britain. In his sixties when the mission began, he assisted Sergeant until his death at the age of seventy-four, in the same year as Sergeant's own death. Working up to the end of his life, he gestured to his own expenditure, noting of his efforts to raise funds for a boarding school at Stockbridge, "It may be my last Service, and I hope will be a good one." Sergeant replied to Colman's foreboding by worrying that he might die before helping the mission, writing, "'Nor would I wish to have your *blessed* MASTER take you from us, 'till you have help'd in laying this *Foundation* also for the Increase of Glory to his *Name*.'"[68] As Eliot did with Baxter, Sergeant expresses affection for Colman through reference to Indians.

A final letter from Colman, written four days before his death, presents a model of dedication to complement Sergeant's. Colman began by marking the letter as the final labor of a fragile body: "With a sick and faint Breast, and a trembling Hand, I now write you (as it seems to me) my last.'" He then related the progress he and Thomas Coram had made with their fund-raising and suggested that Coram's nephew "Mr. Wallis" replace him as a "'minister'" between Coram and Sergeant. Before closing Colman sent his blessing and his farewell, and he promised to write yet another letter on behalf of the mission: "'When I took my Pen in Hand, I fear'd I should not have been able to write at all. My Son, the Lord be with thee, and prosper thou when I am dead. May his holy Pleasure prosper in thy gracious Heart and Hand, which he has sanctified to serve his gracious Purposes. I intend this Hour, God willing, to write to Mr. *Coram*, thank and encourage him, and the Lord reward him; to whom be Glory forever.—It seems to be the last from . . . Benjamin Colman.'" Colman's own words depict him performing his last actions for the salvation of the Indians. Hopkins reiterates this point by observing that his life presented "A rare Instance indeed of a good Man's dying, as it were with his Pen in his Hand, labouring to promote the Good of his Country, the Prosperity of his Friends, and the eternal Salvation of precious Souls!"[69] Alongside the ideal of the missionary, then, he presents a person who supported the missionary from a distance, expending his life to serve God.

Through a sophisticated layering of perspective Hopkins allowed readers to see the experience of converting Indians through the eyes of Sergeant and his supporters. By portraying his biographical subject from without and within, he granted his readers a multidimensional awareness of Sergeant's identity and then used this awareness to generate support. Sergeant's own feelings become prompts to readers' responses, as when Hopkins quotes Colman's observation that the lack of financial support the

mission had received from New England was a "Matter of Stumbling" to
Sergeant.[70] Rather than just presenting arguments for funding Indian conversion or eliciting readers' pity, Hopkins banked on readers' concern for
the missionary they had come to know so well.

While encouraging readers to feel for Sergeant, Hopkins prompted
them to join the network that offered epistolary compensation for the missionary's sacrifice. That Sergeant's identity as depicted in the narrative is
most striking for its eagerness to expend itself for others only heightens the
intersubjective connections that become the real center of the text. Readers
consume Sergeant as they are asked to admire and identify with him, and
they are encouraged to channel these reactions into active support. The
narrative encourages prospective missionaries to anticipate the epistolary
community that will embrace them virtually in their physical isolation. It
also teaches prospective donors that they will receive emotional rewards for
their charity, especially the affection of missionaries and their converts.
Epistolarity in combination with biography invites readers to join a transatlantic community as they all strive to convert America's Indians.

*   *   *

The mid-eighteenth century is well-known as a time when the uninhibited
study of a person's innermost self became both permissible and pleasurable
to a public audience. Hunter has observed that while the Puritan practice
of keeping diaries became widespread during the seventeenth century, "by
the early eighteenth century, this intimate and precise world of privacy
began to shift into the public realm." Events such as the publication of
Colly Cibber's autobiography in 1740 heralded the arrival of the private self
in the realm of secular entertainment in addition to its long-established
role of didactic study, and the culture of sensibility found expression largely
through the exhibition of a subjective interior.[71]

Jonathan Edwards's *Life of David Brainerd* and Samuel Hopkins's *Historical Memoirs* demonstrate that the discourse of Christian mission absorbed widespread cultural shifts and—in the case of Hopkins—turned
them to promotional ends. More intriguingly, they suggest the active contributions that the idea of Indian conversion made to the epistemological
project of charting a self and pondering its connections to other selves. As
they performed the functions of traditional hagiographies, offering models
for spiritual emulation, these narratives used the idea of evangelizing Indians to forward new ways of understanding inter-subjective perception. In

this way they negotiated the intellectual aftermath of the evangelical revivals that swept through Protestant Europe and North America.

They responded to new emphases on both solitary and inter-subjective religious experience, and they absorbed a tendency to translate the structure of a budding consumer culture into a religious paradigm that ostensibly refuted consumer desires. They replaced the excessive emotion linked to revivals with the more moderate force of compassion, an emotion that prevented undue emphasis on the self without neglecting the soul, and that stressed the connections between faith and charitable works as signs of one's salvation. By alternating first-person narration with the second-person address of letters and an editor's third-person observations, they claimed to offer readers unprecedented access to distant missionary endeavor. In these ways they enhanced the sense of community that could be invoked by the textual consumption of vicarious experience.

Stories of efforts to convert Indians in the American wilderness provided an expansive space within which readers could extend sympathy and imagine the unfolding of a Christian community of which they comprised an active part. Indians provided a crucial third point for a triangulation of readers' relations with the texts' main subject, the missionary whom they looked both at and through. While earlier missionary writings sought to generate a sense of community through self-consciously felt pity for Indians, these two biographies linked this evocation of transatlantic community with the experience of peering into the soul of a single minister. Examined against the context of a contemporary secular culture increasingly fascinated with emotion and interiority, they suggest the importance not of Indians or missionaries to the discourse of mission, but rather of the sympathetic network surrounding them. Nurturing missionaries and assisting Indians even as they witness their interactions from afar, the readers from whom these texts seek active involvement become the central figures of the missionary encounter, consuming and emoting over the ensuing narrative whatever its outcome. Rather than being the key figures in dramas of salvation, Indians, as the next chapter will show, become more and more important to this discourse for their tendency to disappear, leaving the British alone to mourn them.

Chapter 6

"Like Snow Against the Sun": The Christian Origins of the Vanishing Indian

One of the most uncertain aspects of missionary writings was their influence. Clearly they intersected in important ways with the discourses of colonialism and sensibility, but did they actually shape how the British thought about and treated Indians? The donations these projects received indicate some influence, but it is not always clear that it reached beyond the religious networks that supported missionaries in the first place. Most strikingly, these texts seem to have had little effect on many colonists who lived near Indians and competed with them for land. When John Sergeant tried to raise funds for an Indian boarding school near the Stockbridge mission, he received far more support from people in Britain than in New England. In his history of this mission Samuel Hopkins chided New Englanders, writing of readers in Britain, "Tho' they are at 3000 Miles Distance, and never beheld, as we do, those miserable Objects; yet, from a truly pious and generous Spirit, they have sent over their liberal Contributions."[1] If pity for Indians did emerge alongside a sympathetic connection with other British people, it seems to have arisen as much from a textually mediated detachment as from access to the spectacle of need. Most missionary programs emerged from what Michael Leroy Oberg has termed the "metropolitan" optimism of colonial overseers in Britain, who looked forward to the peaceful assimilation of Indians into Christian and European mores, rather than from the "frontier" mentality of colonists in America.[2] In many ways missionary sentiments were less characteristic of colonial attitudes than atrocities such as the Paxton Boys' massacre of the Conestoga Indians in 1763 or the murder of ninety-two Moravian Indians in Gnaddenhutten, Ohio, in 1782.[3]

Many missionary writings were not persuasive in the way their writers hoped they would be, especially not in North America. But these texts did exert a significant, if rarely acknowledged, influence on how Britons on both sides of the Atlantic would come to understand Indians. This impact was more vertical than horizontal, exerting a subtle but long-lasting influence on future portrayals rather than having a broad contemporary effect.[4] Even as they criticized and sought to change the hatred with which many colonists viewed Indians, missionary writings helped them accommodate this hatred to a rhetoric of compassion. My project in this chapter is to show how two opposing treatments of Indians converged in sentimental portrayals of Indian death to reinforce the "public transcript" of Anglo domination in America.[5]

The history of the United States is, as we all know, a history of one nation's construction and many native peoples' deaths. Much of American culture is a meditation on this double-edged fact. It is in many ways a long eulogy, voicing the guilt and relief of self-absorbed mourners made wealthy by an unloved relative's death. From James Fenimore Cooper's novel *The Last of the Mohicans* to Kevin Costner's film *Dances with Wolves,* from war narratives to John Wayne films, the non-indigenous peoples of America have remained riveted to the spectacle of indigenous people passing away.[6] Many of the qualities or images we consider essentially "American"— freedom, aggression, virtue, and the frontier—have found expression through reference to Indian deaths. Michael Rogin has argued, "Not the Indians alive, . . . but their destruction, symbolized the American experience."[7] America as we know it would hardly exist, territorially or culturally, without visions of Indian death.

Proof of manifest destiny, dying Indians are also vehicles of affect directed toward varied ideological ends. They were central to sentimental literature, to Jacksonian politics, and more recently to environmental movements and revisionist portrayals of America.[8] Suggesting "an uncompromising power [Americans] deemed benevolent," they catalyzed the process described by Andrew Burstein, in which "Sentiment and coercive power, long seen in opposition, merged into the attractive combination that sentimental democrats have paraded at home and abroad ever since."[9] The range of this image's impact has exceeded the United States, influencing the conflicted emotions of other imperialists.[10] Standing for conquest, dying Indians have helped to rationalize it, absolving responsibility through sad depictions of inevitable demise.[11]

The link between Indians and death is so fixed that texts of recent popular culture have needed only to display Indians to induce melancholy. Consider the "Keep America Beautiful" public service commercials on pollution in the 1970s, which featured the weathered face of Iron Eyes Cody in feathered headdress, shedding a single tear. Consider also the Indian in Oliver Stone's *Natural Born Killers.* He is the only person Mickey and Mallory regret murdering on their ultraviolent killing spree. His death causes a loss of innocence for his killers, and his ghost haunts them, creating rare feelings of remorse.[12] Like the house in Steven Spielberg's *Poltergeist,* America is haunted by the Indian burial grounds on which it is built, the same graveyards upon which Philip Freneau, "The Poet of the American Revolution," built much of his literary reputation.[13]

How is it that this convergence of satisfaction and sorrow, of inevitability and guilt, emerged in representations of American Indians in Britain and the United States? How is it that carnage comes to be rendered with such neatness, with such narrative and affective control? Why are Indians, especially perishing ones, so convenient to the stories and longings of Anglo-American culture?

While much scholarship has pointed out the role that the vanishing Indian played in the assertions of manifest destiny, there is still work to be done on the origins of this image. In particular, we need to consider treatments of dying Indians in missionary writings.[14] Like many writers in colonial America, British missionaries often described Indians as a dying race. They were assiduous witnesses of Indian suffering, and they have given us some of our earliest elegies to the vanishing Indian. "They waste away," wrote SPG minister Thoroughgood Moore of the Iroquois in 1705, "and have done ever since our arrival among them (as they say themselves) like snow against the sun, so that very probably forty years hence there will scarce be an Indian seen in our America."[15] Many more than forty years later Eleazar Wheelock wrote about the Iroquois in much the same way, noting, "They are wasting like the morning dew."[16] The trope of inevitable waste proved to be a persistent one, outlasting deliberate attempts to destroy Indians, such as the British military's strategy—developed in 1763 during Pontiac's Rebellion—of offering smallpox-infected blankets in parleys with Indian insurgents.[17] By the end of the eighteenth century Jeremy Belknap viewed the failure of missionary work entirely in terms of the Indians' fragility: "[T]he number of converts to Christianity, among the Indians, bears but small proportion to those, who have been destroyed either by war, by slavery or by spiritous liquors."[18] Indians are forever dying in these descriptions but never quite extinct. They elicit anticipatory grief from missionaries and their supporters, who watch them ever disappearing into an eternally receding horizon.

Missionaries did more than mourn the Indians' passing, however.

They thought of themselves as running a race to save heathens from a damnation that would be forever sealed by death. In their depictions of dying Indians, then, they often dwelt on the loss of unconverted souls or on the victory of the saved. A preoccupation with the contrasting tropes of waste and conservation guided their descriptions of death, so that they opposed the slaughter of heathens to the recuperation of converted souls. This opposition appeared in their tendency to draw on two genres of writing about death: first, war narratives, which described horrible carnage, often through what Claude Rawson calls a scriptural "language of punitive castigation;"[19] and second, deathbed scenes from the tradition of the *ars moriendi,* or the art of dying. Most of them met the first genre with a sorrow tinged with angry impotence, while they met the second with a pleasing melancholy born of religious accomplishment.

On one level none of this interest in dying Indians is surprising. Obviously many Indians died, and missionaries had to face the task of recording their deaths. Understandably they deplored the carnage of war as much as they took melancholy consolation in the peaceful passing of a convert. Many of them also fought against the insidious but deadly effects of colonial settlement on the Indians' well-being. But the stylized manner in which they described a diminishing population and depicted individual deaths, with a particular emphasis on the search for signs of conversion, requires more study. Missionaries did not just display dying Indians; they also tried to teach readers how to mourn them.

Missionary writings shaped the Anglo-American attachment to the vanishing Indian in a few ways. First, they described British colonization as a recuperative enterprise that would compensate for the destructive tendencies of Indians and Catholics alike. To the gruesome sight of blood spilling over the land they contrasted bucolic images of farmers cohabiting with Christian Indians. Second, by developing a catalog of exemplary Indians to advertise their successes, they prompted readers to attach profound meaning to certain visions of Indian death. Third, by the late eighteenth century they became inclined to defend their failures by citing the obstacle of Indian mortality and by rooting that mortality in what they considered to be a depraved existence. These gestures encouraged readers to transform the destructive impulses of war into the constructive impulses of evangelism, but to mark the dying Indian as the symbol of both impulses.

It is in the combination of these opposing descriptive modes that we first see a gesture so ingrained in Anglo-American culture as to seem natural: the displaying of Indian death as an event laden with rich but imprecise significance. In these texts we first see a tension between a desire to save Indians and a fascination with their demise. Counterintuitive though this idea may seem, the Europeans most concerned with saving Indians—or at least their souls—taught us to feel pleasing melancholy at the sight of Indian death. Only missionaries could have performed this complex and largely unintended task. For only Europeans trying to convert the Indians could have brought a particular set of preoccupations to bear on the spectacle of native demise: a wish to make conquest an act of kindness; a need to scrutinize converts for signs of redemption; and a belief in the Christian paradox of eternal life through death. Only missionaries could have taught us to read Indian death as a sign of the benevolent cultivation of America.

"Blotted out from Under Heaven": Deuteronomic Mandates and the Economy of Waste

The most consistent aspect of the vanishing Indian trope is inevitability. Such an emphasis makes the Indian's sentimental status possible, for sentiment often hinges on a displacement of agency. Describing the "imperialist audience" of Indian death in nineteenth-century "frontier romances," Michelle Burnham explains: "[T]he imperialist nation imagines itself as an unaccountable audience, affected by a tragic disappearing act that no perceptible agent has effected. The convenient elision of agency allows mourning to be free of responsibility."[20] Like bystanders at a fatal accident, Anglo-Americans are constructed as able to do nothing but wring their hands at the spectacle of Indian demise. Inactive except for their emotion, they seem to be absolved of moral implication in the accident's tragic cause. Such is the deft deployment of colonialism's affect in response to its tragic results.

Although the texts Burnham describes were secular, the roots of their assertions are religious. The ability of Anglo-Americans to voice the claims of manifest destiny through sorrow at the enemy's demise developed from a tension between two scripture-based modes of legitimizing the Puritan presence in America. The first was what Alfred A. Cave has called the "deuteronomic vision," in which Puritans were seen as the new Israelites destined to enter the Promised Land and Indians as trials sent by God to his covenanted people.[21] Competing with this outlook drawn from the books of Deuteronomy, Joshua, and Judges was the New Testament's mandate to save the souls of the very people whom the deuteronomic vision marked as condemned to destruction. Both visions legitimated an English presence in

America in different ways, and so the writings of early New England alternated between these modes of describing the colony's mission.

While initially Puritan, this vision influenced broader validations of British empire. Indeed, as Claude Rawson has argued, the deuteronomic model informs many European writings that allude, often under the guise of humor or satire, to the benefits of genocide "of which the various resonances of biblical inculpation and massacre are an allegory."[22] As missionaries sought to accommodate the deuteronomic approach to an evangelical mandate, however, they began to make possible a sentimental response to what was then seen as divinely ordained demise. Trying to persuade readers immersed in a deuteronomic outlook to support missions, they developed a more peaceful and sentimental vocabulary that could be used to justify aggression.

A preoccupation with a contrast between conservation and waste assisted this process. By "waste," I mean a sense of dispersal and unnecessary loss: of objects, lands, or people discarded without purpose, thrown away with unused potential intact.[23] The British hardly were the first to condemn waste, especially when referring to the carnage of war, but they were perhaps the most emphatic. In an era of early capitalism the British desired prosperity but sometimes were uncomfortable with it. They, and Puritans in particular, expressed part of this ambivalence by praising frugality and condemning waste.[24] A tendency to praise Britain as a new Rome, with its power based on peaceful commerce rather than violence, enhanced this trend and tailored it to the slaughter of war.[25] America and its natives were convenient devices for a theorization of needless loss. While Britain saw the emergence of a luxury culture based on colonial commerce, it upheld America as a site of abundant and unused wealth. As Joseph Roach has shown, this wealth sometimes was depicted as a terrifying excess of expenditure, epitomized in depictions of human sacrifices by the Aztecs.[26] Such depictions all but mandated that the British take possession of America, if only to save it and its peoples from destruction.

The identification of Indians with waste particularly shaped Puritan missionary rhetoric. The twelve ministers signing the dedicatory epistle to Parliament that begins *Strength Out of Weakness* (1652), one of the New England Company's tracts, described conversion as the recuperation of spiritual waste: "Behold, then, Right Honourable, a call thereunto, Poore Prodigalls, who have not only with our selves lost that rich Treasure of grace and holinesse, wherewith in our Common roote and Fountaine we were entrusted, but also in a course of Rebellion for many Generations wasted the remainder of Natures Riches."[27] The human condition is predicated on the original lost opportunity of Eden, but Indians have exacerbated their original sin with the "rebellion" of their heathenism. Like the prodigal son, they have wasted their inheritance. Converting Indians thus involves teaching them a frugality based on an understanding of their spiritual worth.

An emphasis on waste also helped demonize Spain. As I suggested in Chapter 1, the idea that the English conserved where the Spanish destroyed was central to England's early imperial ideology. Violence toward Indians was seen to constitute a form of excessive expenditure antithetical to the husbandry the English claimed to embrace.[28] Yet, English violence also could be described in ways that opposed it to waste. While some proponents of mission expanded the rhetoric of husbandry to protest the wartime atrocities of English colonists, others detached English violence from English agency, contrasting it to the gratuitous slaughter by the Spanish and eliding it with images of well-tended land. Thus while the English propagated immense destruction in America, they depicted themselves as the remedy to loss.

This logic appears in one of the earliest English missionary tracts, *New Englands First Fruits* (1643), which meets divinely willed Indian demise with a nurturing, if self-satisfied, response. The tract begins by advertising New England's, and seeking England's, pity for "those poore *Indians* . . . adoring the *Divell* himselfe for their *GOD*." The Indians exist in pain and spiritual exile, while the colonists struggle to save them: "The Lord. . . . hath given us some testimony of his gracious acceptance of our poore endeavours towards them, and of our groanes to himselfe for mercy upon those miserable Soules (the very Ruines of Mankind) there amongst us; our very bowels yerning within us to see them goe downe to Hell by swarmes without remedy." The tract presents compassion and frugal management as central qualities of the colony. Lists of the resources to be reaped from America, such as wheat, furs, and fish, follow descriptions of efforts to convert Indians. Together they buttress the text's assertion of the settlement's peaceful nature: "At our entrance upon the Land, it was not with violence and intrusion, but free and faire, with their consents." This treatment has had a positive effect, so that "The humanity of the English towards them doth much gaine upon them." The closing comments of the tract's first part mirror the opening ones, asking readers "to pitty those poore Heathen that are bleeding to death to eternal death."[29] Wielding their sermons and prayers, the Puritans tend the fields and souls of America. They take what is fallow and make it fruitful.

In spite of this compassion, some of the greatest signs of God's favor are native deaths. These include the eradication of whole villages through disease, as well as the destruction of the Pequots. "Thus farre hathe the good hand of God favoured our beginnings," the text proclaims,

In sweeping away great multitudes of the Natives by the small Pox a little before we went thither, that he might make room for us there. . . .

In . . . that Warre which we made against them Gods hand from heaven was so manifested, that a very few of our men in a short time pursued through the Wildernesse, flew and took prisoners about 1400 of them, even all they could find, to the great terrour and amazement of all the Indians to this day: so that the name of the Pequits (as of Amaleck) is blotted out from under heaven, there being not one that is, or, (at least) dare call himself a Pequit.

Regardless of their cause and manner, Indians' deaths appear in the text as signs of God's approval. Shortly after the English told the Indians not to hunt pigeons on the Sabbath, one man reaching for a nest fell out of a tree and died. Another Indian, "*Sagamore John, Prince of Massaquesers*," who had not converted, "fearfully cryed out of himselfe that he had not come to live with us, to have knowne our God better: *But now* (said he) *I must die, the God of the English is much angry with me, and will destroy me.*"[30] Noting that at his death Sagamore John committed his children to the education of the English, the text implies a spiritually productive outcome even from an unconverted Indian's death. All of these deaths are taken to suggest God's approval of the colony. Here and in succeeding tracts, the colonists take spiritual comfort from indigenous death even as they express their desires to save the Indians' souls.

This affective tension is possible because the text places a missionary mandate within a deuteronomic vision of a covenantal relationship. As the new Israelites stray from their covenant God sends trials, such as Indian attacks. As Puritans overcome these trials—whether through violence or conversion—they earn God's favor. *New England's First Fruits* claims that the Puritans eradicated the Pequots from the Promised Land just as Joshua "mowed down the people of Amalek with the edge of his sword" (Exod. 17:13).[31] As Alfred A. Cave has noted, "The inner logic of Puritan ideology required that the Saints be beleaguered and besieged in this world, and Indians could play the role of foes of God's own people quite admirably."[32]

If Indians are God's punishment for disloyalty, both their destruction and their conversion mark a renewed blessing.

In these tracts the bodies of dying Indians have an impact on the observer that is as forceful as it is imprecise. As they elicit pity for heathens, missionaries shape this emotion, investing it—intentionally or not—with political meaning. This gesture detaches death from its cause, marking it as an unintended result of a well-meaning enterprise. In this way the bodies of dying Indians adopt the function that Elaine Scarry has ascribed to the injured bodies of war. The injuring of war "is relied on as a form of legitimation because, though it lacks interior connection to the issues, wounding is able to open up a source of reality that can give the issue force and holding power. . . . [I]t provides, by its massive opening of human bodies, a way of reconnecting the rerealized and disembodied beliefs with the force and power of the material world." As in any war, "[i]njury becomes the extension or continuation of something else that is itself benign."[33] In this case that thing is a desire to save souls, expressed through an abhorrence of waste. Missionary work in *New England's First Fruits* is not opposed to the deuteronomic vision. Instead, it presents an economic transformation of it.

The deuteronomic treatment of Indians pervaded many Puritan writings. Cotton Mather's sermon *Humiliations Follow'd with Deliverances* (1697), for example, presents a captivity narrative within this framework. Mather related the experience of Hannah Duston, who was captured by Indians after seeing her newborn child killed. One night when the Indians were asleep Duston and two other captives slaughtered them. Preaching to his congregation, Mather compared Duston to Jael, who hammered a tent peg into the head of Sisera, the commander of Israel's enemy forces (Judg. 4:17–22):

She heartened the *Nurse*, and the *Youth*, to assist her, in this Enterprise; and they all furnishing themselves with *Hatchets* for the purpose, they struck such Home Blowes, upon the Heads of their *Sleeping Oppressors*, that e're they could any of them struggle into any effectual resistance, *at the Feet* of those poore Prisoners, *They bowed, they fell, they lay down; at their feet they bowed, they fell; where they bowed, there they fell down Dead.* . . . But cutting off the Scalps of the *Ten Wretches,* who had Enslav'd 'em, they are come off; and I perceive, that newly arriving among us, they are in the Assembly at this Time, to give Thanks unto *God their Saviour.*[34]

Burnham has shown that in this sermon Mather "use[d] . . . a sympathetic identification with a captive's motherhood to sanction a lawless act of female violence."[35] While Mather may have used motherhood to excuse Duston's actions, this excuse does not apply to his own exuberant narration of the scalping. Rather than obscuring the brutality of this event, he reveled in the scene's savage excess. The repetition and spondaic heaviness of his retelling invest the act with the momentousness of epic. He sounds less like a preacher than a bard, describing a battle with Grendel or Goliath. Like many writers of war propaganda, he demonized the enemy and enjoyed its extirpation.

Mather's rhetorical brutality makes more sense when we see that it draws on the parts of Deuteronomy that establish Israel's covenant through the enemy's destruction. Deuteronomy commands that in most wars Israel should practice restraint, enslaving survivors, taking booty, and preserving the trees of a conquered city (Deut. 20:10–22). When the Israelites invade Canaan, however, Moses commands them to purify the Promised Land by purging it: "[T]hou shalt smite them, and utterly destroy them; thou shalt make no covenant with them, nor shew mercy unto them. . . . [Y]e shall destroy their altars, and break down their images, and cut down their groves, and burn their graven images with fire" (Deut. 7:2,5). Mather's description of the scalping is needless and cruel, but in the excess of the event's retelling lies its discursive necessity. This excess signifies the Indians' eradication, echoing the deuteronomic command. As in *New Englands First Fruits*, dead Indians suggest God's favor.

The violence that Mather embellished in 1697 resulted in the same loss of Indian life that he, Increase Mather, and Nehemiah Walker described a few years later in a letter to the president of the New England Company: "The number of Indians in this land is not comparable to what it was fifty years ago. The hand of God has very strangely wasted them; and the war which they began upon the English in the year 1675, hastened a strange desolation upon whole nations of them."[36] Having rejoiced at the Indians' slaughter, Mather and his coauthors then marveled at their near extinction. A fixation on death as waste connects these texts, one supporting the killing of Indians in war, the other attempting their conversion in a time of relative peace. Indians end up dead in both texts, but sadness and loss frame them in this letter, rather than vindication. The loss that the English propagated later provoked their sadness.

Self-Destruction, Sin, and the Search for the Indian Death Song

Horrified descriptions of Spanish cruelties combined with deuteronomic depictions of vanquished Canaanites to cast Indians as a people destined for destruction. Accompanying these accounts was a tendency to see Indians as bound to eradicate themselves. John Sergeant included in his journal a list of causes of the population decline of Indians, ". . . who live bordering upon, and among the *English*. For which divers Reasons may be assign'd, *viz.* Their Intemperance. . . . Their great Irregularity in Diet, . . . [and] when they are sick, they take little or no Care of themselves. . . . It is a Wonder therefore that they be not all sick, and that any recover when they are so!"[37] Sergeant exhibits frustration, blame, and authentic concern, as he explains why the population loss in his mission has not been as severe as that among other native settlements. In so doing he exemplifies much of the ambivalence that would inform missionaries' writings on Indian vulnerability. By presenting Christian conversion as the surest path to survival, the discourse of mission—however sincere and well-intentioned—made easier the replacement of European culpability with pious sorrow.

This shift took place mostly through discussions of Indians' poverty and intemperance. Many forms of metaphorical contagion followed in the wake of the physical infections that swept through native populations as they were weakened by proximity to colonists. Recollecting his introduction in 1757 to the Mashpee congregation to which he would minister for the rest of his life, Gideon Hawley noted that the Mashpee were "in a very abject state in comparison of [*sic*] the Iroquois with whom I had been conversant. They had lost their independence."[38] Some of their greatest concerns related to the excessive consumption of alcohol.[39] In the seventeenth century Daniel Gookin cited alcohol as one of the greatest threats to Indian lives: "Hereby they are made drunk very often; and being drunk, are many times outrageous and mad, fighting with and killing one another."[40] Such worries hardly abated with time, as a report of 1753 from John Ogilvie, the SPG's missionary to the Mohawks since 1747, indicates: "Mr. Ogilvie complains heavily of the shocking effects of strong Liquors among the Indians, which drives them sometimes quite mad, so as to make them burn their Huts, and threaten the Lives even of their wives and Children."[41] Such reports support Peter Mancall's argument that colonists feared Indians could not "control themselves" when they drank.[42]

Missionaries' discussions of alcohol epitomize the complexity of European attitudes to Indian demise. To some degree they simply exemplify the mix of pity and scorn that Europeans tended to express for what Robert Berkhofer terms the image of the "degraded, often drunken, Indian": "Living neither as an assimilated White nor an Indian of the classic image, . . . the degraded Indian exhibited the vices of both societies in the opinion of

White observers."[43] Religious writings sometimes prompted more nuanced treatments of this topic, however. Alcohol constituted a plague Europeans had inflicted on Indians, but it also counted as a sin, providing an obstacle to salvation. Gookin, for example, commented, "This beastly sin of drunkennes [*sic*] could not be charged upon the Indians before the English and other christian nations . . . came to dwell in America."[44] While he held on to the term "sin" to describe the drunkenness, his emphasis was on the role Europeans played in making such sin possible.

Isaac Maddox delivered a more pointed condemnation in his SPG sermon of 1734: "Heavy is their Load of Guilt, who, instead of civilizing and reforming these poor ignorant Creatures, . . . pour in upon them vast Quantities of intoxicating Liqours, to spread the wicked and destructive Practice, that has *already* made *dreadful Havock,* and must in a little Time depopulate whole Countries."[45] Like Gookin, Maddox constructed Indians simultaneously as victims and agents of sin. By making alcohol traders the subject of his verbs—"teach," "learn," "pour,"—and the Indians the objects, he stressed Europeans' responsibility for Indians' behavior. These comments provided one component of his argument, examined in Chapter 4, that Indians needed assistance in finding salvation. His grim forecast stressed Europeans' responsibility for the welfare of their bodies and souls.

This dual condemnation remained a consistent aspect of missionary writings, providing a focal point for frustrations with acquiring few converts. Accompanying this approach was an inclination toward elegy as the prevention of alcohol trade came to be acknowledged as impossible. Maddox's condemnation of alcohol peddlers presents an early example of a phenomenon Lora Romero has noted of the many antebellum novels that depicted vanishing Indians: "The elegiac mode . . . performs the historical sleight of hand crucial to the topos of the doomed aboriginal: it represents the disappearance of the native not just as natural but as having already happened."[46] With this elegiac turn came a tendency to make Indian survival the responsibility of Indians rather than of the colonists who corrupted them. Puritans provided early examples of this elegiac attitude as it grew out of a deuteronomic perspective. In their "Attestation" to Experience Mayhew's *Indian Converts,* the United Ministers of Boston described the Indians' "Love of intoxicating Liquors," as a force of dark magic, *"which marvellously captivates them, and bewitches them, . . . notwithstanding all the Bars laid by our Laws."*[47] In this description alcohol acquires a magical agency of its own, one rooted in the Indians' unquenchable desire. These comments follow a reference to "a strange Blast from Heaven" that has destroyed many Indians, echoing comments made by Cotton Mather. Unlike Gookin and Maddox, the authors of this text avoid the direct assignation of responsibility, replacing European with supernatural agency.

As a colonial presence in America became more powerful, the spectacle of drunken self-destruction increasingly blended with descriptions of Indian death from disease and war. In 1766 the Moravian John Hammerer noted of the Cherokees of Carolina: "They were thought a few years agoe to have . . . upwards of 16,000 Souls; but the Losses they have sustained in the War with the Northern Indians, & the Mortality that [struck] them this Season, must have deminished that Number. [And] their Propensity for strong Liquor in gratifying which is but too much incouraged or indulged by the white Peo[ple and] other bad Customs they are given to are too apt to pre[vent re-]covering from these Losses, they seem to be to be [sic] a fast [illeg] People unless they mend."⁴⁸ Faced with these deaths, most missionaries configured themselves as pitying but powerless, except that they offered conversion as a cure for vices and their effects. As Hammerer suggests, the Cherokees' decimation from "bad customs" is not yet inevitable because he balances this result against the possibility that they will "mend."

However sympathetic missionaries such as Hammerer were to the Indians' plight, the logic of their religious approach to the problem of alcohol, a logic grounded on the principle of free will, left open the possibility of blaming Indians for their destruction. Missionaries often suggested that by choosing Christianity, Indians could choose their physical survival. A correlate of such reasoning was that to decide against conversion was to elect one's death. This reasoning, implicit in many writings, was explicit in others. In 1766 Wheelock, who had founded an Indian school in the 1740s and who later founded Dartmouth College, juxtaposed conversion with destruction, writing, "It looks to me more & more as though God designs to make a Short work with the Natives, that they will soon be christianised, or destroyed. If they will not embrace the Gospel it is likely in a few Generations more, there will be no more an Opportunity to Shew our Charity towards their naked Starving Bodies or perishing Souls. And what a pity that any sho'd have occasion to reflect with Regrett, when it is too late, that they did not improve the Opportunity when they had it."⁴⁹ Only conversion, Wheelock claims, can save the Indians from immediate death. Such a claim makes death the Indians' own responsibility. Rather than feeling culpable for expediting Indian mortality, the British should regret that they did not convert Indians before they died. Ironically, even as he urges his readers in 1771 to "save the poor savages from that temporal and eternal destruction which is so evidently just at their door," Wheelock explains that he has shifted his own focus to English students. This change has been necessary in order to "perpetuate the usefulness of [Dartmouth College] when there shall be no Indians left upon the continent to partake of the [school's] benefit, if that should ever be the case."[50] The object of his anticipatory mourning is not the dying Indian but the chance to show charity to one.

A trace of the deuteronomic paradigm exists in the suggestion that Indians who convert are more likely to escape an early death. Although based on a genuine belief that a Christian Indian would live more healthfully than an unconverted one, such comments implied that unconverted Indians were destined to disappear from America. In this way the logic of Christian mission enabled an elegiac stance. Missionary writings contain some early precursors to Indian death songs, in which Indians are quoted as forecasting their doom before the onslaught of divinely favored invaders. In his history of the SPG, Humphries quotes the dying speech of an Indian in Pennsylvania: "[A]n *Indian* War Captain, in his Sickness made this serious Expostulation with himself, 'What is the matter with Us *Indians*, that we are thus sick in our own Air, and these Strangers well? 'Tis as if they were sent hither to inherit our Lands in our Steads; but the Reason is plain, they love the Great GOD, and we do not.'"[51] Like many Indians of nineteenth-century sentimental poetry, this Indian acknowledges the manifest destiny of Christian settlers with his dying breath. Quoted in a fund-raising text for Anglican missions, he asserts the inevitability of Indian demise, at least for those Indians who will not accept Christianity.

"Poor Despised Indians": Samson Occom's Sermon on Indian Drunkenness

The trope of inevitable demise determined much of the way in which Samson Occom's *Sermon at the Execution of Moses Paul, an Indian* (1772) was summarized in a broadside published shortly after its delivery. A comparison of the two texts suggests how deeply ingrained an elegiac stance was in British colonial attitudes to Indians. Several scholars have noted the skill with which Occom, as a Mohegan Presbyterian minister of international fame, approached the task of preaching at the execution of a fellow Christian Mohegan who, while intoxicated, had killed a white resident of New Haven. Occom's presence at this event held a great deal of "propagandist potential," as Bernd Peyer has noted, of which "the colonial authorities were well aware."[52] As a virtuous Indian, who was reputed to have slipped into drunkenness but reformed,[53] Occom could, as David Murray has written, "stage a sort of moral tableau which encapsulated the moral capacities and disabilities of the Indians."[54]

Occom's address, which is in many ways a traditional execution sermon, does seem at first to denigrate Indians.[55] Occom berated Paul for throwing away the benefits of his Christian education, asking, "What could you say for yourself? for you have been brought up under the bright sunshine . . . of the gospel." He delivered an obsequious address to the white ministers in his audience, and in an address to the Indians he blamed his people's problems, including the hatred whites show toward them, on their drunkenness: "[I]t is this sin . . . that has stripped us of every desirable comfort in this life; by this we are poor, miserable and wretched; by this we have no name nor credit in the world among polite nations."[56] He seemed to use Christianity to articulate an internalized racism, blaming Indians for their own victimhood.

A closer look, however, reveals that Occom did more than ventriloquize a colonialist agenda. Preaching on Romans 6:23, "For the wages of sin is death, but the gift of God is eternal life," he relied on the equalizing message of New Light Calvinism to remind his audience of the universal conditions of sin.[57] He opened the sermon by asking his audience to respond to Paul with compassion, as they were reminded of their common status as sinners: "I suppose the biggest part of you look upon yourselves christians, & as such I hope you will demean yourselves; and that you will have suitable commiseration towards this poor object."[58] Although he presented a familiar trope of racialized pity, he altered its impact on the audience, linking it to the importance of feeling another person's plight. Preventing the alignment of religious with racial difference, he identified Christians through their capacity for emotional engagement. He also conveyed that Paul was pitiable not because he was an Indian, but because he had sinned.

Throughout the sermon Occom stressed the fallenness of the human condition, assuring his listeners that "Negroes, Indians, English, or of what nations soever, all that die in their sins, must go to hell together, for the wages of sin is death."[59] Sin may divide humans from God, but it joins them in a shared condition. He argued that European responsibility accompanies this universal culpability, however. Noting that George Whitefield also had used Romans 6:23 "to criticize British and colonial American con-

sumer society," Sandra Gustafson has observed that "Occom focused on
the image of gift to present a more radical critique of capitalist economy.
This opposition between wages and gift provided Occom with his main
lever for opening up cultural categories." By describing salvation in terms
of an indigenous American gift economy, Occom implicitly aligned European capitalism with the "wages" of sin, rooting Indian dependence on
alcohol in an exploitative colonial economy.[60]

Occom censured Indians for their sins, but he also interrogated the
causes of their sinfulness, among which he included the prejudices of
whites. He said to Paul, "My poor unhappy brother MOSES; . . . You are
the bone of my bone, and flesh of my flesh. You are an Indian, a despised
creature; but you have despised yourself; yea you have despised God
more."[61] As Occom foregrounded his tribal relation to the condemned
man, prompting his readers to consider them both within the category of
Indian, he rooted Paul's crimes in his race by saying that an Indian was "a
despised creature." He rebutted any suggestion of depravity, however, linking Paul's behavior to the hatred others display toward him. As Keely Mc-
Carthy has observed, Occom referred to Paul's first epistle to the
Corinthians in his use of the word despised: "We are fools for Christ's sake,
but ye are wise in Christ . . . ye are honourable, but we are despised" (4:10).
"Occom uses the traditional Christian notion that the true Christian is the
downtrodden to express a more overtly political point. . . . If their status as
despised makes them more like Paul, then it means that the English are
more like the heathen Corinthians."[62]

This approach also guided his address to his Indian audience. By noting that through drink Indians dehumanize themselves, he undercut stereotypes of them as inherently subhuman: "[W]hen we are intoxicated with
strong drink, we drown our rational powers, by which we are distinguished
from the brutal creation."[63] As McCarthy has noted, "Occom distinguishes
between sinfulness and degeneracy, between a natural state according to
theology . . . and a social designation."[64] He saw intemperance in a cycle of
self-hatred, suggesting that Indians despise themselves because they drink,
but they also drink because they despise themselves. He observed, "For this
sin we are despised in the world, and it is all right and just, for we despise
ourselves more; and if we don't regard ourselves, who will regard us?" Even
as he called Indians to be responsible for their own sufferings, he acknowledged the cause of that suffering by noting, "[W]e find in sacred writ, a
woe denounced against men, who put their bottles to their neighbours

mouth to make them drunk."[65] While Indians are responsible for their own drunkenness, so are those who profit from it.

Like many other missionaries, Occom focused on Indian drunkenness as a sin of both the Indians who drink alcohol and the colonists who make it available. His application of Pauline theology to the colonial condition, however, along with his emphasis on his own Indian identity, resulted in a more powerful treatment of this topic. Peyer has argued, "Overall, that section in Occom's sermon directed at the Indian (and African American) audience, which one might justifiably call the 'hidden transcript' within the salvationist discourse, reflects his own belief in Christianity . . . as a guiding force in the will to overcome the spiritual chaos inherent in the colonial encounter."[66] Christianity helped him condemn the effects of colonialism, stress the spiritual equality of his multiracial audience, and exhort Indians to break their dependence on drink.

The *Sermon Preached at the Execution of Moses Paul* presents an Indian confronting, within a Christian framework, his people's destruction through alcohol. In 1773, the year after the sermon was first published, an anonymous broadside titled "Mr. Occom's Address to his Indian Brethren, On the Day that Moses Paul, an Indian, was executed at New-Haven, on the 2d of September, 1772 for the Murder of Moses Cook" appeared in Boston and Newport.[67] Although it appears to paraphrase the sermon, the broadside transforms it into a sentimental meditation on Indian depravity. It revises Occom's text by erasing its religious context, presenting only one section in sixteen ballad verses and neglecting to note that the original text was a sermon. The verses do mention morality, promising that drunken Indians will go to hell, but they ignore Occom's careful unfolding of theological complexities, reducing the urge for repentance to a cliché.

The verses also make important omissions from the section they paraphrase, such as Occom's condemnation of those who sell alcohol to Indians. There is little mention of the Indians' being cheated, and only two references to the prejudice that may motivate them to drink. Even these few references ignore the point of Occom's text. The first stanza reads:

My kindred Indians pray attend and hear,
With great Attention and with godly fear;
This day I warn you of that cursed sin,
That poor despised Indians wallow in. (ll. 1–4)

This compressed discussion of "despised Indians" ignores the scriptural and colonialist contexts of this term, as Occom uses it. Depleted of religious or political meaning, the word *despised* becomes only a signifier of pity and Indians nothing but the "wallow[ing]" subjects of a sentimental scene.

The broadside turns moral outrage into sorrow, and it replaces the exhortation to repent with a distressed wringing of hands. While Occom paired his descriptions of drunken Indians with an emphasis on the heights from which they had fallen, the broadside only delivers a vignette of a drunkard:

Behold a drunkard in a drunken fit,
Incapable to go, stand, speak, or sit;
Deform'd in Soul and every other part,
Affecting sight! enough to melt one's heart. (ll. 33–36)

As the words *behold* and *Affecting sight* indicate, the verse pushes harder for an emotional response from the reader than for a behavioral change from the drunkard. The task of melting the reader's heart replaces Occom's effort to reform his listeners' souls, and the idea of conversion disappears before the imperative of affective response to the static image of a depraved drunkard.

Although there are overtures of reform, the text ends on a note of doom, assuring us that for all these warnings the Indians will drink themselves to damnation:

If you go on and still reject Christ's call,
'Twill be too late his curse will on you fall;
The judge will doom you to that dreadful place,
In Hell, where you shall never see his face. (ll. 61–64)

Even God becomes less involved in the Indians' fate. Whereas in the sermon Christ dies for the Indians' sins, prays for Paul's soul, follows him into prison, and "calls the sinners to himself," in the broadside he only "cr[ies] / With earnestness of Soul, Why will ye die!"[68] The broadside suggests that it is "too late" for the Indians, and Occom only seems to exhort his fellow Indians to repent. His real function is to memorialize the Indians' death and damnation for a British audience.

Since most colonial broadsides were written to commemorate disasters, describe executions, or mourn deaths, it is hardly surprising that this rendition of Occom's sermon would adopt the tones of elegy.[69] It does more than adapt a sermon to a broadside form, however. Most broadsides of execution sermons also preach to the reader. "Advice from the Dead to the

Living: Or, a Solemn Warning to the World, Occasioned by the Untimely
Death of Poor Julian," for example, which also described the execution of
an Indian who had killed a white man, condemned his crimes to dissuade
readers from taking the same path.[70] It begins by advising:

This Day take warning young and old,
By a sad sight we here behold,
Of one whom Vengeance in his Chase
Hath taken in his sinful Race. (ll. 1–4)

Aside from the uncertain meaning of the word *race* in line 4 and an ambig-
uous etching of the murder scene, this broadside does not indicate that
Julian is an Indian. It focuses more on the criminal's class than his race,
noting that he was a bound servant who had tried to kill his employer. The
broadside markets itself as a warning to other servants, saying under the
title, "Very proper to be Read by all Persons, but especially young People,
and Servants of all Sorts." The text directs its moral content to a wide
audience, however, through the penultimate couplet, "Now may the Congregation hear / This awful Voice, and stand in fear." In contrast, "Mr.
Occom's Address" presents no moral to white readers, as it asks them to
view the failings of Indians. Occom is not a respected minister in this text,
preaching to whites as well as Indians and explaining the finer points of
salvation. Instead, he does little but present us with an Indian death song.

As this revision of Occom's sermon suggests, native death came to be
seen in many English writings as the sad but inevitable by-product of progress, so that Indians were described as failing to use their land's resources
and then poignantly embodying the unrecoverable losses endured by primi-
tives overtaken by civilization. Indian death increasingly was depicted as
occurring anonymously, the result of a commercial economic model. Dis-
eases spread, wars break out, and Indians wither from poverty, drink, or
sadness. The inscrutable will of God becomes an invisible hand, granting
wealth to the true caretakers of America. The British, meanwhile, describe
themselves as trying, earnestly but impotently, to save the Indians from
themselves.

Ars Moriendi: From European to Indian

To say that missionaries helped create the trope of the vanishing Indian is
to call into question their intentions. As Mather's and Wheelock's writings

suggest, some missionaries did have ulterior motives informing their mournful descriptions of Indians. Their texts remind us that an emphasis on native demise could provide an excuse for the failure of feeble missionary efforts or rationalize violence. With the benefit of hindsight and the detachment of a secular worldview, it may be tempting to dismiss all missionary writings as rhetorical vehicles for conquest. We could say that these writings just made Indian death palatable to delicate British constitutions, squeamish at the sight of slaughter. Surrounding Indian death with a scriptural framework made it easier for the British to justify the genocide they really desired.

It is important, however, that we not exclude the authentic religious concern that permeated many missionary texts. To do so would be inaccurate, and it would replicate the sentimental dynamic that is the object of my analysis here. It would implicate the early modern British in our own post-imperial guilt, while absolving us through our sorrow and our condemnation of the past. It also would miss the point of how missionary writings influenced their broader culture.

Most missionaries were invested in the colonization of America, many disliked unconverted Indians, and a few may even have wished they would all disappear. But the writings and the actions of many missionaries indicate that they were sincerely concerned with the welfare—both physical and spiritual—of America's natives. They did not all deflect responsibility for Indian deaths from the British, nor did they desert their converts when they became the objects of British aggression. Nonetheless, their writings contributed to the trope of the vanishing Indian.

"It was not in my heart to gather them," John Eliot confessed of the "dying speeches" that Daniel Gookin recorded for him to translate, suggesting authentic grief.[71] Both men, who oversaw the "praying Indians" of New England, risked the wrath of fellow colonists when they protested the Indians' treatment during King Philip's War.[72] As Eliot wrote to Robert Boyle, "I have much to write of lamentation over ye work of Christ among our praying Indians. . . . There are 350 soules thereabout, put upon a bleake bare Island. . . . where yei suffer hunger & cold. . . . Some ungodly and unruly youth, came upon them, . . . shot at them, killed a child of godly parents, wounded his mother and four more. The woman lifted up her hands to heaven and said, Lord thou seest that we have neither done or said anything against the English that yei thus deal on us."[73] Even before Mary Rowlandson's text seared the transatlantic English imagination with images of brutal savages, Eliot overturned the conventions of captivity narratives.[74] He showed the Indians, like Rowlandson, making sense of their unmerited suffering through prayer, as he mourned and protested this atrocity.

Other Congregationalist ministers, such as Solomon Stoddard of North Hampton, Massachusetts, held onto a deuteronomic paradigm but attached it to a missionary mandate. He argued that God had punished New England for not converting more Indians by creating wars between Indians and the English. He also argued that missions would prevent the destruction of war:

[I]f [the Indians] be brought to Religion, then there will be Hopes of a Durable Peace. . . . *That will be much better, than to Destroy them.* Some men in their Rage, meditate nothing but utter Destruction; They throw *Fire-brands, Arrows and Death:* They are like *Edom*, and the *Ishmaelites* that said, *Let us cut them off from being a Nation, that the Name of Israel may be no more in Remembrance,* Psal. 83.4. These men shew a Bloody Spirit: 'Tis much better to convert them: They will do good, they will serve and glorify God, they will help to enlarge his Kingdom, and be a benefit to their Neighbours.[75]

Comparing those colonists who wanted to destroy Indians to the "Ishmaelites" who tried to destroy Israel, Stoddard overturned the inclinations of New England Puritans to see themselves as the new Israelites. He aligned missions with productivity, arguing that converting Indians would transform their violent potential into economic and religious growth.

The Moravians, who began their ministry to Indians in 1735, also condemned the violence that their converts later suffered. This condemnation was consistent with their mission, which involved an intercultural closeness that few British ministers had or desired. When Martin Mack first traveled to the Delaware settlement of Pochgathgoth in January 1743, he described the Indians' shock that he refused nearby lodgings with English people: "[T]hey wonder'd . . . that we slept & eat among them."[76] The closeness that the Moravians promoted with their converts, epitomized in Christian Frederick Post's marriage to Rachel, a Delaware resident of Shekomeko, exposed the dishonesty underlying British claims to be seeking peaceful cohabitation with Indians. The many accusations of treachery that Moravian Indians received near the end of the Seven Years' War, accusations that eventually prompted horrors such as the Gnaddenhutten massacre, revealed the adaptability of the deuteronomic paradigm far beyond its Puritan origin.

Unable to protect their converts from such violence, Moravians were vocal in their protests. "Here they were now murdered!" wrote Heckewelder in his *Narrative of the Mission of the United Brethren,* "Together with the Children!—whose tender years—innocent countenances, and Tears, made no impression on these pretended White Christians: were all butchered with the rest."[77] Heckewelder exposed the brutality of settlers who would slaughter children. Like Eliot, he cast the Indians as martyrs, revealing the outrageousness of claims that the Indians posed a threat to whites' safety.

Protests over Indians' treatment were even voiced by the Society for the Propagation of the Gospel in Foreign Parts, a group often criticized for its failure to engage more actively in missions to Indians. George Berkeley blamed Puritan colonists for alienating Indians and Africans from Christianity because of their cruel treatment:

"[A]n ancient antipathy to the Indians,—whom, it seems, our first planters (therein as in certain other particulars affecting to imitate Jews rather than Christians) imagined they had a right to tread on the foot of Canaanites or Amalekites—together with an irrational contempt of the blacks, as creatures of another species . . . —have proved a main obstacle to the conversion of these poor people."[78] Other Anglican preachers followed Berkeley's example.[79] Berkeley did not have as much to lose for his criticism of Puritans as, say, Gookin and Eliot did, and the Church of England had something to gain from an attack on Puritans. Unsupported though these comments were by much action, they were harsh criticisms of the deuteronomic vision, its hypocritical execution, and its harmful effects.

Even those missionaries who protested British atrocities, however, sometimes unknowingly furthered the trope of the vanishing Indian and the aggression it legitimated. Throughout the colonial period they devoted much of their energy to recording the deaths of the Indians to whom they ministered. Many of these accounts, such as those that appear throughout the Moravian journals, circulated in manuscript among a limited religious community, but many others were printed. Although they exhibit the soteriological concerns of Protestants, they share a great deal with the accounts that Catholic missionaries wrote of Indian converts. These Indians provided readers with a collection of exemplary deaths to complement a European tradition of dying speeches, hagiographies, funeral sermons, and advice manuals outlining the importance of having a "good" death.[80] These texts of the *ars moriendi,* or the art of dying, encouraged readers to see death as a test for which they must prepare themselves and to understand others' deaths as scenes that should be read for signs of that person's salvation or damnation.

Erik Seeman has observed that in the majority of missionaries' accounts, dying Indians are almost indistinguishable from dying Europeans. He has divided these accounts into "model" ones, which exemplify European conventions of a good death, and "unorthodox" ones, which featured indigenous elements.[81] As the preponderance of "model" deaths suggests, most missionaries sought to integrate their Indian converts into a Christian paradigm. One of the many deaths Experience Mayhew describes in *Indian Converts* was that of the minister Wunnanauhkomun: "[H]e called . . . to [his wife and children], and took his Leave of them with Words of Comfort and Counsel; at the same time laying his Hands on each of his Children, and blessing them. Having done this, he immediately began another Prayer, wherein he expressed to *God* his Willingness to leave this World and go to him, which he declared his Hopes that he should, whenever his frail Life ended. And thus resigning up his Spirit to *God* that gave it, he immediately dy'd when his Prayer ended."[82] Wunnanauhkomun's death, like the pious life that Mayhew narrates, reads like an example from an *ars moriendi* manual. Exemplifying the advice given, for example, in *The Rule and Exercises of Holy Dying,* he was "careful that he d[id] not admit of any doubt concerning that which he beleeved." "Mingl[ing] the recital of his Creed together with his devotions," he was "especially active about the promises of grace, and the excellent things of the gospel."[83] He "intreated the Lord, that the Everlasting Covenant of his Grace might be established with his Wife and Children." He "willingly submitted to [God's] good will and Pleasure," blessed his family, and ended his life with a prayer.[84]

The Moravian David Zeisberger displayed a similar set of concerns five decades later when he recorded in his journal the death of the Delaware Indian Lucia: "Our sister and faithful colaborer of many years, Lucia, went to her eternal rest." Like Mayhew, Zeisberger preceded an account of Lucia's death with a summary of her exemplary life. After noting her arrival at Bethlehem during the Easton treaty conference of 1756, he described her conversion and praised her years of service: "She loved the Saviour and his people and was loved by every one. Her life among us was humble and consistent, and for many years, she was a faithful co-laborer among those of her sex." Matching this pious life was a death showing submission to God's will: "[W]ith much patience, resigned to the will of the Saviour, she awaited her call home. Three days before her end, she asked the white brethren and sister to visit her and begged them to greet all the brethren and sisters in Gnadenhutten and in Bethlehem, saying, that she loved them all and rejoiced that she was now soon to go to her Saviour. This happiness she realized today, when, with the blessing of the congregation, she fell gently and happily asleep."[85] Like Wunnanauhkomun, Lucia prepared for her death, sent encouraging messages to loved ones, expressed hope of her salvation, and peacefully met her end. Her death is almost indistinguishable from the model death of a European Christian.

Those missionaries who really cared about Indians thought of conversion as a way to save them from damnation and as a path to survival in their conquerors' world. Their depictions of dying Indians were attempts to mourn them and to prove that Indians were as worthy of salvation as any European. Published versions also inspired the British to fund missionary work. Resisting a deuteronomic vision, they used accounts of good deaths to show that the inhabitation of America could involve benevolence rather than bloodshed. But while conversion projects sought to minimize carnage, they contributed to a developing sentimental discourse of imperial ownership by dwelling on the evidentiary and celebratory aspects of Indian's deaths.[86]

This progression from Christian benevolence to over-determinative imperialist grief offers a striking parallel to the changing modes of punishment Michel Foucault studied in *Discipline and Punish*. During the eighteenth century "a few decades saw the disappearance of the tortured, dismembered, amputated body, symbolically branded on face or shoulder, exposed alive or dead to public view. The body as the major target of penal repression disappeared." Impelling this shift was a growing sense that torturing criminals was uncivilized and cruel, "as if the punishment was thought to equal, if not to exceed, in savagery the crime itself." When reformers pushed for kinder forms of execution, the representation of punishment altered to retain its deterrent goal. "Punishment. . . . leaves the domain of more or less everyday perception and enters that of abstract consciousness; its effectiveness is seen as resulting from its inevitability, not from its visible intensity."[87] The judicial powers that ordered these punishments distanced themselves from the punishments' increasingly sterile enactment, marking them as unpleasant but necessary measures to enforce law and order or to motivate reform.

The consequences of this shift included an abstraction of justice and a new understanding of power, the reinforcement of which was grounded in the individual's psyche and self-regulation. The symbol of governmental legitimacy and power was no longer the tortured body of the condemned but his or her subjective interior. "The expiation that once rained down upon the body must be replaced by a punishment that acts in depth on the heart, the thoughts, the will, the inclinations."[88] The representation of power became more diffuse and hence harder to resist. These alterations occurred, ironically, because of a societal desire to alleviate unnecessary suffering. That the attempt to reform punishment resulted in a redistribution of power does not undermine the sincerity of the intentions that motivated reform. In fact, such a shift of emphasis, from damaging the body of the condemned to reforming the criminal self, could have emerged only from benevolence, or at least from distaste at the sight of state-sanctioned slaughter.

"Real and Undenyable Evidences": Drawing Meaning from Indian Death

A similar process took place in missionaries' treatments of Christian Indians' deaths. These depictions proved the Indians' acceptance into heaven, they offered edification and consolation to readers, and they inspired the British to fund missions. As Samuel Hopkins wrote of John Sergeant, "As Mr. Sergeant was laborious and faithful in the Work to which he was call'd; so there is good Reason to conclude, that he was successful therein: not only from the Increase of Knowledge, and a visible Reformation among the Indians; but also from the Temper of Mind some of them discover'd at the Time of their Death."[89] Good deaths suggested evangelical accomplishment, and they valorized a peaceful colonizing presence in America.

An emphasis on its evidentiary importance led missionaries to see death as an emotionally evocative text that should be read for spiritual signs. Informing this suggestion was a Reformation shift in the understanding of death as a moment of diagnostic, if not determinative, possibility. Claire Gittings has noted, "Protestants of all persuasions agreed that the fate of the soul was sealed at death. . . . The moment of death became more decisive for the dying, particularly since, in a further turn of the Protestant screw, it was essential for salvation to remain perpetually doubtful of your own worthiness."[90] Protestants scoffed at deathbed conversions, but they remained wary of assuming salvation until the moment of death. A good death, following a good life, offered the best assurance of preservation from hell.

When John Eliot reported that "one of [the Indians] I beleeve is verily gone to the Lord," the London preacher John Dury followed Eliot's account of this woman's exemplary death with his own "notes to declare that in truth this work of God is not only in the *Letter*, but in the *Spirit* and power of the *Gospel*." Included in these notes were "the real and undenyable evidences of the work of grace in power upon . . . the *woman* in whom I cannot but note. . . . Her belief that God was well pleased with her in Christ, and hereupon her willingness to dye, in assurance of going to Heaven."[91] Although accounts of Indian death did present examples for their readers to emulate, their primary function usually was to prove the success of missionary projects.[92] Always worried that their converts might backslide into pagan beliefs, missionaries tended to view their deaths with relief, seeing them as the safe deliveries of souls. As a result, they encouraged their readers to see the good deaths of Indians as accomplishments. In these ways even "model" accounts of Indian decease differed from good European deaths.

The hegemonic implications of the Indian deathbed scene are fairly easy to see in a text such as *New Englands First Fruits,* which is littered with Indian corpses as the trophies of war. Interspersed with accounts of vanquished savages are references to one Indian, who "could never be gotten from the English, nor from seeking for their God, . . . died amongst them, leaving some good hopes in their hearts that his soule went to rest."[93] This Indian was Wequash, a Pequot who had defected to the Narragansetts and had played an important role in the Narragansett-English alliance against the Pequots.[94] Supposedly poisoned by other Indians, Wequash died in an exemplary fashion. After noting that Wequesh had been affected by discussions of Christianity, expressed remorse over his sins, and showed signs of repentance, the tract reports: "When he lay upon his death bed, some Indians who were by him wished him according to the Indian manner, to send for *Powow* (that is to say) a Wizzard; he told them, . . . *[I]f Jesus Christ say that Wequash shall dye, then Wequash is willing to dye, and will not lengthen his life by any such meanes.* Before he dyed, he did bequeath his Child to the godly care of the English for education and instruction and so yielded up his soule into Christ his hands." His refusal of a powow's ministrations and the dedication of his child to the English suggest cultural and religious conversion, while his exemplary conduct suggests his salvation. Following this vignette is a quotation from a letter by "a godly Minister in the *Bay* . . . to his Friend in *London*," insisting that "Wequash the famous Indian . . . is dead, and certainly in heaven."[95] The proof of redemption includes his pious conduct in life, but the most important indicator is his death.

Rather than dwelling on Wequash's eschewal of pagan ritual, Roger Williams, Massachusetts's most famous exile, wrote a different account focusing on his internal spiritual state. In his *Key into the Language of America,* published in the same year as *New England's First Fruits,* Williams wrote,

[Wequash] told me that some two or three yeare before, he had lodged at my House, where I acquainted him with the *Condition of all mankind,* & his Own in particular, how God created *Man* and *All things . . .* said *he your words were never out of my heart to this present;* and said hee *me much pray to Jesus Christ:* I told him so did many English, French, and Dutch, who had never turned to God, nor loved Him: He replied in broken English: *Me so big naughty Heart, me heart all one stone! Savory expressions* using to breath *from compunct and broken Hearts,* and a sence of *inward hardnesse* and *unbrokenness.*[96]

These accounts suggest a competition for ownership of Wequash's conversion, and they retrace the disputes that provoked Williams's expulsion from Massachusetts. Critical of his original colony's treatment of Indians and reluctant to credit superficial conversions, Williams displayed caution about declaring Wequash's salvation. Refusing to accept conduct as soteriological proof, he probed Wequash's expressions and emotions for hopeful but uncertain clues to the status of his soul.[97] In so doing he undermined Massachusetts's effort to credit itself with missionary success.[98]

In these texts the death of an Indian becomes contested interpretive territory. Williams and the writers of *New England's First Fruits* struggled to own Wequash as an accomplishment and vehicle of meaning. As these paired descriptions suggest, the intensity and uncertainty of death scenes, especially of conquered peoples, make them unusually pliable. They can suggest violence or peace, kindness or cruelty, conservation or waste. Even when scenes of Indian death did not link Christian mission so obviously to conquest, they reinforced a discourse of benevolent domination. Such was the case with *A True Account of the Dying Words of Ockanickon, an Indian King.* This text was published as a pamphlet in 1682 and 1683, after John Cripps, a Quaker living in New Jersey, sent to another Quaker in London a letter containing "the Dying Words of an Indian King, who died in Burlington, and was Buried amongst his Friends according to his desire."[99] Ockanickon's speech is concerned primarily with establishing the succession of his leadership. He declared that his nephew Jahkursoe should become king after his death and not one Sehoppy, who had previously been appointed king but whom Ockanickon suspected of poisoning him and of not caring for his people.

Underlying these intratribal concerns are references to harmonious relations between Ockanickon's people and his Quaker neighbors. Ockanickon exhorted Jakhursoe to avoid evil and respect their Christian neighbors: "And if any Indians should speak evil of Indians or Christians, do not joyn with it, but . . . look to that which is Good."[100] He did not claim to have adopted the Christian faith, but his speech shows that he had come to value his Quaker neighbors and appreciate much of what they had said. It is hard to know what exactly he meant by his request to be buried among the Friends, but it is clear from the emphasis Cripps places on this request that the Quakers attributed much meaning to it. Pointing out that "Christian burial cut to the heart of the missionary endeavor in North America," Seeman has noted that missionaries emphasized requests for Christian burial in their accounts of Indian deaths.[101]

The Friends did not attempt organized efforts to convert Indians until the late eighteenth century, but the publication of Ockanickon's dying speech suggests an earlier attempt to validate Quaker settlements by connecting them with Indian conversion and peaceful cohabitation. The most Christian statement Ockanickon made was the rather noncommittal request to his nephew, "I desire thee to be plain and fair with all both Indians and Christians," but the textual framing of these words presents a more assertive message. Following the speech are the witnessing signatures of five Quakers and five Indians, including Ockanickon. The two printings of the speech go to some trouble to replicate the Indian marks, the first with woodcuts and the second with the marks copied by hand. This collection of juxtaposed Indian and English signatures, which usually appears in Indian treaties, implies Indian and Quaker consensus. Ockanickon's dying words are made to suggest the possibility of Indians and English peacefully coexisting.

Thomas Budd, one of the witnesses, emphasized the larger implications of this death when he included the dying Indian's speech in his promotional tract, *Good Order Established in Pennsilvania and New-Jersey*. Budd prefaced Ockanickon's speech by noting that a small and peaceful group of Indians lived near his settlement. He described them in admiring terms, mentioning that they listen quietly to each other and that in meetings with Quakers had agreed to "put down the sale of . . . strong Liquors to them, they being a People that have not Government of themselves to

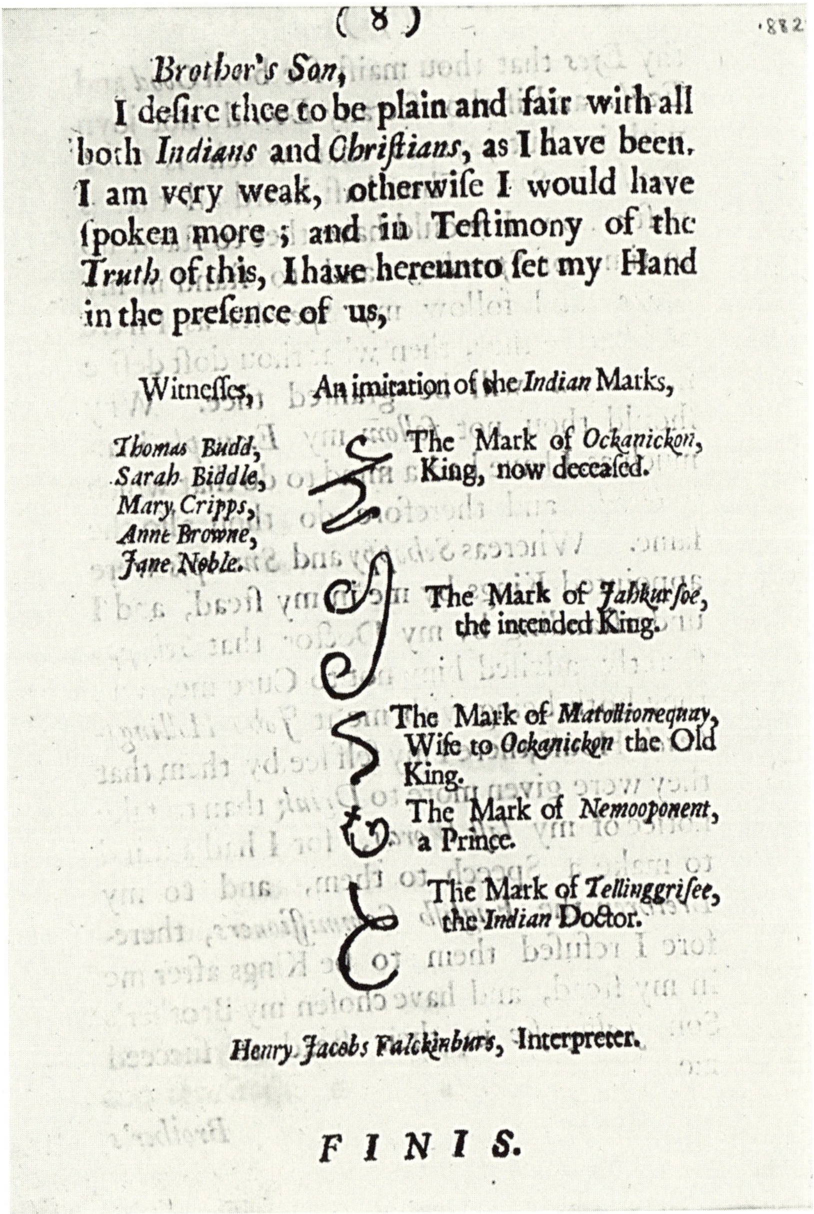

(8)

Brother's Son,

I defire thee to be plain and fair with all both *Indians* and *Chriſtians*, as I have been. I am very weak, otherwiſe I would have ſpoken more ; and in Teſtimony of the *Truth* of this, I have hereunto ſet my Hand in the preſence of us,

Witneſſes,	An imitation of the *Indian* Marks,
Thomas Budd, *Sarah Biddle,* *Mary Cripps,* *Anne Browne,* *Jane Noble.*	The Mark of *Ockanickon,* King, now deceaſed.
	The Mark of *Jahkurſoe,* the intended King.
	The Mark of *Matollioneguay,* Wife to *Ockanickon* the Old King.
	The Mark of *Nemooponent,* a Prince.
	The Mark of *Tellinggriſee,* the *Indian* Doctor.

Henry Jacobs Falckinburs, Interpreter.

F I N I S.

Figure 5. Signature page, The Dying Words of Ockanickon, 1683. The signature page replicates the marks of five Lenni Lenape or Delaware Indians alongside the names of five Quaker witnesses to Ockanickon's death. (The John Carter Brown Library at Brown University)

drink it in moderation." After presenting the dying speech Budd described a conversation he and Ockanickon had:

Friendly Reader, when *Ockanickon* had given his Brothers Son this good Counsel, I thought meet to speak unto him as followeth; *There is a great God, who Created all thing, and this God giveth Man an understanding of what is Good, and what is Bad, and after this Life rewardeth the Good with Blessings, and the Bad according to their Doings;* to which he answered and said, *It is very true, it is so, there are two Wayes, a broad Way, and a strait Way; there be two Paths, a broad Path and a strait Path; the worst, and the greatest Number go in the broad Path, the best and fewest go in the strait Path.*

This dialogue was taken by Budd to suggest the Delawares' openness to Christianity. It also supported his assertion that the Indians and English in these colonies got along because they respected each other.[102] Suggesting the spread of Christianity among his tribe, his words also proved the possibility of a colony founded on mutual respect. On emotional and structural levels dying Indians serve the same purpose in *New England's First Fruits* as they do in Thomas Budd's promotional tract. Although the Quakers no doubt were truly saddened by this death, they presented the speech of a perishing Indian to validate their presence in America.

A "good" death inspires and consoles survivors, and it suggests salvation. Paralleling these soteriological and therapeutic functions is a discursive one. The description of death in British missionaries' texts complements its enactment by suggesting the moral and economic worth of mission. Countering the violence identified with Spanish or brutal British invaders, these accounts argued that colonialism could be spiritually productive. This focus on productivity was especially prominent in the largest catalog of Indian death that emerged from British missions: Experience Mayhew's *Indian Converts.*

Although authored by one missionary, *Indian Converts* was the culmination of a tendency among Congregationalist ministers to collect accounts of Indian conversion and death. John Eliot had started this trend when he collected the "exhortations" of his Massachusett converts as evidence of their readiness to be admitted to full communion. Many of these translated testimonials were published in *A Late and Further Manifestation of the Progress of the Gospel Amongst the Indians in New-England* (1655) and in *A further Accompt of the Progresse of the Gospel amongst the Indians in New-England* (1659). In 1685 Eliot added to these testimonials *The Dying Speeches of Several Indians.* This tract, which presented the last words of eight Massachusett-speaking converts along with brief biographies, offers a precursor to Mayhew's text. Both texts present dying speeches as evidence of missionary accomplishment. The serial structure of both texts also suggests an automatic and ongoing accrual of converts.

Mayhew published *Indian Converts* as a "Discovery of the Efficacy of Divine Grace in the Conversion and Salvation of Sinners" and as a celebration of the lives of the Wampanoags his family had converted.[103] He also prompted his readers to feel a sense of accomplishment at the sight of a dying Indian. The encyclopedic format in which he presented these deaths, sorting them by gender, age, and vocation, added to this effect by suggesting an inventory of spiritual products. This book borrowed much from Protestant hagiographies and martyrologies such as Foxe's *Book of Martyrs*.[104] The colonial framework of the text, however, along with its overriding concern with proving conversion, gives it an added sense of epistemological mastery and suggests a rhetoric of acquisition.

Mayhew proved the Indians' conversions by rendering them transparent to the reader's gaze. I think this is one of the reasons why he made the reader privy to the most intimate information about the Wampanoags, ranging from details about their bodies to gossip about their marriages. The details convey reliability, especially when they show failures with successes, flawed souls alongside paragons of piety. We read that the deacon Jonathan Amos fell into drunkenness, and that the Pastor Japheth Hannit's sermons "were not very accurate." Of Rachel Amos, Mayhew is self-consciously forthcoming: "[S]he was once suffered to drink to Excess; and having done so, made a most humble and affecting Confession of her Sin therein, and never was known to do any more: which Fault of hers, if I had not thought here to have mention, would perhaps . . . have weakened the Credit of my whole History."[105] Frank admissions of Indians' lapses, combined with scrupulous descriptions of their lives and deaths, mark Mayhew's honesty.

The precise data of *Indian Converts* suggest trustworthiness and epistemological control. Readers are made to feel they know these Indians inside and out. They are privy to their personal quirks, fears, sicknesses, marital problems, feelings, and flaws. Mayhew displayed their injured bodies in detail, noting that Mary Coshomon died after a crib of harvested corn "did most grievously crush and bruise her, insomuch that, besides several other Hurts, some of the Joints of her Back were somewhat displaced." Readers learn gossip about relationships, hearing that Hannah Sissetom had a terrible marriage to an alcoholic, and that Sarah Peag suffered "sad jars betwixt her and her Husband." Besides baring their bodies, emotions, and intimate relations to us, Mayhew opened their souls. Abigail Kesoehtaut "was very deeply sensible of the Sins of her Nature and Life, and Jannohquissoo "was in great distress about his Soul." The communication of particular knowledge becomes intertwined with the repeated experience of seeing them die. James Nashompait "came in and laid himself on his Bed; and then turning his Face to the side of the House, and calling on his God, immediately resigned up his Spirit to him."[106] This vision of an Indian emptying himself to God and to the reader's gaze appears repeatedly. It anchors affective and aggressive impulses, which inform the trope of the dying Indian, to a discourse of careful management.

Indian Converts rewrites the deuteronomic narrative in a more efficient form. The text converts potential enemies into loyal servants and then directs us to watch their religiously sanctioned deaths. Encouraging his readers to gain an intimate, if formulaic, knowledge of these Indians, Mayhew implied that the British (or, more particularly, the Congregationalists of New England) were worthy stewards of America. He preserved images of dead Indians, repeatedly asserting the power of Protestant Christianity over them. He also encouraged his readers to peer inside Indians at the moment of death, glimpsing the state of their souls. In these ways Mayhew taught readers to think of Indian death as a rich repository of spiritual meaning.

Perhaps the desire to counter violence explains why we sometimes see the Christian dying Indian appearing in contrast to the carnage of war. In 1757 Timothy Horsfield, justice of the peace in the Moravian town of Bethlehem, interrupted his reports of Indian raids on Pennsylvania's frontier to inform Governor Denny that "the Indian Man John Smalling has deceased." Horsfield's letters were often rushed, as he coped with the urgent circumstances of the Seven Years' War, but he paused to deliver a detailed account of an Indian convert's death from smallpox:

Some time before his death he desired one of the Brethren to visit him & speak something to him of our Saviour, he said he Remembered, he had been Baptized by the Brethren, and wished he could feel so in his Heart as he did at that Time, the Brother that visited him Informed me, that he was a real Penitant, and that shortly before his Departure he spoke with much Confidence that he should soon go to Rest. He instructed his wife, his Mother, and Father in Law Geo: Hoys, to leave off the Indian ways, and to hear what the Brethren would tell them of our Saviour.[107]

The depth of Horsfield's feeling for Smalling is easy to understand, given the connections between the Moravian community he oversaw and the Delawares they had converted. That he would communicate this death in such detail to Pennsylvania's governor, and in a separate letter to Benjamin Franklin and other members of the Pennsylvania assembly, is more surprising.[108]

Most likely Horsfield presented this deathbed speech as evidence of the loyalty of the Moravian Indians, who already had been accused by panicked colonists of supporting enemy Indians' attacks. But an emotional component supplements this evidentiary function. Horsfield asks the governor to share his mourning for Smalling, but his description also opposes the carnage of war. Denny and Franklin hardly had close involvement in the missionary work, but they are drawn into this moment of mourning, asked to commemorate the Christian death of one Indian even as they offer bounties for the scalps of countless others.[109] If the men overseeing the defense of Pennsylvania's frontier outposts in wartime took consolation in an Indian ally's Christian death, it can hardly be surprising that the broader Anglo-American culture soon would do the same.

The link between Christian Indians' deaths and the carnage of war is more emotional than logical, but it is not weaker for this fact. Whether authentic or corrupt, missionary sentiment made possible the complex emotions with which Anglo-American readers would meet the sight of Indian death. Confronted elsewhere with blood and violence, Horsfield and his readers took refuge by dwelling for a moment on the poignant aspects of a Christian Indian's death. In reply to the waste of war appeared the possibility of peaceful cohabitation and spiritual productivity. Signifying all these desirable goals was the death of an Indian.

"No Blood We Shed"

The influence of missionary writings on broader treatments of Indians has been a subtle but palpable one. We do not often find the writers of "dying Indian" poems quoting missionaries, nor do we see soldiers expressing regrets that they haven't saved more Indian souls. What we do see, however, are many texts talking about Indian death in ways developed by missionaries. We see the expression of an apparently self-contradictory logic in the depiction of Indian death, a logic that gathers validation from the Christian paradox of life from death, as well as from the claim that British colonialism, if combined with conversion, is an act of benevolent recuperation. We also see the tendency to turn the scene of Indian death into a sentimental spectacle, and to meet that spectacle with intense but ineffectual emotion. Missionaries were the ones who assembled the economic and emotional framework that made possible the simultaneous sense of loss and gain—as well as the pairing of pleasure and sadness—that British and American audiences have expressed—and still express—at the sight of a dying Indian. Even as it manifests a fascination with waste, Indian death suggests moral accomplishment and conveys narrative closure. Death amounts to spiritual production, associating British settlement with cultivation and care.

This immersion in a missionary vision was pervasive enough that elements of it are present in texts by antireligious writers. Philip Freneau ridiculed Indians and their missionaries in "The Indian Convert," but in his treatment of Indian death he reveals the subtle influence of missionary writings. *The Rising Glory of America,* first written with his Princeton classmate Hugh Henry Brackenridge in 1771, exhibits this influence.

But why, to prompt your tears, should we resume,
The tale of *Cortez,* furious chief, ordained
With Indian blood to dye the sands, and choak,
Famed Mexico, thy streams with dead?
. . . .
Better these northern realms demand our song,
Designed by nature for the rural reign,
For agriculture's toil.—No blood we shed
For metals buried in a rocky waste.—[110]

Brackenridge and Freneau displayed sadness at the carnage of colonialism, aligning indigenous Americans and Spanish invaders with waste. *The Rising Glory of America* begins by averting the reader's eye from Mexico, a land where blood flows from corpse-filled streams, staining the barren land. Tears threaten to flow in response to this river of blood, but the poets stem both streams by turning our attention to the "northern realms" of America.

Northern America is a land of labor and abundance, set against a southern "rocky waste." It is a place of conservation where, as the poets note, no blood is shed. What violence there has been is marked as necessary, and it is appropriately mourned. One of the poem's speakers does mourn the violence of the Seven Years' War, exclaiming, "[W]hat streams / of blood were shed! What Indian hosts were slain." As Susan Castillo has pointed out, though, another speaker "immediately steps in to justify the necessity for violence by alleging that the Indians had been in cahoots with the French."[111] Northern America is, most of all, a country ordained by nature, not ruined by an invader. Indians—or, more accurately, their bodies—display these differences, validating the British. The Indians of British America are just as dead as those of Mexico. Instead of bleeding over the earth, however, they are neatly buried within the "rural reign" of America.

Brackenridge and Freneau implemented a missionary logic, transforming native death so that it signified first waste and then productivity, changing a symbol of loss into one of conservation. The dying Indian is a vehicle for sentiment and a symbol of manifest destiny. This figure also links British colonialism and, later, the United States, with Indian deaths that are so clean and so suggestive of profound change as to imply the beneficence of the forces that caused them. Searching for signs of conversion, missionaries probed Indians' sufferings for deeper meanings. They greeted converts' deaths with joy and abundant narration, matching death with an outpouring of affect and text. They made this loss a source of spiritual gain. Far as Freneau —a well-known Deist—later felt from Christian faith, he and Brackenridge imitated and extended the missionaries' project so that death songs supersede death, and Indians perish into poetry.

Fifteen years after cowriting this poem, Freneau published a revision of it in a collection of his work. As Julie Ellison has noted, most of these revisions "replac[ed] attacks on the British in the name of liberty and by new visions of a Pax Americana. . . . revers[ing] the moral status of Britain between the first and second versions."[112] The poem's deployment of Indian demise, however, remained the same. That the dying Indian can legitimate Freneau's America as easily as it does the young Freneau's and Brackenridge's Britain, that it can implicate Britain or Spain, reveals this trope's most important quality. It is a productive image, creating an abundance of both meaning and affect, a natural resource that writers can use for several ends. Indian death is about stoicism, sentiment, and inevitable loss, but it is also about the efficient management of wealth. Describing Indian death, it seems, has always been the way to own America.

Conclusion

By the second half of the eighteenth century British missionary writings exhibited a preoccupation with what had become a necessary task: explaining the failure of most efforts to convert Indians. From this anatomy of defeat a familiar catalog of blame emerged: writers in Britain accused colonists of alienating or corrupting Indians, and Nonconformists, especially in the colonies, blamed the Church of England for its feeble conversion attempts. Clergy on both sides of the Atlantic derided merchants for selling alcohol to Indians, and everyone blamed the Spanish and the French—even after France lost Canada in the Seven Years' War—for seducing natives with the superstitions of Catholicism.

Above all, these writings blamed Indians for refusing the blessings of Protestant Christianity. These analyses echoed earlier speculations that Indians could or would not convert. Before he founded the SPG Thomas Bray had explained why he thought efforts to establish missionary schools for Indians were a waste of time: "When our Instructed Indians do Return among them, what will it signify to the Conversion of their Fellow Indians, when they are almost always found, either for Fear of being Murdered, or out of a violent Inclination to Idleness and Hunting, and perhaps to a Bestial Sensual Way of Living, to Return, like the Dog to his Vomit, to the former Wild and Savage Ways of the Indians?"[1] Such sentiments appeared throughout the century, evolving into an explanation for the Indians' demise. In 1773 Jonathan Shipley speculated in his SPG sermon that Indians could not be separated from their "untameable savage spirit": "The sagacity for which they are remarkable seems to be of a partial kind, and to partake of more instinct than of reason. . . . [T]heir passions and habits proceeding always in one track, they have neither relish nor discernment for the clearest truths."[2] Samuel Halifax, preaching before the SPG in 1789, claimed that Indians are "generally insusceptible of religious impressions," and he concluded that in spite of the society's efforts "most of them have relapsed into their original barbarism."[3] The SPG, like many other groups, ended the eighteenth century where it had started, contemplating the moral depravity of Indians. The main difference was that they could assure themselves of their own benevolence because of their failed exertions.

Samson Occom punctured this rhetoric of failed benevolence when he discovered that the money he had raised in Britain was going to be used to educate white missionaries. He wrote to his teacher, Eleazar Wheelock: "I am very jealous that instead of your semenary becoming alma mater, she will be too alba mater to suckle the Tawnees, for she is already adorned up too much like the Popish Virgin Mary."[4] Occom overturned the image of the nursing parent, one often used by British missionaries to describe themselves, their supporters, or institutions such as Wheelock's Dartmouth College, as he compared the school to the maternal icon of Roman Catholicism. In so doing he undercut the very terms by which British missionaries had distinguished themselves from Catholics, showing how an abandonment of Indians invalidated the entire rhetoric of Protestant virtue. Occom eventually broke ties with Wheelock and cast his lot with his fellow Christian Indians. Having been offered a deed of land from the Oneidas, Occom, his son-in-law Joseph Johnson, and David Fowler (also former students of Wheelock) organized a voluntary removal of Native Americans from several tribes along the eastern seaboard to Brothertown, New York.[5]

As the Brothertown movement suggests, much of the commentary from late eighteenth-century white missionaries overlooked the ways in which Indian communities had absorbed Christianity. Such willful ignorance contributed to an erasure—political if not physical—of Indians from the eastern seaboard, as communities moved westward or receded into the background of colonial society. From 1765 to 1776 Joseph Fish, a Congregationalist minister of North Stonington, Rhode Island, tried to "convert" a Narragansett community that criticized his theology and eventually shunned him for his unwillingness to assist them in their efforts to retain their land. In his diary and letters Fish interpreted a clash between a conservative minister and an evangelical congregation, as well as the tension between a native community and its white advocate, as the Narragansetts' unwillingness to accept Christianity. Hearing them question his status as a standing minister funded by his nearby white parish rather than as a true itinerant minister, and even learning that an elderly woman of the church had complained, "Can't that old Creature preach no better?" failed to convince him that these Indians were anything other than heathens refusing conversion. In a letter written near the beginning of this ministry Sewall claimed, "The poor people are not fit to be left alone, Not being Equal to the Important affair of Conducting their Religious and ecclesiastical Matters, agreeable to the Gospel Order."[6] He continued to maintain this point of view until the community persuaded him to end his ministry there.

In spite of a growing tendency on the part of Anglo-Americans and Britons to regard Indians as doomed to vanish because of their unwillingness to accept civilization or Christianity, missionary efforts did continue. Some white ministers had successful and long-lasting relationships with their communities, while others repeated the cycle of optimism, frustration, and defeat expressed by missionaries in the colonial period. In particular, evangelical Christians in North America accepted the mandate of mission with unprecedented fervor. Led by figures such as William Carey, they imitated the self-sacrifice of David Brainerd, accompanying the building of a modern imperial infrastructure as they spread the gospel throughout the world. Expanding the fund-raising strategies of earlier movements, they depicted themselves and their readers as part of a global Christian community.[7] The rhetoric of mission, in a sense, moved beyond the Indians that used to be at its center, leaving many of them behind even as it continued to proclaim the importance of saving them.

Seventeenth- and eighteenth-century British missionary writings had a limited impact on their contemporaries, persuading some readers to contribute substantial sums of money but influencing general attitudes to Indians less obviously than captivity narratives and depictions of noble savages did. The true impact of these texts has been more apparent in nineteenth- and twentieth-century depictions of Indians, in treatments of colonialism, and in the fraught engagement of privileged spectators with the sufferings of others. Missionaries themselves have continued to describe Indians in many of the ways their predecessors did, especially those most sincerely concerned for Indians.

The archives of the New England Company, which has continued to fund missions to Indians in Canada, suggest some ways in which this discourse has altered but also remained the same. In 1975 H.V.R. Short, Bishop of Saskatchewan, transformed the longstanding trope of trade in a way early modern missionaries may well have found inconceivable, writing to Sir John Winnifrith, president of the New England Company, of the Indians he periodically visited, "I often think that . . . I receive far more from them than I give." While he replaced the notion of spiritual wealth compensating for material exploitation, and while he suggested a far more reciprocal relationship than many earlier missionaries would have, Short did retain the elegiac tones of earlier writings. He distinguished, for example, between "the Indians in the north," who "are still truly Indians," and those who are "a poor replica of a white man." He went on to explain, "The Indian, as an Indian, is a beautiful person; but unfortunately many of them have been destroyed by the impact of the very worst aspects of white society."[8] The resemblance of this commentary to, say, Gideon Hawley's depiction of the Mashpee Indians of Massachusetts in 1794, who were "in a very abject state in comparison of the Iroquois with whom I had been conversant," with its distinction between wild and settlement Indians, is hard to miss.[9] While Short displays more genuine affection for the Indians than this earlier employee of the New England Company, the two men express the same affective response of a concerned witness to a scene of unstoppable decline.

Short was hardly alone in this twentieth-century inclination toward tropes of impoverishment, diminishment, and loss. In 1976 the Bishop of Keewatin, Canada, wrote of Indians in a letter to Miss Mary S. Kearney of the New England Company: "The people themselves are, for the most part, lovely, faithfully-committed Christians." He continued to praise qualities such as their kindness and hospitality. Like Short, though, he saw Indians as a fragile people, who, "when they are exposed to the inroads of what we sometimes call 'civilization'," are likely to "succumb to the worst influences." As a result, "[N]orthern development often leaves a tragic wake behind it."[10] That these two bishops described Indians through tropes of decline hardly diminishes the concern they clearly felt, as well as their authentic efforts to meet Indians' material and spiritual needs. It also does not detract from the reality of the decline they observed. As with the earlier writings, however, the authenticity of missionaries' compassion for Indians, as well as their frustration with their inability to help more than they did, does not prevent such writings from contributing to a broader tendency to think of Indians as diminished or vanished. The prominence of such tendencies has been so great that it has overdetermined the ways in which Indians are depicted in both religious and secular contexts.

As I have argued throughout this book, missionary writings had an importance that exceeded actual efforts to Christianize Indians. They did more than offer a moral validation for colonial expansion or raise money for their projects. Sent eastward across the ocean, descriptions of Indians became items of evangelical exchange, constituting returns on the money, emotions, and prayers of British readers. They provided textual arenas where readers in Britain could become involved imaginatively with colonial activity. They asserted that readers could play an active role in distant evangelical labor, and they suggested an affective basis for the building of transatlantic communal ties. Perhaps most remarkably, they made pity one of the most important, if troubled, aspects of Britain's self-image. Compassion in these texts acquired the power to define self and other, to forge ties across distances, to propel action and cement religious belief.

The discourse of empire has been an intellectual preoccupation of at least the past three decades, as scholars in many fields have pondered the ways in which modern Europe not only conquered foreign peoples but also made the contemplation of conquest a font of artistic and humanistic pursuit. Far more than exotic backdrops for the enactment of adventures, accounts of intercultural contact, accommodation, exploitation, and war have been revealed as complex and potent influences on Western European culture. Even our interpretations of texts and issues apparently rooted in the domestic realm are enriched now by understanding how they were inflected by the implications of Europe's interactions with the peoples of Africa, Asia, and the Americas.

Steeped as we are in an awareness of empire's impact, we still have yet to untangle the more complex aspects of a postcolonial legacy, especially its emotional ones. It is arguable that the more we are aware of empire's influence, the more we are in danger of being entrapped by its emotional expressions, if not its assumptions. It is not entirely clear at this moment whether the hegemony of postcolonial critique will in the long run collapse into a continuation of Europe's fraught fascination with its own domination, or will emerge as a confrontation with the most subtle manifestations of power. Achieving the latter result requires a critical engagement with colonialism in all its ambivalence, not just revealing the ways in which Europeans eloquently excused violence but also the doubt, condemnation, and guilt that provoked such excuses. The rhetoric of British and Anglo-American hegemony is all the more impenetrable for its undercurrents of mourning and remorse, and a retrospective critique of it is always in danger of slipping into a reiteration of elegy. Acquiring critical traction must involve an analysis of the emotions that British writers attached to the idea of conquering foreign lands. This study of missionary writings has attempted to undertake a part of that project. It has explored some of the ways in which the hopes and desires that attended efforts to save Indians from their own sins as well as from the encroachments of colonists enhanced the affective framework of imperialist discourse by making it more fraught.

Enriching imperial rhetoric, missionary writings also forged new ways of thinking about the role that compassion could play in linking people across greater distances and cultural divides, for better or worse. The relevance of this topic to the present day, when "compassion fatigue" is a widely acknowledged result simply of watching or reading too much news, is obvious. These religious texts arguably were the first concerted attempts to raise funds from groups of people for charitable causes, especially for activities in lands removed from the immediate perception of those contributors. In order to raise such funds these texts had to bring distant cases of need to the attention of readers, convince them they should care about that suffering, and persuade them that their contributions would, when pooled together, have a good result. This line of argument—so familiar in the twenty-first century—was rather new in the seventeenth century, and it provoked much reconsideration of the practical and moral capacity of feeling.

Because they presented a cause so faraway, so immaterial, and so entangled in political complexity, missionaries' fund-raising publications could at times justify both the optimism and the caution that attended theories about the ethical value of emotion. Just as the launching of missions in North America suggested what could happen when faraway cases of spiritual suffering were brought before the eyes of Britons, and when those readers were made to feel connected to their distant compatriots, the failures of these projects heightened concerns about the feeble power or the unintended side effects of benevolence. Efforts to convert Indians provoked debate about the inherent cruelty or kindness of humans, about the justice and compassion of God, and about the relation between feeling and doing. They also produced many questions about the responsibilities humans have to each other and the role that emotion plays in determining those responsibilities. These writings, and the projects they promoted, do not provide clear or uniform answers to these difficult questions, which are still of the greatest relevance today. They do, however, show us how those questions developed, and they remind us how deep and tangled the roots of these issues are. Seeing how pity became such a powerful component of fund-raising texts in the early modern period, how it emerged from a Christian context and then spread into secular discourse, and how it intertwined with aggression, sadness, and eventually fatigue may help us come to terms with the conflicted affect that must meet any contemplation of suffering in the present day.

As I conclude this book my eyes fall upon a letter from Raymond C. Offenheiser, the president of Oxfam America, opened the month before and pushed to the dusty edge of my desk. It presents contrasting vignettes of two communities in Ethiopia, separated from each other by only five miles. The first scene is of a group of farmers who are surviving a terrible drought through the intercession of Oxfam's Action for Africa campaign. Their "peppers, tomatoes and onions have grown big and healthy," and they have progressed from desperate poverty to subsistence because of a new irrigation system. The second scene is of a woman, Tadese Konta, who "sits in a small clinic cradling her severely malnourished son," while the rest of her family languishes in poverty, ill health, and debt.[11] The difference between these two scenes, the letter asserts, is me.

Offenheiser proceeds to explain all the ways in which contributions to this campaign can help individuals in Africa. One of his projects is to make almost infinite suffering epistemologically manageable for me, his reader. As he describes the poverty, drought, and disease over-running this continent, he tells me enough about this suffering that I can envision it, without letting me be overpowered by my inability to address such vast pain. Portraits of individuals anchor me amid general references to famine, drought, illiteracy, and AIDS. While prompting my pity, the letter insists on bolstering my hope in my effectiveness, showing how small groups connected with Oxfam make small but important changes. I am introduced to the leader of a grassroots organization in Zimbabwe that is assisting rural women, and I am told how this group delivers maize to "[s]everal orphaned children, a man in a wheelchair, a terminally-ill woman with HIV/AIDS." Offenheiser and his colleagues promise to transform my emotion into benevolent action on a distant continent, channeling my small donation toward a larger end. He concludes by assuring me, "[T]he role you play is indispensable."[12]

I experience predictable emotions as I skim this letter: sadness, pity, and faint hope. These feelings flit quickly through me, for my exhaustion with the discourse of philanthropy preemptively contains them. My deepest feeling is the guilt that occurs when I realize how hard it is for me to comprehend hunger. I sit back and wonder if it is odd that emotion would emerge from a failure of imagination, and then decide that it actually has followed from my conceptualizing something else: the gap separating my privilege from this distant African's desperate need. As I wonder how much money it would take to do any good, I try to envision my own small donation traveling along a chain of intermediaries and agents, finally purchasing food or medicine for someone else. This feels rather ridiculous, and I begin to contemplate, with growing discomfort, the stage this letter has constructed in my mind. How is it that I can just sit here envisioning people in desperate need, prompted by the letter in my hand? How can I imagine that whatever money I give will do anything to narrow that gap between us, a gap evidenced most of all in my position as imaginative spectator and reader? And why is it that I cannot contemplate this situation of suffering without slipping into conflicted self-consciousness?

But then, how can I not do any of these things? In a sense, to be a middle-class resident of a wealthy nation, whatever one's religious position, is to be the offspring of missionaries. Often reluctant or overwhelmed, we sometimes experience imagined empowerment and connection with others through the mere acts of reading letters and donating funds. We are, inevitably, connoisseurs of suffering, filled with occasional fantasies of saving others. We wring our hands, we impotently mourn, and we make feeble gestures toward collective acts of benevolence. These efforts sometimes go wildly astray, and sometimes they do a bit of good. The suffering goes on no matter what, and we keep witnessing it.

Notes

Introduction

1. Daniel Defoe, *Robinson Crusoe: An Authoritative Text, Background, and Sources,* ed. Michael Shinagel, 2nd ed. (New York: W. W. Norton, 1994), 122–24.

2. Ibid., 125.

3. Ibid., 156.

4. Ibid., 158–59.

5. I use the words *English* and *England,* or *Scottish* and *Scotland,* when referring to texts written before the Act of Union between England and Scotland in 1707, and *British* or *Britain* when referring to texts appearing during or after 1707. When commenting on groups of texts, ideas, or images that span that date, I usually choose the more inclusive term, *British,* especially when that comment applies equally well to the writings, people, or sentiments of England and Scotland. I also use the word *English* as a linguistic term, especially when distinguishing them from French or Spanish writings.

6. Joseph Conrad, *Heart of Darkness,* ed. Robert Kimbrough, 3d ed. (New York: W. W. Norton, 1988), 28, 51, 72.

7. Two recent dissertations offer exceptions to the dearth of literary scholarship on this topic. Keely McCarthy, " 'Reducing Them to Civilitie': Religious Conversions and Cultural Transformations in Protestant Missionary Narratives, 1690–1790" (Ph.D. diss., University of Maryland, 2000), and Kristina Kae Bross, " 'That Epithet of Praying': The Praying Indian Figure in Early New England Literature" (Ph.D. diss., University of Chicago, 1997).

8. Thomas Scanlan, *Colonial Writing and the New World, 1583–1671* (New York: Cambridge University Press, 1999); Gordon M. Sayre, *Les Sauvages Américains: Representations of Native Americans in French and English Colonial Literature* (Chapel Hill: University of North Carolina Press, 1997).

9. Joshua Bellin, *The Demon of the Continent: Indians and the Shaping of American Literature* (Philadelphia: University of Pennsylvania Press, 2001); Sandra Gustafson, *Eloquence Is Power: Oratory and Performance in Early America* (Chapel Hill: University of North Carolina Press, 2000); Hilary E. Wyss, *Writing Indians: Literacy, Christianity, and Native Community in Early America* (Amherst: University of Massachusetts Press, 2000).

10. Toni Morrison, *Playing in the Dark: Whiteness and the Literary Imagination* (Cambridge, Mass.: Harvard University Press, 1992), 11.

11. Ibid., 44.

12. Matthew 28:19. Unless noted otherwise all Bible quotes are taken from the Authorized King James Version (New York: Family Library, 1973).

13. James I to Toby Matthew, Archbishop of York, February 26, 1615, in "The Collections for Henrico College," by Peter Walne, *Virginia Magazine of History and Biography* 80 (1972): 260.

14. Richard W. Cogley, *John Eliot's Mission to the Indians before King Philip's War* (Cambridge, Mass.: Harvard University Press, 1999); James A. De Jong, *As the Waters Cover the Sea: Millennial Expectations in the Rise of Anglo-American Missions, 1640–1810* (J. H. Kok N. V. Kampen, 1970).

15. Margaret Connell Szasz, *Indian Education in the American Colonies, 1607–1783* (Albuquerque: University of New Mexico Press, 1988), 62–64.

16. On the centrality of Protestantism to British unity, see Linda Colley, *Britons: Forging the Nation, 1707–1837* (New Haven: Yale University Press, 1992), 11–54.

17. William Castell, *A Petition of W.C. Exhibited to the High Covrt of Parliament now assembled, for the propagating of the Gospel in America, and the West Indies; and for the setling of our Plantations there; which Petition is approved by 70 able English Divines. Also by Master Alexander Henderson, and some other worthy Ministers of Scotland* (N.p., 1641).

18. Ibid., 6.

19. Ibid., 8–9.

20. See, e.g., Norman Fiering, "Irresistible Compassion: An Aspect of Eighteenth-Century Sympathy and Humanitarianism," *Journal of the History of Ideas* 37 (1976): 195–218.

21. Thomas Haskell, "Capitalism and the Origins of the Humanitarian Sensibility, Part One," in *The Antislavery Debate: Capitalism and Abolitionism as a Problem in Historical Interpretation,* ed. Thomas Bender (Berkeley: University of California Press, 1992), 111, 130.

22. *The Geneva Bible: A Facsimile of the 1560 Edition,* intro. Lloyd E. Berry (Madison: University of Wisconsin Press, 1969). On the differences among English Bible translations, see Lisa M. Gordis, *Opening Scripture: Bible Reading and Interpretive Authority in Puritan New England* (Chicago: University of Chicago Press, 2003); Marvin W. Anderson, "The Geneva (Tomson/Junius) New Testament among Other English Bibles of the Period," in *The Geneva Bible: The Annotated New Testament 1602 Edition,* ed. Gerald T. Sheppard (New York: Pilgrim, 1989), 5–17; S. L. Greenslade, "English Versions of the Bible, 1525–1611," *The Cambridge History of the Bible: The West from the Reformation to the Present Day,* ed. S. L. Greenslade (Cambridge: Cambridge University Press, 1963), 141–74.

23. J. R. Willis notes, under the entry for "pity," "This word is entirely synonymous with compassion both in OT and NT, except, perhaps, in 1 Pet 3.8, where 'sympathetic' would better express the meaning of the original word." Willis, *Dictionary of the Bible,* ed. James Hastings, rev. ed. Frederick C. Grant and H. H. Rowley (New York: Charles Scribner's Sons, 1963), 774. In *The Interpreter's Dictionary of the Bible,* J. M. Ward includes compassion and pity under the entry for "mercy." There is no entry for "sympathy," but Ward does mention that "when applied to God or to Jesus Christ, it can denote an inner feeling of sympathy or

love." *The Interpreter's Dictionary of the Bible,* ed. George Arthur Buttrick et al. (New York: Abington Press, 1962), 3:352.

24. John Milton, *Paradise Lost,* ed. Alastair Fowler, 2d ed. (London: Longman, 1988), X, ll. 211–12.

25. Ibid., 246–49.

26. Cotton Mather, fn. to *A Letter Concerning the Success of the Gospel amongst the Indians in New England,* by Increase Mather, in *Magnalia Christi Americana,* ed. Thomas Robbins (1702; Hartford, 1853), 2:574.

27. Janet Todd, *Sensibility: An Introduction* (London: Methuen, 1986), 7. On sensibility generally, see G. J. Barker-Benfield, *The Culture of Sensibility: Sex and Society in Eighteenth-Century Britain* (Chicago: University of Chicago Press, 1992). On emotion in eighteenth-century British colonial culture, see Nicole Eustace, "Passion is the Gale': Emotion and Power on the Eve of the American Revolution" (Ph.D. diss., University of Pennsylvania, 2001).

28. Thomas Randall, *Christian Benevolence. A Sermon Preached before the Society in Scotland for Propagating Christian Knowledge, at their Anniversary Meeting, in the High Church of Edinburgh* (Edinburgh, 1763), vi, 2.

29. Ibid., 105, 98.

30. Ibid., 114, 29.

31. Fiering, "Irresistible Compassion."

32. Ibid., 207.

33. Ned C. Landsman, "Witherspoon and the Problem of Provincial Identity in Scottish Evangelical Culture," in *Scotland and America in the Age of the Enlightenment,* ed. Richard B. Sher and Jeffrey R. Smitten (Edinburgh: Edinburgh University Press, 1990), 29–45.

34. This was especially true of New England until the mid-eighteenth century. Conrad Edick Wright, "Christian Compassion and Corporate Beneficence: The Institutionalization of Charity in New England, 1720–1810" (Ph.D. diss., Brown University, 1981), 11–35.

35. David Hume, *A Treatise of Human Nature,* ed. L. A. Selby-Bigge and P. H. Nidditch (1739; Oxford: Clarendon, 1978), 369–70 (book II, part 2, section 7).

36. Adam Smith, *Theory of Moral Sentiments,* ed. D. D. Raphael and A. L. Macfie (Indianapolis: Liberty Fund, 1984), 139.

37. Julie Ellison has pointed out the "ambivalence" with which Smith "crafted the culture of systems that is so important to the modern individual's feeling of being meaningfully related to remote locations and cultures." *Cato's Tears and the Making of Anglo-American Emotion* (Chicago: University of Chicago Press, 1999), 10–12.

38. Smith, *Theory,* 140.

39. Ibid., 235.

40. For Smith's definitions of these terms, see *Theory,* 10. As Gillian Skinner writes of Smith, "The idea of community is, like the sentimental circle, restricted to those who will understand." *Sensibility and Economics in the Novel, 1740–1800: The Price of a Tear* (New York: St. Martin's Press, 1999), 13.

41. "Let pity be [defined as] a certain pain at an apparently destructive or painful evil happening to one who does not deserve it and which a person might

expect himself or one of his own to suffer." Aristotle, *On Rhetoric*, trans. and ed. George A. Kennedy (New York: Oxford University Press, 1991), II.8.1. Skinner writes that Smith's definition of sympathy came "perilously close to Mandeville's formulations." *Sensibility*, 13.

42. William Kellaway, *The New England Company, 1649–1776, Missionary Society to the American Indians* (London: Longmans, Green and Co., 1961), 5–20; George Parker Winship, *The New England Company of 1649 and John Eliot: The Ledger for the Years 1650–1660 and the Record Book of Meetings between 1656 and 1686 of the Corporation for the Propagation of the Gospel in New England* (Boston: Prince Society, 1920), vi–vii. On Occom's journey to Britain, see Harold Blodgett, *Samson Occom* (Dartmouth College Manuscript Series, 1935); Leon Burr Richardson, ed., *An Indian Preacher in England* (Hanover, N.H.: Dartmouth College Publications, 1933); W. DeLoss Love, *Samson Occom and the Christian Indians of New England*, intro. Margaret Connell Szasz (1899; reprint, Syracuse: Syracuse University Press, 2000), 130–51. The "Reports" or "Abstracts of Proceedings" of the SPG, which usually were attached to the anniversary sermons after the society's first decade, routinely included accounts of contributions and expenditures. In 1715, for example, the "Abstract" noted that a nationwide parish collection ordered by Queen Anne just before her death had gathered £3,423 with more money still coming in. *An Abstract of the Proceedings of the Society for the Propagation of the Gospel in Foreign Parts*, in George Ash, *A Sermon Preached before the Incorporated Society for the Propagation of the Gospel in Foreign Parts; At their Anniversary Meeting in the Parish Church of St. Mary-le-Bow, on Friday the 18th of February, 1714* (London, 1715), 31.

43. Ann Jessie Van Sant, *Eighteenth-Century Sensibility and the Novel: The Senses in Social Context* (New York: Cambridge Univeristy Press, 1993), 16–17.

44. Ibid., 17.

45. Eric Hinderaker, "The 'Four Indian Kings' and the Imaginative Construction of the First British Empire," *William and Mary Quarterly*, 3d ser., 53 (1996): 487–526; Richmond P. Bond, *Queen Anne's American Kings* (Oxford: Oxford University Press, 1952); John Wolfe Lydekker, *The Faithful Mohawks* (Cambridge: Cambridge University Press, 1938).

46. Polly Stevens Fields, "Samson Occom and/in the Missionary's Position: Consideration of a Native-American Preacher in 1770's Colonial America," *Wordsworth Circle* 32 (2001): 16.

47. Samson Occom to Eleazar Wheelock, July 24, 1771. Quoted in Blodgett, *Samson Occom*, 124. Michael Elliott has presented a compelling reading of one copy of this letter that replaces the word *Buck* with *Bait*. "'This Indian Bait': Samson Occom and the Voice of Liminality," *Early American Literature* 29 (1994): 233–53.

48. Joseph Caryl, preface, *A Late and Further Manifestation of the Progress of the Gospel Amongst the Indians in New-England*, by John Eliot (London, 1655).

49. Thomas Thorowgood, *Iewes in America, or, Probabilities That the Americans are of that Race. With the removal of some contrary reasonings, and earnest desires for effectual endeavors to make them christian* (London, 1650), preface.

50. Ibid., 77.

51. Ibid., 92.

52. Eve Kosofsky Sedgwick, *Between Men: English Literature and Male Homosocial Desire* (New York: Columbia University Press, 1985); René Girard, *Deceit, Desire, and the Novel: Self and Other in Literary Structure*, trans. Yvonne Freccero (Baltimore: Johns Hopkins University Press, 1972).

53. Aristotle, *On Rhetoric*, I.2, pp. 37–39.

54. Benedict Anderson, *Imagined Communities: Reflections on the Origin and Spread of Nationalism*, rev. ed. (New York: Verso, 1991).

55. See, e.g., Philip H. Round, *By Nature and By Custom Cursed: Transatlantic Civil Discourse and New England Cultural Production, 1620–1660* (Hanover, N.H.: University Press of New England, 1999); Scott Black, "Social and Literary Form in the Spectator," *Eighteenth-Century Studies* 33 (1999): 21–42; David S. Shields, *Civil Tongues and Polite Letters in British America* (Chapel Hill: University of North Carolina Press, 1997); Michael Warner, *Letters of the Republic* (Cambridge, Mass.: Harvard University Press, 1990).

56. Anderson, *Imagined Communities*, 26.

57. My focus on religion as a unifying force owes much to Adrian Hastings, *The Construction of Nationhood: Ethnicity, Religion and Nationalism* (New York: Cambridge University Press, 1997), and Colley, *Britons*.

58. Although my work covers the pre-Revolutionary period and has a transatlantic range, it shares with David Waldstreicher's work on the early United States an effort to see nationalism as imagined and enacted. *In the Midst of Perpetual Fetes: The Making of American Nationalism, 1776–1820* (Chapel Hill: University of North Carolina Press, 1997), 3.

59. See Kant's dismissal of benevolence that results from sympathy: "To be beneficent when we can is a duty; and besides this, there are many minds so sympathetically constituted that, without any other motive of vanity or self-interest, they find a pleasure in spreading joy around them, and can take delight in the satisfaction of others so far as it is their own work. But I maintain that in such a case an action of this kind, however proper, however amiable it may be, has nevertheless no true moral worth." Immanuel Kant, *Theory of Ethics*, I.2, in *Kant: Selections*, ed. and trans. Theodore Meyer Greene (New York: Charles Scribner's Sons, 1929), 276.

60. Joseph Conrad to T. Fisher Urwin, July 22, 1996, in Conrad, *Heart*, 199.

61. Karen Halttunen, "Humanitarianism and the Pornography of Pain in Anglo-American Culture," *American Historical Review* 100 (1995): 303–334; 309.

62. Ibid., 309.

63. June Howard, "What Is Sentimentality?" *American Literary History* 11 (1999): 63–81; John Mullan, "Sentimental Novels," in *The Cambridge Companion to the Eighteenth Century Novel*, ed. John Richetti (New York: Cambridge University Press, 1996), 236–54.

64. Richard W. Pointer has attended to the importance of this adjective in "'Poor Indians' and the 'Poor in Spirit': The Indian Impact on David Brainerd," *New England Quarterly* 67 (1994): 403–26.

65. Caryl, preface.

66. Alexander Pope, *An Essay on Man* (1733–34), in *The Twickenham Edition of the Works of Alexander Pope*, ed. John Butt, vol. 3, ed. Maynard Mack (London: Methuen, 1951–69), epistle I, ll. 99–112.

67. Paulino Castañeda Delgado, "La condición miserable del indo y sus privilegios," *Anuario de Estudios Americanos* 28 (1971): 245–335. My thanks to Beth Penry for calling my attention to the Spanish usage of this term.

68. John Eliot, ed., *A further Accompt of the Progresse of the Gospel amongst the INDIANS in New-England,* with Abraham Pierson's "Some Helps for the Indians" (Boston, 1659), 17–18.

69. Samson Occom, Journal, pp. 91–92. Occom Papers, Dartmouth College Baker Library, Hanover, N.H.

70. Daniel Defoe, *The Farther Adventures of Robinson Crusoe* (New York: W. W. Norton, 1953), 369.

71. On Henrico College, the massacre of 1622, and the publications of the Virginia Company, see Michael Leroy Oberg, *Dominion and Civility: English Imperialism and Native America, 1585–1685* (Ithaca: Cornell University Press, 1999), 8–80; Scanlan, *Colonial Writing*; Alden T. Vaughan, *Roots of American Racism: Essays on the Colonial Experience* (New York: Oxford University Press, 1995), 105–21; Szasz, *Indian Education,* 46–77; Walne, "Collections for Henrico," 259–66; Louis B. Wright, *Religion and Empire: The Alliance between Piety and Commerce in English Expansion, 1558–1625* (Chapel Hill: University of North Carolina Press, 1943); Robert Hunt Land, "Henrico and Its College," *William and Mary Quarterly,* 2d ser., 18 (1938): 453–98.

72. Walne, "Collections for Henrico," 259–66.

73. Nigel Smith, *Literature and Revolution in England, 1640–1660* (New Haven: Yale University Press, 1994).

74. Women played important but silent roles in the earlier organizations. See, e.g., Winship, *New England Company,* v. On the distinction between earlier and later missionary movements, cf. Andrew Walls, "The Eighteenth-Century Protestant Missionary Awakening in its European Context," in *Christian Missions and the Enlightenment,* ed. Brian Stanley (Grand Rapids: Eerdmans, 2001), 22–44.

75. Gustav Warneck, *Outline of a History of Protestant Missions from the Reformation to the Present Time. With an Appendix Concerning Roman Catholic Missions,* ed. and trans. George Robson, 3d ed. (Edinburgh, 1906), 56.

76. John Dryden, trans., *The Life of St. Francis Xavier, of the Society of Jesus, Apostle of the Indies, and of Japan, Written in French by Father Dominick Bohours, of the Same Society,* vol. 19 of *The Works of John Dryden* (1688; Berkeley: University of California Press, 1979). My thanks to Anne Barbeau Gardiner for calling my attention to this text.

77. For an overview of many of these groups and their approaches to missionary work, see Szasz, *Indian Education*; R. Pierce Beaver, "Methods in American Missions to the Indians in the Seventeenth and Eighteenth Centuries: Calvinist Models for Protestant and Foreign Missions," *Journal of Presbyterian History* 47 (1969): 124–48.

78. *An Act for the Promoting and Propagating the Gospel of Jesus Christ in New England. Acts and Ordinances of the Interregnum, 1642–1660,* vol. 2, 197, July 27, 1649; Patent of incorporation of the Company for Propagation of the Gospel in New England and the parts adjacent in America, *Calendar of State Papers, Colonial Series, America and West Indies, 1661–1668,* ed. W. Noel Sainsbury (London, 1880), §223;

Cogley, *John Eliot's Mission*; Szasz, *Indian Education*, 101–28; Kellaway, *The New England Company*; Henry William Busk, *A Sketch of the Origin and the Recent History of the New England Company by the Senior Member of the Company* (London, 1884).

79. Busk, *A Sketch*, 20 ff.; Beaver, "Methods," 125.

80. Gideon Hawley Collection, 1754–94, Massachusetts Historical Society, Boston; William S. Simmons and Cheryl L. Simmons, eds., *Old Light on Separate Ways: The Narragansett Diary of Joseph Fish, 1765–1776* (Hanover, N.H.: University Press of New England, 1982).

81. Kellaway, *The New England Company*, 194–96, 282–83.

82. George Parker Winship, *The Eliot Indian Tracts* (Cambridge, Mass.: Harvard University Press, 1925).

83. Szasz, *Indian Education*, 113–20.

84. Daniel O'Connor et al., *Three Centuries of Mission: The United Society for the Propagation of the Gospel, 1701–2000* (London: Continuum, 2000); Margaret Dewey, *The Messengers: A Concise History of the United Society for the Propagation of the Gospel* (London: Mowbrays, 1975); Hans Cnattingius, *Bishops and Societies: A Study of Anglican Colonial and Missionary Expansion, 1698–1850* (London: SPCK, 1952), 7–37; H. P. Thompson, *Into All Lands: The History of the Society for the Propagation of the Gospel in Foreign Parts, 1701–1950* (London: Billing and Sons, 1951); Samuel Clyde McCulloch, "The Foundation and Early Works of the Society for the Propagation of the Gospel in Foreign Parts," *Huntington Library Quarterly* 8 (1945): 244–58; Frank J. Klingberg, *Anglican Humanitarianism in Colonial New York* (Philadelphia: Church Historical Society, 1940); G. E. Edwards, "Life in Old Documents," *SPG Archives Lectures* (Westminster: SPG, 1936–37); E. C. Midwinter, "The SPG in America," *SPG Archives Lectures*, 3–12; C. F. Pascoe, *Two Hundred Years of the SPG* (London, 1901); W. O. B. Allen and Edmund McClure, *Two Hundred Years: The History of the Society for Promoting Christian Knowledge, 1698–1898* (London, 1898); Earnest Hawkins, *Historical Notices of the Church of England in the North American Colonies* (London, 1845); David Humphries, *An Historical Account of the Incorporated Society for the Propagation of the Gospel in Foreign Parts* (London, 1730), 13–22.

85. April 21, 1710, p. 474, April 28, pp. 478–82, May 19, pp. 483–85, June 16, p. 487, September 15, pp. 502–3, vol. 1A; February 16, 1711, p. 1, March 16, p. 6, March 22, p. 10, vol. 2; Journals Series A, USPG Archives, Bodleian Library of Commonwealth and African Studies at Rhodes House, Oxford, UK (hereafter Journals A); Hinderaker, "'Four Indian Kings'"; Daniel K. Richter, "Some of them . . . Would Always Have a Minister With Them': Mohawk Protestantism, 1683–1719," *American Indian Quarterly* 16 (1992): 471–84; Szasz, *Indian Education*, 129–38, 149–72; S. Charles Bolton, *Southern Anglicanism: The Church of England in Colonial South Carolina* (Westport, Conn.: Greenwood, 1982), 102–20; Bond, *Queen Anne's American Kings;* John Wolfe Lydekker, "The Mohawk Alliance in the Eighteenth Century," *SPG Archives Lectures*, 35–42; Lydekker, *Faithful Mohawks*; Frank J. Klingberg, "The Efforts of the SPG to Christianize the Mosquito Indians, 1742–1785," *Historical Magazine of the Protestant Episcopal Church* 9 (1940): 305–21.

86. Henry Hunter, *A Brief History of the Society in Scotland, for Propagating*

Christian Knowledge in the Highlands and Islands; and of the Correspondent Board in London (London, 1795).

87. Frederick V. Mills, Sr., "The Society in Scotland for Propagating Christian Knowledge in British North America, 1730–1775," *Church History* 63 (1994): 15–30; Szasz, *Indian Education*, 218–32.

88. Richardson, *Indian Preacher*; Love, *Samson Occom*, 130–51.

89. Mills, "The Society in Scotland."

90. Beaver, "Methods," 125.

91. Rayner Wickersham Kelsey, *Friends and the Indians, 1655–1917* (Philadelphia: Associated Executive Committee of Friends on Indian Affairs, 1917), 19–37.

92. Karl-Wilhelm Westmeier, *The Evacuation of Shekomecko and the Early Moravian Missions to Native North Americans* (Lewiston: Edwin Mellen Press, 1994); Allen W. Schattshneider, *Through Five Hundred Years* (Bethlehem: Comenius Press, 1990); Edwin Welch, ed., *The Bedford Moravian Church in the Eighteenth Century* (Northamptonshire: Stanley L. Hunt, 1989); Daniel B. Thorpe, *The Moravian Community in Colonial North Carolina: Pluralism on the Southern Frontier* (Knoxville: University of Tennessee Press, 1989); Elma E. Gray, *Wilderness Christians: The Moravian Mission to the Delaware Indians* (1956; reprint, New York: Russel and Russel, 1973); William M. Beauchamp, ed., *Moravian Journals Relating to Central New York, 1745–66* (1916; reprint, New York: AMS Press, 1976); Joseph Mortimer Levering, *A History of Bethlehem, Pennsylvania, 1741–1892 with Some Account of its Founders and their Early Activity in America* (1903; reprint, New York: AMS Press, 1971); George Henry Loskiel, *History of the Mission of the United Brethren among the Indians in North America* (London, 1794).

93. Klingberg, "Mosquito Indians."

94. Szasz, *Indian Education*, 201, citing Levering.

95. J. H. [John Heckewelder], *A Letter to a Friend; in which Some Account is Given of the Brethren's Society for the Furtherance of the Gospel among the Heathen* (London, 1769).

96. Szasz, *Indian Education*, 202–5.

97. Roxann Wheeler assigns this alignment of categories in the third quarter of the eighteenth century. *The Complexion of Race: Categories of Difference in Eighteenth-Century British Culture* (Philadelphia: University of Pennsylvania Press, 2000). On the apparent invisibility of Indians within African communities, see Ruth Wallis Herndon and Ella Wilcox Sekatau, "The Right to a Name: The Narragansett People and Rhode Island Officials in the Revolutionary Era," in *After King Philip's War: Presence and Persistence in Indian New England*, ed. Colin G. Calloway (Hanover, N.H.: University Press of New England, 1997), 132.

98. Since the New England Company's ledgers contain no record of book sales, and since "none of those issued after 1652 are found in the Thomason Catalogue or on the Stationers' Registers," Winship suggested that these texts were distributed among company members and prospective contributors rather than sold to the public. *Eliot Indian Tracts*, 12.

99. The society printed 500 copies of its first sermon, none of its second, 1,500 of its third, and 750 of the rest preached in the first decade. In 1710 it began publishing larger quantities, especially with famous preachers such as William Fleetwood,

whose sermon of 1711 was first printed with 750 copies in quarto and 3,000 in octavo. March 17, 1703/4, p. 142, March 2, 1704/5, p. 185, February 28, 1705/6, p. 225, April 18, 1706/7, p. 288, vol. 1, Journals A; March 16, 1711, p. 7, vol. 2, Journals A.

100. Kellaway, *The New England Company*, 22.

101. Jonathan Edwards, *An Account of the Life of the Late Reverend Mr. David Brainerd, Minister of the Gospel, Missionary to the Indians, from the honourable Society in Scotland, for the Propagation of Christian Knowledge, and Pastor of a Church of Christian Indians in New-Jersey. Who died at Northampton in New-England, Octob. 9th 1747. in the 30th Year of his Age: Chiefly taken from his own Diary, and other private Writings, written for his own Use* (Boston, 1749) (hereafter *Life of David Brainerd*). All citations to this text will be to *The Life of David Brainerd*, ed. Norman Pettit, vol. 7 of *The Works of Jonathan Edwards*, (New Haven: Yale University Press, 1985).

102. See, e.g., *Mercurius Politicus, Severall Proceedings in Parliament, Lloyd's Evening Post*, vol. 18, Wednesday, June 4 to Friday, June 6, 1766, SPG Journals A; Winship, *Eliot Indian Tracts* 5–18; Winship, *The New England Company*.

103. Kellaway, *The New England Company*, 131–33. Wyss, *Writing Indians*, 1.

Chapter 1

1. *An Act for the promoting and propagating the Gospel of Jesus Christ in New England. Acts and Ordinances of the Interregnum, 1642–1660*, 2:197, July 27, 1649.

2. Winship, *The New England Company*, vi–vii.

3. Kellaway, *The New England Company*, 42–46, describes legal contests over such lands after the Restoration.

4. Caryl, preface.

5. Scanlon, *Colonial Writing*, 165. See also Joyce E. Chaplin's reading of Caryl's letter in *Subject Matter: Technology, the Body, and Science on the Anglo-American Frontier, 1500–1676* (Cambridge, Mass.: Harvard University Press, 2001), 301.

6. Louis B. Wright, *Religion and Empire: The Alliance between Piety and Commerce in English Expansion, 1558–1625* (Chapel Hill: University of North Carolina Press, 1943).

7. Vine Deloria, Jr., *Custer Died for Your Sins: An Indian Manifesto* (London: Macmillan, 1969), 101.

8. Scanlon has argued that "attempts by New England's clergy to convert the Indians could and did function within a symbolic economy, in which people in England donated money and materials in return for being able to lay claim to the harvest of souls for their nation." *Colonial Writing*, 165. See also his study of William Crashaw's sermon promoting the Virginia plantation (1610), (p. 113); Roy Harvey Pearce, *Savagism and Civilization* (1953; reprint, Baltimore: Johns Hopkins University Press, 1965), 8; L. Wright, *Religion and Empire*, esp. ch. 4.

9. Christopher Columbus, *Letter to the King and Queen of Castile (First Voy-*

age), 1493, in *The English Literatures of America, 1500–1800,* ed. Myra Jehlen and Michael Warner (New York: Routledge, 1997), 13.

10. Ibid., 13–14.

11. Daniel K. Richter, *Facing East from Indian Country: A Native History of Early America* (Cambridge, Mass.: Harvard University Press, 2001), 6–7; Michael P. Morris, *The Bringing of Wonder: Trade and the Indians of the Southeast, 1700–1783* (Westport, Conn.: Greenwood Press, 1999), 1–3; Daniel K. Richter, *The Ordeal of the Longhouse: The Peoples of the Iroquois League in the Era of European Colonization* (Chapel Hill: University of North Carolina Press, 1992), 22–23.

12. Christopher L. Miller and George R. Hamell, "A New Perspective on Indian-White Contact: Cultural Symbols and Colonial Trade." *Journal of American Studies* 23 (1986): 311–28.

13. Bellin, *Demon,* 42–43.

14. Stephen Greenblatt, *Marvelous Possessions: The Wonder of the New World* (Chicago: University of Chicago Press, 1991), 110, quoted in Bellin, *Demon,* 42.

15. Columbus, *Letter,* 14.

16. This vision of unequal exchange occasionally appeared in reference to Asians or Africans. Joanna Lipking mentions the "promise that opens a 1665 collection called *The Golden Coast* that 'a man may gain an estate by a handful of beads, and his pocket full of gold for an old hat.'" "The New World of Slavery — An Introduction." in *Oroonoko,* by Aphra Behn, ed. Joanna Lipking (New York: Norton, 1997), 76.

17. There continues to be uncertainty about the reference to the "Indian," as the folio edition of Shakespeare's plays refers to "the base Iudean," while the quarto edition substitutes "the base Indian." E. A. J. Honigmann has concluded, "The best analysis, is, I think, Richard Levin's 'The Indian/Iudean crux in *Othello*' [SQ 33 (1982), 60–7], which ends with a telling point. It is appropriate for Othello to compare himself with the Indian, whose action results from ignorance, and 'very inappropriate for him to compare himself to Judas, whose action was regarded as a conscious choice of evil.'" "Longer Notes," in William Shakespeare, *The Arden Shakespeare "Othello,"* ed. E. A. J. Honigmann (Surrey: Thomas Nelson and Sons, 1997), 342–43. My thanks to Lars Engle for suggesting this connection.

18. Eliza Haywood, *The City Jilt,* in *Three Novellas by Eliza Haywood,* ed. Earla A. Wilputte (1726; East Lansing: Michigan State University Press, 1995), 105.

19. John Milton, *Complete Poems and Major Prose,* ed. Merritt Y. Hughes (Indianapolis: Odyssey Press, 1957), 665 (emphasis mine).

20. On the changing meaning of the word factory, connoting both consular outpost for trade and site of production, see Jean-Christophe Agnew, *Worlds Apart: The Market and the Theater in Anglo-American Thought, 1550–1750* (New York: Cambridge University Press, 1986), 143.

21. Robert Boyle, "The Aretology" (1645), in *The Early Essays and Ethics of Robert Boyle,* ed. John T. Harwood (Carbondale: Southern Illinois University Press, 1991), 73–74. See a similar reference to Indians in "The Doctrine of Thinking," *Early Essays,* 196.

22. John Hall, "Of Felicity," in *Horae Vacivae, Or, Essays. Some Occasional Considerations* (London, 1646), 25–27.

23. [Richard Allestree], *The Whole Duty of Man; Laid Down in a Plain and*

Familiar Way for the Use of All, but Especially the Meanest Reader (1658; Williamsburg, 1746), 129.

24. Samuel Sewall, *Phaenomena quaedam Apocalyptica Ad Aspectum Novi Orbis configurata. Or, some few Lines towards a description of the New Heaven as it makes to those who stand upon New Earth* (Boston, 1697), 5. Patricia Seed has shown that the building of houses and fences, as well as the visible cultivation of land within an enclosure, constituted a distinctively English approach to "creat[ing] political authority over New World peoples." *Ceremonies of Possession in Europe's Conquest of the New World, 1492–1640* (New York: Cambridge University Press, 1995), 3, 16–40.

25. John Dury, preface to *The Glorious Progress of the Gospel, amongst the Indians in New England. Manifested by three Letters, under the Hand of that famous Instrument of the Lord Mr. John Eliot, And another from Mr. Thomas Mayhew jun.*, ed. Henry Winslow (London, 1649), 22. Cogley identifies J. D. as "John Dury, the Scottish-born ecumenist then residing in England." *John Eliot's Mission,* 67.

26. Henry Whitfield, ed., *The Light Appearing more and more towards the perfect Day. or, a farther Discovery of the present state of the Indians in New-England, Concerning the Progresse of the Gospel amongst them. Manifested by Letters from such as preacht to them there* (London, 1651), 13.

27. Cotton Mather, *India Christiana. A Discourse, Delivered unto the Commissioners, for the Propagation of the Gospel among the American Indians. Which is Accompanied with several Instruments relating to the Glorious Design of Propagating our Holy Religion, in the Eastern as well as the Western, Indies* (Boston, 1721), 20.

28. John Wynne, *A Sermon Preached before the Incorporated Society for the Propagation of the Gospel in Foreign Parts, At the Parish-Church of St. Mary-le-Bow, on Friday, the 19th of February, 1724. Being the Day of their Anniversary Meeting* (London, 1725), 30.

29. Robert Millar, *The History of the Propagation of Christianity, and the Overthrow of Paganism, wherein the Christian Religion is Confirmed,* 3d ed. (London, 1731), 354.

30. George Muir, *The Conversion of the Gentiles illustrated. A Sermon Preached Before the Society in Scotland, for propagating Christian Knowledge, At their Anniversary Meeting* (Edinburgh, 1766), 43.

31. Colin G. Calloway, *New Worlds for All: Indians, Europeans, and the Remaking of Early America* (Baltimore: Johns Hopkins University Press, 1997), 55; James Axtell, "The Invasion Within: The Contest of Cultures in Colonial North America," in *The European and the Indian: Essays in the Ethnohistory of Colonial North America* (New York: Oxford University Press, 1981), 39–86; James P. Ronda, "'We Are Well As We Are': An Indian Critique of Seventeenth-Century Christian Missions," *William and Mary Quarterly,* 3d ser., 34 (1977): 66–82.

32. Claire Jowitt, "Radical Identities? Native Americans, Jews, and the English Commonwealth," *Seventeenth Century* 10 (1995): 107.

33. Solomon Stoddard, *QUESTION: Whether GOD is not Angry with the Country for doing so little towards the Conversion of the Indians?* (Boston, 1723), 10–11.

34. C. Mather, *India Christiana,* 28–29.

35. On Native resistance to English planting, see Jonathan Field, "Peculiar Manuerance': Puritans, Indians, and the Rhetoric of Agriculture, 1629–1654," *Annual Proceedings of the Dublin Seminar for New England Folklife* 20 (1995): 12–24.

36. Cotton Mather et al., "An Attestation by the United Ministers of Boston," in *Indian Converts: or, some Account of the Lives and Dying SPEECHES of a considerable Number of the Christianized INDIANS of Martha's Vineyard, in New-England,* by Experience Mayhew (London, 1727), xvii.

37. Samuel Hopkins, *Historical Memoirs, Relating to the Housatunnuk Indians: Or, An Account of the Methods used, and Pains taken, for the Propagation of the Gospel among that heathenish-Tribe, and the Success thereof, under the Ministry of the late Reverend Mr. John Sergeant: Together, with the Character of that eminently worthy Missionary; and an Address to the People of this Country representing the very great Importance of attaching the Indians to their Interest, not only be treating them justly and kindly, but by using proper Endeavours to settle Christianity among them* (Boston, 1753), 51.

38. E. Mayhew, *Indian Converts,* 180.

39. John Locke, *An Essay Concerning the True Original, Extent and End of Civil Government,* in *Two Treatises of Government,* intro. W. S. Carpenter (London: Everyman, 1986), V, #40–42.

40. Stephen Marshall et al., "A Letter to the Christian Reader," in *The Clear Sun-shine of the Gospel Breaking Forth upon the Indians in New-England,* ed. Thomas Shepard (London, 1648), n.p.

41. Charles Gibson, *The Black Legend: Anti-Spanish Attitudes in the Old World and the New* (New York: Knopf, 1971).

42. On the use of Las Casas for English propaganda, see Scanlon, *Colonial Writing,* 19–28.

43. Bartolomé de Las Casas, *The Tears of the Indians: BEING an Historical and true Account Of the Cruel Massacres and Slaughters of above Twenty Millions of innocent People; Committed by the Spaniards In the Islands of Hispaniola, Cuba, Jamaica, &c. As also, in the Continent of Mexico, Peru, & Other Places of the West-Indies, to the total destruction of those Countries,* trans. J. Phillips (London, 1656), 20.

44. Phillips, preface to *Tears of the Indians,* n.p.

45. Humphries, *Historical Account,* 279.

46. John Dryden, *The Indian Emperour* (Menston: Scholar Press, 1971), V, 2.

47. Thomas Shepard, *The Day-Breaking, if not the Sun-Rising of the Gospell With the Indians in New-England* (London, 1647), 15.

48. Ibid., 16.

49. Ibid., 15.

50. Whitfield, *Light Appearing,* 18.

51. John Eliot to Sir Robert Boyle, April 22, 1684, Misc. Letters and Documents, Royal Society of London, 1684–1788. Microfilm in History of Science Collection, American Philosophical Society, Philadelphia.

52. Elkanah Settle, *A Pindaric Poem on the Propagation of the Gospel in Foreign Parts. A Work of Piety so Zealously Recommended and Promoted by her Most Gracious Majesty* (London, 1711), iv.

53. Howard Weinbrot, *Britannia's Issue: The Rise of British Literature from Dryden to Ossian* (New York: Cambridge University Press, 1993), 348.

54. Settle, *Pindaric Poem,* v.

55. Martin Benson, *A Sermon Preached before the Incorporated Society for the Propagation of the Gospel in Foreign Parts; at their Anniversary meeting in the Parish-Church of St. Mary-le-Bow, on Friday, February 15, 1739–40* (London, 1740), 10.

56. Nathaniel Eells to Nathaniel Whitaker, Stonington, January 12, 1767, in Richardson, *Indian Preacher,* 198.

57. The latter claim was, however, present in earlier publications. In *A Good Speed to Virginia,* one of many sermons commissioned by the Virginia Company in 1609 to promote its colony, Robert Gray argued that God would repay the Indians for being conquered by offering them salvation. L. Wright, *Religion and Empire,* 93.

58. J. D., afterword to Winslow, *Glorious Progress.*

59. On the fate of the praying Indians in King Philip's War, see Jill Lepore, *The Name of War: King Philip's War and the Origins of American Identity* (New York: Vintage, 1998), chs. 1, 5; Jenny Hale Pulsipher, "Massacre at Hurtleberry Hill: Christian Indians and English Authority in Metacom's War," *William and Mary Quarterly* 3d ser., 53 (1996): 459–86.

60. There is a large body of scholarship on the philosophical implications of the development of modern finance and public debt, beginning with the work of J. G. A. Pocock. See his *Virtue, Commerce, and History: Essays on Political Thought and History, Chiefly in the Eighteenth Century* (New York: Cambridge University Press, 1985); and *The Machiavellian Moment: Florentine Political Thought and the Atlantic Republican Tradition* (Princeton: Princeton University Press, 1975).

61. O'Connor et al., *Three Centuries,* 5–6.

62. Patrick Gordon, *Geography Anatomized: Or, A Compleat Geographical Grammer . . . with a Reasonable Proposal for the Propagation of the Blessed gospel in all Pagan Countries* (London, 1693), 208.

63. "Proposals for Propagating the Gospel in all Pagan Countreys," by Mr. Patrick Gourdon [*sic*]. Item 7, Appendix A, USPG Journal. See reference to "Proposals," January 16, 1701, vol. 1, Journal A, USPG Papers.

64. O'Connor et al., *Three Centuries,* 5–6.

65. Gilbert Burnet, *Of the Propagation of the Gospel in Foreign Parts. A Sermon Preach'd at St. Mary-le-Bow, Feb. 18. 1703/4. Before the Society Incorporated for that purpose. Exhorting all Persons in their Stations, to assist so Glorious a Design* (London, 1704), 22.

66. George Stanhope, *The early Conversion of Islanders, a wise Expedient for Propagating Christianity. A Sermon Preached before the Incorporated Society for the Propagation of the Gospel in Foreign Parts; at their Anniversary Meeting in the Parish-Church of St. Mary-le-Bow; on Friday, the 19th of February, 1713/14* (London, 1714), 23.

67. Edward Chandler, *A Sermon Preached before the Incorporated Society for the Propagation of the Gospel in Foreign Parts; At Their Anniversary Meeting in the Parish-Church of St. Mary-le-Bow; On Friday the 20th of February, 1718* (London, 1719), 25.

68. William Dawes, *A Sermon Preach'd before the Society for the Propagation*

of the Gospel in Foreign Parts, At the Parish-Church of St. Mary-le-Bow, on Friday February 18. 1708/9 (London, 1709), 22.

69. Benson, *SPG Sermon*, 12.

70. John Waugh, *A Sermon Preached before the Incorporated Society for the Propagation of the Gospel in Foreign Parts; at their Anniversary Meeting in the Parish-Church of St. Mary-le-Bow; On Friday the 15th of February, 1722* (London, 1723), 30–31.

71. Philip Bisse, *A Sermon Preach'd before the Incorporated Society for the Propagation of the Gospel in Foreign Parts; At their Anniversary Meeting in the Parish Church of St. Mary-le-Bow, On Friday the 21st of February, 1717* (London, 1718), 4.

72. Eleazar Wheelock, *A Plain and Faithful Narrative of the Original Design, Rise, Progress, and Present State of the Indian Charity-School at Lebanon, in Connecticut* (Boston, 1763), 11.

73. Eleazar Wheelock, *A Continuation of the Narrative of the Indian Charity-School, in Lebanon, in Connecticut, From the Year 1768, to the Incorporation of it with Dartmouth-College, And Removal and Settlement of it in Hanover, in the Province of New-Hampshire, 1771* (Hartford, 1771), 17–18.

74. On the weakening of transatlantic ties, see generally Fred Anderson, *Crucible of War: The Seven Years' War and the Fate of Empire in British North America, 1754–1766* (New York: Vintage, 2000); David Armitage, *The Ideological Origins of the British Empire* (New York: Cambridge University Press, 2000).

75. William Warburton, *A Sermon Preached before the Incorporated Society for the Propagation of the Gospel in Foreign Parts; at their Anniversary Meeting in the Parish Church of St. Mary-le-Bow, on Friday, February 21st, 1766* (London, 1766), 16.

76. George Herbert, "The Church Militant," in *The Works of George Herbert*, ed. F. E. Hutchinson (Oxford: Clarendon Press, 1941), 190–98, ll. 247–54.

77. David S. Shields, "Then Shall Religion to America Flee," in *Like Season'd Timber: New Essays on George Herbert*, ed. Edmund Miller and Robert DiYanni (New York: Peter Lang, 1987), 282.

78. Daniel Gookin, *Historical Collections of the Indians in New England* (wr. 1674; Boston, 1792), 20.

79. Randall, *SSPCK Sermon*, 109.

80. On Dryden's adaptation of Isaiah 60, see Michael McKeon, *Politics and Poetry in Restoration England: The Case of Dryden's "Annus Mirabilis"* (Cambridge, Mass.: Harvard University Press, 1975), 152–90; Steven N. Zwicker, *Dryden's Political Poetry: The Typology of King and Nation* (Providence: Brown University Press, 1972), 82–83.

81. Christopher Smart, "On the Goodness of the Supreme Being," in *Christopher Smart: Religious Poetry*, ed. Marcus Walsh (New York: Carcanet Press, 1988), 28, ll. 106–15.

82. Laura Brown, *Ends of Empire: Women and Ideology in Early Eighteenth-Century English Literature* (Ithaca: Cornell University Press, 1993), 45; Laura Brown, *Alexander Pope* (New York: Basil Blackwell, 1985), 11; Louis Landa, "Pope's Belinda, the General Emporie of the World, and the Wondrous Worm," in *Essays in Eighteenth-Century English Literature* (Princeton: Princeton University Press, 1980), 178–98.

83. Bond, *Queen Anne's American Kings*, 11–12.

84. In 1711 the SPG's secretary, John Chamberlayne, referred to the Iroquois' request in an address to Queen Anne, requesting that she authorize a citywide parish collection so the society could establish a mission in Albany. Tenison Papers, f. 100, Lambeth Palace Library, London; SPG Journals A, April 28, 1710; Several Indians to Archbishop Tenison and the SPG, Boston, July 21, 1710, Tenison Papers, f. 711, num. 17, p. 198, Lambeth Palace Library, London; Hinderaker, "'Four Indian Kings,'" 492; Richter, *Ordeal of the Longhouse*, 227.

85. *Dawks's News Letter*, April 29, 1710, quoted in Bond, *Queen Anne's American Kings*, 7, and Hinderaker, "'Four Indian Kings,'" 497.

86. Gideon Hawley to Dr. Thacher, January 1794, Letters of Gideon Hawley, Gideon Hawley Papers, Massachusetts Historical Society, Boston.

87. Thomas Jefferson, Address to Congress, January 18, 1803, in *Documents of United States Indian Policy*, ed. Francis Paul Prucha, 3d ed. (Lincoln: University of Nebraska Press, 2000), 21–22.

88. Thomas Jefferson to William Henry Harrison, February 27, 1803, *Documents*, ed. Prucha, 22.

89. Greenblatt, *Marvelous Possessions*, 71.

Chapter 2

1. Walne, "Collections for Henrico."

2. "Accounts" of the society were published in 1704, 1705, and 1706. A *Collection* of these accounts along with other documents also was published in 1706. The titles of the letters were *A Letter from a Member of the Society for Propagating the Gospel in Foreign Parts, to an Inhabitant of the City of London; Giving an Account of the Late Address from the Said Society to the Queen, for Causing their Designs to be Recommended to the Citizens of London, by the Ministers of London and Westminster, and Burrough of Southwark, in their Sermons on Trinity Sunday Next, &c.* (London, 1708); *A Second Letter from a Member of the Society for Propagation of the Gospel in Foreign Parts, to his Friend in London* (London, 1714); *A Third Letter from a Member of the Society for Propagation of the Gospel in Foreign Parts, to his Friend in London; On Occasion of his Majesty's Gracious Letters Newly Granted to the Said Society* (London, 1718). Some of these letters were not published independently but were attached to the anniversary sermons for that year or informally distributed to supporters.

3. James G. Watson, *William Faulkner: Letters and Fictions* (Austin: University of Texas Press, 1987), 10.

4. Julia A. Stern, *The Plight of Feeling: Sympathy and Dissent in the Early American Novel* (Chicago: University of Chicago Press, 1997), 16–17.

5. Elizabeth Heckendorn Cook, *Epistolary Bodies: Gender and Genre in the Eighteenth-Century Republic of Letters* (Stanford: Stanford University Press, 1996), 7.

6. Cook, *Epistolary Bodies*, 6.

7. John Eliot to Jonathan Hanmer, Roxbury, July 19, 1652, in *John Eliot and the Indians, 1652–1657. Being Letters Addressed to Rev. Jonathan Hanmer of Barnstaple, England. Reproduced from the Original Manuscripts in the possession of Theodore N. Vail*, ed. Wilberforce Eames (New York, 1915), 11.

8. Eliot to Hanmer, October 7, 1652, in Wilberforce, *John Eliot and the Indians*, 6.

9. John Eliot to the Corporation, Roxbury, October 8, 1652. No. 6, Ms. 07938, Papers Relating to the Proceedings of the Company, 1649–56, New England Company Collection, Guildhall Library, London.

10. Richard Baxter, *Reliquiae Baxterianae: Or, Mr. Richard Baxter's Narrative of the Most Memorable Passages of his Life and Times* (London, 1696), sec. 148.

11. John Eliot to Richard Baxter, October 16, 1665, Massachusetts, in *Some Unpublished Correspondence of the Reverend Richard Baxter and the Reverend John Eliot, the Apostle of the American Indians, 1656–1682*, ed. F. J. Powicke (Manchester: Manchester University Press, 1931), 19.

12. Baxter to Eliot, January 20, 1657, Worcestershire, in Powicke, *Some Unpublished Correspondence*, 21.

13. Eliot to Baxter, October 7, 1657, in Powicke, *Some Unpublished Correspondence*, 22.

14. Eliot to Baxter, January 22, 1668, in Powicke, *Some Unpublished Correspondence*, 32.

15. George Winship noted that these tracts "were issued . . . to induce people charitably inclined to give money to be sent to New England." *Eliot Indian Tracts*, 9.

16. Kellaway notes that the first of the tracts were published after the General Court of Massachusetts had sent Hugh Peter and William Hibbins to London to placate creditors over late payments and raise funds for the colony. The two agents first tried to gather funds for the transportation of poor children to the colonies. *The New England Company*, 8–9. On the misapplication and theft of these funds, see Cogley, *John Eliot's Mission*, 69, citing Raymond P. Stearns, "The Weld-Peter Mission," *Publications of the Colonial Society of Massachusetts* 32 (1937): 193, 214–16.

17. Bross, "'Epithet of Praying,'" abstract; Kellaway, *The New England Company*, xv.

18. Scanlan, *Colonial Writing*, 155–86.

19. *New Englands First Fruits* (1643), the earliest of the "Indian Tracts," promoted Harvard College and the Massachusetts Bay Colony as much as it did missionary work. In assuming Shepard's authorship of this tract I am following Cogley, *John Eliot's Mission*, who notes that "the evidence in Shepard's favor is extremely strong" (278), citing Thomas Werge, *Thomas Shepard* (Boston: Twayne, 1987).

20. Shepard, *Day-Breaking*, 2.

21. G. J. Barker-Benfield has discussed the eighteenth-century interpretation of weeping as a sign of grace and virtue. *Culture of Sensibility*, 67.

22. Shepard, *Day-Breaking*, 9.

23. Ibid., 14.

24. Scanlan makes a similar point about Indian "self-loathing" in Eliot's *Indian Dialogues*. *Colonial Writing*, 181.

25. Shepard's mix of investigative and emotional language offers an early example of a tendency Ann Jessie Van Sant has noticed in eighteenth-century philanthropic discourses and experimental observation. *Eighteenth-Century Sensibility*, 16–44.

26. Shepard, *Day-Breaking*, 14.

27. Ibid., 18.

28. Ibid., 23.

29. Shepard, *Clear Sun-shine*, 6.

30. Ibid., preface, 35, 36, 37.

31. Ibid., 24, 27–29, 6.

32. Winslow, *Glorious Progress*, 12, 14.

33. Ibid., preface.

34. *Strength out of Weakness; or a Glorious Manifestation of the Further Progresse of the Gospel among the Indians in New-England. Held Forth in Sundry Letters from Divers Ministers and Others to the Corporation Established by Parliament for Promoting the Gospel among the Heathen in New-England* (London, 1652); *Collections of the Massachusetts Historical Society*, 3d ser., 4 (1834): 185, 169.

35. I have borrowed the term *supra-national* from Jonathan Scott, *England's Troubles: Seventeenth-Century English Political Instability in European Context* (Cambridge: Cambridge University Press, 2000).

36. The author of the text often is listed as Caspar Sibellius, whose Latin epistle describing the Dutch missionary work Jessey translated and edited. The full title is *Of the Conversion of Five Thousand and Nine Hundred East-Indians, in the Isle of Formosa, neere China, to the Profession of the True God, in Jesus Christ, By Meanes of M. Ro: Junius, a Minister lately in Delph in Holland. Related by his good Friend, M.C. Sibellius, Pastor in Daventrie there, in a Latine Letter. Translated to further the Faith and Joy of many here, by H. Jessei, a Servant of Jesus Christ. With a Post-Script of the Gospels good succese also amongst the West-Indians, in New-England* (London, 1650).

37. As Richard Cogley notes, Jessey's text gave "free publicity" to the New England Company. *John Eliot's Mission*, 207.

38. On Jessey's life, see B. R. White, "Henry Jessey and the Great Rebellion," in *Reformation, Conformity, and Dissent*, ed. R. B. Knox (London: Epworth Press, 1977), 132–53; *The Dictionary of National Biography*, s.v. "Jessey, Henry"; Edward Whiston, *The Life and Death of Mr. Henry Jessey, late Preacher of the Gospel of Christ in London* (London, 1671).

39. J. F. McGregor, "The Baptists: Fount of All Heresy," in *Radical Religion in the English Revolution*, ed. J. F. McGregor and B. Reay (New York: Oxford University Press, 1984), 38.

40. On Jessey's millenarian views see B. R. White, "Henry Jessey: A Pastor in Politics," *Baptist Quarterly*, 25(1973): 98–110. On millenarianism generally, see Keith Lindley, *Popular Politics and Religion in Civil War London* (Aldershot: Scolar Press, 1997), 292; Jowitt, "Radical Identities," 103; Richard Popkin, "Seventeenth-Century Millenarianism," in *Apocalypse Theory and the Ends of the World*, ed. Malcolm Bull (Cambridge, Mass.: Blackwell, 1995), 112–34; E. Brooks Holifield, *Era of Persuasion: American Thought and Culture, 1521–1680* (Boston: Twayne, 1989), 52–55. Christo-

pher Hill, " 'Till the Conversion of the Jews,' " in *The Collected Essays of Christopher Hill*, vol. 2: *Religion and Politics in 17th Century England* (Amherst: University of Massachusetts Press, 1986), 274. On John Eliot's millenarian theology, see Cogley, *John Eliot's Mission*, esp. ch. 5.

41. Hill, " 'Till the Conversion,' " 275.

42. Jessey, *Of the Conversion*, 13, A2.

43. Ibid., 7–9, 5–6, 5, 10.

44. William Campbell, ed., *Formosa under the Dutch, Described from Contemporary Records* (1903; reprint, Taipei: Ch'eng-Wen Publishing, 1967); C. R. Boxer, *The Dutch Seaborne Empire: 1600–1800* (New York: Knopf, 1965), 133, 132–46.

45. Governor Putmans to Governor-general J. Specx, February 22, 1631, in Campbell, *Formosa*, 102.

46. Warneck, 45; Boxer, *Dutch Seaborne Empire*, 145.

47. Jessey, *Of the Conversion*, A3, A4.

48. Pieter Geyl, *The Netherlands in the Seventeenth Century, Part Two: 1648–1715* (New York: Barnes and Noble, 1964), 12–18; J. L. Price, *Culture and Society in the Dutch Republic during the 17th Century* (New York: Charles Scribner's Sons, 1974), 5–7, 25–27; Jonathan Israel, *The Dutch Republic: Its Rise, Greatness, and Fall 1477–1806* (Oxford: Clarendon Press, 1995), 595–609.

49. Jowitt, "Radical Identities," 101–19.

50. Thorowgood, *Iewes in America*, c4.

51. Philip J. Anderson, "Letters of Henry Jessey and John Tombes to the Churches of New England, 1645," *Baptist Quarterly* 28 (1979): 30.

52. Cogley, *John Eliot's Mission*, 69–70, 207–8. On Peter's reputation, see Louise Breen, "Cotton Mather's *Magnalia Christi Americana* and the Creation of a Usable Massachusetts Past" (paper presented at the annual meeting of the American Society for Eighteenth-Century Studies, Colorado Springs, April 2002), 5.

53. Eliot, *A Late and Further Manifestation of the Progress of the gospel Amongst the Indians in New-England. Declaring their constant Love and Zeal to the Truth: With a readinesse to give Accompt of their Faith and Hope; as of their desires in Church Communion to be Partakers of the Ordinances of Christ*, 3–4.

54. Winslow, *Glorious Progress*, 2.

55. Reynolds, preface to Eliot, *Further Accompt*.

56. There were exceptions to this trend. The radical Puritan clergyman John Oxenbridge combined missionary impulses with antiroyalist sentiment and Puritan ideals after the Restoration, fleeing England and attempting to establish a missionary college in British Surinam. Louise A. Breen, "On Becoming Marginal in the British Atlantic World: The Strange Career of John Oxenbridge" (paper presented at the annual meeting of the Society of Early Americanists, Providence, R.I., April 2003).

57. Matthew Mayhew, *The Conquests and Triumphs of Grace: Being a Brief Narrative of the Success which the Gospel hath had among the INDIANS of Martha's Vineyard (and the Places adjacent) in New-England* (London, 1695), 61. Dellius later was approached by the Church of England's Society for the Propagation of the Gospel in Foreign Parts to continue this work. In its "Account" of 1706 the SPG claimed that it had offered to hire him to preach to the Iroquois but that it could

not meet his demands. *An Account of the Society for Propagating the Gospel in Foreign Parts, Established by the Royal Charter of King William III. With their Proceedings and Success, and Hopes of continual Progress under the Happy Reign of Her most Excellent Majesty Queen Anne* (London, 1706), 41. For the society's correspondence with and discussions of Dellius, see June 18, 1703, p. 111, August 20, p. 114, October 15, p. 122, November 17, 1703, p. 126, February 18, 1703/04, p. 139, June 16, 1704, p. 154, May 30, 1707, p. 293, vol. 1, Journals A.

58. The signers of the opening endorsement were George Griffith, Matthew Mead, John How, Vincent Alsop, Isaac Chauncy, and Nathaniel Miller.

59. John Spurr, "'Latitudinarianism' and the Restoration Church," *Historical Journal* 31 (1988): 61–82.

60. As he petitioned that Queen Mary remove Andros as Governor of the Massachusetts colony in 1689, Abraham Kick emphasized that the people of the colony "have erected a University amongst them, that hath produced very many able Divines, who have been very Instrumental in the Conversion of many, of the Indians, to the Christian Faith, having for the furtherance of that good Work, Translated the Bible into the Indian Tongue," and he enclosed a copy of Increase Mather's *De Successu Evangelij Apud Indos in Nova-Anglia Epistola* (1688). Burt Franklin, ed., *The Andros Tracts. Being a Collection of Pamphlets and Official papers Issued during the Period Between the Overthrow of the Andros Government and the Establishment of the Second Charter of Massachusetts* (Boston: Prince Society, 1869). Thanks to Brendan McConville for suggesting this text.

61. Louise Breen, *Transgressing the Bounds: Subversive Enterprises among the Puritan Elite in Massachusetts, 1630–1692* (Oxford: Oxford University Press, 2001), 13.

62. Breen, "Cotton Mather's *Magnalia*," 7.

63. M. Mayhew, *Conquests and Triumphs,* 38.

64. Nathaniel Mather, preface to N. Mayhew, *Conquests and Triumphs.*

65. Bruce Tucker, "The Reinvention of New England, 1691–1770," *New England Quarterly* 59 (1986): 315–40.

66. Ned Landsman, *From Colonials to Provincials: American Thought and Culture, 1680–1760* (1997; New York: Twayne, 2000), 29, 3. On this shift in New England's identity, see 10–12, 24–29.

Chapter 3

1. Ernst Benz, "Pietist and Puritan Sources of Early Protestant World Missions (Cotton Mather and A. H. Francke)," in *Christianity and Missions, 1450–1800,* ed. J. S. Cummins (Aldershot: Ashgate Variorum, 1997), 315–29; F. W. B. Bullock, *Voluntary Religious Societies, 1520–1799* (St. Leonards on Sea: Budd and Gillatt, 1963), 99.

2. E. Mayhew, *Indian Converts,* xvii. The ministers who signed the preface were Cotton Mather, Benjamin Colman, Peter Thacher, Joseph Sewall, Thomas

Prince, John Webb, William Cooper, Thomas Foxcroft, Samuel Checkley, William Waldron, and Joshua Gee.

3. C. Mather, *India Christiana*, 58.

4. On efforts to increase Protestant unity, see William Gibson, *The Church of England, 1688–1832: Unity and Accord* (London: Routledge, 2001), 182–215. On voluntary societies, see Karl Hertz, "The Nature of Voluntary Associations," in *Voluntary Associations: A Study of Groups in Free Societies. Essays in Honor of James Luther Adams,* ed. D. B. Robertson (Richmond: John Knox Press, 1966), 17–39. Louise Breen has made a similar observation of Cotton Mather's ecumenical approach to Christian mission, linking this impulse to his desire to "enhance his own and the colony's image abroad." "Cotton Mather's *Magnalia*," 2.

5. C. Mather, *Magnalia*, 2:582.

6. David Owen, *English Philanthropy, 1660–1960* (Cambridge, Mass.: Belknap Press, 1964), 3. See also Paul Langford, *A Polite and Commercial People: England, 1727–1783* (Oxford: Clarendon Press, 1989), 125–50.

7. Bullock, *Voluntary Religious Societies,* ix–x, 3, 27, 52. On the influence of German pietism on British missions, see Andrew F. Walls, "The Eighteenth-Century Protestant Missionary Awakening in Its European Context," in *Christian Missions and the Enlightenment,* ed. Brain Stanley (Grand Rapids: Eerdmans, 2001), 22–44.

8. Gibson, *Church of England,* 150; Barker-Benfield, *Culture of Sensibility,* 55–65; Thomas A. Horne, *The Social Thought of Bernard Mandeville: Virtue and Commerce in Eighteenth-Century England* (New York: Columbia University Press, 1978), 1–18; Josiah Woodward, *An Account of the Religious Societies in the City of London, &c. And of Their Endeavours for Reformation of Manners,* 4th ed. (London, 1712).

9. Roger D. Lund, "Guilt by Association: The Atheist Cabal and the Rise of the Public Sphere in Augustan England," *Albion* 34 (2002): 391–421; Peter Clark, *British Clubs and Societies 1580–1800* (Oxford: Clarendon Press, 2000).

10. Margaret C. Jacob, "Money, Equality, Fraternity: Freemasons and the Social Order in Eighteenth Century Europe," in *The Culture of the Market: Historical Essays,* ed. Thomas L. Haskell and Richard F. Teichgraeber III (New York: Cambridge University Press), 129. See also Clark, *British Clubs and Societies.*

11. On eighteenth-century clubs, see Richard D. Brown, *Knowledge Is Power: The Diffusion of Information in Early America, 1700–1865* (New York: Oxford University Press, 1989), 120–23; Jacob, "Money, Equality." On this distinction between earlier and later missionary groups, see Susan Thorne, " 'The Conversion of Englishmen and the Conversion of the World Inseparable': Missionary Imperialism and the Language of Class in Early Industrial Britain," in *Tensions of Empire: Colonial Cultures in a Bourgeois World,* ed. Frederick Cooper and Ann Laura Stoler (Berkeley: University of California Press, 1997), 238–62.

12. W. O. B. Allen and Edmund McClure, *Two Hundred Years: The History of the Society for Promoting Christian Knowledge, 1698–1898* (London, 1898); William Kemp Lowther Clarke, *A History of the SPCK* (London: SPCK, 1959); Craig Rose, "The Origins and Ideals of the SPCK, 1699–1716," *The Church of England c. 1689–c. 1833,* 172–90.

13. The SPG did not have jurisdiction over Virginia, Maryland, or the West Indies, where the need for Anglican ministers was perceived to be less than in colonies with a smaller Anglican presence. Edward L. Bond, *Damned Souls in a Tobacco Colony: Religion in Seventeenth-Century Virginia* (Macon, Ga.: Mercer University Press, 2000); Joan R. Gundersen, *The Anglican Ministry in Virginia, 1723–1766: A Study of a Social Class* (New York: Garland, 1989), 32.

14. On Bray's approach to Indian conversion see McCarthy, "'Reducing,'" 18–65.

15. Brendan McConville, *These Daring Disturbers of the Public Peace: The Struggle for Property and Power in Early New Jersey* (Ithaca: Cornell University Press, 1999), 69.

16. William C. Watson, "Rethinking the Late Stuart Church: The Extent of Liberal Anglicanism, 1688–1715," *Anglican and Episcopal History* 70 (2001): 143–68; Geoffrey Holmes, *The Trial of Doctor Sacheverell* (London: Eyre Methuen, 1973), 21–47.

17. For an overview of these issues, see Gibson, *Church of England*.

18. L. Wright, *Religion and Empire*.

19. Owen, *English Philanthropy*, 3.

20. Thomas Sprat, *The History of the Royal Society* (London, 1667), 53.

21. Steven Shapin, *A Social History of Truth: Civility and Science in Seventeenth-Century England* (Chicago: University of Chicago Press, 1994); Steven Shapin and Simon Schaffer, *Leviathan and the Air-Pump: Hobbes, Boyle, and the Experimental Life* (Princeton: Princeton University Press, 1985); Michael Hunter, *Science and Society in Restoration England* (New York: Cambridge University Press, 1981).

22. Warneck, *Outline*, 41–42. On Jablonski's letter, see May 18, 1711, pp. 46–47, Journals A.

23. Baxter, *Reliquiae Baxterianae*, sec. 148. Kellaway notes that Boyle's "religious convictions and his strong family ties with the Anglican Church did something to obscure the Company's true religious complexion and helped to make it more widely acceptable." *The New England Company*, 48.

24. Busk, *Sketch*, appendix.

25. April 20, 1705, pp. 192–93, August 17, p. 201, September 21, p. 202, October 19, p. 204, November 16, p. 205, December 21, 1705, p. 207, January 18, 1705/6, p. 211, February 1, 1705/6, p. 215, vol. 1, Journals A.

26. Bray, "A Memorial Prepar'd to be sent to the Clergy of Maryland . . . ," F. 33, Christian Faith Society, Letters and Papers, Lambeth Palace Library, London. Kellaway notes that the proceeds from an estate purchased with Boyle's bequest were sent to Harvard as well as William and Mary. *The New England Company*, 173–74. H. P. Thompson also suggested that the Governors of the Charity for the Reliefe of the poore Widdowes and Children of Clergymen, founded in 1678, provided a model for the SPG. *Into All Lands*, 18–19.

27. Hunter, *Brief History*; Edwin Welch, *Popish and Infidel Parts of the World: Dr. Daniel Williams & the Scottish SPCK* (London: Dr. Williams's Trust, 1996).

28. Mills, "Society in Scotland."

29. Robert Kent Donovan, "The Popular Party of the Church of Scotland and the American Revolution," in *Scotland and America in the Age of Enlightenment*, ed.

Richard B. Sher and Jeffrey R. Smitten (Edinburgh: Edinburgh University Press, 1990), 81–85.

30. Kellaway, *The New England Company*, 187; Hunter, *Brief History*, 22–27.

31. Mills," Society in Scotland," 15–30; Hunter, *A Brief History*, 52–77.

32. June 27, 1701, pp. 1–3; July 8, 1701, pp. 4–7; July 10, 1701, pp. 8–9, vol. 1, Journals A.

33. March 6, 1702, p. 39, Journals A.

34. See, e.g., "Orders Relating to Members," in *A Collection of Papers Printed by Order of the Society for the Propagation of the Gospel in Foreign Parts* (London, 1741), 31.

35. Richard Willis, *A Sermon Preach'd before the Society for the Propagation of the Gospel in Foreign Parts, At Their First Yearly Meeting* (London, 1702), 17.

36. John Moore, *Of the Truth and Excellency of the Gospel. A Sermon Preach'd before the Society for the Propagation of the Gospel in Foreign Parts; At their Anniversary Meeting in the Parish-Church of St. Mary-le-Bow* (London, 1713), 7.

37. Burnet, *SPG Sermon*, 24.

38. Philip Stubs, *An Account of the Propagation of the Gospel in Foreign Parts. What the Society Establish'd in* England *by ROYAL CHARTER hath done since their* Incorporation, *June the 16th 1701* (London, 1704); Philip Stubs, *An Account of the Propagation of the Gospel in Foreign Parts. Continued to the Year of Our Lord 1705. Representing what the Society Established in England by Royal Charter hath Done Since their Incorporation June 16. 1701. in Her Majesty's Plantations, Colonies, and Factories: As Also What they Design to Do upon Further Encouragement from their Own Members and Other well-disposed Christians, either by Annual Subscriptions, Present Benefactions, or Future Legacies* (London, 1705); *An Account of the Society for Propagating the Gospel in Foreign Parts, Established by the Royal Charter of King William III. With their Proceedings and Success, and Hopes of Continual Progress under the Happy Reign of Her Most Excellent Majesty Queen Anne* (London, 1706); David Humphreys, *An Historical Account of the Incorporated Society for the Propagation of the Gospel in Foreign Parts. Containing Their Foundation Proceedings, and the Success of their Missionaries in the British Colonies, to the Year 1728* (London, 1730).

39. Stubs, *SPG Account 1705*.

40. Humphreys, *Historical Account of the Incorporated Society*, 15.

41. Lund, "Guilt."

42. *An Account of the Rise, Constitution and Management, of the Society in Scotland, for Propagating Christian Knowledge* (London, 1714), 6.

43. *An Account of the Society in Scotland for Propagating Christian Knowledge* (Edinburgh, 1741), 20–21.

44. *An Abridgment of the Statutes and Rules of the Society in Scotland for Propagating Christian Knowledge* (Edinburgh, 1732), 3–10.

45. *An Abridgement*, 10–11.

46. *An Abridgement*, 11.

47. Colley, *Britons*, 55–60.

48. See, e.g., Martin Benson's commemoration of Lady Elizabeth Hastings shortly after her death, for her annual gifts to the society. *SPG Sermon*, 26; See also, e.g., the Scottish Society's acknowledgment of a "considerable" gift from "a Widow

Lady of Great Quality, whose Modesty forbids us to Name her here." *SSPCK Account* 1714, 31.

49. List of "Ladies Annual Subscribers," in Anthony Ellis, *A Sermon Preached before the Incorporated Society for the Propagation of the Gospel in Foreign Parts, at their Anniversary Meeting* (London, 1759), 64.

50. Barker-Benfield, *Culture of Sensibility*, 37–103.

51. Settle, *Pindaric Poem*, ii.

52. John F. O'Brien, "The Character of Credit: Defoe's 'Lady Credit,' The Fortunate Mistress, and the Resources of Inconstancy in Early Eighteenth-Century Britain," *English Literary History* 63 (1996): 603–31; Sandra Sherman, *Finance and Fictionality in the Early Eighteenth Century: Accounting for Defoe* (New York: Cambridge University Press, 1996), 40–54. On the gendering of benevolence and its links with latitudinarian thought, see Elizabeth Hedrick, "Gender, Moderation, and Liberalism Reconsidered," in *Gone Critical: Feminism and the Academic Disciplines* (work-in-progress).

53. *The Spectator*, no. 324, in Joseph Addison, Richard Steele, et al., *Selections from "The Tatler" and "The Spectator,"* ed. Robert J. Allen, 2d ed. (Fort Worth: Holt, Rinehart and Winston, 1970), 380–81. See also Barker-Benfield, *Culture of Sensibility*, 45–46.

54. Barker-Benfield, *Culture of Sensibility*, 43.

55. Richard Trevor, *A Sermon Preached before the Incorporated Society for the Propagation of the Gospel in Foreign Parts; at Their Anniversary Meeting* (London, 1750), 17, 18.

56. John Ewer, *A Sermon Preached before the Incorporated Society for the Propagation of the Gospel in Foreign Parts; at Their Anniversary Meeting in the Parish-Church of St. Mary-le-Bow* (London, 1768), 18–19.

57. Willis, *SPG Sermon*, 8, 6.

58. Geoffrey Holmes notes that while High Church clergy were indifferent or even hostile to most of the voluntary societies founded at this time, "only the SPG (1702) had something like broad-based support." *Trial*, 305 n. 38.

59. Gibson, *Church of England*, 80; Holmes, *Trial*, 245, 258.

60. Gibson, *Church of England*, 80; Holmes, *Trial*, 237, 239.

61. John Hough, *Of the Propagation of the Gospel in Foreign Parts. A Sermon Preach'd at St. Mary-le-Bow, Feb. 16. 1704/05. Before the Society Incorporated for that purpose. Exhorting All Persons, in Their Stations, to Assist so Glorious a Design* (London, 1705), 23.

62. Charles Trimnel, *A Sermon Preached before the Society for the Propagation of the Gospel in Foreign Parts. At the Parish-Church of St. Mary-le-Bow* (London, 1710).

63. Philip Bisse, *A Sermon Preach'd before the Incorporated Society for the Propagation of the Gospel in Foreign Parts; At Their Anniversary Meeting in the Parish Church of St. Mary-le-Bow* (London, 1718), 2.

64. Gibson, *Church of England*, esp. 185.

65. Stanhope, *SPG Sermon*, 30.

66. See, e.g., Trimnel, *SPG Sermon*, 22; *Relation de la société etablie pour la Propagation de l'Evangile dans les Pays Etrangers, par les Lettres Pattentes du Roi*

Guillaume III (Rotterdam, 1708); William Fleetwood, *A Sermon Preached before the Society for the Propagation of the Gospel in Foreign Parts, At the Parish Church of St. Mary-le-Bow,* with *A Short Abstract of the Most Material Proceedings and Occurrences in the Society, for the Propagation of the Gospel in Foreign Parts; Between February 1709/10 and February 1710/11* (London, 1711), 37; May 18, 1711, p. 33, vol. 2, Journals A; on Prussia's new society, see May 18, 1711, pp. 46–47, June 6, 1712, p. 197, vol. 2, Journals A. On the Tranquebar mission, see Brijrah Singh, *The First Protestant Missionary to India: Bartholomaeus Ziegenbalg (1683–1719)* (New York: Oxford University Press, 1999), 8, 30, 36–37.

67. *An Abstract of the Proceedings of the Society for the Propagation of the Gospel in Foreign Parts,* in George Ash, *A Sermon Preached before the Incorporated Society for the Propagation of the Gospel in Foreign Parts; At their Anniversary Meeting* (London, 1714), 41.

68. John Gowdie, *The Propagation of the Gospel, and the Blessed Effects thereof: A Sermon preached in the High Church of Edinburgh, Monday, January 6. 1735, upon occasion of the Anniversary Meeting of the Society in Scotland for propagating Christian Knowledge* (Edinburgh, 1735), 13.

69. Ibid., 11.

70. *An Account of the Rise, Constitution and Management, of the Society in Scotland, for Propagating Christian Knowledge. second edition. Enlarged by a Member of the Society* (Edinburgh, 1720), 22.

71. Hunter, *Brief,* 19.

72. Philip Doddridge, ed., *An Abridgment of David Brainerd's Journal among the Indians. Or, the Rise and Progress of a Remarkable Work of Grace among a Number of the Indians. In the Provinces of New-Jersey and Pennsylvania* (London, 1748), iv–v, v, vi.

73. Thomas Newton, *On the imperfect Reception of the Gospel. A Sermon Preached Before the Incorporated Society for the Propagation of the Gospel in Foreign Parts; at their Anniversary meeting in the Parish Church of St. Mary-le-Bow* (London, 1769), 21.

74. Randall, *SSPCK Sermon,* 106–7.

75. Bisse, *SPG Sermon 1718,* 2–3.

76. Arthur Lyon Cross, *The Anglican Episcopate and the American Colonies* (1902; reprint, Hamden, Conn.: Archon Books, 1964); Carl Bridenbaugh, *Mitre and Sceptre: Transatlantic Faiths, Ideas, Personalities, and Politics 1689–1775* (New York: Oxford University Press, 1962); John Frederick Woolverton, *Colonial Anglicanism in North America* (Detroit: Wayne State University Press, 1984); Patricia U. Bonomi, *Under the Cope of Heaven: Religion, Society, and Politics in Colonial America* (New York: Oxford University Press, 1986); Peter M. Doll, *Revolution, Religion, and National Identity: Imperial Anglicanism in British North America, 1745–1795* (Madison, N.J.: Fairleigh Dickinson University Press, 2000).

77. Mills, "Society in Scotland," 17–18.

78. Landsman, *From Colonials,* esp. 129–32.

79. *An Abstract of the Most Material Proceedings and Occurences within the Last Years Endeavours,* in White Kennett, *The Lets and Impediments in Planting and Propagating the Gospel of Christ. A Sermon Preach'd before the Society for the Propa-*

gation of the Gospel in Foreign Parts; At their Anniversary Meeting (London, 1712), 43–44.

80. *Strength out of Weaknesse,* 168.

81. John Brainerd, *A Genuine Letter from Mr. John Brainard [sic], Employed by the Scotch Society for Propagating the Gospel, A Missionary to the Indians in America, and Minister to a Congregation of Indians, at Bethel in East Jersey, To his Friend in England* (London, 1752), 16.

82. Christopher Hill, "Sin and Society," in *The Collected Essays of Christopher Hill* (Amherst: University of Massachusetts Press, 1986), vol. 2, 117–40.

83. Samson Occom, "An Extract of a Sermon, Preached August 10, 1766, at Tucker-Street meeting, by the Rev. Mr. Samson Occom, the Indian," in *Extracts of Several Sermons, Preached Extempore at Different Places of Divine Worship, in the City of Bristol, by the Rev. Mr. Nathaniel Whitaker, Minister of the Gospel at Norwich, in New-England, and the Rev. Mr. Samson Occom, An Indian Minister, Who are Appointed to Solicit Benefactions from the People of this Island, for the Establishing, &c. Of an Indian School in America, as taken down by a Youth* (Bristol, 1766), 7.

84. Winslow, ed. *Glorious Progress of the Gospel,* 98.

85. Shepard, *Day-Breaking,* 18.

86. On the religious origins and shifting meanings of "vicariousness," see Julie Ellison, "A Short History of Liberal Guilt," *Critical Inquiry* 22 (1996): 357.

87. William Beveridge, *A Sermon Preach'd before the Society for the Propagation of the Gospel in Foreign Parts, At the Parish Church of St. Mary le Bow; February 21st, 1706/7* (London, 1707), 1, 21–22, 22–23.

88. Dawes, *SPG Sermon,* 17. This hierarchy of participation imitated an approach taken in an *Account* published in 1705.

89. Dawes, *SPG Sermon,* 18–19, 25.

90. George Ash, *A Sermon Preached before the Incorporated Society for the Propagation of the Gospel in Foreign Parts; At their Anniversary Meeting in the Parish Church of St. Mary-le-Bow* (London, 1715), 14–15.

91. John Leng, *A Sermon Preached before the Incorporated Society for the Propagation of the Gospel in Foreign Parts; At the Parish-Church of St. Mary-le-Bow* (London, 1727), 32.

92. Joseph Sewall and Benjamin Colman, pref. to Joseph Sewall, *CHRIST Victorious over the Powers of Darkness, by the Light of His preached Gospel. A Sermon Preached in Boston,* December 12. 1733. *At the ORDINATION of the Reverend Mr. Stephen Parker, Mr. Ebenezer Hinsdell, and Mr. Joseph Seccombe, Chosen by the Commissioners to the Honourable SOCIETY for Propagating Christian Knowledge, at Ed-* inburgh, *to carry the Gospel to the Aboriginal Natives on the Borders of New England. To which are annexed, A brief Account of the Honourable SOCIETY and of the present Mission, with an Abstract of the Ordination Prayers, and the Charge given by the Reverend Dr. COLMAN. And the Right Hand of Fellowship given by the Reverend Mr. PRINCE* (London, 1733).

93. Ibid., 13, 16–17, 25, 35–36.

94. Ibid., 45.

95. Landsman, *From Colonials,* 129. See also Donovan, "Church of Scotland," 84.

96. Timothy D. Hall, *Contested Boundaries: Itinerancy and the Reshaping of the Colonial American Religious World* (Durham: Duke University Press, 1994), 84. See also Frank Lambert, *Inventing the "Great Awakening"* (Princeton: Princeton University Press, 1999), 164. See also Susan O'Brien, "A Transatlantic Community of Saints: The Great Awakening and the First Evangelical Network, 1735–1755," *American Historical Review* 91 (1986): 811–32.

97. Hall, *Contested Boundaries,* 106, 78.

98. Landsman, *From Colonials,* 124–32.

99. William Carey, *An Enquiry into the Obligation of Christians to use Means for the Conversion of the Heathen,* ed. Ernest A. Payne (1792; London: Kingsgate Press, 1961), 81. On the links between early missionary movements and the later ones launched by Carey, see Walls, "Missionary Awakening," 22–44.

Chapter 4

1. Morgan Godwyn, *The Negro's & Indians Advocate, Suing for Their Admission into the Church* (London, 1680); Vaughan, *Roots of American Racism,* 55–81, 105–27.

2. Hinderaker, "'Four Indian Kings'"; Bond, *Queen Anne's American Kings*; Lydekker, *Faithful Mohawks*; April 21, 1710, p. 474, April 28, pp. 478–82, May 19, pp. 483–85, June 16, p. 487, September 15, pp. 502–3, vol. 1A, Journals A; February 16, 1711, p. 1, March 16, p. 6, March 22, p. 10, vol. 2, Journals A; Klingberg, "Mosquito Indians."

3. Szasz, *Indian Education,* 129–47; S. Charles Bolton, *Southern Anglicanism: The Church of England in Colonial South Carolina* (Westport, Conn.: Greenwood Press, 1982), 102–20; Frank J. Klingberg, ed., *Carolina Chronicle: The Papers of Commissary Gideon Johnston, 1707–1716* (Berkeley: University of California Press, 1946); June 19, 1713, p. 297, October 2, 1713, p. 315, October 30, 1713, p. 333, November 20, 1713, p. 336, December 18, 1713, p. 346, August 20, 1714, p. 395, vol. 2, Journals A; January 21, 1714/15, p. 33, vol. 3, Journals A. Johnston and "Prince George" returned to South Carolina in the midst of the Yamasee war, and discovered that George's father had been enslaved. The SPG's contact with "Prince George" ended with Johnston's death in 1716.

4. On the mission to the Mohawks, see Kirk Swinehart, "Indians in the House: Race, Empire, and Aristocracy in Mohawk Country" (Ph.D. diss., Yale University, 2001); William B. Hart, "For the Good of Our Souls: Mohawk Authority, Accommodation, and Resistance to Protestant Evangelism, 1700–1780" (Ph.D. diss., Brown University, 1998); Richter, *Ordeal of the Longhouse*; Richter, "Some of them," 471–84; Isabel Thompson Kelsay, *Joseph Brant, 1743–1807: Man of Two Worlds* (Syracuse: Syracuse University Press, 1984).

5. On the SPG's efforts to convert slaves, see Gundersen, *Anglican Ministry in Virginia;* Mechal Sobel, *The World they Made Together: Black and White Values in Eighteenth-Century Virginia* (Princeton: Princeton University Press, 1987); John C. Van Horne, ed., *Religious Philanthropy and Colonial Slavery: The American Corre-*

spondence of the Associates of Dr. Bray, 1717–1777 (Urbana: University of Illinois Press, 1985); Bolton, *Southern Anglicanism,* 102–21; Sheldon S. Cohen, "Elias Neau, Instructor to New York's Slaves," *New York Historical Society Quarterly* 55 (1971): 7–27; Denzil T. Clifton, "Anglicanism and Negro Slavery in Colonial America," *Historical Magazine of the Protestant Episcopal Church* 39 (1970): 29–70; Frank J. Klingberg, ed., *The Carolina Chronicle of Dr. Francis le Jau, 1706–1717* (Berkeley: University of California Press, 1956); Klingberg, *Carolina Chronicle: The Papers of Commissary Gideon Johnston.* The SPG also has received some attention in studies of African-American history and abolition movements, such as Peter H. Wood, *Black Majority: Negroes in Colonial South Carolina from 1670 through the Stono Rebellion* (New York: Norton, 1974), 132–42.

6. For a summary of approaches to these missions, see Daniel O'Connor, "Red, Black and White—the Society in Mission," in O'Connor et al., *Three Centuries,* 31–44.

7. Noel Titus, "Concurrence without Compliance: SPG and the Barbadian Plantations, 1710–1834," in O'Connor et al., *Three Centuries,* 249–61; Frank J. Klingberg, *Codrington Chronicle: An Experiment in Anglican Altruism on a Barbados Plantation, 1710–1834* (Berkeley: University of California Press, 1949).

8. Jon Butler, *Becoming America: The Revolution before 1776* (Cambridge, Mass.: Harvard University Press, 2000), 192.

9. Deborah Mathias Gough describes the difficulties that Christ Church in Philadelphia had in retaining a minister, for example. *Christ Church, Philadelphia: The Nation's Church in a Changing City* (Philadelphia: University of Pennsylvania Press, 1995), 29–38. On the exaggerated but not entirely inaccurate reputation of Anglican ministers for poor conduct, see Gundersen, *Anglican Ministry in Virginia,* 119–47; S. Charles Bolton also has discussed the approximately 10 percent of Anglican clergy in South Carolina who had to be removed from their posts. *Southern Anglicanism,* 86–101.

10. See, e.g., Bolton's account of Samuel Thomas in *Southern Anglicanism,* 103–4. See also Szasz, *Indian Education,* 132–33. On the society's recruitment and training of missionaries, see Daniel O'Connor, "Orthodox Clergy, Schoolmasters, Two Creditable White Women and a Surgeon," in O'Connor et al., *Three Centuries,* 23–30.

11. Willis, *SPG Sermon,* 17.

12. George Berkeley, *A Proposal for the Better Supplying of Churches in our Foreign Plantations, and for Converting the Savage Americans to Christianity,* in *The Works of George Berkeley,* ed. Alexander Campbell Fraser (Oxford, 1871), 4:341–64.

13. Edwin S. Gaustad, *George Berkeley in America* (New Haven: Yale University Press, 1979).

14. Thomas Bray, *Missionalia: Or, A Collection of Missionary Pieces Relating to the Conversion of the Heathen; both the African Negroes and American Indians* (London, 1727).

15. [Thomas Wilson], *An Essay Towards an Instruction For the Indians; Explaining the Most Essential Doctrines of Christianity* (London, 1740).

16. See, e.g., Cotton Mather's complaints to Sir William Ashurst about the SPG, Boston, January 30, 1709/10, No. 33, MS. 07936, Artificial collection of original

correspondence relating to affairs in New England, 1657–1714, New England Company Collections, Guildhall Library, London.

17. On Scottish Presbyterian worries about an American episcopate, see Donovan, "Popular Party."

18. J. Brainerd, *A Genuine Letter,* 15.

19. Hopkins, *Historical Memoirs,* 69.

20. Doll, *Revolution, Religion.* On this topic see also Bonomi, *Under the Cope of Heaven;* Woolverton, *Colonial Anglicanism in North America;* Bridenbaugh, *Mitre and Sceptre;* John Wolfe Lydekker, "The American and Colonial Episcopates," *SPG Archives Lectures,* 32–44; Arthur Lyon Cross, *The Anglican Episcopate and the American Colonies* (1902; reprint, Hamden, Conn.: Archon Books, 1964).

21. "A Letter from the Lords Commissioners of Trade & Plantations to the Arch Bishop of Canterbury concerning the Conversion of the Indians," October 25, 1700, Number 5, Appendix A, Journals A; Stubs, *SPG Account 1704.*

22. Landsman, *From Colonials,* 30; George Keith, *A Journal of Travels from New-Hampshire to Caratuck, on the Continent of North-America* (London, 1706). Gough, *Christ Church,* 15–17; Stubs, *SPG Account 1705;* February 27, 1702, pp. 32–33, vol. 1, Journals A.

23. Thomas Secker, *A Sermon Preached before the Incorporated Society for the Propagation of the Gospel in Foreign Parts; at their Anniversary Meeting* (London, 1741). See also Doll, *Revolution, Religion,* 165–67.

24. Jonathan Mayhew, *Observations of the Charter and Conduct of the Society for the Propagation of the Gospel in Foreign Parts; Designed to Shew their Non-Conformity to Each Other* (Boston, 1763). This was a reply to *Considerations on the Institution and Conduct of the Society for the Propagation of the Gospel in Foreign Parts* (Boston, 1763) by East Apthorpe. Apthorpe, an SPG missionary in New England, had interpreted the society's goals as oriented primarily toward English colonists.

25. Kellaway, *New England Company,* 194–96.

26. J. Mayhew, *Observations of the Charter,* 30–31.

27. Ibid., 109–10.

28. Stanhope, *SPG Sermon,* 25.

29. E.g., Charles Trimnel, the Bishop of Norwich, said, "I do believe none of us pretend to any immediate and extraordinary Call from God to preach the Gospel to any particular Part of the Heathen World." *SPG Sermon,* 11.

30. William Fleetwood, *A Sermon Preached before the Society for the Propagation of the Gospel in Foreign Parts, At the Parish Church of St. Mary-le-Bow, on Friday the 16th of February, 1710/11. Being the Day of their Anniversary Meeting* (London, 1711), 14.

31. Klingberg, *Anglican Humanitarianism,* 22.

32. Gerald R. McDermott, *Jonathan Edwards Confronts the Gods: Christian Theology, Enlightenment Religion, and Non-Christian Faiths* (New York: Oxford University Press, 2000), citing Bruce Marshall, *Christology in Conflict: The Identity of a Saviour in Rahner and Barth* (New York: Basil Blackwell, 1987).

33. W. M. Spellman, *The Latitudinarians and the Church of England, 1660–1700* (Athens: University of Georgia Press, 1993); John Walsh, Colin Haydon, and

Stephen Taylor, eds. *The Church of England c. 1689–c. 1833: From Toleration to Tractarianism* (New York: Cambridge University Press, 1993); J. A. I. Champion, *The Pillars of Priestcraft Shaken: The Church of England and its Enemies, 1660–1730* (New York: Cambridge University Press, 1992); Henry R. McAdoo, *The Spirit of Anglicanism: a Survey of Anglican Theological Method in the Seventeenth Century* (New York: Scribner, 1965); See Stephen Neill, *Anglicanism* (1958; New York: Oxford University Press, 1977).

34. Gerard Reedy, *The Bible and Reason: Anglicans and Scripture in Late Seventeenth-Century England* (Philadelphia: University of Pennsylvania Press, 1985).

35. James H. Averill, *Wordsworth and the Poetry of Human Suffering* (Ithaca: Cornell University Press, 1980), 13. See also Fiering, "Irresistible Compassion," 212–13; Laura Hinton, *The Perverse Gaze of Sympathy: Sadomasochistic Sentiments from Clarissa to Rescue 911* (Albany: State University of New York Press, 1999).

36. Waugh, *SPG Sermon*, 33.

37. Henry Egerton, *A Sermon Preached before the Incorporated Society for the Propagation of the Gospel in Foreign Parts; at their Anniversary Meeting in the Parish-Church of St Mary-le-Bow* (London, 1729), 11.

38. John Spurr, "The Church, the Societies and the Moral Revolution of 1688," in *The Church of England, c. 1689–c. 1833*, 127–42; Bullock, *Voluntary*; William Kemp Lowther Clarke, *Eighteenth Century Piety* (New York: Macmillan, 1944).

39. Thomas Bray began *A Short Account of the Several Kinds of Societies, Set up of Late Years, for Carrying on the Reformation of Manners, and for the Propagation of Christian Knowledge* (London, 1700) by citing "the infamous Clubbs of Atheists, Deists, and Socinians, who . . . have endeavour'd to destroy in themselves, and others, all Notions of Divine Things" (1). Craig Rose also has shown that concerns about Deism motivated Bray to found the SPCK. "Origins and Ideals of the SPCK," 178.

40. McDermott, *Jonathan Edwards*, 17–33; James Herrick, *The Radical Rhetoric of the English Deists: The Discourse of Skepticism, 1680–1750* (Columbia: University of South Carolina Press, 1997); J. A. Leo Lemay, ed., *Deism, Masonry, and the Enlightenment: Essays Honoring Alfred Owen Aldridge* (Newark: University of Delaware Press,1987); Robert E. Sullivan, *John Toland and the Deist Controversy: A Study in Adaptions* (Cambridge, Mass.: Harvard University Press, 1982); John Redwood, *Reason, Ridicule, and Religion: The Age of Enlightenment in England, 1660–1750* (Cambridge, Mass.: Harvard University Press, 1976); Peter Gay, ed., *Deism: An Anthology* (Princeton: D. Van Nostrand, 1968); E. Graham Waring, ed., *Deism and Natural Religion: A Source Book* (New York: Frederick Ungar Publishing, 1967); A. Owen Aldridge, *Shaftesbury and the Deist Manifesto* (Philadelphia: American Philosophical Society, 1951); Leslie Stephen, *History of English Thought in the Eighteenth Century* (London, 1876), 1:62–211.

41. Matthew Tindal, *Christianity as Old as the Creation: Or, the Gospel, a Republication of the Religion of Nature* (London, 1731), 119.

42. Roger Lund, ed., *The Margins of Orthodoxy: Heterodox Writing and Cultural Response, 1660–1750* (New York: Cambridge University Press, 1995).

43. Bolton, *Southern Anglicanism*, 105.

44. For a summary of the varieties of Deism, see *The Catholic Encyclopedia,* 1ˢᵗ ed., s.v. "Deism."

45. Stephen, *History of English Thought,* 1:70.

46. Ibid., 1:161–62.

47. Herrick, *Radical Rhetoric,* 53–54.

48. Kerry S. Walters, *Rational Infidels: The American Deists* (Durango, Colo.: Longwood Academic, 1992); C. J. Betts, *Early Deism in France: from the So-Called 'Deistes' of Lyon (1564) to Voltaire's Lettres philosophiques (1734)* (Boston: M. Nijhoff, 1984); Alfred Owen Aldridge, *Benjamin Franklin and Nature's God* (Durham, NC: Duke University Press, 1967); Herbert Montfort Morais, *Deism in Eighteenth Century America* (New York: Russell and Russell, 1960).

49. Gibson, *Church of England,* 92–93; Gay, *Deism,* 140; cf. Herrick, *Radical Rhetoric,* 21, 125–44.

50. Thomas Sherlock, *A Sermon Preached before the Incorporated Society for the Propagation of the Gospel in Foreign Parts; At Their Anniversary Meeting in the Parish Church of St. Mary-le-Bow* (London, 1716). Sherlock published *The Use and Intent of Prophecy, in the Several Ages of the World* (London, 1724) against Collins and *The Trial of the Witnesses to the Resurrection of Jesus* (London, 1729) against Woolston. Henry Stebbing replied to Woolston with *A Discourse on our Saviour's Miraculous Power of Healing* (London, 1730) and delivered the society's sermon of 1742. George Berkeley, who delivered the sermon of 1732, published A*lciphron, Or, the Minute Philosopher* (London, 1732), a dialogue against Deism and other heterodox thought. Many other SPG sermons, like John Moore's of 1713, placed the Deist controversy in a global arena: "So that while you are setting up the Gospel abroad, . . . these ill Men, Sinners against their own Souls, are trying to subvert it at Home." *Of the Truth and Excellency of the Gospel. A Sermon Preach'd before the Society for the Propagation of the Gospel in Foreign Parts; At their Anniversary Meeting in the Parish-Church of St. Mary-le-Bow, on Friday the 20th of February, 1712/11* [sic] (London, 1713), 10.

51. Roger L. Emerson, "Latitudinarianism and the English Deists," in Lemay, *Deism, Masonry,* 19–48. See generally Reedy, *Bible and Reason.*

52. See, e.g., J. A. Leo Lemay, "The Amerindian in the Early American Enlightenment: Deistic Satire in Robert Beverly's *History of Virginia* (1705)," in Lemay, *Deism, Masonry,* 79–92.

53. Robert F. Berkhofer, Jr., *The White Man's Indian* (New York: Knopf, 1978), 72–75.

54. John Toland, "An Account of the Indians at Carolina," *A Collection of Several Pieces of Mr. John Toland* (London, 1726), 2:425. See Lemay, "Amerindian," 79.

55. Abbé Pestré, "Philosophy of the Canadians," *Encyclopedia: Selections,* ed. Denis Diderot et al., trans. Nelly S. Hoyt and Thomas Cassirer (Indianapolis: Bobbs-Merrill, 1965), 26–27.

56. Benjamin Franklin, "Remarks Concerning the Savages of North-America," in *Benjamin Franklin: Writings,* ed. J. A. Leo Lemay (New York: Library of America, 1987), 969–74.

57. McDermott, *Jonathan Edwards,* citing Marshall, *Christology in Conflict.* Although McDermott uses the term "scandal of particularity" to discuss the problem of peoples excluded from knowledge of the gospel, this term usually applies not to the object of salvation but rather to the particular, and thus scandalous, instrument of it, i.e., Christ. Thanks to Kerry Walters for this clarification.

58. Shepard, *Day-Breaking,* 18–19.

59. Winslow, *Glorious Progress,* 9.

60. Phillip Harth, *Contexts of Dryden's Thought* (Chicago: University of Chicago Press, 1968), 149.

61. See J. B. Schneewind, *The Invention of Autonomy: A History of Modern Moral Philosophy* (New York: Cambridge University Press, 1998) 17–19, on the role of Paul's formulation in natural law theory.

62. Dante Alighieri, *The Divine Comedy,* trans. Charles S. Singleton (Princeton: Princeton University Press, 1970), vol. 1, canto 4, ll. 25–42.

63. Harth, *Contexts;* McDermott, *Jonathan Edwards.*

64. Shepard, *Day-Breaking,* 10.

65. C. Mather, *Magnalia,* 2:556.

66. Schneewind, *Invention of Autonomy;* Evan Radcliffe, "Revolutionary Writing, Moral Philosophy, and Universal Benevolence in the Eighteenth Century," *Journal of the History of Ideas* 54 (1993), 221–40; Barker-Benfield, *Culture of Sensibility,* 65–77.

67. Fiering, "Irresistible Compassion," 215–16.

68. Judith Shklar, *Ordinary Vices* (Cambridge, Mass.: Belknap, 1984).

69. Ava Chamberlain, "The Theology of Cruelty: A New Look at the Rise of Arminianism in Eighteenth-Century New England," *Harvard Theological Review* 85 (1992): 335–56.

70. On the eighteenth-century permutations of this debate, see Isabel Rivers, *Reason, Grace, and Sentiment: A Study of the Language of Religion and Ethics in England, 1688–1780* (Cambridge: Cambridge University Press, 1991).

71. John Matthisen, *The Necessity of divine Revelation, and Knowledge thereof, in order to Salvation. A Sermon Preached in the High Church of Edinburgh, Munday* [sic] *5 January 1730. Upon Occasion of the anniversary Meeting of the Society in Scotland for Propagating Christian Knowledge* (Edinburgh, 1730), 4–6.

72. David Plenderleath, *Religion a Treasure to Men, and the Strength and Glory of a Nation. A Sermon Preached in the High-Church of Edinburgh, January 7. 1754. Before the Society in Scotland for propagating Christian Knowledge* (Edinburgh, 1754), 32.

73. Robert Wallace, *Ignorance and Superstition a Source of Violence and Cruelty, and in Particular the Cause of the Present Rebellion. A Sermon Preached in the High Church of Edinburgh, Monday January 6, 1745–46. Upon Occasion of the Anniversary Meeting of the Society in Scotland for Propagating Christian Knowledge* (Edinburgh, 1746).

74. William Robertson, *The Situation of the World at the Time of Christ's Appearance, and its Connection with the Success of his Religion, Considered; A Sermon, Preached before the Society in Scotland for Propagating Christian Knowledge, January 6, 1755* (Edinburgh, 1755), 4.

75. Thomas Fuller, *The Just Mans Funeral. Lately Delivered in a Sermon at Chelsey, before Several Persons of Honour and Worship* (London, 1649), 24–25.

76. Richard Reynolds, *A Sermon Preached before the Incorporated Society for the Propagation of the Gospel in Foreign Parts; At Their Anniversary Meeting in the Parish-Church of St. Mary-le-Bow, On Friday, the 16th of February, 1727* (London, 1728), 19.

77. Thomas Hahn, introduction to *Upright Lives: Documents Concerning the Natural Virtue and Wisdom of the Indians, 1650–1740* (Los Angeles: William Andrews Clark Memorial Library, 1981), iv.

78. George Fox, *The Journal*, ed. Nigel Smith (London: Penguin, 1998), 470.

79. Anthony Benezet, *Collection of Religious Tracts* (Philadelphia, 1773), vi.

80. Benezet, *Collection*, ix.

81. Charles Blount, *The Oracles of Reason* (London, 1693), 196.

82. Tindal, *Christianity as Old*, 360.

83. Ibid., 360.

84. Fiering, "Irresistible Compassion," 196.

85. Burnet, *Of the Propagation of the Gospel*, 11–12.

86. John Dryden, *Religio Laici*, in *The Works of John Dryden*, ed. H. T. Swedenberg et al., vol. 2, *Poems, 1681–1684*, ed. H. T. Swedenberg (Berkeley: University of California Press, 1972), 114, ll. 168–79. Dryden also discussed this problem in the poem's preface, 99–101.

87. Dryden, *Religio Laici*, l. 185.

88. Dryden, *Religio Laici*, l. 189. Harth, *Contexts of Dryden's Thought*, 60–61, 147–73; Sanford Budick, *Dryden and the Abyss of Light: A Study of "Religio Laici" and "The Hind and the Panther"* (New Haven: Yale University Press, 1970), 97–115.

89. Daniel Defoe, "An Essay on the Present State of Religion in the World," in *The Serious Reflections of Robinson Crusoe*, vol. 3 of *Romances and Narratives by Daniel Defoe*, ed. George Aitken (New York: AMS Press, 1895), 111. On Defoe's views on Deism, see Maximillian E. Novak, "Defoe, the Occult, and the Deist Offensive during the Reign of George I," in Lemay, *Deism, Masonry*, 93–108.

90. Shepard, *Day-Breaking*, 9–10.

91. Barker-Benfield, *Culture of Sensibility*, 37–103; Lawrence E. Klein, *Shaftesbury and the Culture of Politeness* (New York: Cambridge University Press, 1994); Bullock, *Voluntary*.

92. Klein, *Shaftesbury*. On the uncertain political alignment of sentimental and gentlemanly rhetoric, see Ellison, *Cato's Tears*, 23–47.

93. See generally R. S. Crane, "Suggestions Toward a Genealogy of the 'Man of Feeling,'" *English Literary History* 1 (1934): 205–30; Barker-Benfield, *Culture of Sensibility*; Ellison, *Cato's Tears*.

94. Frank Klingberg did note the apologetic function of the sermons in *Anglican Humanitarianism*, 11–48.

95. Richard Smallbroke, *Reflections on Mr. Whiston's Conduct* (London, 1711); *Dictionary of National Biography*, s.v., "Moore, Jonathan," "Smallbroke, Richard."

96. *Dictionary of National Biography*, s.v. "Waddington, Edward"; Lund, "Guilt," 3–6.

97. Moore, *SPG Sermon*, 16.

98. Hough, *SPG Sermon*, 8, 11.

99. William Stanley, *A Sermon Preach'd Before the Society for the Propagation of the Gospel in Foreign Parts, At the Parish Church of St. Mary le Bow, February 20th, 1707/8* (London, 1708), 10.

100. Moore, *SPG Sermon 1713*, 34.

101. Nicholas Clagget, *A Sermon Preached before the Incorporated Society for the Propagation of the Gospel in Foreign Parts; At Their Anniversary Meeting in the Parish-Church of St. Mary-le-Bow* (London, 1737), 22.

102. Smith, *Theory of Moral Sentiments*, 235–37.

103. John Williams, *A Sermon Preached before the Society for the Propagation of the Gospel in Foreign Parts. At the Parish Church of St. Lawrence Jewry, February 15, 1705/6* (London, 1706), 16–17.

104. Klingberg, *Anglican Humanitarianism*, 15.

105. Williams, *SPG Sermon*, 16.

106. Ibid., 18.

107. Ibid., 18, citing Rom. 1:20 and Eph. 2:12.

108. Zachary Pearce, *A Sermon Preached before the Incorporated Society for the Propagation of the Gospel in Foreign Parts; At the Parish Church of Mary-le-Bow, On Friday the 20th of February, 1729, being the day of their Anniversary Meeting* (London, 1730), 11–12.

109. John Denne, *Want of Universality no Just Objection to the Truth of the Christian Religion. A Sermon Preached before the Incorporated Society for the Propagation of the Gospel in Foreign Parts; At their Anniversary Meeting in the Parish-Church of St* [sic] *Mary-le-Bow, on Friday the 19th of February, 1730* (London, 1730), 13.

110. Benson, *SPG Sermon*, 14–15.

111. Jonathan Edwards, *Works*, vol. 3, 151–52, cited in Norman Pettit, introduction to *The Life of David Brainerd*, by Jonathan Edwards, ed. Norman Pettit, vol. 7 of *The Works of Jonathan Edwards* (New Haven: Yale University Press, 1985), 11.

112. Thomas Aquinas, *Summa Contra Gentiles*, book 4, trans. C. J. O'Neil (Garden City, N.Y.: Hanover House, 1975).

113. Secker, *SPG Sermon*, 8–9.

114. Isaac Maddox, *A Sermon Preached before the Incorporated Society for the Propagation of the Gospel in Foreign Parts; at their Anniversary Meeting in the Parish-Church of St. Mary-le-Bow, On Friday, February 15.* [sic] *1733* (London, 1734), 11.

115. Moore, *SPG Sermon*, 17.

116. Maddox, *SPG Sermon*, 11.

117. Ibid., 30.

118. Denne, *SPG Sermon*, 23.

119. Thomas Herring, *A Sermon Preached before the Incorporated Society for the Propagation of the Gospel in Foreign Parts; at their Anniversary Meeting in the Parish-Church of St. Mary-le-Bow, on Friday, February 17, 1737–38* (London, 1738), 22–23.

120. Quoted in Barker-Benfield, *Culture of Sensibility*, 109.

121. Fiering, "Irresistible Compassion," 212–13.

122. Stephen Cox, "Sensibility as Argument," in *Sensibility in Transformation:*

Creative Resistance to Sentiment from the Augustans to the Romantics: Essays in Honors of Jean H. Hagstrum (Cranbury, N.J.: Associated University Press, 1990), 64, 78.

123. Bernard Mandeville, "An Essay on Charity, and Charity Schools," in *The Fable of the Bees,* ed. Phillip Harth (1723; New York: Penguin, 1970), 263. On Mandeville's critique of charity, see Thomas Horne, *The Social Thought of Bernard Mandeville: Virtue and Commerce in Early Eighteenth-Century England* (New York: Columbia University Press, 1978), 67.

124. Mandeville, "Essay on Charity," 264.

125. Fleetwood, *SPG Sermon,* 17.

126. Clagget, *SPG Sermon,* 36.

127. Joseph Butler, *A Sermon Preached before the Incorporated Society for the Propagation of the Gospel in Foreign Parts; at their Anniversary Meeting in the Parish Church of St. Mary-le-Bow, on Friday, February 16, 1738–39* (London, 1739), 13.

128. Joseph Butler, *The Analogy of Religion, Natural and Revealed, to the Constitution and the Course of Nature* (London, 1736).

129. Francis Hare, *A Sermon Preached before the Incorporated Society for the Propagation of the Gospel in Foreign Parts; At their Anniversary Meeting in the Parish-Church of St. Mary-le-Bow; On Friday the 21st of February, 1734* (London, 1735), 31–32.

130. Ibid., 26.

131. Secker, *SPG Sermon,* 10.

132. Trimnel, *SPG Sermon,* 12.

133. Emerson, "Latitudinarianism," 40.

134. "[T]he *first* and *principal* End of this Corporation is, not to plant Christianity among the Heathens, but, to restore, or to preserve it among Christians. . . . The converting Heathens is a *secondary, incidental* Point." Henry Stebbing, *A Sermon Preached before the Incorporated Society for the Propagation of the Gospel in Foreign Parts; at their Anniversary Meeting in the Parish-Church of St. Mary-le-Bow, on Friday, February 19, 1741–42* (London, 1742), 18.

135. See Van Sant, *Eighteenth-Century Sensibility,* for a useful discussion of curiosity and pity as parallel responses to the sight of suffering.

136. Chester Chapin, "Shaftesbury and the Man of Feeling," *Modern Philology* 81 (1983): 47–50; Elizabeth Duthie, "The Genuine Man of Feeling," *Modern Philology* 78 (1981): 279–85; Donald Greene, "Latitudinarianism and Sensibility: The Genealogy of the "'Man of Feeling.'" *Modern Philology* 75 (1977): 159–83; Crane; Marjorie Nicolson, "Christ's College and the Latitude-Men." *Modern Philology* 27 (1929): 35–53.

Chapter 5

1. See generally Patricia Meyer Spacks, *Imagining a Self: Autobiography and Novel in Eighteenth-Century England* (Cambridge, Mass.: Harvard University Press, 1976).

2. Dryden, *Life of St. Francis Xavier.*

3. On Mather's attempts to present an appealing New England to England, see Breen, "Cotton Mather's *Magnalia.*"

4. J. Paul Hunter notes, "To some extent English Protestantism had always licensed the publication of lives, although it had no hagiographic tradition to match the saints' lives that Roman Catholicism had fostered." *Before Novels: The Culture of Eighteenth-Century English Fiction* (Chicago: University of Chicago Press, 1990), 313–14.

5. David Brainerd's journal was published in two parts during his lifetime. Part 1 was titled *Mirabilia Dei inter Indicos; or the Rise and Progress of a Remarkable Work of Grace, Among a Number of Indians,* and part 2 was titled *Divine Grace Displayed; or the Continuance and Progress of a Remarkable Work of Grace among Some Indians Belonging to the Provinces of New Jersey and Pennsylvania* (Philadelphia, 1746).

6. On the later influence of this text, see A. de M. Chesterman, "The Journals of David Brainerd and William Carey," *Baptist Quarterly* 19 (1961): 147–56; Joseph Conforti, "David Brainerd and the Nineteenth Century Missionary Movement," *Journal of the Early Republic* 5 (1985): 309–29.

7. Joseph Conforti, "Jonathan Edwards's Most Popular Work: 'The Life of David Brainerd' and Nineteenth-Century Evangelical Culture," *Church History* 54 (1985): 188–201.

8. Samuel Hopkins, *Historical Memoirs.*

9. On the origins and different names of the Housatonic Indians, see Szasz, *Indian Education,* 205; Wyss, *Writing Indians,* 83.

10. Samuel Hopkins, *An Abridgment of Mr. Hopkins's Historical Memoirs, Relating to the Housatunnuk, or Stockbridge Indians. Or, a Brief Account of the Methods Used, and Pains Taken, for Civilizing and Propagating the Gospel among the Heathenish Tribe, and the Success thereof, under the Minister of the Late Rev. Mr. John Sergeant* (Philadelphia, 1757).

11. Hunter, *Before Novels,* 343.

12. William Allen, *The American Biographical and Historical Dictionary* (Boston, 1832), s.v. "Hopkins, Samuel"; S. A. Allibone, *A Critical Dictionary of English Literature and British and American Authors* (London, 1859–71), s.v. "Hopkins, Samuel."

13. Szasz, *Indian Education,* 205–17.

14. Samuel Hopkins, *Life of the Rev. Jonathan Edwards, President of Princetown College, New Jersey* (1765; London, 1799).

15. While Brainerd published his journal, John Sergeant authored a letter to be published for fundraising, titled, *A Letter From the Revd Mr. Sergeant of Stockbridge, to Dr. Colman of Boston; Containing Mr. Sergeant's Proposal of a More Effectual Method for the Education of Indian Children* (Boston, 1743).

16. Szasz, *Indian Education,* 191–92.

17. Ian Douglas Maxwell, "Civilization or Christianity? The Scottish Debate on Mission Methods, 1750–1835," in *Christian Missions and the Enlightenment,* ed. Brian Stanley (Grand Rapids: Eerdmans, 2001), 123–40.

18. On the history of this term, see Lambert, *Inventing the "Great Awakening."*

19. On the syncretic reception of revivalist Christianity among indigenous

groups, see Gustafson, *Eloquence*, 75–110; Hall, *Contested Boundaries*, 1–15, 134–35; Simmons and Simmons, introduction to *Old Light on Separate Ways*; William S. Simmons, "The Great Awakening and Indian Conversion in Southern New England," *Papers of the Tenth Algonquian Conference* (1979): 25–36.

20. Frank Lambert has written, "While aiming their message at each person individually, the revivalists sought to convey the gospel to all." *Inventing the "Great Awakening*," 51.

21. Hall, *Contested Boundaries*, 6–7.

22. Bruce M. Metzger and Roland E. Murphy, *The New Oxford Annotated Bible* (New York: Oxford University Press), 279.

23. Paul Harris, "David Brainerd and the Indians: Cultural Interaction and Protestant Missionary Ideology," *American Presbyterian* 72 (1994): 2.

24. Gustafson, *Eloquence*, 83.

25. Brainerd to Eleazar Wheelock, December 30, 1745, Crossweeksung, N.J., in Edwards, *Life of David Brainerd*, 584.

26. Gustafson, *Eloquence*, 81.

27. On Brainerd's performance strategies, see Gustafson, *Eloquence*, 81–90; on Moses Tatamy, see Harris, "David Brainerd and the Indians," 1–9.

28. Richard W. Pointer, "'Poor Indians' and the 'Poor in Spirit': The Indian Impact on David Brainerd," *New England Quarterly* 67 (1994): 418.

29. Sunday, February 3, 1745, Edwards, *Life of Brainerd*, 285.

30. Pointer, "Poor Indians," 415. See also Conforti, "David Brainerd," 321.

31. Edwards, *Life of David Brainerd*, 90–91.

32. Norman Pettit, introduction to Edwards, *Life of David Brainerd*, 1.

33. McCarthy, "'Reducing,'" 95–132.

34. Edwards, *Life of David Brainerd*, 93–94.

35. Joseph A. Conforti, *Samuel Hopkins and the New Divinity Movement: Calvinism, the Congregational Ministry, and Reform in New England between the Great Awakenings* (Grand Rapids: Christian University Press, 1981).

36. September 21, 1745, p. 327, June 14, 1742, p. 170, Edwards, *Life of David Brainerd*.

37. Edwards, *Life of David Brainerd*, 91. On Edwards's editing of Brainerd's diary, see Norman Pettit, "Prelude to Mission: Brainerd's Expulsion from Yale," *New England Quarterly* 59 (1986): 28–50.

38. May 10, 1742, p. 167, February 17, 1743, p. 198, Edwards, *Life of David Brainerd*.

39. March 18, 1743, p. 207, March 6, 1745, p. 289, April 17, 1743, p. 204, April 26, 1744, p. 292, Edwards, *Life of David Brainerd*.

40. May 18, 1743, p. 207, n.d., p. 144, May 13, 1742, p. 167, Edwards, *Life of David Brainerd*.

41. Augustine, *Confessions*, trans. R. S. Pine-Coffin (New York: Penguin, 1961), 75–80, 21.

42. August 21, 1744, p. 317, March 24, 1745, p. 378, Edwards, *Life of David Brainerd*.

43. April 19, 1742, p. 162, April 28, 1742, p. 165, June 26, 1743, p. 255, Edwards, *Life of David Brainerd*.

44. Edwards, *Life of David Brainerd,* 245 n. 8.

45. April 6, 1742, p. 159, September 20, 1743, p. 221, Edwards, *Life of David Brainerd.*

46. Hopkins, *Historical Memoirs,* 152, 13, 10.

47. Hopkins notes, "He was of a most sweet, kind and benevolent natural Temper; without the least Constitutional Turn towards Gloominess, Melancholy." *Historical Memoirs,* 149. He also expressed regret that Sergeant had left few journals or copies of letters (ii–iii).

48. Hopkins, *Historical Memoirs,* 14, 22–26, 39–40, 47, 54; Szasz, *Indian Education,* 209; Wyss, *Writing Indians,* 84.

49. Szasz, *Indian Education,* 206.

50. Hopkins, *Historical Memoirs,* 7; Szasz, *Indian Education,* 9–11. Wyss provides a convincing reading of the concern that Sergeant's marriage to Abigail Williams, which allied Sergeant more strongly to the Williams family's interests, created among the native community of Stockbridge. *Writing Indians,* 95–105.

51. Wyss, *Writing Indians,* 81–140.

52. Hopkins, *Historical Memoirs,* 72, 79, 90, 1–2, 164–82.

53. Wyss, *Writing Indians,* 82, 87. On this topic, see generally 86–95.

54. Evan Haefeli and Kevin Sweeney, *Captors and Captives: The 1704 French and Indian Raid on Deerfield* (Amherst: University of Massachusetts Press, 2003); John Demos, *The Unredeemed Captive: A Family Story from Early America* (New York: Knopf, 1994).

55. Hopkins, *Historical Memoirs,* 5, 6.

56. Ibid., 17, 20, 25, 29.

57. Ibid., 129, 155, 116.

58. Ibid., 149, 158–59.

59. Ibid., 128, 159.

60. Ibid., 150, 151, 148, 153.

61. Ibid., 152–53.

62. Ibid., 25, 29–30, 39.

63. Ibid., 30, 39–40.

64. Ibid., 40, 41.

65. Ibid., 41.

66. Ibid., 55, 56.

67. Ibid., 90.

68. Ibid., 96, 101.

69. Ibid., 132–33.

70. Ibid., 105.

71. Hunter, *Before Novels,* 303, 324–25, 330–31, 338–39.

Chapter 6

1. Hopkins, *Historical Memoirs,* 182.

2. Michael Leroy Oberg, *Dominion and Civility: English Imperialism and Native America, 1585–1685* (Ithaca: Cornell University Press, 1999).

3. On the Paxton Boys, see Richter, *Facing East,* 201–16; Vaughan, *Roots of American Racism,* 82–102. On the Gnaddenhutten massacre, see Richter, *Facing East,* 221–23.

4. My thanks to Matthew Dennis for suggesting this distinction.

5. This term is taken from James C. Scott, *Domination and the Arts of Resistance: Hidden Transcripts* (New Haven: Yale University Press, 1990), 2.

6. Many scholars have commented on the racist dynamics of a nostalgic attachment to Indians in the United States. Peter Matthiessen has written, "American hearts respond with emotion to . . . modern films and television dramas in which the nineteenth-century Indian is portrayed as the tragic victim of Manifest Destiny . . . .Our nostalgia comes easily, since those stirring peoples are safely in the past, and the abuse of their proud character . . . can be blamed on our roughshod frontier forebears." *In the Spirit of Crazy Horse* (1980; New York: Viking, 1991), xxii. Daniel R. Mandell has shown that many more Indians lived within eighteenth-century British territories than we usually think, because the U.S. attachment to visions of dying Indians has precluded studies of Indian assimilation and survival. *Behind the Frontier: Indians in Eighteenth-Century Eastern Massachusetts* (Lincoln: University of Nebraska Press, 1996). See also Colin G. Calloway, ed., *After King Philip's War: Presence and Persistence in Indian New England* (Hanover: University Press of New England, 1997); Brian Dippie, *The Vanishing American: White Attitudes and U.S. Indian Policy* (Middletown, Conn.: Wesleyan University Press, 1972).

7. Michael R. Rogin, "Liberal Society and the Indian Question," in *"Ronald Reagan," the Movie, and Other Episodes of Political Demonology* (Berkeley: University of California Press, 1987), 137–38. See also Lepore, *Name of War,* 224; Laurence M. Hauptman, *Tribes and Tribulations: Misconceptions about American Indians and Their Histories* (Albuquerque: University of New Mexico Press, 1995), 39–48; Richard Slotkin, *Regeneration through Violence: The Mythology of the American Frontier, 1600–1860* (Middletown, Conn.: Wesleyan University Press, 1973); G. Harrison Orians, *The Cult of the Vanishing American: A Century View* (Toledo: H. J. Chittenden, 1934).

8. Of Jackson's speech on the removal of indigenous peoples, Roy Harvey Pearce noted, "Jackson's . . . rhetoric amounts to formal public expression of American regret in the face of the tragic and triumphant progress of civilization over savagism." *The Savages of America: A Study of the Indian and the Idea of Civilization* (Baltimore: Johns Hopkins Press, 1953), 58. On the coincidence of sentimental images of "vanishing Indians" with the Indian removals, see Philip J. Deloria, *Playing Indian* (New Haven: Yale University Press, 1998), 64–65. Also see Deloria generally for the varying ideological applications of vanishing Indians.

9. Andrew Burstein, *Sentimental Democracy: The Evolution of America's Romantic Self-Image* (New York: Hill and Wang, 1999), xiii, xx.

10. Renato Rosaldo, "Imperialist Nostalgia," in *Culture and Truth: The Remaking of Social Analysis* (1989; Boston: Beacon Press, 1993), 69–70.

11. Of vanishing Indians in poems of the early republic, see Ellison, *Cato's Tears,* 140. On dying Indians in nineteenth-century literature, see Robert Berkhofer, Jr., *The White Man's Indian* (New York: Knopf, 1978), 86–91.

12. *Natural Born Killers,* prod. by Jane Hamsher, Don Murphy, and Clayton

Townsend, dir. by Oliver Stone, story by Quentin Tarantino, Warner Brothers, 1985, videocassette. In an interview from prison, Mickey says that the Indian is the only person he regrets killing. The film also suggests a biblical fall through the Indian's death, as the shaman's rattlesnakes bite Mickey and Mallory just after he is killed, debilitating them so that the police can catch them. For a recent scholarly treatment of the theme of haunting in portrayals of Indians, see Renee L. Berglund, *The National Uncanny: Indian Ghosts and American Subjects* (Hanover, N.H.: University Press of New England, 2000).

13. *Poltergeist,* prod. by Steven Spielberg and Frank Marshall, dir. by Tobe Hooper, Metro-Goldwyn-Mayer, 1982, videocassette; Philip Freneau, "Indian Burial Ground," in vol. 2 of *The Poems of Philip Freneau, Poet of the American Revolution,* ed. Fred Lewis Pattee (Princeton: Princeton University Library, 1902), 2:369. On the preoccupation of Anglo-America with Indian remains, see Matthew Dennis, "Patriotic Remains: Bones of Contention in the Early Republic," in *Mortal Remains: Death in Early America,* ed. Nancy Isenberg and Andrew Burstein (Philadelphia: University of Pennsylvania Press, 2003), 136–48.

14. Joyce E. Chaplin has pointed out the importance of missionaries to colonial readings of Indian death, noting that "missionaries associated Indians' sickness and dying with their acceptance of the gospel." *Subject Matter,* 301–2. Kristina Kae Bross recently has explored the contribution that Puritan missionaries, especially Eliot, made to the trope of the vanishing Indian. "Dying Saints, Vanishing Savages: 'Dying Indian Speeches' in Colonial New England Literature," *Early American Literature* 36 (2002): 325–52. Her observations coincide with many of mine about seventeenth-century writings from New England. See also David Murray's reading of John Eliot's collection of dying Indian speeches. *Forked Tongues: Speech, Writing and Representation in North American Indian Texts* (Bloomington: Indiana University Press, 1991), 34–39. For a comparison of Spanish and English interpretations of Indian deaths, see Seed, *Ceremonies.*

15. Thoroughgood Moore to John Chamberlayne, Secretary, November 13, 1705, #122, Letterbook A2, USPG Archives, Rhodes House Library, Oxford. The SPG often paraphrased this line in its publications. See, e.g., *SPG Account 1706,* 53.

16. Wheelock, *Continuation* (1768), 22.

17. Anderson, *Crucible of War,* 541–43.

18. Jeremy Belknap, *A Discourse Intended to Commemorate the Discovery of America by Christopher Columbus* (Boston, 1792) 51.

19. Claude Rawson, *God, Gulliver, and Genocide: Barbarism and the European Imagination, 1492–1945* (New York: Oxford University Press, 2001), 12.

20. Michelle Burnham, *Captivity and Sentiment: Cultural Exchange in American Literature, 1682–1861* (Hanover, N.H.: University Press of New England, 1997), 94.

21. On the "deuteronomic vision," see Alfred A. Cave, *The Pequot War* (Amherst: University of Massachusetts Press, 1996), 171; Greenblatt, *Marvelous Possessions,* 80–81.On the scriptural justification of Puritan violence, see E. Brooks Holifield, *Era of Persuasion: American Thought and Culture, 1521–1680* (Boston: Twayne, 1989), 43, 51; Wright, *Religion and Empire,* 157.

22. Rawson, *God, Gulliver,* 310.

23. My emphasis is not so much on the object that is depleted of value but more on the object whose potential value has been neglected. I focus on this connotation because it elicits the elegiac response and the fear of loss that were present in missionaries' and in sentimental British treatments of dying Indians. I have learned much from but not adopted Michael Thompson, *Rubbish Theory: The Creation and Destruction of Value* (Oxford: Oxford University Press, 1979). Rather, I have drawn some of my ideas from Georges Bataille's theories of waste as unnecessary expenditure of resources ranging from food and capital to human beings. *The Accursed Share: An Essay on General Economy,* vol. 1: *Consumption,* trans. Robert Hurley (New York: Zone Books, 1991), 9.

24. This ambivalence is one aspect of Weber's Protestant ethic as it applies to the New England Puritans and their concerns over the corruptive effects of prosperity. See Edmund S. Morgan, "The Puritan Ethic and the American Revolution," *William and Mary Quarterly,* 3d. ser., 24 (1967): 4; Perry Miller, *The New England Mind: From Colony to Province* (Cambridge, Mass.: Belknap Press, 1953).

25. Weinbrot, *Britannia's Issue,* 348.

26. Joseph Roach, *Cities of the Dead: Circum-Atlantic Performance* (New York: Columbia University Press, 1996), 131.

27. *Strength out of Weakness,* 151.

28. In *The Curse of Cain: The Violent Legacy of Monotheism* (Chicago: University of Chicago Press, 1997), Regina M. Schwartz confronts the problem of identity formation through violence in the Bible. My theory of waste overlaps with her argument that violence emerges from the sense of scarcity that pervades the Bible. If violence is the response to scarcity, so also is the effort to dole out violence in less destructive forms.

29. *New Englands First Fruits,* 1, 22–23, 8, 19.

30. *New Englands First Fruits,* 20–21, 4, 3.

31. These words are not an exact quotation from the Geneva or the King James translations, which both read, "discomfited Amalek and his people with the edge of his sword."

32. Cave, *Pequot War,* 19.

33. Elaine Scarry, *The Body in Pain: The Making and Unmaking of the World* (New York: Oxford University Press, 1985), 124, 128, 77.

34. *Humiliations Follow'd with Deliverances* in *Days of Humiliation, Times of Affliction and Disaster. Nine Sermons for Restoring Favor with an Angry God* (1696–1727), by Cotton Mather, intro. George Harrison Orians (Gainesville, Fla.: Scholars' Facsimiles and Reprints, 1970), 132–33.

35. Burnham, *Captivity,* 52.

36. John W. Ford, ed., *Some Correspondence between the Governors and Treasurers of the New England Company in London and the Commissioners of the United Colonies in America, The Missionaries of the Company and Others Between the Years 1657 and 1712 to which are added the Journals of the Rev. Experience Mayhew in 1713 and 1714* (London, 1896), 84.

37. Hopkins, *Historical Memoirs,* 82.

38. Gideon Hawley to Dr. Thacher, January 1794, Letters of Gideon Hawley.

39. Wyss, *Writing Indians,* 98.

40. Gookin, *Historical Collections,* 11.

41. *An Abstract of the Charter, and of the Proceedings of the Society for the Propagation of the Gospel in Foreign Parts, from the 21st of February 1752, to the 16th of February 1753,* in Edward Cressett, *A Sermon Preached before the Society for the Propagation of the Gospel in Foreign Parts, at their Anniversary Meeting* (London, 1753), 48.

42. Peter C. Mancall, *Deadly Medicine: Indians and Alcohol in Early America* (Ithaca: Cornell University Press, 1995), 21, 65.

43. Berkhofer, *White Man's Indian,* 30.

44. Gookin, *Historical Collections,* 11.

45. Maddox, *SPG Sermon,* 31.

46. Lora Romera, "Vanishing Americans: Gender, Empire, and New Historicism," in *The Culture of Sentiment: Race, Gender, and Sentimentality in Nineteenth-Century America,* ed. Shirley Samuels (New York: Oxford University Press, 1992), 115.

47. United Ministers of Boston, "Attestation" to E. Mayhew, *Indian Converts,* xvii.

48. John Hammerer, Report on Cherokees in Carolina, n.p., 1766, orig. English, reel 24, box 191, folder 3, item 1, n.p., Records of the Moravian Mission among the Indians of North America, Moravian Church Archives, Bethlehem, Pa. Microfilm publication of Research Publications, Inc., of New Haven, Conn., at American Philosophical Society, Philadelphia. The right edge of this paper has been cut off, and the letters in brackets are my guesses for missing text.

49. Eleazar Wheelock to Nathaniel Whitaker, December 21, 1766, Lebanon, Conn., in Richardson, *Indian Preacher,* 193.

50. Wheelock, *Continuation* (1771), 24.

51. Humphries, *Historical Account,* 283, citing *English Empire in America,* 162.

52. Bernd Peyer, *The Tutor'd Mind: Indian Missionary-Writers in Antebellum America* (Amherst: University of Massachusetts Press, 1997), 92.

53. Peyer notes that when Occom returned from England he "may have sought solace in alcohol, as he immediately penned two letters of confession, one to the Suffolk Presbytery and another to the SSPCK. The former . . . came to the conclusion that his intoxication came not from intemperance 'but from having Drank a small quantity of Spirituous Liquor after having been all day without food.'" *Tutor'd Mind,* 78. See also Love, *Samson Occom,* 162–67.

54. Murray, *Forked Tongues,* 45.

55. On execution sermons, see Daniel A. Cohen, *Pillars of Salt, Monuments of Grace: New England Crime Literature and the Origins of American Popular Culture, 1674–1860* (New York: Oxford University Press, 1993); Ronald A. Bosco, "Early American Gallows Literature: An Annotated Checklist," *Resources for American Literary Study* 8 (1978): 81–105; Wayne C. Minnick, "The New England Execution Sermon, 1639–1800," *Speech Monographs* 35 (1968): 77–89. On the relation of Occom's sermon to the genre, see A. LaVonne Brown Ruoff, "Introduction: Samson Occom's *Sermon Preached by Samson Occom . . . at the Execution of Moses Paul, an Indian,*" *Studies in American Indian Literatures,* 2d ser., 4, no. 2 (1992): 78–80; Peyer, *Tutor'd Mind,* 90–92.

56. Samson Occom, *A Sermon, Preached at the Execution of* Moses Paul, *an Indian. Who was executed at* New-Haven, *on the 2d of* September, *1772, for the Murder of Mr Moses Cook, Late of* Waterbury, *on the* 7th *of December, 1771. Preached at the Desire of said Paul* (New-London, 1772), 26.

57. Gustafson, *Eloquence*, 98; Ruoff, "Samson Occom's *Sermon*," 78–79.

58. Occom, *Execution*, 3.

59. Occom, *Execution*, 15.

60. Gustafson, *Eloquence*, 98–99.

61. Occom, *Execution*, 19–20.

62. Keely McCarthy, "Samson Occom's Purpose: The Execution Sermon as Social Critique" (paper presented at the National Conference of the American Society for Eighteenth-Century Studies, April 21, 2001, New Orleans), 6.

63. Occom, *Execution*, 27.

64. McCarthy, "Samson Occom's Purpose," 8.

65. Occom, *Execution*, 29.

66. Peyer, *Tutor'd Mind*, 95.

67. The Boston edition adds to this title the phrase, "Put in Metre."

68. Occom, *Execution*, 21–22; "Mr. Occom's Address," ll. 57–58.

69. Ola Elizabeth Winslow, introduction to *American Broadside Verse: From Imprints of the 17th and 18th Centuries* (New Haven: Yale University Press, 1930).

70. "Advice from the Dead to the Living: Or, a Solemn Warning to the World, Occasioned by the Untimely Death of Poor Julian, Mar. 22, 1733" (Boston: Thomas Fleet, 1733), in *American Broadside Verse*, ed. Winslow, 82–83.

71. John Eliot, *The Dying Speeches of Several Indians* (Cambridge, 1685).

72. Louise A. Breen, "Praying with the Enemy: Daniel Gookin, King Philip's War and the Dangers of Intercultural Mediatorship," in *Empire and Others: British Encounters with Indigenous Peoples, 1600–1850*, ed. Martin Daunton and Rick Halpern (Philadelphia: University of Pennsylvania Press, 1999), 101–22; Lepore, *Name of War*, esp. 21–47; James Drake, "Restraining Atrocity: The Conduct of King Philip's War," *New England Quarterly* 70 (1997): 33–56; Pulsipher, "Massacre at Hurtleberry Hill."

73. John Eliot to Robert Boyle and the Commissioners of the New England Company, October 17, 1675, in Ford, *Some Correspondence*, 54–55.

74. Mary Rowlandson, *The Sovereignty and Goodness of God, together with the Faithfulness of his Promises Displayed; being a Narrative of the Captivity and Restoration of Mrs. Mary Rowlandson*, in *Narratives of Indian Wars 1675–1699*, vol. 14 of *Original Narratives of Early American History*, ed. C. H. Lincoln (New York, 1913).

75. Stoddard, *QUESTION*, 11–12.

76. Martin Mack, Travel Diary, Pochgathgoth, February 6, 1743, German, trans. 1743, Records of the Moravian Mission among the Indians of North America, reel 1, item 3.

77. John Heckewelder, *A Narrative of the Mission of the United Brethren Among the Delaware and Mohegan Indians From its Commencement in the Year 1740 to the Close of the Year 1808*, ed. William Elsey Connelley (Cleveland, 1907), 427.

78. George Berkeley, *A Sermon Preached before the Incorporated Society for the*

Propagation of the Gospel in Foreign Parts; At the Parish-Church of St. Mary-le-Bow (London, 1732), 19–20.

79. See, e.g., Herring, *SPG Sermon,* 28–29.

80. L. M. Beier, "The Good Death in Seventeenth-Century England," in *Death, Ritual, and Bereavement,* ed. Ralph Houlbrooke (New York: Routledge, 1989), 43–61; Philip Morgan, "Of Worms and War, 1380–1558," Clare Gittings, "Sacred and Secular, 1558–1660," and Ralph Houlbrooke, "The Age of Decency, 1660–1760," in *Death in England: An Illustrated History,* ed. Peter C. Jupp and Clare Gittings (New Brunswick: Rutgers University Press, 1999), 119–74.

81. Erik R. Seeman, "Reading Indians' Deathbed Scenes: Ethnohistorical and Representational Approaches," *Journal of American History* 88 (2001): 17–47. See also Hilary Wyss's study of transcultural influences on Mayhew's text. "'Things that Do Accompany Salvation': Colonialism, Conversion, and Cultural Exchange in Experience Mayhew's *Indian Converts,*" *Early American Literature* 33 (1998): 39–61.

82. E. Mayhew, *Indian Converts,* 20.

83. *The Rule and Exercises of Holy Dying. In which are Described the Means and Instruments of Preparing Our Selves, and Others Respectively, for a Blessed Death* (London, 1651), 178–81.

84. E. Mayhew, *Indian Converts,* 20.

85. David Zeisberger, Diary of the Schonbrun on the Ohio, September 1778, English, Records of the Moravian Mission among the Indians of North America, box 141, folder 12, in microfilm reel 8.

86. As David Murray has said, these dying narratives "fix[ed] [Indians] in a certain safe and comforting role for a white readership." *Forked Tongues,* 35.

87. Michel Foucault, *Discipline and Punish: The Birth of the Prison,* trans. Alan Sheridan, 2d ed. (New York: Vintage Books, 1995), 7, 9.

88. Ibid., 16.

89. Hopkins, *Historical Memoirs,* 117.

90. Gittings, "Sacred and Secular," 153.

91. Winslow, *Glorious Progress,* 6, 25, 26.

92. Seeman, "Reading Indians' Deathbed Scenes," 9.

93. *New Englands First Fruits,* 2.

94. Cave, *Pequot War,* 120.

95. *New Englands First Fruits,* 15.

96. Roger Williams, *A Key into the Language of America,* 1643, ed. John J. Teunissen and Evelyn J. Hinz (Detroit: Wayne State University Press, 1973), 88.

97. On Williams's approach to Indian conversion, see his *Christenings Make Not Christians, or a Briefe Discourse Concerning that name Heathen, Commonly Given to the Indians. As Also Concerning that Great Point of their Conversion* (1645), ed. Sidney Rider (Boston, 1881).

98. See generally Anne G. Myles, "Dissent and the Frontier of Translation: Roger Williams's *A Key into the Language of America,*" in *Possible Pasts: Becoming Colonial in Early America,* ed. Robert Blair St. George (Ithaca: Cornell University Press, 2000), 88–108.

99. *A True Account of the Dying Words of Ockanickon, an Indian King, Spoken*

to Jahkursoe, His Brother's Son, Whom he Appointed King After Him (London, 1682), 4.

100. *Ockanickon,* 5.

101. Seeman, "Reading Indians' Deathbed Scenes," 11.

102. Thomas Budd, *Good Order Established in Pennsilvania & New-Jersey in America, Being a True Account of the Country; With its Produce and Commodities there Made* (London, 1685), 28–29, 32, 33–34.

103. E. Mayhew, *Indian Converts,* 6.

104. John Foxe, *Acts and Monuments of these Latter and Perilous Days. . . .* (London, 1563). This text is commonly called *The Book of Martyrs.*

105. E. Mayhew, *Indian Converts,* 20, 49, 154.

106. Ibid., 181, 185, 205, 146, 125, 101.

107. Timothy Horsfield to Governor Denny, January 21, 1757, number 353, Horsfield Papers, American Philosophical Society, Philadelphia, Pa.

108. Timothy Horsfield to Benjamin Franklin and others, January 21, 1757, number 351, Horsfield Papers.

109. Anderson, *Crucible of War,* 162.

110. Hugh Henry Brackenridge and Philip Freneau, *The Rising Glory of America,* in *Poems of Philip Freneau,* 1.49.10–13, 19–22.

111. Susan Castillo, "Imperial Pasts and Dark Futurities: Freneau and Brackenridge's 'The Rising Glory of America,'" *Symbiosis* 6 (2002): 34.

112. Ellison, *Cato's Tears,* 143.

Conclusion

1. Thomas Bray, *A Memorial, Representing the Present State of Religion, on the Continent of North-America* (London, 1700), 40.

2. Jonathan Shipley, *A Sermon Preached before the Incorporated Society for the Propagation of the Gospel in Foreign Parts; at their Anniversary Meeting* (London, 1773), v–vi.

3. Samuel Halifax, *A Sermon Preached before the Incorporated Society for the Propagation of the Gospel in Foreign Parts; at their Anniversary Meeting* (London, 1789), n.p.

4. Samson Occom to Eleazar Wheelock, July 24, 1771, Wheelock Papers (ms. 771424), Baker Library, Dartmouth College, Hanover, N.H., reprinted in Blodgett, *Samson Occom,* 122–24, and in Peyer, *Tutor'd Mind,* 78–79.

5. Thomas Commuck, "Sketch of the Brothertown Indians," *Reports and Collections of the State Historical Society of Wisconsin* 4 (1859): 291–98.

6. Simmons and Simmons, *Old Light,* 58–60, 94, 6.

7. Chesterman, "Journals of David Brainerd and William Carey"; Conforti, "David Brainerd and the Nineteenth Century Missionary Movement."

8. Right Reverend H. V. R. Short, D.D., Bishop of Saskatchewan to Sir John Winnifrith, New England Company, September 4, 1975, New England Company Papers, Documents Relating to Missions, 1961–68, Guildhall Library, London, UK.

9. Hawley to Dr. Thacher, January 1794, Letters of Gideon Hawley.

10. Bishop of Keewatin to Mary S. Kearney, New England Company, March 31, 1976, New England Company Papers, Documents Relating to Missions, 1961–68, Guildhall Library, London, UK.

11. Raymond C. Offenheiser to Oxfam America Supporters, May 2003, Boston, Mass., 1.

12. Offenheiser, 4.

Index

1 Corinthians: 4:10, 175; 9:11, 38
1 Peter 3:8, 8
2 Corinthians: 12:15, 142; 9:2, 104

abolitionism, 7
Abridgement of the Statutes and Rules of the Society in Scotland for Propagating Christian Knowledge, An, 94
Account of the Life of the Late Reverend Mr. David Brainerd, An (Edwards), 143–48; depictions of Indians in, 143–44, 147–48; refutation of Arminianism, 144–45; spiritual significance of solitude in, 147–48; spiritual struggles in, 143
Act for the Promoting and Propagating the Gospel of Jesus Christ in New England, An (1649), 35, fig. 1, 208 n.78, 211 n.1
"Action for Africa" (Oxfam fundraising campaign), 200–202
Acts: 10:34–35, 150; 16:9, 129
alcohol, 162, 170–78, 195; as Indian vice, 170–78; understood as sinful, 171–74
Allestree, Richard, *The Whole Duty of Man*, 43
American Revolution: as end-date for book's study, 3, 22–24, 109; Freneau as poet of, 162; and Indian migration, 149; and SPG, 102, 111, 115
Anderson, Benedict, 15
Anne (queen of Great Britain), as patron of SPG, 49–50, 93, 96–99, 217 n.84
anti-Catholic rhetoric, 46–49, 103
anti-Spanish rhetoric, 37, 46–47, 49, 166, 169–70; in SPG sermons, 95–96, 125. *See also* Black Legend
apologists, 129–30
Appleton, Nathan, 155
Aristotle, 15
Arminianism, 123, 127, 135, 144–45
Arminius, Jacobus, 123
ars moriendi tradition, 181–82; and missionary depictions of Indian deaths, 163; as

trope in missionary writing, 178–84; as resistance to deuteronomic vision of American colonization, 183. *See also* deuteronomic vision; Indian death
Ash, George (Bishop of Clogher), 105–6
Augustine, *Confessions*, 146–47
autobiography, as popular genre, 158

Bank of England, founding of, 52
Baptist Missionary Society, 109
Barker-Benfield, G. J., 98
Baxter, Richard, 64, 88
Belcher, Jonathan (Governor of Massachusetts), 154–55
Belknap, Jeremy, 162
Bellin, Joshua, 39
Benezet, Anthony, *A Plain Path to Christian Perfection*, 124
Benson, Martin (Bishop of Gloucester), 50–51; attacks on Deism by, 130–31
Berkeley, George (Dean of Derry), 114; attacks on Puritans for cruelty to Indians, 181
Berkhofer, Robert, 170–71
Beveridge, William (Bishop of St. Asaph), praise for SPG, 104–5
Bible: Indians, absence from, 4; Indian ignorance of, 119, 126; translation into Indian languages, 24. *See also* Deism
Bisse, Philip (Bishop of Hereford), 55, 101–2
Black Legend, 47, 126. *See also* anti-Spanish rhetoric
Blount, Charles, *Works* (1695), 120
Boehm, Anthony, 84
Bolton, S. Charles, 120
Book of Martyrs, The (Foxe), 190
Boyle, Robert, 24, 42; leadership positions in Royal Society and New England Company, 88–89, 223 n.23
Brackenridge, Hugh Henry, *The Rising Glory of America*, 193–94. *See also* Freneau, Philip

Brainerd, David: correspondence of, 146–47; dislike of Indians, 145–46; journal of, 26; solitude of, 145–47; as SSPCK missionary, 26, 139. *See also* Edwards, Jonathan, *Account of the Life of the Late Reverend Mr. David Brainerd*

Brainerd, John, 26, 115; *A Genuine Letter from Mr. John Brainard* [sic], 62

Bray, Thomas, 86, 89, 195; *Missionalia* (1727), 114

British identity, 4, 15–17, 23, 125; as defined in missionary writing, 16; defined by reference to Indians, 4

broadsides, 177–78

Bross, Kristina Kae, 66, 203 n.7, 241 n.14

Brothertown, New York, 149, 196. *See also* Occom, Samson

Budd, Thomas, conversations with Ockanickon, 189; *Good Order Established in Pennsilvania and New-Jersey*, 187–89

Bullock, F.W.B., 85

Burnet, Gilbert, 53, 93; as historian of SPG, 93

Burnham, Michelle, 164

Burstein, Andrew, 161

Butler, Joseph (Bishop of Bristol), *The Analogy of Religion*, 134

Calvinism, 24

Cambridge Platonists, 10

Canaanites, Indians described as, 119, 169–70, 181. *See also* deuteronomic vision

capitalism, 7

captivity narratives, 150, 168, 179

Carey, William, 23, 109, 197; and Christian fellowship, 109; and earlier missionary movements, 228 n.99

Cary, Mary, *The Little Horns Doome and Downfall*, 73

Caryl, Joseph, 14, 18, 34–37, 42; as Independent preacher, 14; use of images of husbandry, 36

Castell, William, 5–6

Castillo, Susan, 193

Cave, Alfred A., 164, 167

Chamberlain, Ava, 123

Chandler, Edward (Bishop of Coventry and Litchfield), 54

charity, 7, 12; and British national identity, 7;

as collective missionary endeavor, 15, 106; and Protestant internationalism, 100

Charles I, execution of, 12, 34

Charles II, impact of Restoration on missionary activity, 78. *See also* Restoration

Christianity, "unfairness" of God and question of heathen salvation, 125, 128–36, 233 n.57

Church of England, 23, 229 n.9

Church of Ireland, relations with SPG, 100

Cibber, Colly, 158

City Jilt, The (Haywood), 42

"city on a hill," as image in missionary texts, 101–2

civil society, 16

Clagget, Nicholas (Bishop of St. Davids), 129, 133

Clear Sun-shine of the Gospel, The, 46

Codrington plantation, 113

Colley, Linda, 95

Collins, Anthony, *Discourse on the Grounds and Reasons of the Christian Religion*, 120

Colman, Benjamin, 154–57

Columbus, Christopher, 38–39, 40–43; descriptions of Taino culture, 38–39

compassion, 7–11; defined, 7–8; equated with pity, 8; extent of as assumed by missionaries, 8–11. *See also* pity

compassion fatigue, 200–202

concerts of prayer, 108; Concert for United Extraordinary Prayer, 108

Conforti, Joseph, 139

Congregationalism, 24, 189; collections of accounts of Indian conversion and death by Congregationalist ministers, 189

Conquests and Triumphs of Grace: Being a Brief narrative of the Success which the Gospel hath had among the Indians of Martha's Vineyard, The (Matthew Mayhew), 79; anti-Catholic rhetoric of, 81; on Dutch in transatlantic Protestant community, 79–80; on Indian politics, 81; on interdenominational relationships, 81–82; internationalism of, 84

Conrad, Joseph, *Heart of Darkness*, 2–3, 17

conversion: as alternative to destruction by alcohol, 172; as benevolent act, 2; as compensation for Indian suffering, 60–61

Cook, Elizabeth Heckendorn, 63

Cooper, Anthony Ashley (Third Earl of

Shaftesbury), *Characteristics of Men, Manners, Opinions and Times* (1711), 120, 132

Cooper, James Fenimore, *The Last of the Mohicans*, 161

Coram, Thomas, 95, 154, 157

Coshomon, Mary, 45

Costner, Kevin, *Dances with Wolves*, 161

Cripps, John, *A True Account of the Dying Words of Ockanickon, an Indian King*, 26, 186–87

Dante Aligheri, on pagan entrance to Heaven, 122

Dawes, William (Bishop of Chester), 55, 99, 105

Day-Breaking, if not the Sun-rising, of the Gospell, The (Shepard), 48–49, 104, 121, 126–27; emotional language of, 219 n.25; rhetorical strategies in, 67–69

debt, philosophical implications of, 215 n.60

Defoe, Daniel, 1–2, 21, 126; *The Farther Adventures of Robinson Crusoe*, 21; *The Life and Strange and Surprizing Adventures of Robinson Crusoe*, 1–2; *The Review*, 97; *The Serious Reflections of Robinson Crusoe*, 126

Deism, 117–21, 194; as challenge to British identity, 125–26, 136; as challenge to Church of England, 117, 119, 133–35; as challenge to SPG, 117–18; distinguished from Latitudinarianism, 135–36; and Indian conversion, 117–18; rhetoric of, 125; theological arguments for, 119–21; on universal salvation and question of pagan entrance to Heaven, 121, 125, 127, 129. *See also* Christianity

de las Casas, Bartolomé, *Brief relation of the Destruction of the Indies*, 46

Deloria, Vine, 38

Denne, John (Archdeacon of Rochester), *Want of Universality no Just Objection to the Truth of the Christian Religion*, 130, 132

deuteronomic vision of colonization, 164–68, 173, 180–83, 242 nn.23–24, 28; as legitimation of British imperialism, 165; resistance to in accounts of Indian deaths, 183

Deuteronomy 7:16, 8

diary-keeping, as Puritan practice, 158

discursive communities, definition of, 15–16

dissenting churches, legalization of, 87. *See also* Toleration Act

Doddridge, Phillip, 100–101

Doll, Peter M., 115

Donovan, Robert Kent, 89

Dryden, John: *Annus Mirabilis*, 57; *The Indian Emperour*, 47; *Religio Laici*, 126; translation of Dominick Bohours's *Life of St. Francis Xavier*, 23, 139

Dury, John: accounts of exemplary deaths, 185; description of Indian prayer, 104; *The Glorious progress of the Gospel amongst the Indians in New England*, 44, 52. *See also ars moriendi* tradition

Duston Hannah, captivity of, 168. *See also* captivity narratives

Dutch missions in Taiwan, 74–75

Dying Speeches of Several Indians, The, 189–90

Edwards, Jonathan: *Account of the Life of the Late Reverend Mr. David Brainerd*, 29, 32, 139–48; *The Doctrine of Original Sin Defended*, 131; as missionary to Stockbridge, 140; theology of, 144–45

Eells, Nathaniel, 51

Eliot, John, 20, 24–25, 34, 67; accounts of exemplary Indian deaths, 184–85; *A Brief Narrative of the Progress of the Gospel*, 71; as collector of Indian death accounts, 189–90; correspondence of, 28, 49, 64–65, 179; *The Dying Speeches of several Indians*, 25, 71; *A further Accompt of the Progrese of the Gospel*, 20; *Indian Dialogues*, 25, 138; *A Late and Further Manifestation of the Gospel*, 77–78; on pagan entrance to heaven and "scandal of particularity," 121–22; role in New England Company, 24; role in publication of Indian tracts, 24; *Tears of Repentance*, 71; on transatlantic link between readers and Indian converts, 71–72; translations of deathbed speeches of Indians, 179. *See also* New England Company

Ellison, Julie, 194, 205 n.37

Emerson, Roger L., 135

emotion: appeals to in missionary texts, 7; as defining British identity, 16, 205 n.27; shared emotions, 110. *See also* sensibility

Encyclopédie (Diderot), 121

English Civil War, 22–23, 66, 78, 88

Enlightenment, the, 123

epistolary literature, 62–63, 66

ethos, as shared *pathos*, 15
evangelical Christianity: missionary efforts of, 197; revivals of, 108–9
Ewer, John (Bishop of Llandaff), 98

Fields, Polly Stevens, 13
Fiering, Norman, 10, 132
Fish, Joseph, 14, 196. *See also* Narragansett Indians
Fleetwood, William, 116, 133
Flint, Thomas, 69–70
Foucault, Michel, *Discipline and Punish*, 183
Fox, George, *Journal*, 26, 124
Foxe, John, *Book of Martyrs*, 190
France, British competition with, 9–10, 94
Francke, August Hermann, *Missionsnachrichten*, 23, 84
Franklin, Benjamin: correspondence with Timothy Horsfield, 192; influence of Deism on, 121
Freneau, Philip, 162; "The Indian Convert," 193; *The Rising Glory of America*, 193–94
Fuller, Thomas, 124
fundraising, 12–13; in articulation of public and private spheres, 86; discourse of, 200; emotional appeals in, 20; use of Indians in, 12; use of portraits of suffering individuals in, 201
Further Accompt of the Progresse of the Gospel amongst the Indians in New-England, A, 78–79, 189

Genuine Letter from Mr. John Brainard [sic], *A*, 62
Girard, Rene, 15
Gittings, Claire, 184
Glorious Progress of the Gospel, The, 44, 52, 71, 73, 78, 121–22
Glorious Revolution, 80, 87; and Deism, 127; impact on New England missionaries' relations with Dutch colleagues, 80
Gnaddenhutten, Ohio, massacre of Moravian Indians, 160, 180. *See also* Moravian Indians; Moravians
Godwyn, Morgan, 111
"gold for glass": image used by Columbus, 39–40; used by Robert Boyle, 42; used by Eliza Haywood, 41; used by John Milton, 41; persistence of image in eighteenth-century writings, 60–61; as trope in missionary writings, 37–43, 53–54
Gookin, Daniel: collections of Indian deathbed speeches, 179; *Historical Collections of the Indians in New England*, 57; on Indian alcoholism, 170–71
Gordon, Patrick, 53; *Geography Anatomized*, 53
Gowdie, John, 100
Great Awakening, 32, 115, 141–42, 237–38 nn.18–20; expansion of epistolary networks during, 141–42; influence on discourse of Christian mission, 32; revival of missionary efforts during, 141
Greenblatt, Stephen, 39, 60
Gustafson, Sandra, 143, 175

Hahn, Thomas, 124
Halifax, Samuel, 195
Hall, John, "Of Felicity," 42
Hall, Timothy, 141
Halttunen, Karen, 18
Hammerer, John, 172
Hare, Francis, 128, 134; condemnation of, 128
Harris, Paul, 143
Harth, Phillip, 122
Haskell, Thomas, 7
Hawley, Gideon, 24, 59, 170, 198; letters to the Massachusetts Historical Society, 59; on Mashpee Indian alcoholism, 170
Haywood, Eliza, *The City Jilt*, 42
Heckewelder, John, *A Letter to a Friend*, 27; *Narrative of the Mission of the United Brethren*, 180–81. *See also* Moravians
Henrico College, 22, 57, 208 n.71
Herbert, George, "The Church Militant," 57, 59
heroism, as trope in fundraising efforts, 96
Herring, Thomas (Bishop of Bangor), attacks on Deism by, 132
Historical memoirs, relating to the Housatunnuk Indians (Hopkins), 25, 32, 115, 148–53; compared to *Life of David Brainerd*, 148–49, 153; as hagiography of John Sergeant, 150–53; Muhhakaneok Indians represented in, 149–50, 151–52; pity in, 149; rhetorical differences from captivity narratives, 150; Stockbridge mission described in, 150
Hobbes, Thomas, 10
Hopkins, Samuel: as biographer of John Ser-

geant, 139; *Historical memoirs, relating to the Housatunnuk Indians*, 25, 32, 115, 148–53; on Indian deaths, 184; as reformist, 145; rhetorical strategies of, 157–58, 160

Horsfield, Timothy, 191–92

Hosea: 1:6, 8; 2:23, 8

Hough, John (Bishop of Litchfield and Coventry), 128–29

Hume, David, 10

Humiliations Follow'd with Deliverances (Mather), 168

Humphreys, David, 47, 93; as chronicler of SPG, 93

Hus, John, 26–27. *See also* Moravians

husbandry: in anti-Catholic propaganda, 47; English methods taught to Indians, 44, 214 n.35; images of in sermons, 44–45; Indians identified with organic abundance, 58–59; Indians seen as lacking ability in, 44–46; as metaphor for missionary work, 48, 59; as trope in missionary writings, 43–49, 55, 59; understood as element of British culture, 44–45

Hutchinson, Francis, 10

imperialism, 17

India Christiana (Mather), 25

Indian Charity School, 51–52, 56. *See also* Wheelock, Eleazar

Indian Converts (Experience Mayhew), 25, 45, 171; deuterononomic imagery used in, 191; exemplary Indian death as defense of British colonialism in, 189. *See also* deuteronomic vision

Indian death: accounts of as "safe" for white readership, 245 n.86; and concept of the American frontier, 161; and concept of manifest destiny, 161, 164; "good" deaths as proof of missionary success, 184, 189, 192; influence of depiction on development of American identity, 192, 240 n.6, 241 n.14; portrayal in missionary writing, 161, 177–78; scriptural allusions in depictions of, 179; sentimentalized, 164; as sign of God's favor of British colonists, 163–64, 167–69, 172, 194; as trope in Romantic literature, 32. See also *ars moriendi* tradition; deuteronomic vision

Indian death songs, 173

Indian policy (of early United States), 59

Indian removal, 21, 60, 196, 240 n.8

Indian tracts, 24; as collections of letters, 62; emphasis on reliability of accounts in, 65–66; New England Company's publication of, 65; portrayal of conversions in, 66; rhetorical strategies of, 67–69; role of emotion in, 67; role in inclusion of readers in transatlantic community, 66–83

Iron Eyes Cody, 161–62

Iroquois: letter to Archbishop of Canterbury, 112 fig. 3; visit of representatives to London (1710), 12, 59, 61, 111–12

Isaiah 59:19, 74

Jablonsky, Daniel Ernest, 84. *See also* Moravians

Jacob, Margaret, 85

James I, 5, 23; authorization of parish collections to support missions, 23

Jefferson, Thomas, on United States Indian policy, 59–60

Jessey, Henry: advocacy of Anglo-Dutch collaboration, 84; appeals to international Christian community, 73, 76–77; biblical allusions by, 74; *Of the Conversion of Five Thousand and Nine Hundred East-Indians, in the Isle of Formosa, neere China, to the Profession of the True God, in Jesus Christ*, 73–77; epistolary techniques of, 74–77; inclusion of personal correspondence as verification of accounts, 75–76; millenarian beliefs of, 73–77, 219 n.40

Jesuits, 23, 94; accusations of deception against in British texts, 5

Jesuit Relations, The, 62

Jowitt, Claire, 44, 77

Junius, Robert, 74–75. *See also* Jessey, Henry

Kant, Immanuel: dismissal of benevolence resulting from sympathy, 207 n.59; exclusion of emotions from morality, 17

"Keep America Beautiful" (advertising campaign), 161–62

Kellaway, William, 29, 66

Kenosis, and genre of missionary biography, 142

Kick, Abraham, petition to remove Edmund Andros, 221 n.60

King Philip's War, 57, 71, 179

Klingberg, Frank, 117

Landsman, Ned, 181, 108

Late and Further Manifestation of the Progress of the Gospel Amongst the Indians in New-England, A, 34, 36–37, 77–78, 189

Latitudinarianism, 117

Leng, John (Bishop of Norwich), 106

letters: in building of transatlantic communities, 62–63, 157–58; importance in fundraising, 62

Licensing Act, 87, 120

Light Appearing More and More Towards the Perfect Day, The, 44

Locke, John, 46

London Missionary Society, 109

Lord Herbert of Cherbury, *De Veritae*, 120. *See also* Deism

lost tribes of Israel, Indians as, 5, 14, 46, 119

Mack, Martin, 180. *See also* Moravians

Maddox, Isaac (Dean of Wells), 131–32; criticism of alcohol trade, 171

Magdalen House, 12

Magnalia Christi Americana (Mather), 80–81, 139; anti-Catholic rhetoric of, 80–81; internationalism of, 84–85; interpretation of Indian rejection of the Gospel, 123

Mahican Indians, 139–40

Mancall, Peter, 170

Mandeville, Bernard, 10; distinction between charity and pity, 133

manifest destiny, 161, 173; and Indian death, 161

masculinity: Christian ideals of, 98, 125, 127; differing models of, 97–98; eighteenth-century ideals of, 86; in missionary rhetoric, 97

Mashpee Indians, 59

Massachusetts Bay Colony, 24–25, 48, 57, 65, 67, 69, 78–80

Massachusetts Bay Company, 69, 71

Massachusetts Historical Society, 59

Massachusetts Indians, 20, 24, 34, 71, 78, 121, 189–90

Mather, Cotton, 9, 44, 45, 178–79; deuteronomic imagery used by, 168–69; *Humiliations Follow'd with Deliverances*, 168; *India Christiana*, 25; *Magnalia Christi Americana*, 80–81, 139

Mather, Increase, 80; internationalism of, 84

Matthew: 13:44–46, 51; 19:24, 51

Matthisen, John, 123

Mayhew, Experience: depictions of Wampanoag Indians, 190; description of death of Wunnanauhkomun, 182; *Indian Converts*, 25, 45, 171, 189; use of Indian death as image, 191

Mayhew, Jonathan, criticism of SPG, 115–17, 135

Mayhew, Matthew, anti-Catholic rhetoric of, 81; concerns about interdenominational relationships, 81–82; *The Conquests and Triumphs of Grace: Being a Brief narrative of the Success which the Gospel hath had among the Indians of Martha's Vineyard*, 79; on inclusion of Dutch in transatlantic Protestant community, 79–80; internationalism of, 84; observations of Indian politics, 81

Mayhew, Thomas, 34, 72

Mayhew, Thomas, Jr., *The Light Appearing More and More Towards the Perfect Day*, 44

Mayhew family, 24

McCarthy, Keely, 175, 203 n.7

McDermott, Gerald, 121

Mexico, as compared to New England, 46–47, 193–94. *See also* anti-Spanish rhetoric

Millar, Robert, 44

Milton, John: *Paradise Lost*, 8; *The Reason of Church Government Urg'd against Prelaty*, 41

missionary biography, 139; British identity in, 143; and building of transatlantic Christian community, 158–59; circulation in consumer culture, 159; in context of secular biographies, 158–59; as hagiography, 142–43, 237 n.4; impact of Great Awakening on, 141–42; as literary genre, 140–41; representation of epistolary networks, 142–43. *See also* missionary writing

missionary efforts: and British identity, 98; Catholic, 23; failure of, 11; failure explained in light of Indian death, 162–63; as mercantile activity, 26, 38–41

missionary letters: allusions to biblical epistles, 64, 70–71; in establishment of spiritual community, 64–83; as fundraising tools, 65; and inclusion of readers in transatlantic community, 66–83; nature of communities defined by, 82–83; rhetorical strategies of, 63–64. *See also* missionary writing missionary memoir, 139–40. *See also* missionary writing

missionary societies: competition between, 84, 88–89; as conduits for prayer, 104; in context of secular clubs and societies, 85–86; as example for individuals, 101–2; history of publications by, 206 n.42; impact on Anglican theology, 136–37; Indians as part of missionary networks, 156; internationalism of, 109–10, 222 n.4; links between, 90; origins of, 222 n.11; publicity efforts of, 94–95; responses to Deism, 119; suitability of for transatlantic projects, 101; women's roles in, 208 n.74. *See also* New England Company; Society for the Promotion of Christian Knowledge; Society for the Propagation of the Gospel in Foreign Parts; Society in Scotland for the Propagation of Christian Knowledge

missionary writing: appeals to shared feeling, 106–7; compared to secular literature, 16; contemporary influence of, 3–4, 6, 29–33, 160, 197; in development of British imperialism, 33, 37; elision of missionaries' identities in, 139; genres of, 29, 62–64; images of husbandry in, 36, 35; images of trade in, 37, 51–52; influence on eighteenth- and nineteenth-century literature and thought, 197, 199, 200; influence on secular literature, 192–94; rhetoric of domesticity in, 49–50; women as audience, 23

Mohawk Indians, 49, 111, 228 n.4

Moore, John (Bishop of Ely), 93, 127–28

Moore, Thoroughgood, reaction to Indian death, 162

Moravian Indians, 180–83, 191–92

Moravians (United Brethren): attitudes toward Indian deaths, 191–92; individual missionaries, 62, 111; journals kept by, 181; massacre of, 160, 180–81; origins of, 26–27; texts produced by, 27, 62

Morrison, Toni, *Playing in the Dark*, 4

Muhhakaneok Indians, 139, 149, 154, 156. See also *Historical memoirs, relating to the Housatunnuk Indians*

Muir, George, 44

Murray, David, 174

Narragansett Indians, 24, 185; refusal of Christianity by, 196–97

natural religion, 119. *See also* Deism

networks of feeling, 15, 31

New England clergy, social context of, 140–41

New England Company (Society for the Propagation of the Gospel in New England), *An Act for the Promoting and Propagating the Gospel of Jesus Christ in New England*, 35; history of, 11, 12, 24, 34, 49, 64, 88–89, 165, 197–98; nationalism of, 77; publication records of, 210 nn.98–99; tracts published by, 71, 218 nn.15–16

New Englands First Fruits, 44, 166–69, 185, 218 n.19

New Light Calvinism, 174

Newton, Thomas (Bishop of Bristol), 101

noble savages, 19. *See also* "poor Indians"

Oberg, Michael Learoy, 160

Occom, Samson, 11–12, 20; affiliation with SSPCK, 26; on European complicity in Indian "sinfulness," 176, 196; on Indian alcoholism, 173–78, 243 n.53; *A Sermon, Preached at the Execution of Moses Paul*, 26, 173–78; use of "poor Indians" as trope in writing, 20–21; visit to London, 13, 30, 61

Of the Conversion of Five Thousand and Nine Hundred East-Indians, in the Isle of Formosa, neere China, to the Profession of the True God, in Jesus Christ (Jessey), 73–77. *See also* Dutch missions

Othello (Shakespeare), 40, 42

Owen, David, 85

Pamela (Richardson), 6

Paradise Lost (Milton), 8

parish collections, support of American missions by, 23, 34, 211 n.2

pathos, as constitutive of *ethos*, 15

Paxton Boys, massacre of Conestoga Indians, 160

Pearce, Zachary (Vicar of St. Martins-in-the-Fields), 130

Pestré, Abbé, 121

Peter, Hugh, 77

Peyer, Bernd, 176

Phaenomena quaedam Apocalyptica (Sewall), 43

philanthropic discourse, emergence of, 85–86

Philippians 2:1, 8

Pindaric Poem on the Propagation of the Gospel in Foreign Parts, A (Settle), 25, 49, 50, 95–96; nationalism of, 95–96

pity: in British identity, 1–4; discussed by Aristotle, 205–6 n.41; distinguished from charity, 133–34; as doctrinal concern of SPG, 134–35; and donations, 160; moral definition of, 7–9, 17, 204–5 n.23; negative interpretation of by Indians, 20–21; "poor" as term of, 18; relationship to obligation, 9; as shared emotion, 15; as trope in sermons, 174, 200; visual understanding of, 12–13

Piumbubbon, 20; use of "poor Indian" trope, 20–21

Plenderleath, David, 123

Pontiac's Rebellion, 162

"poor Indians," 18–21; as equivalent to Spanish term *miserable*, 19; as image in philanthropic discourse, 85; image used by Milton, 41–42; Indian interpretations of concept, 20–21; relation to material poverty, 59–60, 170

Pope, Alexander, *Essay on Man*, 18–19

Post, Christian Frederick, 27, 111; marriage to Rachel (Delaware Indian), 180. *See also* Moravians

postcolonial studies, 199

poverty, Indians described as living in, 59–60, 170. *See also* "poor Indians"

Powhatan massacre, 22

prayer: economic models of, 38–39, 103; as link between readers and missionaries, 103–6; in missionary rhetoric, 107–9; requests for, 103

praying Indians, 20–22; British readers' familiarity with, 71; described in fundraising publications, 34–37, 44–46, 52, 64–73, 77–82, 121–22, 165–68, 179–80, 184–86, 189

predestination, and interpretations of Indian salvation, 121–24. *See also* Christianity

Prince George, letter to SPG, 113 fig. 4

print culture, origins of, 23

propagation of the Gospel, as obligation for Christians, 5

Psalm 74:20, 123–24

Puritans: described as Israelites, 164, 167; political position of, 76; understanding of pity, 18

Quakers: beliefs about Indian salvation, 124; conversion efforts of, 187; missions in North America, 26; texts produced by, 26

racial difference, fascination with, 13

Randall, Thomas, 9, 10; sermon delivered to SSPCK, 57, 101

Rawson, Claude, 163

Reason of Church Government Urg'd against Prelaty, The (Milton), 41

Reedy, Gerard, 117

Reformation, 5; attitudes toward death during, 183–84

requests for prayers: as appeal to individuals, 103; distinguished from fundraising, 103, 107–9

Restoration: images of American riches during, 57; impact on missionary discourse, 78; reorganization of New England Company under, 88

Review, The (Defoe), 97

Reynolds, Richard (Bishop of Lincoln), 124

Richardson, Samuel, *Pamela*, 6

Rising Glory of America, The (Freneau and Brackenridge), 193–94

Roach, Joseph, 165

Robertson, William, and Church of Scotland policy, 124

Rogin, Michael, 161

Roman Catholic Church, British missionaries' rivalry with, 9–10, 23, 94. *See also* anti-Catholic rhetoric

Romans: 1:19, 122; 2:1, 122; 2:13–16, 122; 2:14–15, 126; 6:23, 174; 10:14–15, 64; 13:3, 64; 15:25–27, 38, 51; 15:27, 38

Romero, Lora, 171

Rowlandson, Mary, 179. *See also* captivity narratives

Royal Society, 88

Rule and Exercises of Holy Dying, The, 182. *See also* *ars moriendi* tradition

Sacheverell, Henry, trial of, 87, 99

Sagamore, John, death of depicted in *New Englands First Fruits*, 167

savages: images of in British culture, 13; as objects of pity, 2–3

Sayre, Gordon, 4

Scanlan, Thomas, 4, 36, 66, 211 n.8

Scarry, Elaine, 168

Secker, Thomas, 131, 134

Sedgwick, Eve, 15, 110

Seeman, Erik, 182
sensibility: culture of, 32, 116–18, 136, 158–59; as literary era, 6, 9; and responses to Deism, 132–33
separation of church and state, development of concept in New England, 81–82
Sergeant, John: correspondence of, 151, 153–58; correspondence with Muhhaka-neok Indians, 154, 156; as New England Company missionary, 24, 32, 139–40; as portrayed in *Historical Memoirs, relating to the Housatunnuk Indians,* 139, 148–58; rationalism of, 148–49
Settle, Elkanah: nationalism of, 95–96; *A Pindaric Poem on the Propagation of the Gospel in Foreign Parts,* 25, 49, 50, 95–96
Seven Years' War, 12, 56, 193; and weakening of transatlantic ties, 216 n.74
Sewall, Joseph, requests for prayers, 107–8
Sewall, Samuel, *Phaenomena quaedam Apocalyptica,* 43
Shaftesbury, Third Earl of, and Deism, 10, 120, 132. *See also* Cooper, Anthony Ashley
Shakespeare, William, *Othello,* 40, 212 n.17
Shepard, Thomas, *The Day-Breaking, if not the Sun-Rising, of the Gospell,* 48–49, 104, 121, 126–27; emotional language of, 219 n.25; rhetorical strategies in, 67–69
Shipley, Jonathan, 195
Shklar, Judith, 123
Short, H.V.R. (Bishop of Saskatchewan), twentieth-century missionary efforts, 197–98
simony, 42
slaves, African, 27–29, 87, 89, 111, 113–14, 228 n.5
Smallbroke, Richard (Bishop of Litchfield and Coventry), 128
Smart, Christopher: "On the Goodness of the Supreme Being," images of wealth in, 57–58
Smith, Adam, and culture of sensibility, 129, 205 n.40; *Theory of Moral Sentiments,* 6, 10–11, 13; *Wealth of Nations,* 55
Society for the Furtherance of the Gospel, 27. *See also* Moravians
Society for the Promotion of Christian Knowledge (SPCK): founding of, 86–87; as model for SSPCK, 89; response to Deism, 231 n.39
Society for the Propagation of the Gospel in Foreign Parts (SPG), 12, 25, 44, 49–50; acknowledgment of gifts, 224–35 n.48; activities in Canada, 24; as Anglican organization, 25, 87, 99, 114–17, 135–36, 225 n.58, 230 n.24; anniversary sermons, 25, 31–32, 87, 92, 98, 115–16; annual reports of, 62; attempts to convert Indians, 114, 116–17; conflicts with American Dissenters, 102, 114–17; conversion efforts among Dissenters, 87; criticisms of, 102; discourse of associated philanthropy used by, 62; failure of conversion efforts, 102, 111–14; institutional organization of, 31, 90–93; international cooperation of, 99–100, 102; jurisdiction of, 223 n.13; nationalism of, 99; protests at mistreatment of Indians, 181; publications of, 25, 29, 92, 217 n.2; publications in epistolary form, 62; on question of heathen salvation, 131–35; responses to Deism, 117–18, 127–37; responses to skepticism, 136–37; seal of (described), 90–92, 91 fig. 2; sermons delivered to, 55–56; Standing Committee of, 29; theology of, 118–19, 135. *See also* Bray, Thomas
Society in Scotland for the Propagation of Christian Knowledge (SSPCK): adoption of SPG strategies, 93; British identity of, 94; compared to SPG, 102, 107; discourse of associated philanthropy used by, 85; Indian missions of, 90; institutional organization of, 31; internationalism of, 100, 102; missionary work in Scotland, 89, 94, 100; origins of, 9, 12, 26, 89; as Presbyterian organization, 26, 89, 107; publications of, 26; and question of heathen salvation, 123–24; role in Scottish politics, 89–90; seal of (described), 94; sermons delivered to, 44; transatlantic networks of, 107
South Sea Bubble, 12
Spain, British competition with in the Americas, 1, 5–6, 9, 10, 20, 37. *See also* anti-Spanish rhetoric
Spectator, The (Addison and Steele), 97
Spielberg, Steven, *Poltergeist,* 162
spiritual debt, concept of, 54
spiritual factory, metaphor of, 34, 36, 42
Sprat, Thomas, *History of the Royal Society,* 88
Spurr, John, 80
Stanhope, George (Dean of Canterbury), 53–54, 100, 116

Stanley, William (Dean of St. Asaph), attacks on Deism by, 128–29

Stebbing, Henry (Chancellor of Sarum), on SPG's abandonment of Indian conversion efforts, 136, 236 n.134

Steele, Richard, 97

Stephen, Leslie, 120

Stern, Julia, 63

Stockbridge mission, 140, 149; described in biblical terms, 150

Stoddard, Solomon, 45, 180

Stone, Oliver, *Natural Born Killers*, 162, 240–41 n.12

Strength out of Weakness, 72, 165

structures of feeling, 3

Succinct View of the Missions Established Among the Heathen by the Church of the Brethren, or Unitas Fratrum, 62. *See also* Moravians

sympathy, distinguished from pity, 8

Taino Indians, 38–39

Taiwanese converts, 74–75

tears, as image of Indian repentance, 67

Tears of the Indians, The, translation of de las Casas's *Brief relation of the Destruction of the Indies*, 46

Thorowgood, Thomas, 14; *Jewes in America, or, Probabilities That the Americans are of that Race* (1650), 25, 77; nationalism of, 77

Thorpe, George, 111

Tindal, Matthew: *Christianity as Old as the Creation*, 121; and Deism, 120–21; on pagan entrance to Heaven, 125

Todd, Janet, 9

Toland, John, *Christianity Not Mysterious*, 120; "Account of the Indians at Carolina," 121

Toleration Act, 87

trade: Indians as naive traders, 38–42; as metaphor for missionary work, 52–56, 59; as trope in missionary writings, 54–55; relation between commerce and philanthropy, 106

Trimnel, Charles (Bishop of Norwich), 99, 230 n.29

True Account of the Dying Words of Ockanickon, an Indian King, The, 186–87; image of signature page, 188 fig. 5. *See also* Budd, Thomas; Cripps, John

Tucker, Bruce, 81

Unio Fidelium (Union of the Faithful), concept of, 84

United Ministers of Boston, on Indian alcoholism, 171–72

vanishing Indians: and concept of manifest destiny, 162; as trope in Romantic literature, 110. *See also* Indian death

Van Sant, Ann Jessie, 12

Virgil, 122

Virginia Company: development of joint-stock company model, 88; promotional writings, 22

voyeurism, and pejorative connotations of "sentimentality," 18

Wallace, Robert, 123–24

Wampanoag Indians, 190

Warburton, William (Bishop of Gloucester), 56

Warneck, Gustav, 75

wastefulness, British colonialism as opposed to, 165–66. *See also* husbandry

Watson, James, 63

Watts, Isaac, correspondence of, 154

Waugh, John (Dean of Gloucester), 55

Wayne, John, 161

Weinbrot, Howard, 49–50

Wequash (Pequot Indian), deathbed scene described in *New Englands First Fruits*, 185–86

Wesley, Charles, 25

Wesley, John, 25

Wheelock, Eleazar, 13, 162, 172, 178–79; Indian School of, 51–52; *Narrative[s] of the Indian Charity-School*, 26; as SSPCK missionary, 26. *See also* Indian Charity School

Whiston, William, 128

Whitaker, Alexander, 111

White, Andrew, Jesuit attempts to convert Algonquian Indians, 5

Whitefield, George, 174–75

Whitfield, Henry, *The Clear Sun-shine of the Gospel Breaking Forth upon the Indians in New-England*, 69–71; correspondence of, 69–71

Whole Duty of Man, The (Allestree), 43

Willard, Simon, 69–70

Williams, Eunice, 150. *See also* captivity narratives

Williams, John (Bishop of Chichester), 129

Williams, Roger: account of Wequash's death as criticism of Massachusetts Bay colony, 186; *A Key into the Language of America,* 25, 186

Willis, Richard (Dean of Lincoln), 92–93

Wilson, Thomas (Bishop of Sodor and Man): *An Essay Towards an Instruction For the Indians* (1740), 25, 114

Winslow, Edward, *The Glorious Progress of the Gospel amongst the Indians in New England,* 71–72, 78

Woodbridge, Timothy, 149

Woolston, Thomas: *Discourse on the Miracles of our Saviour,* 120–21; imprisonment for blasphemy, 128

Wynne, John (Bishop of Asaph), 44

Wyss, Hilary, 149

Yale University, 140

Zeisberger, David, description of death of Lucia, 182. See also *ars moriendi* tradition; Moravians

Acknowledgments

I cannot help thinking that many years of studying the circulation of affect in missionary writings should have left me better able to express my gratitude to the institutions and people who have helped me write this book. I find myself unable to do more than compose the usual acknowledgments, however, and I hope the recipients will understand that my appreciation is hardly expressed by these words. Thanks must go first to Julie Ellison of the University of Michigan, who was present at the inception of this project, who has continued to be a font of inspiration and support, and who has become a valued friend. Lincoln Faller, Sue Juster, and James Winn suffered through early drafts of this book, and they have continued to provide me with valuable assistance and advice. I also am grateful to Anne Krook and David Porter, who helped me formulate parts of this project. I owe thanks to Lee Behlman, Jim Blenko, Jessica Printz, Michael Sowder, Shaun Strohmer, and John Su for commenting on early drafts of this book. The University of Michigan provided many years of financial support, especially through a Mellon Fellowship and a Rackham Fellowship.

I would like to thank several scholars at Villanova University. Through their work on early modern Europe, Michael Burke, Colleen Sheehan, and John Immerwahr introduced me to the texts that kindled my interest in depictions of American Indians. They and many others at Villanova, including Jack Caputo, Jack Doody, Seth Koven, Marie McAllister, Hugh Ormsby-Lennon, the late Phil Pulsiano, Evan Radcliffe, and Vince Sherry instilled in me a love of teaching and scholarship. I will always be grateful to them.

I benefited from the support of several other institutions. The University of Tulsa has helped my work in many ways, not least through several Faculty Development Summer Fellowships and additional assistance provided by Al Soltow and the Office of Research. Tom Horne, as dean of the College of Arts and Sciences, and Roger Blais, as provost, helped me take a semester of research leave by matching an external short-term grant. As current dean of the college, Tom Benediktson also has assisted me through generous travel grants. I was able to complete research for this book thanks to a Summer Stipend from the National Endowment for the Humanities, a Center for New World Comparative Studies Fellowship from the John Carter Brown Library, a Phillips Fund Research Fellowship from the American Philosophical Society (perhaps the only library where one can see Revolutionary War enactments through the window while reading manuscripts from the same era), and two research grants from the Oklahoma Humanities Council.

I owe particular thanks to Norman Fiering and the John Carter Brown Library, which, through its weekly lunches, wonderfully helpful staff, and friendly environment, provided an unsurpassed setting for research and intellectual exchange. I also would like to thank the McNeil Center for Early American Studies, especially its past and present directors, Richard Dunn and Dan Richter, who offered me an academic home for several months in 2000. They, the center coordinator Amy Baxter, the center's fellows, and the participants in the McNeil consortium welcomed me into their community, offering an island of stability—not to mention free use of their computers and copiers—in the midst of my itinerant research. I treasure the intellectual community and the resources they provided while I was on leave from my teaching position. I am most grateful for the suggestions I received there on my work, especially on a seminar paper that became the basis for this book's sixth chapter.

I could not have written this book without the research I was able to do at several libraries. I would like to thank the librarians and staff of the Harlan Hatcher Graduate Library and the Clements Library of the University of Michigan, the McFarlin Library at the University of Tulsa (especially Lori Curtis, the staff of Special Collections, and the interlibrary loan department), the American Philosophical Society (especially Rob Cox, Roy Goodman, and Alison Lewis), the Huntington Library, the Massachusetts Historical Society (especially Virginia Smith), the Dartmouth College Baker Library (with thanks to Anne Ostendarp), the John Hay Library at Brown University, the Library Company of Philadelphia (especially Jim Greene), the Penn Library and Special Collections at the University of Pennsylvania, and the Presbyterian Historical Society of Philadelphia. I owe thanks to several libraries in Britain: the Friends' House Library, Dr. Williams's Library, Lambeth Palace Library, the Guildhall Library, the British Library, the Bodleian Library of Commonwealth and African Studies at Rhodes House, the New College Library at the University of Edinburgh (especially Eileen Dickson), and the Central Library of Edinburgh. I would also like to thank the United Society for the Propagation of the Gospel, which generously allowed me to reproduce illustrations from its eighteenth-century publications and manuscripts.

My present and past colleagues in the Department of English at the University of Tulsa—Kate Adams, Hermione de Almeida, Susan Belasco, Becky Damron, Lars Engle, George Gilpin, Grant Jenkins, Joseph Kestner, Bill Kupinse, Holly Laird, Sean Latham, Grace Mojtabai, Bob Spoo, Anne Stavney, Gordon Taylor, and Jim Watson—have provided one of the most supportive environments imaginable. They have been generous with their time and their thoughts, offering useful advice on many aspects of this project. As department chairs, Jim Watson, Holly Laird, and Lars Engle have been especially helpful to me. I also have been lucky enough to work in a vibrant interdisciplinary setting, where colleagues from other departments have read parts of this book and helped me think through difficult ideas. These include Jane Ackerman, John Bowlin, Andy Burstein, Alfred Corn, Eldon Eisenach, Don Gilbert, Richard Grounds, Jake Howland, Nancy Isenberg, Ron Jepperson, Michael Mosher, and Paul Rahe. I thank the Graduate Student Association for inviting me to deliver a talk at their colloquium, which prompted me to try out some new ideas in a public forum. Under the auspices of the Tulsa Undergraduate Research Challenge, Mara Delcamp and Anthony Quinn proved to be invaluable research assistants. Scott Roberts, the college computer guru, quickly solved any problems that arose with my campus computer. Finally, I must thank the English department secretary Sandy Vice, who has helped me in more ways than I can count.

While working on this book I received assistance from scholars in several fields who read sections of my work or discussed aspects of my project with me. They include Louise Breen, Konstantin Dierks, Jim Egan, John C. English, Norman Fiering, Evan Haefeli, Sarah Knott, Ned Landsman, Roger Lund, Brendan McConville, Jim Muldoon, Erik Seeman, Jonathan Sweet, Kirk Swinehart, Fredrika Teute, and Mike Zuckerman. I have experienced some of the most exciting moments of working on this project through exchange with them, and I am deeply grateful for the generosity and thoughtfulness they have shown through their comments on my work. Christopher Grasso, Kerry Walters, and four anonymous readers for the *William and Mary Quarterly* helped with an early draft of Chapter 4. I owe particular thanks to Matt Dennis and Michelle Burnham, who read this manuscript for the University of Pennsylvania Press, and to Dan Richter and Kathy Brown, who as editors of the Early American Studies series at the Press, offered indispensable help with several stages of the manuscript's preparation. Their suggestions improved the book a great deal, and I am most grateful for their feedback. Bob Lockhart has been a remarkable and supportive editor. I would like to thank him, Erica Ginsburg, Jennifer Backer, and the staff of the University of Pennsylvania Press for their work in seeing this manuscript through to publication.

Parts of Chapter 6 were published previously as "The Christian Origins of the Vanishing Indian," in *Mortal Remains: Death in Early America*, edited by Andrew Burstein and Nancy Isenberg (Philadelphia: University of Pennsylvania Press, 2002), 17–30.

Family members and friends have helped me in numerous ways over the past few years, making it possible for me to complete this project. As they did earlier in my career, Mary and Arthur O'Brien opened their house in London to me for several months, offering me a true home abroad. Linda Bachman and Doug Toma, Konstantin Dierks, and Denny Schmidt graciously offered me housesitting opportunities in Philadelphia, allowing me to extend my stay there and complete necessary research. Many colleagues supported me through their advice about academia and their friendly inquiries about my work. These include Garrick Bailey, Susan Chase, Kevin Cope, John Coward, Holly Kruse, Lamont Lindstrom, Elana Newman, Alex Pettit, Jim Ronda, Chris Ruane, and Tod Sloan, as well as the colleagues I mention above. Lee, Elise, Tara, Michael, Nancy, Katy, Miranda, Christine, Sean, and Muriel have been true friends, talking me through rough moments of work and putting it all into perspective.

My brother, Matt, not only assisted in the purchase of my laptop computer but also provided heroic technical support, going so far as to Express Mail a replacement computer to London in a moment of dire need. I can't imagine the fragments this book—and I—would have fallen into without his help. I will always be grateful to him and to my sister-in-law, Tara, for their unfailing support and for the perspective that only those outside the academy can give to those working in it. My nephews, Matthew and Jack, have given me many moments of joy over the past few years, pulling me from work into playtime on my visits to them. My parents, Mary Nixon Stevens and Thomas Stevens, have offered me their constant love and support, unstinting interest in my esoteric labors, and countless gifts of books I will always treasure. As professorial role models, my uncle Richard Cobb-Stevens and my aunt Helen Ahearn have inspired me more than they realize. Finally, I owe a world of thanks to Thomas Buoye, my partner and husband, who knows my feelings better than I can describe them here. This book is dedicated with love to him.